ENVIRONMENTAL LAW

THE LAW AND POLICY RELATING TO THE PROTECTION OF THE ENVIRONMENT

ENVIRONMENTAL LAW

THE LAW AND POLICY RELATING TO THE PROTECTION OF THE ENVIRONMENT

Simon Ball, BA, BCL
Stuart Bell, LLB Hons, Barrister

BLACKSTONE PRESS LIMITED

First published in Great Britain 1991 by Blackstone Press Limited, 9–15 Aldine Street, London W12 8AW. Telephone: 081–740 1173

© S. Ball and S. Bell, 1991

ISBN: 1 85431 117 4

British Library Cataloguing in Publication Data
A CIP catalogue record for this book is available from the British Library

Typeset by Kerrypress Ltd, Luton, Beds
Printed by BPCC Wheatons Ltd, Exeter

This book is printed on recycled paper

Contents

The scope of this book—Some themes of the book—The shape of the book—The history of environmental law—The modern age of environmental law—The future of environmental law—Policy and environmental law

Some major features of environmental legislation—Informal sources of law and practice—European Communities (EC) law—International law—Judicial review—Remedies—Procedure—Restrictions on judicial review—The Ombudsman

Department of the Environment (DoE)—Other parts of Central Government—Parliamentary Select Committees—Royal Commission on Environmental Pollution—Her Majesty's Inspectorate of Pollution (HMIP)—National Rivers Authority (NRA)—Sewerage undertakers—General environmental duties and the water industry—Countryside bodies—Local authorities—Decision-making in local authorities—The future: an environmental protection agency?

The nature of the EC—The institutions of the EC—The European Commission—The Council of Ministers—The European Parliament—The European Court of Justice—The European Environment Agency—Sources of EC law—Validity of EC legislation—Compliance by Member States with EC law—The common market—The EC's environmental policy—The constitutional basis of the EC's environmental policy—Articles 100 and 100A—Articles 130R, 130S and 130T—Article 235—Qualified majority voting—Is uniformity required?—The *Danish Bottles* case—The scope of EC environmental policy—The range of environmental Directives—Framework Directives—The future of EC environmental policy—EC environmental law and Britain

Administrative regulation—The processes of regulatory decision-making—Anticipatory and continuing controls—Planning and prevention—Standards in environmental law—Interrelationship of standards—Other characteristics of standards—Strengths and weaknesses of different types of standard—Locally set and centrally set standards: Britain versus the EC—Why Britain and the EC differ—The 'British approach' to regulation—Decentralisation—Discretion—Gradualism and reliance on scientific evidence—The importance of context—Market mechanisms or the use of economic tools—Future uses of economic instruments—The polluter pays principle—The criminal law as a tool for environmental protection

The British approach to enforcement—The nature of enforcement mechanisms in environmental protection—The legal context—The attitude towards the offence—Attitudes towards the offender—The use of sanctions other than prosecution—The process of enforcement—Lack of public confidence in the enforcement system—Differing levels of enforcement—Administrative difficulties—Staffing and funding levels—Changes in attitudes to enforcement—The redefinition of the regulatory role—The redefinition of the enforcement agencies' relationship with industry—The redefinition of the importance of environmental protection—Public participation in the enforcement process

The development of a general environmental secrecy policy—Mechanisms

of secrecy—Commercial confidentiality—'Green nutters'—Administration costs—The Royal Commission's approach—The effect of secrecy
upon risk perception—Environmental rights—The recommendations of
the Royal Commission—Water pollution—Waste disposal—Exclusions—
Integrated pollution control—Air pollution—EC Directive on
environmental information—The public's utilisation of registers

8 The common law and the protection of the environment 128

Hybrid nature of the common law's role—Controls are not purely
environmental—Is the common law as a protection mechanism dead?—
Civil liability in statutes—The law of tort and environmental protection—
The law of nuisance—Defences to a claim for nuisance—An assessment
of nuisance as a tool for environmental protection—Public nuisance—
The distinction between public and private nuisance—Trespass—
Negligence—The rule in *Rylands* v *Fletcher*—Defences—The usefulness
of the rule in *Rylands* v *Fletcher*—The protection of riparian rights—
Civil law remedies—Statutory nuisance—The control of statutory
nuisances—The categories of statutory nuisance—What is required to
satisfy the local authority?—Who is the 'person responsible'?—The
abatement notice—Defences—The right of appeal against an abatement
notice—Individual actions by any person—Sentencing powers for
contravention of an abatement notice—The use of injunctions and
proceedings in the High Court.

Part II Sectoral Coverage of Environmental Law 159

9 Town and country planning 159

The main features of town and country planning—Town and country
planning as a tool of environmental policy—Town and country planning
and some themes of this book—The planning legislation—What is town
and country planning?—Planning policy—Deregulation—Local planning
authorities—Forward planning: development plans—The Planning and
Compensation Act 1991 and development plans—Development plans and
development control—Non-statutory plans and guidance—The history
and future of development plans—Development control: definition of
development—Material change of use—Use Classes Order—Existing
uses—General Development Order—Is planning permission required?—
Applying for planning permission—Decisions by the local planning
authority—Alternative and special procedures—Special areas—The
Secretary of State's powers—Summary of rights of third parties—The
local planning authority's discretion—The new presumption in favour
of the development plan—Conditions—Legal tests for the validity of
conditions—Conditions and policy—Planning conditions and pollution
control—Planning agreements—Planning appeals—Procedure on
appeals—Challenging the decision of the Secretary of State—Enforcement

of planning law—Enforcement notices—Stop notices—Injunctions—New enforcement powers—Enforcement where there is no breach of planning law—Environmental assessment

Pollution of the atmosphere—Pollution on land—Control of water pollution—The administrative jungle and the mechanisms of protection—Consequences of the fragmented approach—Time for a change—Best practicable environmental option—The EC's role in change—*Vorsorgeprinzip*: anticipation through foresight—HMIP—a unified body—The introduction of integrated pollution control—Organisation and administration of the system of integrated pollution control—The requirement for authorisation—Prescribed processes—Meaning of process—Release of prescribed substances—Exceptions—Overlapping controls—Applications for authorisation—Authorisation fees and charges—Public participation and other consultation procedures—Call-in procedure—Commercial confidentiality and national security—The determination of an application—BATNEEC—Integrated pollution control notes—Implementation of the IPC system—Transfer of authorisations—Enforcement powers—Offences and remedies—Corporate liability—Crown immunity—Appeals—Modes of appeal

Local atmospheric pollution—International difficulties: acid rain—Global issues: ozone depletion and global warming—The control of smoke under the Clean Air Acts—Control of smoke from chimneys—Strict liability—Exemptions and defences—Enforcement and offences—Emissions of dark smoke from industrial plants—The control of grit, dust and fumes—The control of height of chimneys—Miscellaneous controls—Smoke control areas—The control of noxious emissions to the atmosphere other than smoke, dust, grit and fumes—Air pollution guidance notes—Enforcement provisions—Public registers—Overlap with other controls—The control of emissions from motor vehicles—Control by the European Community—The Air Quality Standards Regulations 1989—Control over global warming

History—Waste disposal and planning law—Development plans—Development control matters—Waste disposal under the Control of Pollution Act 1974—The organisation of waste disposal administration—What is waste?—Waste disposal licences—Exemptions—Applications for a waste disposal licence—Statutory consultees—Conditions—Supervision of licences—Variation and revocation of licences—The transfer and surrender of licences—Appeals—Miscellaneous powers—The Control of

Pollution (Special Waste) Regulations 1980—The failings of the Control of Pollution Act 1974—The Environmental Protection Act 1990—closing the loophole?—Implementation of the Environment Protection Act 1990—Reorganisation of the waste disposal authorities—The licensing system—Application procedures—The criteria for the grant of a licence—The grant of a licence—Supervision and enforcement—Appeals—The duty of care—Miscellaneous powers—Powers to require removal of unlawful waste—Duties of WRAs in respect of closed landfills—Contaminated land registers—Overlap with integrated pollution control—Future changes

13 Water pollution

Water pollution—The water industry—The Water Act 1989—Water pollution controls—Scotland—Pollution policy—The EC and water pollution—Dangerous substances—Quality approaches—Water supply—Consents for the discharge of trade or sewage effluents—General pollution offence—Defences—Meaning of 'cause or knowingly permit'—The consent system—Revocation and variation—Transitional provisions—Annual charges for discharge consents—The role of the Secretary of State—Appeals—How are consents set?—Water quality standards—Public registers—Integrated pollution control—Sewage discharges—Radioactive discharges—Sampling and enforcement powers—Enforcement policy—Preventative and remedial powers—Precautions against pollution—Water protection zones—Nitrate sensitive areas—Planning controls—Other water pollution offences—Statutory nuisances—Water pollution and the common law—Postscript

14 Disposal of waste to sewers

Trade effluent discharges—Applying for a trade effluent consent—How are consents set?—Trade effluent charges—Public participation—'Red List' substances—Enforcement—Discharges from sewage works—Domestic sewage discharges

15 The conservation of nature

History—Nature Conservancy Council (NCC)—The protection of individual animals and plants—Habitat protection—Sites of special scientific interest (SSSIs)—Nature conservation orders—National nature reserves (NNRs)—Local nature reserves—Marine nature reserves (MNRs)—Limestone pavements—EC Wild Birds Directive 79/409—Draft Habitats Directive—The Ramsar Convention—Management agreements—Planning permission—Loss and damage to SSSIs

Preface

Writing a book on environmental law is rather like trying to hit a moving target. One reason for this is the amount of new legislation being produced, such as the Water Act 1989, the Environmental Protection Act 1990 and the Planning and Compensation Act 1991. Another is the immense amount of activity within the EC on environmental matters, which has an impact on British developments that is hard to underestimate. A third factor is the tendency for policy to change rapidly in response to pressure from the public, industry, the EC and the international community.

As this book tries to emphasise, in the environmental area, policy is of crucial importance. An understanding of the law is incomplete without an equal understanding of how it operates and where its future directions are likely to be. There are clear signs that the attitudes of the current Government (the Conservative Government that has been in power for 12 years) are being re-assessed under John Major's Prime Ministership, although most of the now-familiar ideologies from the Thatcher years still remain in place. This means that the next few years may well see a number of radical changes in the direction of the law, whether the Conservatives stay in power or are replaced.

There are also likely to be changes in the nature of the legal mechanisms which make up environmental law. This book, as the sub-title suggests, looks at the law from the point of view of the *protection of the environment*. It is not a book on environmental *liability* law, but it is clear that this may well be a growth area in the next few years. Subjects such as environmental auditing and reporting, civil actions for environmental degradation, judicial review of the actions of environmental protection agencies, directors' liability for environmental harm and environmental insurance all look ripe for development. At present, it is arguable that the law is relatively under-developed in these areas. For example, the use of the civil law is limited by the law's refusal to accept the environment as an entity capable of legal protection in its own right, and by restrictions on class actions. The rules on administrative protection are also limited by restrictive rules on standing and delay and the width of the discretions granted to many decision-makers. In both cases the cost of an action is also a significant factor.

However, this is not a book written for the practitioner experienced in environmental law, so many of these features have not been covered in detail. This book is aimed more at anyone who wishes to gain an introductory understanding of the basic concepts of environmental law, both in relation to its general principles and in relation to particular sectors. Thus, students on law courses, practitioners seeking such an introduction and, we hope, non-lawyers searching for an explanation of the law should all find this book useful.

The book is organised in two parts. The first is on the general principles and context within which environmental law operates, whilst the second looks at some of the key issues of environmental protection by reference to various sectors. Readers will find that an understanding of those things covered in the first part will enhance their understanding of the law in the second part and are encouraged to cross-refer between the two. An explanation should also be made about the contents of the book. There is a clear difference between what a book on the environment would include and what a book on environmental law may include. Some of the major issues of environmental policy, such as global warming and the reduction of CFCs, have very little formal law attached to them. In any case there is no room to write on every subject, and a number of issues are omitted on grounds of space. These include international law and the environment, radioactivity, the protection of the countryside, the protection of the cultural heritage and the developing area relating to genetically modified organisms.

It is important to be up-to-date on environmental law. Accordingly, every attempt has been made to include changes to the law up to 31 July 1991. This means that the Planning and Compensation Act 1991 is covered. The consolidation of the legislation on water has not been included on the grounds that it does not effect any changes to the substance of the law and does not come into force until 1 December 1991. Two particular difficulties which should be noted are those of explaining an area of law where laws have been passed but are not yet in force (such as on waste disposal), and having to comment on legislation which is in force, but where the implications have not yet become clear (as in relation to integrated pollution control). We hope we have succeeded in explaining these areas as clearly as possible.

Every attempt has also been made to be accurate in the statement of the law, but this is an area which is an art rather than a science and there is inevitably a certain amount of subjective opinion about what a particular provision means in practice. In any case, we strongly believe that lawyers should have opinions about the adequacy of the law: in relation to environmental protection this is quite literally of life-saving importance.

In such a confusing area of law the onus falls upon the authors to state that any mistakes made are our responsibility. Similarly, any views expressed (either explicitly or otherwise) are our own and not necessarily those of our respective employers.

In preparing the manuscript for publication we would like to thank the following people: Suzanne Phillips for her good natured hard work in converting incomprehensible tapes and computer print-outs into a proper manuscript; our friends and colleagues at the Universities of Sheffield, Leeds, East Anglia and

Dibb Lupton Broomhead and Prior for their helpful comments and support; our publishers for their understanding in what has been a book of numerous re-writes; Carolyn Shelbourn who has either worked with or taught both authors and thus has played an important part in both the conception and completion of this book.

Finally, we have found that writing a book is a profoundly anti-social experience and therefore Simon would like to thank Frances and Stuart would like to thank Philippa and his mother and father, without whom, as the saying goes, none of this would have been possible!

Simon Ball
Stuart Bell
October 1991

Abbreviations

APC	air pollution control
BATNEEC	best available techniques not entailing excessive cost
BOD	biochemical oxygen demand
BPEO	best practicable environmental option
BPM	best practicable means
COPA	Control of Pollution Act 1974
COSHH	Control of Substances Hazardous to Health
DoE	Department of the Environment
EC	European Communities
EPA	Environmental Protection Act 1990
HMIP	Her Majesty's Inspectorate of Pollution
HSE	Health and Safety Executive
IPC	integrated pollution control
MAFF	Ministry of Agriculture, Fisheries and Food
MHLG	Ministry of Housing and Local Government
MNR	marine nature reserve
NCC	Nature Conservancy Council
NNR	national nature reserve
NRA	National Rivers Authority
SSSI	site of special scientific interest
WRA	waste regulation authority

Table of Cases

Table of Statutes

Table of Statutory Instruments

PART I GENERAL PRINCIPLES OF ENVIRONMENTAL LAW

ONE

What is environmental law?

The 1990s are already being called 'The Green Decade' by some commentators. Whilst this may be somewhat premature, there is little doubt that 'the environment' will be a big issue, perhaps the big issue, of the decade.

It is a big issue in political terms, since protection of the environment is high on most people's priorities for the 1990s. As a result political parties and Governments are falling over each other in their eagerness to appear green, even if as yet their actions rarely match their rhetoric. It is big in terms of the size of the problems faced and the solutions required; global warming, the destruction of the ozone layer, acid rain, deforestation, overpopulation and toxic waste are all global issues which require an appropriately global response. It is big in terms of the range of problems and issues—air pollution, water pollution, noise pollution, waste disposal, radioactivity, pesticides, countryside protection, conservation of wildlife—the list is virtually endless. In the words of the recent White Paper on the Environment, *This Common Inheritance* (Cm. 1200, 1990) the issues range 'from the street corner to the stratosphere'. Finally, it is big in terms of the knowledge and skills required to understand a particular issue. Law is only one element in what is a major cross-disciplinary topic. Lawyers need some understanding of the scientific, political and economic processes involved in environmental degradation. Equally, all those whose activities and interests relate to the environment need to acquire an understanding of the structure and content of environmental law, since it has a large and increasing role to play in environmental protection.

The scope of this book

Faced with all these elements of 'bigness', authors of books on environmental law have to make many choices, otherwise each book would become unmanageably large. Inevitably what is included in this book reflects the personal interests and prejudices of the authors. The shape and structure of this book— what is included, what is omitted, what is covered in detail, what is covered in outline, how it is put together—must therefore be explained.

The book is entitled 'Environmental Law' and an explanation of these two words will clarify some preliminary points about its content.

Environmental

This is a difficult word to define. Its normal meaning relates to 'surroundings', but obviously that is a concept that is relative to whatever object it is which is surrounded. Used in that sense environmental law could include virtually anything; indeed, as Einstein once remarked, 'The environment is everything that isn't me'. However, 'the environment' has now taken on a rather more specific meaning, though still a very vague and general one, and may be treated as covering the physical surroundings that are common to all of us, including air, space, waters, land, plants and wildlife.

A definition of this nature is used in the Environmental Protection Act 1990 s. 1, which defines the environment as consisting of 'all, or any, of the following media, namely, the air, water and land'. Rather than offering a hostage to fortune by attempting to lay down some impossibly precise definition, we propose to adopt this one for the general description of the book's content. A more precise description can be given simply by stating what is and what is not covered by the book. We intend to concentrate on those laws and practices which relate primarily to the protection of the whole or part of the general surroundings, as opposed to those where the true objective is the protection of public health, or individual people such as workers or consumers.

Obviously, it is not possible to consign some areas of law with certainty to one category or another and, as a result, the exact dividing line between what is and what is not included is rather artificial. But a line has to be drawn somewhere. Accordingly, we cover the law and practice on the protection of air, water and land against pollution, and the protection of the ecosystem, together with those ancillary issues which help to explain these areas, such as public participation, access to information, remedies and procedures.

Such things as consumer protection laws, product liability laws, health and safety legislation and animal protection laws are not covered, although they can often be relevant to solving environmental problems. There are also a number of areas of what is undeniably environmental law which are omitted on grounds of space. The law on the protection of trees and the landscape is omitted, as is the growing package of legislation on the protection of the cultural heritage. Little will be said about radioactivity, where the law is very complex indeed and where there is a large overlap between the environmental and human protection parts of the law. The new provisions in the Environmental Protection Act 1990 on the introduction of genetically modified organisms into the environment and on litter are also omitted.

Law

This book is not intended to be merely a description of the various rules and regulations, although obviously that is a part of any useful book on the law. Such a description would give little clue to what happens in practice. Whether, and how, the law is enforced is just as important as what the law is. Indeed, given the discretionary nature of many of the powers and duties imposed on environmental decision-makers, it is unreal to draw a hard and fast distinction between what the law is and how it is used. This book will therefore seek to emphasise policy as much as law, and practice as much as principle.

There are some other general limitations on the subject matter of the book in addition to the ones mentioned above. It is not about all those laws which 'relate to' the environment, since that too could cover virtually anything. We intend to concentrate on those laws and practices which have as their object or effect the *protection* of the environment. Those things which merely have an indirect impact on the state of the environment, such as tax levels, grants and incentives, are thus excluded from full coverage, although their relevance is referred to in passing and they may frequently be of crucial importance to the policy-maker.

In addition, for reasons of space, we intend to concentrate on domestic laws and practices. We will not attempt to deal with truly international problems in any detail. Even so, the importance of international agreements in influencing and moulding our domestic law should be recognised.

The crucial relevance of European Communities (EC) law must be emphasised. We adopt the attitude that EC law *is* domestic law in the sense that it cannot be ignored even though it does not always give rise to enforceable obligations and remedies. Therefore EC controls, both current and proposed, will be integrated into each part of the book where relevant. In addition, there is a separate chapter on the basic constitutional rules of the EC and on the history, philosophy and current direction of its environmental policy. It is hard to overestimate the central importance of EC law and policy to British environmental law. This importance is often masked by the fact that in the environmental field EC law tends to require some form of implementation in this country before it is formally recognised. Once implemented, the EC derivation of the rule is then frequently forgotten because the domestic law is cited as the applicable law.

Some themes of the book

This description of the scope of the book highlights a number of important themes. One is that there is a great deal of interaction between rules which have as their main objective the protection of the environment and those which aim to protect people. Just as in nature conservation it has become accepted in the last 30 years that there is no use in protecting individual animals or species unless you also protect their habitats, in all matters we now accept that protection of human beings involves protection of their environment. The converse is also true in that many rules originally aimed at protection of people end up protecting the environment. For example, standards in relation to radioactivity are often set with the protection of humans in mind, but have an important impact on environmental levels of radiation. Similarly, the presence or absence of laws on cruelty to animals has a significant impact on nature conservation even though that is not their primary motive.

A related theme is that the rules are simply the tools of the trade of law-makers, environmental protection agencies and environmentalists. A rule which has as its objective one goal is frequently of enormous use in an entirely different way. For example, the law of nuisance owes its existence and shape to the objective of protecting property rights, but it still has an important, though often unpredictable, part to play in regulating environmental standards in the interests of the community. This is one of the major themes of this book: that there is often more than one way of tackling a problem and that the environmental lawyer must be seen as a problem-solver who chooses the most appropriate tool for the particular problem encountered. Often this will involve using a combination of different tools. As an example, many rules of property law may be used to further environmental ends: the Royal Society for the Protection of Birds follows a policy of buying land for nature reserve purposes on the principle that the exercise of ownership rights will often provide a better method of protection than many statutory designations or protections. This is not to say that the whole of property law must be somehow annexed as a part of environmental law, but that environmental lawyers should make use of any piece of law which has a relevance to the problem in hand.

A further issue relates to the nature of law. It is often stated that law is not constructive; that it does not build houses or plant trees. We regard this as an inaccurate notion. There is no doubt that many laws do lay down straightforward negative rules restricting specified forms of behaviour. But many laws lay down rights as well as wrongs. Much of environmental law consists of setting out a framework for behaviour—who should make decisions, how they should make them, what procedures must be followed. Such law is clearly not just negative.

In *Countryside Conflicts* (Lowe et al, 1986), the authors state that, 'planning control is no more than an essentially negative power; a device for stopping objectionable proposals'. This pessimistic view, which is undoubtedly widespread (especially amongst non-lawyers), seems to miss the point that planning law, like much of environmental law, is also about positive concepts, as expressed in the word 'planning' and illustrated by the production of development plans as an integral part of the process. In relation to pollution control, a similar point can be made by noting that the regulatory agencies spend a far greater proportion of their time providing positive advice on how to reach the standards they set than on enforcing those standards through legal threats and remedies.

This distinction between negative and positive tools links to a division in the subject matter of environmental law. It is common to equate environmental protection with pollution control. However, whilst pollution control undoubtedly represents a major part of environmental law, there are many other issues, such as the retention of biological diversity and the preservation of landscape, which also make up the subject. These issues often require slightly different legal mechanisms.

Finally, and perhaps most importantly, the law provides remedies. To many people, whether they are environmentalists or industrialists or lawyers giving advice, this is the most central aspect of law, since they want to know what they can do about a situation. One of the interesting developments of recent years has been the search for adequate remedies for environmental problems. Legal tools have been accepted as legitimate devices for helping to solve environmental problems. Law plays an often underrated but enormously important role, alongside scientific, technological, social and economic solutions, in helping to combat environmental degradation. In this role, many novel legal concepts have been developed.

The shape of the book

A major aim of this book is to illustrate the proposition that there is developing such a thing as environmental law. Most lawyers are brought up on the idea that there are a number of core, or basic, subjects which are essentially about techniques and in which a set of central organising principles can be distilled from the law. Criminal law, constitutional law, public law, contract law, torts, equity and property law would be good examples. The traditional view would then be that, alongside those basic subjects, are as many areas of law as there are areas of life, in each of which the techniques of the basic subjects are used; for example, the law relating to family relationships, the law relating to housing. But over a period of time, there is no doubt that these topic-related areas build up their own principles and reasoning processes. A good example of this process would be the development of the principles of public law over the last 40 years.

We would argue that environmental law is starting to acquire its own conceptual apparatus, in the sense that there is being built up a set of principles and concepts which can be said to exist across the range of the subjects covered. This is very much at an early stage, but the process of establishing environmental law as a separate discipline has begun. This makes it important to explain some general concepts, such as the 'polluter pays' principle, near the beginning of the book (see p. 85). It also explains the division of the book into two parts, one on the general themes of environmental law and the other on specific environmental issues. As suggested above, an environmental lawyer ideally needs to understand both parts in order to possess the tools required to carry out the task of solving particular problems properly.

Part I of the book looks at those general issues which cut across all issues of environmental protection, but which are in practice an essential part of any understanding of the law. The discussion in this part should also provide a form of vocabulary to help with an understanding of the context of the specific laws and practices which are dealt with in Part II.

Part I thus covers the nature of the regulatory systems adopted for environmental protection, the sources of the law, the institutions and agencies involved in environmental protection, the process of setting environmental standards and the different types of standard that may be adopted, the role of the EC, secrecy and freedom of access to information, the role of the common law and the important question of how environmental laws are actually enforced.

In *Part II* the specific laws relating to particular environmental issues are treated on a chapter by chapter basis. However, there is a significant problem of organisation here. Should the law be divided up according to the medium in which the environmental threat manifests itself (i.e. air, water, land etc.)? Should it be divided according to the identity of the polluter (e.g. cars, factories, power stations etc.)? Should it be divided according to the nature of the pollutant (e.g. radiation, lead, pesticides, CFCs etc.)? Or should it even be divided according to the nature of the target which is being protected (e.g. people, animals, ecosystems, the atmosphere)?

There is no single answer. The laws are not designed on any one of these four axes, but on all four at once. The best that can be done is to select groupings of laws that more or less hang together in a way that makes sense to someone faced with a problem. It must then be remembered that in reality all these things interrelate, so that a problem on the disposal of waste to land cannot be considered without some consideration of the law on incineration, or discharges to water, or recycling. Integrated pollution control and the adoption of the related concept of best practicable environmental option in the Environmental Protection Act 1990 are explicit recognitions of this interrelation.

Certain issues also play a role which it is impossible to explain in terms of any one of the four axes set out above. The law on town and country planning is an example. It clearly has a central role in protecting against threats to amenity and is in other ways an important part of the law on environmental protection. For example, hazardous or undesirable developments can be prevented or subjected to conditions, making the need for planning permission an essential part of most systems of pollution control. But it also has a role in organising economic development which is outside environmental law in its strict sense.

As a result the chapter divisions in Part II may be seen as artificial in a number of ways. We try to cover the protection of the major environmental media—air, land and water—from pollution, at the same time as considering the various means of disposing of waste—sewage disposal, incineration, landfill, discharge to rivers, discharge to the sea, reuse and recycling.

Environmental protection law is undoubtedly undergoing a period of unprecedentedly rapid change (see below). It is therefore intended to give special prominence to those areas where there have been recent changes and to refer to potential future developments wherever possible. In a subject area such as this, where activities have to be planned reasonably far in advance, it is always best to know what is likely to happen in the future as well as what is actually the law at the time. In this sense environmental law is forward-looking law.

The history of environmental law

An understanding of the current state of environmental law requires some understanding of its history. Not surprisingly for such a densely populated country, environmental controls have a long history, going back to medieval statutes on small-scale pollution and the development of private law principles to deal with threats to communal assets such as water. Of course, until recently, few would have thought of these laws as part of something called 'environmental law', since their main focus was on the protection of private and common property.

Britain's position as the cradle of the Industrial Revolution led to the very early development of public controls specifically related to environmental protection. The most significant provisions were developed in response to public health problems in the mid-nineteenth century, culminating in the landmark Public Health Act 1875.

Britain can boast what is normally considered the world's first national public pollution control agency, the Alkali Inspectorate, which was established by the Alkali Act 1863 to control atmospheric emissions primarily from the caustic soda industry. Water pollution controls followed in the Rivers Pollution Prevention Act 1876, although these proved to be virtually unenforceable in practice. Britain also introduced some of the earliest provisions on town planning. The first legislation to cover this subject was the Housing, Town Planning etc. Act 1909, which again derived from public health pressures and which vested controls in local authorities, at this stage on a non-obligatory basis. Obligatory town and country planning controls were introduced on a nationwide scale in 1947—again early in world terms.

In addition to these public controls, the law of nuisance was developed (especially in the nineteenth century) as a means of providing private redress for environmental harm, although on a very selective basis. Britain also had some of the earliest voluntary bodies concerned with environmental protection.

National, centralised control of problems (such as through the Alkali Inspectorate) was very much the exception in this period of development, and most public health and environmental protection was carried out at a local level by a vast array of local boards and, at a later stage, local authorities. Some uniformity was effected by the Public Health Act 1875, which produced model by-laws for such things as the design and layout of housing, but most of the early provisions reflect a tendency (which is still apparent) to regulate only the most dangerous or sensitive matters at a central level.

In these formative years, law-making tended to be ad hoc in the extreme. This is self-evident with case law, which by its very nature must react to the facts of cases brought. But legislative changes were also reactive, with Parliament tending to legislate for problems on an individual basis, in isolation from other areas and without any thought for wider development or consolidation of the law. For example, one effect of the early Alkali Acts and the controls over atmospheric emissions is reputed to have been an immediate worsening of water quality as industries chose liquid discharge as a replacement method for the disposal of their wastes. The same reactive tendency can be seen more recently. A good modern example is the enactment of the Deposit of Poisonous Wastes Act 1972, which passed through Parliament in only a few days in response to a much-publicised discovery of the fly-tipping of poisonous waste near a school playground.

As a result, environmental law has traditionally been split amongst a number of statutes, many of them covering much other material with little to do with environmental protection. Grandiose titles have often concealed the fact that an Act only covers part of the law on a particular area. For example, the Wildlife and Countryside Act 1981 did not really have much to offer for the protection of the wider countryside outside sites protected for nature conservation and landscape purposes, and even the Control of Pollution Act 1974, which was the first of the modern breed of large statutes concerned exclusively with pollution control, had very little to say about air pollution.

One reason for this fragmentation was often lack of Parliamentary time provided by the Government of the day, fuelled by the perceived lack of importance of environmental issues. This is undoubtedly changing rapidly as the political importance of environmental protection has grown immensely in recent years. But many environmental measures in the past have resulted from single issue campaigns, or from Private Members' Bills. For example, one of the reasons why the protection of birds has always been at a greater level than the protection of animals and plants is the passage of the Protection of Birds Act 1954 as a Private Member's Bill sponsored by the Royal Society for the Protection of Birds. A further example to show that this still happens is the Control of Pollution (Amendment) Act 1989, a Private Member's Bill to require the registration of carriers of controlled waste, passed in response to fly-tipping in London.

One effect of this long, and unplanned, history is that modern Britain has inherited a far less coherent system of pollution control than many other countries. The same historical factors also explain the relatively large number of agencies dealing with environmental matters, although recent changes in institutional responsibility have significantly improved matters in this respect.

A further effect is the survival of anachronisms. The name 'Alkali Inspectorate' lasted until the 1980s (it is now part of Her Majesty's Inspectorate of Pollution) and, although there have been changes in the Environmental Protection Act 1990, we still have laws on statutory nuisances which retain the essential shape they were given in the Public Health Act 1875. Anachronisms may also be seen in the limitations on access to environmental information and public participation in environmental decision-making (see Chapter 7) and in the still widespread immunity of the Crown in relation to environmental regulation.

Of course, as well as a long history of pollution control, Britain has a long history of pollution. This has left a legacy of problems that require urgent action, such as abandoned waste tips, derelict land, discharges of toxic wastes and untreated sewage into estuaries and the sea, and a host of other matters. There are other problems, stemming from the fact that many matters were not perceived as problems in the past, or that lower standards were accepted then. For example, perpetual planning permissions for peat extraction or gravel extraction were commonly granted in the 1940s and 1950s. Many of these are in areas now accepted as sensitive and worthy of protection, but under the current law the permission may only be removed by the payment of compensation for the loss of potential development rights.

Britain's ageing industrial base also creates difficulties when new, improved controls and standards are introduced. Fairness requires that existing producers are given some time to adapt to new standards, yet there is at the same time a problem of unfairness if controls are introduced so as to produce an inequality between new and existing producers.

The modern age of environmental law

Environmental law has changed rapidly in the last few years, and further change can be expected in the future to reflect the vastly increased prominence of environmental issues. Although it is not possible to specify a precise date or event, the modern age of environmental law can tentatively be said to have begun some time in the early 1970s.

There has been an obvious shift in the emphasis of the law since then to reflect newer environmental concerns. Many problems were simply not perceived as such in the 1960s, or were subordinated to other more pressing matters, such as the raising of living standards or the provision of full employment. The emphasis at that stage was on health and safety matters, a point well illustrated by the placing of the Alkali and Clean Air Inspectorate within the Health and Safety Executive when it was established in 1974. Land use was also emphasised; indeed, it could be argued that the very fact that Britain had (and still has) what is probably the world's most advanced system of land use planning led to the concentration of controls at that stage rather than to encouraging the development of adequate continuing pollution controls.

By comparison, the focus of modern legislation is on the control of pollution, and growing concern is being expressed about global and transfrontier problems, the control of hazardous substances and processes, the minimisation and management of waste, and the conservation of natural resources and protection of ecosystems. In short, current concerns tend to reflect the need to control the almost inevitable by-products of the modern, technological, industrial age.

In terms of legislation, the law is becoming more concentrated in a smaller number of Acts. Four in particular require some comment.

The *Environmental Protection Act 1990* contains the main bulk of provisions on air pollution from stationary sources, waste management and disposal, the integrated control of the most potentially polluting processes, litter, the environmental impact of genetically modified organisms, noise and statutory control of environmental nuisances. The *Water Act 1989* includes most of the law on water pollution. It is currently being consolidated (see Chapter 13, postscript). The *Wildlife and Countryside Act 1981* includes much of the relevant law on nature conservation in Parts I and II. The *Town and Country Planning Act 1990* includes in consolidated form most of the relevant statutory law on town and country planning and tree protection, though the related Planning (Listed Buildings and Conservation Areas) Act 1990 and Planning (Hazardous Substances) Act 1990 now include separate treatment of listed buildings and hazardous substances consents. There is also the Planning and Compensation Act 1991, which makes some significant amendments to the 1990 Acts.

None of these Acts are full codes in relation to the relevant subject matter. There are numerous individual issues which are dealt with by separate pieces of legislation, such as on mobile sources of pollution, or on pesticides. There are other issues where the controls are still spread amongst a large number of Acts, such as in relation to landscape protection, or the control of radioactivity. It is also necessary to point out that much of the detailed law in any area is actually provided in statutory instruments and a wide range of other documents made under the relevant Acts. The process of producing a coherent body of environmental law, begun in the Control of Pollution Act 1974 (which put most of the law on water pollution and waste disposal in one place, but which is now virtually replaced by later legislation in England and Wales), has certainly moved forward some distance.

One of the important features of this process is that the development and direction of the statutory controls is more planned than before. The four main Acts referred to above are all Government-sponsored Acts, illustrating an increasing tendency to plan and interlink legislation properly, although there is still a habit of including unrelated matters in legislation just in case no other opportunity arises in a packed Parliamentary timetable. For example, the Environmental Protection Act 1990 includes miscellaneous provisions on the control of dogs, the dismantling of the Nature Conservancy Council and the prospective prohibition of straw and stubble burning. The publication of the wide-ranging White Paper on the environment, *This Common Inheritance* (Cm. 1200, 1990), underlines this commitment to a planned development of environmental policy. The important aspect of the White Paper is not the new policies it includes (these are very limited and many of the proposals have a distinctly recycled feel to them), but its mere existence as a declaration of the importance of the environment and of having a definite set of policies towards its protection.

There is also an increasing institutional coherence, though the process is not complete (see Chapter 3). The National Rivers Authority has been established as a national body regulating water pollution and a number of other activities affecting water quality. Her Majesty's Inspectorate of Pollution has been established to bring together a number of sectoral Inspectorates, and now has integrated powers over the most hazardous industrial processes. The Environmental Protection Act 1990 has also created greater coherence in relation to the control of air pollution by local authorities and the management of waste and waste disposal. Once again it is clear that controls over stationary sources of pollution are more coherent than those over mobile or non-point sources. It will be surprising if the next few years do not see the creation of a unified Environmental Protection Agency with responsibility for most of the matters covered in this book. There is also the possibility that the European Environment Agency, the creation of which was agreed in 1990, will expand its role from that of information broker to that of European environmental police force.

A different aspect of developments in relation to institutional responsibilities is the Government's policy of splitting production from regulation. This may be termed the need to differentiate the poachers from the gamekeepers. In recent years this has been achieved by the creation of the National Rivers Authority. Prior to that the regulation of water pollution was the responsibility of the regional water authorities, who were also responsible for causing pollution from sewage works which they operated. A more recent example is the enforced separation of waste regulation authorities from waste disposal authorities in the Environmental Protection Act 1990 (see Chapter 12).

A final change, which may be seen from the examples referred to, and also from the recent history of town and country planning (see Chapter 9), is that environmental protection is becoming increasingly centralised, although this must be seen against the perspective that, as stated above, the system inherited from earlier years was particularly decentralised. There are many reasons for this—the increasing technological and scientific demands on pollution controllers, Central Government antipathy towards local government, increased emphasis on uniform and integrated planning of solutions to problems, and the impact of EC membership. This issue is considered further at p. 75.

A most important factor in all of these changes has been the influence of the European Communities (EC). The EC has a well-developed environmental policy and has passed numerous pieces of environmental law. At a general level, membership of the EC has led to the consideration and adoption of new methods of control and to the need to confront environmental issues in an organised way at Central Government level. More specifically, EC legislation and pressure has led to many actual and proposed changes in the law (often after British resistance), for example, on sulphur dioxide emissions, the dumping of sewage sludge in the sea and reductions in emissions from vehicles. Other changes have been more indirect. The Wildlife and Countryside Act 1981 was necessary to comply with EC Directive 79/409 on Wild Birds, and the opportunity was taken to modify other areas of the law at the same time. Without the EC obligation there must be some doubt whether any legislation would have been brought forward at that time—and even greater doubt as to whether it would have been persevered with in the light of the widespread opposition to the Government's original proposals, which were significantly altered as the Bill passed through Parliament.

The future of environmental law

In the light of EC membership, and the pressure now brought to bear by the whole international community on environmental issues, it is difficult to disentangle future British policies from global and regional ones. It is also difficult to predict the future accurately in this area because environmental policy is currently a highly political area. The present British Government has some highly individual attitudes towards policy and these will change if a different administration is elected. Indeed, the signs are that a number of attitudes have changed within the Conservative Government in the last few months. Nevertheless, a number of key directions for future policy present themselves.

The emphasis is shifting away from the more traditional reactive methods of solving environmental problems towards the prevention of harm. This is illustrated by the progressive adoption of laws that set standards for products, or the processes by which they are made, rather than for discharges or emissions. The introduction of integrated pollution control, a process-based control, is an important step in this direction.

The importance of the market in controlling environmental problems is being stressed. Partly this stems from the philosophical obsessions of the Conservative Government, but it is also related to the preference for preventative mechanisms, since there is little doubt that market mechanisms may help to prevent pollution occurring. Examples may be seen in the proliferation of schemes for charging for environmentally harmful activities, in the frequent references nowadays to the 'polluter pays' principle, and in proposals for such things as 'carbon taxes'.

A separate strand of policy is the emphasis on the conservation of natural resources. The current buzz-phrase is 'sustainable development', and steps are being taken to reduce waste by tackling the issue of waste production at source. However, 'sustainable development' still represents a commitment to growth: *This Common Inheritance* stresses that continued growth is necessary for maintaining the quality of life although it does not guarantee it.

A further point is the internationalisation of problems. A number of high-profile issues, such as global warming, depletion of the ozone layer, the protection of the rainforest, the Gulf smoke plumes and oil slick, and the saving of the whales, have galvanised interest in environmental issues, and there is no doubt that the future agenda will increasingly be set on the international stage. This point has not been lost on the Government, which devoted a significant proportion of *This Common Inheritance* to international issues.

There are a number of more technical areas where environmental law can be expected to develop. It was suggested earlier that environmental law is about using various legal tools to solve problems. It is obvious from a comparative study of the law that some mechanisms which are used in one area would be of great use in others. For example, a vast array of enforcement devices is available to Her Majesty's Inspectorate of Pollution for dealing with scheduled processes, and there seems very little reason why the arguments in favour of these methods in that arena should not apply to planning control or water pollution control. It is therefore suggested that the next few years will see the development of remedies for securing compliance with environmental requirements. Another example is the development of a means of legal redress for purely environmental harm. Private individuals are able to recover for loss to their property, but no damages are payable for harm to the environment as such. Fines levied for environmental offences are not even paid into a special fund for the enhancement of the environment. The development of some concept of environmental rights may well be something which occurs in the not-too-distant future.

A separate, though connected, development will relate to the provision of information about the environment. Increased interest in environmental issues leads not only to a need for more information and greater powers for individuals to take matters into their own hands, but also to a need for greater openness in decision-making. This issue will be discussed further in Chapter 7, but it seems crucial for the future of environmental law that there is greater accountability to the public for decisions made in their name by public bodies.

Whatever the exact direction that the law takes, one thing is clear about the future; the cost of compliance with the law is going to rise sharply, both for polluters and for society in general. This is mainly because regulatory standards are getting stricter and are being enforced more rigorously. But there are other factors, such as a heightened perception of the true environmental cost of many activities and the greatly increased pressure that is being brought to bear by the public, environmental groups and green consumers and investors. For example, charges are also being introduced for the first time for a number of discharges and emissions, in line with the Government's commitment to require charges for services provided by public bodies.

The cost of sewage disposal also illustrates the point. Disposal to the sewers has traditionally been thought of as a fairly cheap and efficient way of disposing of wastes. But the introduction of integrated pollution control means that increased controls will be applied to discharges of prescribed substances to the sewers. The costs of sewage treatment are also increasing because of changes relating to the disposal of their own wastes by sewage works. For example, the standards set for discharges to controlled waters are being tightened as the National Rivers Authority reviews existing consents, and this will carry a new urgency in the light of the need to meet the requirements of the newly agreed EC Directive 91/271 on Urban Waste Water Treatment. These discharges are also to be subject to new charges levied by the National Rivers Authority.

The cost of disposal of sewage sludge will also rise. Not only is the cheap option of dumping sewage sludge in the sea being phased out, after strong international pressure, but the cost of disposal to landfill sites is likely to rise significantly, and will rise even faster when the new regulatory framework in Part II of the Environmental Protection Act 1990 is brought into force. Incineration is another possibility for disposal of sludge, but that too is coming under increasingly tight regulation.

The privatised nature of the sewerage undertakers emphasises the need to take these factors into account. At the moment these sewerage undertakers are reviewing existing trade effluent consents for discharges to the sewers, and it is clear that in the next few years conditions restricting the discharge of certain substances will increasingly be imposed and that charges for discharges to sewers will rise.

Apart from the direct cost to business of tighter regulatory controls, the potential liabilities are also increasing. A good example in this respect is the cost of cleaning up contaminated land, but the draft EC Directive on Civil Liability for Damage Caused by Waste (COM (91) 219 final) will also increase the options for bringing a civil claim. Many businesses would be well advised to carry out environmental audits of their activities and to check on their insurance cover against such environmental claims. It is significant that a draft British Standard on environmental management systems was issued in June 1991.

Policy and environmental law

A final thought, but a most important one, is that environmental law is a political discipline. It is political in the narrow sense that major differences can be discerned between political parties as to the correct policy to apply. These differences do not normally relate to the ends to be achieved, but to the methods to be adopted in doing so, and the costs to be incurred. A clear example is the controversy provoked by the passage of the Wildlife and Countryside Act 1981 over whether voluntary or compulsory controls should be adopted in relation to the protection of important natural sites (see p. 348). A further example relates to the whole history of town and country planning in the 1980s, when the very dramatic changes to planning policy led to disagreement and dispute. In one way this is the clearest example of the application of 'Thatcherism' to the environment, as a Government with a deep suspicion of planning and regulation sought to grapple with a system based on coherent planning for the future, though the signs for the 1990s are that these attitudes are being subtly altered.

But environmental law is also political in the wide sense that it involves the making of policy decisions about the best way to achieve certain objectives. This is emphasised in this book by looking at law as being about techniques or tools for solving problems. It is not just lawyers and environmentalists who have a choice of tools they may use to achieve a particular objective. Legislators and policy-makers also have a range of tools available to them. The law is one tool alongside such things as fiscal policy, education, research, and voluntary solutions. There are different types of legal mechanism that may be used, such as the setting of environmental quality objectives, or of strict limits on emissions, or controls attached to processes or products. These various possibilities are discussed in detail in Chapter 5, but it ought to be recognised that, in order to combat complex problems of pollution and environmental harm, a combination of methods is often required.

It is impossible to say that Britain always adopts one method rather than another, but it is clear that the tendency has been to adopt flexible mechanisms of control, where what is permitted is judged by reference to its effect on the receiving environment. As a result, the British approach to pollution control tends to be fairly pragmatic, and involves a great deal of discretion. This discretion is normally exercised by specialist regulatory agencies, although local authorities also have very significant environmental protection functions. An important point is that this discretion is exercised on grounds that are not restricted to environmental factors. There is a traditionally close connection in British environmental regulation between social, political and economic factors and decisions on environmental protection.

This emphasis on taking into account a wide range of factors before making a decision links to a fundamental point about the way that 'pollution' and 'environmental harm' are defined. Once again, it is difficult to formulate precise definitions, but a general guide would be to say that they cover situations where there is an excess of something over what is desirable. There is no doubt that they are relative concepts; one person's waste is another's raw materials. As a result, Nicholas Ridley's famous comment that 'Housing is not a form of environmental pollution' can be seen as inaccurate in some cases.

The level of pollution is also relative. For example, because of the self-cleansing properties of the environment, it may well be said to be less polluting to discharge into a large fast-flowing river than into a small sluggish one, and higher levels of pollution from industrial sources may be tolerated in one area than in another because of the corresponding advantages of the economic prosperity that the industries bring. It is nonsensical to talk of getting rid of pollution. It only makes sense to consider how to reduce it and the levels which are acceptable.

Everything therefore depends on what is considered acceptable. This involves economic, political, social and cultural criteria as well as scientific and environmental ones. It is therefore important to understand that, in implementing environmental protection policies, regulatory agencies are effectively carrying out a political balancing process. As Hawkins puts it in *Environment and Enforcement* (1984), 'The power to define and enforce consents is ultimately a power to put people out of business, to deter the introduction of new business or to drive away a going concern'.

TWO

Sources of environmental law

Most of the formal sources of environmental law are statutory. Compared with subjects such as contract or tort there is very little judge-made law, and most of what there is consists of interpretations of statutory provisions. Obviously there are areas of the common law which can be used to promote environmental protection, such as the law of nuisance, or the rules on restrictive covenants, but the environmental advantages they bring tend to be incidental to the main purpose of the law concerned. For a discussion of the common law's contribution to environmental protection see Chapter 8.

Some major features of environmental legislation

Environmental statutes tend to exhibit a number of features:

(a) they are often framework Acts requiring delegated legislation to be effective;
(b) their commencement is often delayed or staged;
(c) they include unclear definitions;
(d) they confer wide discretions.

Delegated legislation

Much of the detail of environmental statutes is left to be worked out in various forms of delegated legislation, such as regulations, rules, orders and schemes. This is particularly true of three of the main pieces of legislation in environmental law—the Environmental Protection Act 1990, the Water Act 1989 and the Town and Country Planning Act 1990. In each case a person who read the Act on its own would get a very limited view of the law. For example, the general requirement that an authorisation must be obtained from Her Majesty's Inspectorate of Pollution before 'prescribed processes' are carried on is laid down in the Environmental Protection Act 1990, s. 6, but the list of processes is prescribed in Regulations, as are the detailed procedures for acquiring an authorisation. In the Town and Country Planning Act 1990, the central definition of what requires planning permission owes just as much to two statutory instruments—the General Development Order and the Use Classes Order—as to the general definition laid down in s. 55 (see Chapter 9).

Delegated legislation may take a number of forms. In most cases, it is made by the Secretary of State or some other member of the Government (such as the Minister of Agriculture). But this is not necessarily the case, and it does not always involve the use of statutory instruments laid before Parliament. In the last year a number of charging schemes for pollution control have either been made or are being introduced. Some of these are made by the relevant regulatory body. For example, the National Rivers Authority's Scheme for Charges in Respect of Applications and Consents for Discharges to Controlled Waters is made by the Authority, although it does require certain publicity procedures and the approval of the Secretary of State. (It also involved very lengthy consultation even before the draft Scheme was published.)

Very wide powers are often granted in relation to matters that are delegated. In some cases, such as the General Development Order and the Use Classes Order, this virtually amounts to giving the Secretary of State a power to rewrite the Act. There are obvious problems of accountability with such an approach, since far less Parliamentary scrutiny is given to delegated legislation than to Acts of Parliament. There is also the problem that the powers may not be used. Under the Control of Pollution Act 1974, powers were given to the Secretary of State to make regulations on precautions to be taken over the control of potentially polluting matter, and on water protection zones (s. 31(4) and s. 31(5) respectively), yet none were ever made.

Commencement
Legislation often requires implementation by statutory instrument before it comes into force. The Control of Pollution Act was enacted in 1974, yet Part II relating to water pollution was not brought into force until 1986, and then only in a piecemeal and gradual manner. Some parts of the Act were never brought into force (e.g. ss. 46(1)–46(3) on the powers of water authorities to vary consents after an act of pollution). Apart from the suspicion that such delays are used for political purposes, this gradualist approach obscures what the law is and brings it into disrepute by creating uncertainty for the public, regulatory bodies and industry alike.

The Environmental Protection Act 1990 includes a provision for most of it to be brought into force by commencement order. This has already happened for much of the Act, but the precise timetable for the introduction of Part II of the Act on waste regulation is still unclear. As far as integrated pollution control is concerned, the provisions of the Act have been brought into force, but are not applicable to individual processes until a separate commencement order is made. A timetable for this has been published (see p. 241). It seems contrary to the rule of law that the decision on whether, and how far, to implement enacted legislation should be left entirely to the discretion of the Secretary of State, but that is the position.

Definitions
Definitions are often left unclear in the legislation. Normally this is to preserve flexibility in the application of the law. For example, until the enactment of the Environmental Protection Act 1990, the central concept in the law on air

pollution was that of Best Practicable Means (BPM). This phrase was never statutorily defined. Instead, it was explained in relation to different processes in BPM Notes published by Her Majesty's Inspectorate of Pollution (HMIP) and its predecessors. Even these were not comprehensive, since an important feature of BPM is that it allows flexibility to cater for local and individual circumstances. Interestingly, the BPM Notes were often drawn up in consultation with interested parties, including representatives of the industry concerned.

The same approach is being adopted for the definition of the key phrase in Part I of the Environmental Protection Act 1990—Best Available Techniques Not Entailing Excessive Cost (BATNEEC). Integrated pollution control (IPC) Guidance Notes explaining the content of BATNEEC are being prepared and published by Her Majesty's Inspectorate of Pollution for each prescribed process, although in this case they are being set with less reliance on the industries concerned (see p. 233).

A similar process can be seen in the Town and Country Planning Act 1990, where fundamental concepts such as development and material change of use have deliberately been left as open as possible in the legislation. In this case, they have been further defined by the courts in numerous cases, but the original flexibility has been retained by the courts' insistence that the application of the law to the facts of any individual case is a matter for the relevant decision-maker (the so-called 'fact and degree' test).

As a final example, in the Water Act 1989 it is provided that the normal publicity requirements for an application for a discharge consent can be disregarded where the National Rivers Authority 'considers that the discharges in question will have no appreciable effect' on the receiving waters (sch. 12, para. 1(4)). This phrase is not defined in the legislation, but it is defined quite specifically in Department of the Environment Circular 17/84. Whilst this advice has no strict legal force, and the ultimate definition of the phrase is a matter for the courts, it is clearly followed in most cases. What should be determined as a matter of law is thus relegated to a matter of administrative discretion. It has been estimated that the majority of applications for consent (possibly up to 90%) have not been publicised in the past on the basis that the 'no appreciable effect' exemption applies. This suggests a significant reduction in potential public involvement in standard-setting (see Howarth, 'Water Pollution: Improving the Legal Controls', [1989] 1 *Journal of Environmental Law* 33-5).

Discretions
Wide discretions are frequently given in the legislation. This is a particularly clear feature of British environmental law (see p. 76). There are many examples, ranging from the discretion given to the Secretary of State on the form of delegated legislation, through discretion as to whether an area should be designated for special protection, discretion on the setting of standards (e.g. in the permitted level of a pollutant discharged or emitted), to discretion over the enforcement of the law. In all areas of environmental law it is hard to get away from discretionary decision-making.

These features of environmental legislation help to explain some of the essential characteristics of the 'British approach' to environmental protection, such as flexibility and pragmatism (see p. 73). The width of the discretions given also militates against uniformity in either the definition or the application of the law.

Informal sources of law and practice

One particular result of giving wide discretion to decision-makers is that the concept of environmental 'law' expands to include a wide range of matters. For example, the BPM and IPC Guidance Notes mentioned above are crucial to any understanding of what is actually required of industry in relation to air pollution, even though they have no formal legal effect. Similarly, in areas of the law that depend on the discretionary balancing of policy factors, an understanding of the sources of policy is central. In many cases, prevailing policies effectively make or change the law. One of the most famous of policies in town planning—the Green Belt—has no statutory foundation at all (apart from around London). It stems entirely from a Central Government restraint policy dating back to the 1950s, which has been applied on a local basis in many areas. In theory, the whole idea of Green Belt could be amended, or even scrapped, tomorrow merely by a change in Government policy.

The story of town planning in the 1980s illustrates this point graphically, since what amounted virtually to a revolution in town planning law took place with very few changes to the legislation and delegated legislation. The main vehicle of change was Central Government Circular guidance on policy, which could be imposed on local authorities through the appeal system. It is arguable that a student of current planning law would learn more about what will happen in practice by reading Government policy documents than by reading the legislation.

The range of what must be considered as law is also widened by some of the features of environmental law. It is law in action rather than law for lawyers. It involves the solving of practical problems, so everything which is likely to have an impact on the solution of a problem should be understood, including policy and evidence of practice. It is also a forward-looking law; because of the need to plan for the future, it is desirable to know what the law is going to be as well as what it is.

Thus, the sources of environmental law are far wider than Acts of Parliament, delegated legislation and cases. Much of what constitutes law in its wider sense is in Circulars and policy documents issued by Central Government or the regulatory agencies. (It should be noted that there are normally different Circulars issued by the Department of the Environment and the Welsh Office, but these normally say the same things. In this book references to Circular numbers are to those issued by the Department of the Environment.)

It may also be argued that 'law' should include the actual practice of agencies with responsibilities in the environmental field; an argument which is at its strongest when dealing with enforcement. This makes it desirable that as much as possible about the practice and policy actually relied upon by decision-makers is published officially, an aim which (sadly for writers of environmental law books) is not yet met in practice.

European Communities (EC) law

It would not be proper to conclude a discussion of the sources of the law without a reference to EC law, which is of enormous importance in the environmental field. Membership of the EC has clearly involved a distinct loss of sovereignty for Member States, and in this country this is given constitutional force by the European Communities Act 1972. Section 2(1) provides that EC legislation is recognised as law in Britain, although very little EC environmental legislation is directly effective in the sense that it can be relied upon by individuals before it is implemented by domestic measures (see p. 43).

By virtue of the European Communities Act 1972, s. 2(2), EC legislation can be transposed into domestic law by delegated legislation even if there is no parent statute authorising it. For example, Directive 85/337 on Environmental Impact Assessment was implemented in British law through the passage of regulations by reference to that subsection. This power has a technical limitation, since no provisions extra to the EC legislation may be added without a new piece of enabling legislation. This explains why the domestic regulations on environmental assessment go no further than required by the Directive, but that limitation has now been removed by a new statutory power to make regulations on environmental assessment under the Planning and Compensation Act 1991, s. 15.

EC law is explained in greater detail in Chapter 4, but an important point to establish here is that, as with the position in domestic law, EC environmental law consists of far more than legal rules. It is as necessary to understand the policies, principles and future direction of EC law as it is to understand its current legal content.

International law

International law governs relations between states. Unlike EC law, it has no direct effect on domestic law or on individuals. However, it will often have an indirect effect, for example by publicising a particular issue, by laying down generally accepted standards, or by imposing political pressure on states to change their laws or practices. Thus the North Sea Conferences have had an important impact on British domestic policies in relation to the dumping of sewage sludge in the North Sea, which will now cease. Many pieces of legislation include powers for the Government to introduce changes into domestic law in order to comply with international obligations. For example, the Environmental Protection Act 1990, s. 156 enables the Secretary of State to make regulations to modify other parts of the Act in order to comply with EC or international obligations.

For the most part, international environmental law consists of Conventions agreed by signatory states, such as the Ramsar Convention on Wetlands of

International Importance (see p. 357) or the Vienna Convention for the Protection of the Ozone Layer. These may provide general guidance on activities or they may lay down precise standards and requirements (for example, the Montreal Protocol to the Vienna Convention does this—see p. 261). The important point is that such law is not ultimately binding, except in a political sense, because of the lack of sanctions available for non-compliance. However, it is often implemented by domestic or EC legislation, a process which is now happening to the Montreal Protocol. It is anticipated, by analogy with the development of international law in other spheres, that it will develop some generally agreed principles to cover such things as trans-boundary pollution, that will apply even without the need for a treaty.

Judicial review

Environmental enforcement authorities are public bodies exercising public powers. Mostly, these powers are exercised under statute and consequential delegated legislation. However, in exercising these powers, it may be that such bodies do not follow statutory procedures, that they arrive at decisions unfairly, or that they attempt to make decisions which they have no power to make. The High Court oversees the exercise of these powers by administrative bodies by means of judicial review. The main ground for judicial review is that an administrative body has made a decision which was outside the statutory powers given to it (i.e. *ultra vires*). This may happen in one of three ways.

(a) No power to make the decision itself
If the National Rivers Authority decided to issue a trade effluent discharge consent for a discharge made to a sewer, a matter which is controlled by the privatised water services company, then the decision would be subject to judicial review because it could not be made within the National Rivers Authority's powers under the Water Act 1989.

(b) The improper exercise of discretion
This principle was first expounded by Lord Greene MR in the case of *Associated Provincial Picture Houses Limited* v *Wednesbury Corporation* [1948] 1 KB 223:

> . . . a person entrusted with a discretion must, so to speak, direct himself properly in law. He must call his own attention to the matters which he is bound to consider. He must exclude from his consideration matters which are irrelevant to what he has to consider. If he does not obey those rules, he may truly be said, and often is said, to be acting 'unreasonably'. Similarly there may be something so absurd that no sensible person could ever dream that it lay within the powers of the authority. Warrington LJ in *Short* v *Poole Corporation* gave the example of the red-haired teacher, dismissed because she had red hair. That is unreasonable in one sense. In another it is taking into account extraneous matters. It is so unreasonable that it might almost be described as being done in bad faith; and, in fact, all these things run into one another.

Therefore, the improper exercise of discretion can be subdivided into a number of different categories: taking into account irrelevant considerations, failing to take into account relevant considerations, and acting so irrationally that the decision could only have been made in bad faith. Examples include taking into account the political party that an applicant supported when deciding an application for a waste disposal licence, and failing to consider the special attention to be paid to the desirability of preserving or enhancing the character or appearance of a conservation area on a planning application.

(c) Procedural unfairness

Although, in theory, the review of decisions made with procedural impropriety falls within the unreasonableness ground above, it is distinct enough to form its own head of review. There are two elements making up procedural fairness. These are that every person has a right to a fair hearing and that there should be no bias in a decision-making process. The right to a fair hearing includes the right to meet any case put against an applicant and the right to present cogent and coherent evidence in support of a case. The prohibition against bias covers such situations as local authority planning committee members participating in decisions to grant planning applications on land which a planning committee member owns. In such circumstances it is impossible for the decision-maker to reach a fair decision.

When a decision is made in any of the above circumstances, an aggrieved person has the right to apply to the High Court for judicial review. Such a right should not be confused with any statutory right of appeal, which may give rise to a reconsideration of the merits of a case, rather than consideration of questions of law. Indeed, theoretically, a court exercising its power of judicial review is not entitled to substitute its own decision for that of the administrative body.

Remedies

The High Court has several remedies available to it to overturn a decision made unlawfully.

(a) Certiorari

An order of certiorari is used to quash an administrative decision made unlawfully. Thus, where a noise abatement order has not been made correctly because of procedural defects, the order itself would be declared null and void.

(b) Prohibition

Where there is a threat that a statutory power will be unlawfully exercised then a prohibition forbids a statutory body from exercising its power in the threatened way.

(c) Mandamus

An order for mandamus forces a statutory body to carry out its statutory duty. For example, where a waste disposal authority is under a statutory duty to supervise sites governed by a waste management licence under the Environmental Protection Act 1990, such an order would force them to carry out this supervision properly. This is perhaps the remedy which is most obviously concerned with the control of environmental bodies. Many authorities are under a duty to carry out activities which have a consequential effect on environmental protection. A failure to carry out these duties may be due to the 'unreasonableness' of the body making the decision. Thus, the rights of people aggrieved by such a lack of activity are considerably enhanced.

(d) Declaration

The reform of judicial review procedures in 1977 added the remedy of declaration and/or injunction to the other remedies. When a declaration is sought the court seeks to give a statement as to the legal relations between the parties, but that is all it does and the declaration cannot be enforced. A declaration seeks no more than to state the legal position and does not seek to change the respective legal positions of the parties. Thus, a declaration is suitable for a situation where there are uncertainties over whether or not a certain set of facts falls within a category of law.

(e) Injunctions

Although an injunction is available as a remedy under the judicial review procedure, it is the least used remedy, since it is not available against the Crown. As much of environmental protection is carried out by Crown bodies, such a remedy is limited.

Procedure

The procedure for judicial review is contained within the Rules of the Supreme Court, Order 53. An application has to be made within three months from the date when the grounds of the application first arose, unless the court considers that there is good reason for extending the period (Ord. 53, r. 4). This time limit does not apply where there is any other statutory provision which has the effect of limiting the time within which an application for judicial review may be made (Ord. 53, r. 4(3)). In addition, the court may refuse to hear an application if there has been undue delay in bringing it, even if it is brought within the three months period (see, for example, *R v Swale BC, ex parte Royal Society for the Protection of Birds* [1991] JPL 40).

However, in order to bring a claim for judicial review, the applicant must show a 'sufficient interest' in the decision or power to which the application relates (Supreme Court Act 1981, s. 31(3)). There has been some suggestion that this interest has to be greater where the application is for the remedies of prohibition or certiorari, but it is generally accepted that the only test is to show a sufficient interest for remedies. The phrase 'sufficient interest' is of tremendous importance in matters of environmental protection. As will be shown in Chapter 8, the protection of private law rights is contained within the common law and thus anyone seeking to protect their own private interests in land may resort to the common law rather than going through the even more expensive procedure of judicial review. But it is clear that somebody with a private interest in land affected by an administrative decision would have 'sufficient interest' or *locus standi*. It is more difficult to show that a person has the necessary standing by virtue of an interest in the environment as a whole, as it is not generally accepted that there are 'environmental rights' available to the public at large. The basis of the law on standing is contained in *IRC* v *National Federation of Self Employed and Small Businesses Ltd* [1982] AC 617, where Lord Wilberforce said that the decision as to who had a 'sufficient interest' under the Supreme Court Act 1981, s. 31 had to be considered with the known merits of a case:

> It will be necessary to consider the powers or the duties of those against whom the relief is asked, the position of the applicant in relation to those powers or duties, and to the breach of those duties said to have been committed. In other words, the question of sufficient interest cannot, in such cases, be considered in the abstract, or as an isolated point: it must be taken together with the legal and factual context.

In the planning system many actions have been brought by interest groups, where sufficient interest can be demonstrated by objecting to proposals or giving evidence at a local inquiry (see *Save Britain's Heritage* v *Secretary of State* [1991] 2 All ER 10 or *R* v *Hammersmith LBC ex parte People Before Profit* (1982) 80 LGR 322). In purely environmental matters, however, it is suggested that such an interest would be more difficult to show. In *R* v *Secretary of State for the Environment ex parte Rose Theatre Trust Company* [1990] 1 All ER 754, Schiemann J considered an application made by the Theatre Trust Company in relation to the Secretary of State's refusal to schedule the site of the Rose Theatre in Southwark (which was being developed) as an ancient monument under the Ancient Monuments and Archaeological Areas Act 1979. In deciding whether or not the company had any standing to bring an action in judicial review, he decided that, although it was not necessary for an applicant to demonstrate a financial or legal interest in the matter complained of, the statute giving rise to the power or duty had to be examined and the question asked as to whether or not the construction of that statute gave the applicant a right to have a duty performed. As the power confirmed by the Act in that case was specifically to be exercised by the Secretary of State in the public interest, on the construction of the Act the judge decided that no individual citizen or company had the right to challenge the decision in any event.

This decision is perhaps not as wide-ranging as it would seem. In many environmental regulations the purpose of the legislation is to protect certain groups or certain areas. For instance, under the Clean Air Acts, it is clear that protection is to extend to a local authority's area and therefore a resident within that area would be entitled to expect that the statutory obligations would be carried out properly under that Act. Similarly, the waste disposal regime contained within Part II of the Environmental Protection Act seeks to control the disposal of waste so that it does not cause harm to the environment or to human health. This may be given a broad construction by the courts and it would, it is suggested, give wide rights of standing to all those who were intended to be protected. Guidance on this matter was given recently in another decision of Schiemann J, *R v Poole BC, ex parte Beebee* [1991] JPL 643. In this case he considered whether various environmental groups had sufficient standing to challenge a decision by Poole BC to grant itself planning permission for housing on a site of special scientific interest. The British Herpetological Society was held to have standing because of its long association with the site (indeed, one of the conditions of the planning permission was that the Society would be allowed to mount a rescue of reptiles and amphibians from the site). The World Wide Fund for Nature, which was involved mainly to fund the action, was stated not to have standing. It was made clear, however, that the Nature Conservancy Council would also have standing in such a case because of its official responsibilities for nature conservation.

Restrictions on judicial review

There are a number of restrictions on the use of judicial review as a method of controlling the activities of enforcement bodies. Firstly, as stated previously, the matter is not a hearing of the merits of a case. Thus, when a decision is quashed or a duty is enforced, it does not necessarily mean that the final decision of the administrative body will be to the liking of the person seeking judicial review. A good example of this is in the case of the judicial review of planning decisions. If an Inspector, on appeal, makes a decision which is contrary to the Inquiries Procedure Rules (for instance by not taking into account written representations from objectors), the resulting decision may be challenged. The Inspector's decision in those circumstances could be overturned by the High Court, but the final decision would be referred back to a fresh Inspector, who could very well arrive at the same decision as the first Inspector, even though taking into account the representations made.

Furthermore, where individuals with 'sufficient interest' apply for judicial review of a decision they have to be able to show that they have suffered prejudice. Therefore, although the court is not entitled to make a judgment on the merits of the individual case, it may well be that the substance of the point raised by the interested party shows an unlawful act, but, on the facts of the individual case, the applicant did not suffer any prejudice from the decision itself. Thus, where an interested party was not entitled to put its views across at a planning inquiry, there may well be a breach of the right to a fair hearing. However, where it could be shown that other people had put over a similar case, a judicial review remedy may be refused.

Where there are other remedies available, the court has a discretion to refuse an application for judicial review. Therefore, in the situation where an applicant is seeking an injunction and also has private rights which could give rise to a similar remedy under the common law, a court can refuse to exercise its discretion in relation to the public law remedy.

Overall, the role of judicial review in controlling administrative actions has grown in importance over the past twenty years. The introduction of new concepts to govern the full breadth of administrative action gives rise to an important avenue of redress to the private individual.

The Ombudsman

There may be instances where, although there is no abuse of the statutory power which would render a decision reviewable, there is some maladministration which could give rise to a public complaint. In such cases a complaint can be made to the Ombudsman in control of those activities. In the case of Central Government activities (e.g. the Department of the Environment) the investigating Ombudsman is the Parliamentary Commissioner for Administration, whereas in the case of complaints against a local authority or the National Rivers Authority, the matter is dealt with by the Commissioner for Local Administration. The governing factor in such complaints is whether or not the authority concerned have acted within appropriate standards of administrative conduct, rather than whether or not they have acted lawfully.

Complaints to the Ombudsman normally go through either a local councillor or an MP (depending upon the level of authority concerned). The nature of the Ombudsman remedy is both singular and advisory. Therefore, an aggrieved party who has other rights of action, whether under the common law or by means of judicial review, must pursue that particular avenue, as long as it is realistic to do so. Secondly, an Ombudsman has no statutory power to impose an award of damages. Normally, the Ombudsman will make a recommendation for compensation which, although having no statutory backing, is normally accepted by the statutory body concerned. The role of the Ombudsman should not be underestimated. The incidence of complaints to the Ombudsman has risen in recent years because it is a quick, cheap, and often effective mechanism for channelling complaints about public authorities. It is a mechanism which the public are happy to utilise because of its informal nature and simple procedure. It is perhaps worthwhile to point out that the stages of a complaint are relatively straightforward and provide an adequate opportunity for the proper presentation of grievances. It is also important that the Ombudsman has significant investigatory powers: these will have an impact on the practices of the public bodies over which jurisdiction is exercised.

THREE
Environmental protection agencies

The number of different agencies involved in environmental protection reflects the fragmented nature of policy-making and law enforcement in this area. Whilst there has been some rationalisation in recent years with the establishment of the National Rivers Authority (NRA) and Her Majesty's Inspectorate of Pollution (HMIP), environmental responsibilities remain spread amongst a wide range of bodies.

Some of these bodies exercise purely policy-making functions, whilst others carry out specific regulatory ones. One of the key features of the British system of environmental protection is that powers are, in a sense, decentralised by being given to a range of regulatory agencies, although it must be admitted that often this is only a matter of implementing and enforcing policies decided centrally, or by the EC.

A distinction also needs to be drawn between those bodies which are elected and those which are not. With the exception of local authorities, British regulatory agencies tend not to be elected. In the light of the wide discretions given to most public bodies in environmental matters, and the tradition of making decisions in a secretive manner (see Chapter 7), the accountability of some of these bodies becomes a central question.

Department of the Environment (DoE)

As its name suggests, the DoE has the major responsibility within Central Government for environmental matters. This is mainly manifested at the level of policy, but since environmental law is essentially about the taking of discretionary, political decisions, this means that the DoE has an enormous impact, even if this is not always apparent from a bare statement of the law. However, three important qualifications must be made about the role of the DoE.

First it is not the only part of Central Government which sets policy in relation to environmental matters. Indeed, it is arguable whether there is such a thing as a national environmental policy, as opposed to a set of individual policies for individual issues. Other Government Departments, such as the Ministry of Agriculture, Fisheries and Food (MAFF), the Department of Energy and the Department of Transport, exercise enormous influence in their own fields. The Welsh, Scottish and Northern Ireland Offices also exercise responsibility within their own geographical areas. It is clear that the DoE is not a particularly strong Department within Central Government, even in relation to environmental matters.

Secondly it has few operational powers relating to environmental protection. Those that it does have are often delegated to others. For example, although planning appeals are made to the Secretary of State, in the vast majority of cases they are decided by members of the Planning Inspectorate (although the Inspectorate is formally a part of the DoE).

Thirdly it is not concerned simply with environmental protection. It has a very wide portfolio which includes responsibility for local government (including the vexed question of local government finance), housing, the water industry, sport and recreation. It is fairly clear that some of these areas take priority over environmental protection at present.

Some of these points require amplification. The Secretary of State has very wide legislative and quasi-legislative powers which stem from the framework nature of the main environmental protection legislation, and also from the need to update legislation in the light of EC requirements. Very wide discretionary powers are also granted: for example, the decision whether to declare an area an urban development area is virtually an unfettered discretion given to the Secretary of State.

There are also very wide powers in relation to appeals against decisions made by the regulatory bodies. This is most obvious in the planning area, but an appeal to the Secretary of State is a common feature of many of the regulatory systems covered in this book. This reflects the political (i.e. policy based) nature of much of this area of law. For example, it is significant that the Planning Inspectorate has always been kept within the DoE, rather than being moved to the Lord Chancellor's Department. This reflects the fact that the important feature of its decisions is that they are based on policy rather than on any notion of judicial fairness, despite the increasing formality of planning procedures.

The DoE may impose its policies in a number of ways. Obviously, one is by changing the law (a feature of the British system of Government is that the Government is rarely defeated in Parliament). Another is through exercising powers granted under the legislation. This may include the making of directions, the power to approve actions of regulatory bodies, the power to make appointments to the various regulatory bodies, or the power to hear appeals. Interference has been at its clearest in town planning, where there is the greatest opportunity to disagree over matters of policy (see p. 162). A third method is by the manipulation of available resources. The DoE and the Treasury have complete responsibility for the budgets of a number of the regulatory agencies (e.g. HMIP, the Countryside Commission and the Nature Conservancy Councils). They also control local government finances very tightly. One avenue for future development here is the way that regulatory agencies, such as the NRA, are being encouraged to acquire some financial independence by charging for parts of their work.

Given the importance of independent regulatory agencies in environmental law, it is also significant that the DoE is the channel through which Parliamentary accountability of a number of these agencies, such as the National Rivers Authority and the Countryside Commission, is provided.

Internally, the DoE has four Directorates in its Environmental Protection Group (see Burr, The Department of the Environment, in *Environmental Challenges: The Institutional Dimension*, ICCET, 1990). These are the Directorate of Rural Affairs, with responsibility for the countryside, conservation and rural development, the Directorate of Air, Noise and Wastes, the Central Directorate of Environmental Protection, and Her Majesty's Inspectorate of Pollution.

Other parts of Central Government

Important roles are played by other Government Departments in particular sectors. For example, control of pollution from vehicles is largely the responsibility of the Department of Transport, whilst many policy decisions of central importance to global warming and acid rain are made by the Department of Energy.

An important aspect of decisions is how far they take into account environmental considerations. A number of pieces of legislation now include general requirements to take the environment into account. For example, there is a very vague, but potentially useful, duty imposed on all public bodies in the Countryside Act 1968, s. 11. This states 'In the exercise of their functions relating to land under any enactment every Minister, government department and public body shall have regard to the desirability of conserving the natural beauty and amenity of the countryside'.

This has perhaps been overtaken by a more significant proposal in the White Paper, *This Common Inheritance* (Cm. 1200, 1990). This is that each Government Department should have a nominated Minister responsible for considering the environmental implications of its policies and programmes. These Ministers have now been nominated. There is a strong link with a second proposal that there should be an appraisal of the policies of each Department in the light of their environmental implications.

Parliamentary Select Committees

Parliamentary Select Committees may be said to perform the functions of scrutinising the day-to-day activities of Government. They also, in the environmental field, help to inform public debate outside Parliament. In the House of Lords, the European Communities Sub-Committee has been especially important in analysing the potential impact of proposed EC legislation. In the House of Commons, the Select Committees are organised so as to mirror Government Departments. There is thus a House of Commons Select Committee on the Environment. This body has had a large impact on the direction of environmental policy, and can be said to be influential in this area. Sir Hugh Rossi has been the Chairman since 1983 and in that time the Committee has concentrated on environmental (as opposed to local government or housing) issues, conducting inquiries into Acid Rain (September 1984), the Operation and Effectiveness of Part II of the Wildlife and Countryside Act 1981 (January 1985), Pollution of Rivers and Estuaries (May 1987), Air Pollution (June 1988), Toxic Waste (March 1989) and Pollution of Beaches (July 1990).

There is little doubt that the reports of these inquiries, all of which have been unanimous on a cross-party basis, have an influence on Government. As an example, the Report on Contaminated Land (January 1990) recommended the creation of public registers of contaminated land, a recommendation that was introduced into the Environmental Protection Act 1990, although some of the accompanying proposals were not.

Royal Commission on Environmental Pollution

This is a rather rare beast, a standing Royal Commission with its own Secretariat. It has been in existence since 1970 and has produced 13 Reports on a variety of matters. These Reports have enormous authority in relation to the subject matter discussed and exert a significant influence on the direction of future policy, although by no means all the recommendations of the Royal Commission are implemented. The Royal Commission has been a particularly strong supporter of the widening of access to environmental information, and can also claim to have popularised the concept of 'Best Practicable Environmental Option'. Important Reports have been the Fifth Report, *Air Pollution Control: An Integrated Approach* (Cmnd. 6371, 1976), the Tenth Report, *Tackling Pollution—Experiences and Prospects* (Cmnd. 9149, 1984), the Eleventh Report, *Managing Waste: The Duty of Care* (Cmnd 9675, 1985) and the Twelfth Report, *Best Practicable Environmental Option* (Cm. 310, 1988).

Her Majesty's Inspectorate of Pollution (HMIP)

HMIP has responsibility in England and Wales for operating the system of integrated pollution control introduced by the Environmental Protection Act 1990, the control of scheduled processes under air pollution legislation (until this system is replaced by integrated pollution control), the control of radioactive substances and the monitoring of waste disposal. It therefore has effective responsibility for the regulation of pollution from the most hazardous activities. It also has planning and research functions in relation to these tasks. Despite its name, it has few operational responsibilities for most types of water pollution, waste disposal to land or other polluting activities such as noise. For HMIP's specific powers in relation to integrated pollution control (IPC), see p. 218.

HMIP was established in 1987 with the intention of providing a more integrated and coherent approach to pollution control, particularly through the introduction of such concepts as best practicable environmental option. It brought together the Industrial Air Pollution Inspectorate of the Health and Safety Executive (previously called the Alkali and Clean Air Inspectorate), and the Radiochemical, Hazardous Waste and embryonic Water Inspectorates of the DoE. It is a part of the DoE.

In its short existence it has been dominated by the air pollution and radioactivity functions, though this is set to change as the integrated nature of its new responsibilities has an effect on its operation. This domination is important in view of the history of controls in those areas, where the tradition has been for a somewhat secretive and conciliatory approach to be taken to polluters.

A problem for HMIP since its creation has been a shortage of resources, particularly staff. This was a major reason for the introduction of IPC being delayed to April 1991. It is reported as having a staff complement of 223 in January 1991, with approval given for an expansion to over 300 by the end of 1991/2 and over 400 when IPC is fully operational. However, in September 1990, HMIP reported vacancies for 24 Inspectors out of a total complement of 135. One reason has been thought to be the low pay relative to equivalent jobs in industry, so pay increases have been introduced in an attempt to rectify the problem. The adequate funding of HMIP remains one of its major difficulties.

Until October 1989, HMIP was organised in four divisions, dealing with air, water, radioactivity and hazardous wastes. In preparation for IPC, it was reorganised into three Regions (East, based in Bedford; West, based in Bristol; and North, based in Leeds), which deal with all aspects of pollution in their areas. These regional offices are supported by a central Regulatory Standards Division, which coordinates guidance and technical standards. There are also five industry groups which cover the main sectors within IPC.

The current responsibilities of HMIP are as follows:

(a)   In relation to air pollution, it has responsibility for 2,000 works operating 3,000 scheduled processes under the provisions of the Health and Safety at Work etc. Act 1974 and the Alkali etc. Works Regulation Act 1906. This will be replaced over the next five years by responsibility for around 5,000 works under the IPC system. The remaining air pollution matters will be the responsibility of local authorities.

(b)   In relation to water pollution, HMIP exercises control over discharges from processes covered by IPC, though it is subject to a degree of interference from the National Rivers Authority (NRA). It also licences aqueous radioactive discharges. All other discharges are the responsibility of the NRA (for controlled waters) and the relevant sewerage undertaker (for discharges to sewers). Prior to the Water Act 1989, HMIP was responsible for granting discharge consents to water authorities; this function has now been taken over by the NRA.

(c)   In relation to radioactive emissions, HMIP operates the authorisation procedures under the Radioactive Substances Act 1960. These cover the registration of 6,000 premises and the authorisation of over 1,000 waste disposal processes.

(d)   On waste disposal, HMIP has a largely supervisory and research role. Its functions include monitoring the management of hazardous wastes, publishing waste management papers and giving advice to waste disposal authorities.

National Rivers Authority (NRA)

The NRA is an independent, non-departmental public agency which has been in existence since 1 September 1989, when it was established under the Water Act 1989. It has taken over many of the regulatory powers of the old regional water authorities and has responsibility in England and Wales for a wide range of water matters. Included within this is primary responsibility for dealing with pollution of inland, underground and coastal waters, although HMIP takes over whenever a process is subject to IPC.

The other functions of the NRA relate to flood defence and land drainage, water resources and the licensing of abstractions, salmon and freshwater fisheries, navigation, conservancy and harbour authority functions. In addition, it has environmental duties set out in the Water Act 1989, s. 8 and a number of ancillary powers. These relate to such things as the acquisition of information (s. 118), and powers of entry and taking of samples (s. 147).

The NRA must have a minimum of 8 and a maximum of 15 members, who are to be appointed by the Secretary of State for the Environment, the Secretary of State for Wales and the Minister of Agriculture, Fisheries and Food. At present there are 15 members. Other provisions relating to its structure, including its powers to employ people and a wide power to delegate, are set out in the Water Act 1989, sch. 1. It is not a Crown body and therefore does not benefit from Crown immunity.

The NRA has a regional structure, based on the old regional water authority regions. Each of these regions has a consultative Regional Rivers Advisory Committee established under the Water Act, s. 2. There is a further Advisory Committee for Wales established under s. 3. Nevertheless, one of the strengths of the NRA is its national status and it is striving to build up a uniform system of pollution control throughout the country. This is to be achieved by the establishment of uniform policies and practices on setting discharge consents and on enforcement.

The financing of the NRA is quite complex, since it varies for each of its functions. For flood defence, money is raised by a levy on county and metropolitan councils, who will recoup this through drainage charges. For water resources, the cost of the system is recovered through charges for abstractions. The NRA is also undergoing a period of change as far as the financing of water pollution control is concerned. In relation to pollution control, the main source of money in the first year of operation was Treasury grant, but a scheme for charging for discharges to controlled waters has now been introduced. It came into force on 1 July 1991 and is expected to raise £41m per year (see p. 314).

Sewerage undertakers

In relation to discharges to sewers, the licensing body is the privatised sewerage undertaker, which grants what are called trade effluent consents. This is an unusual example of a private body undertaking an environmental regulation function, although it is arguable that a sewerage undertaker is in reality doing little different from a private waste disposal contractor in providing a method of waste disposal through privately owned facilities. Appeals against trade effluent consent decisions go to the Director General of Water Services, who was appointed under the Water Act 1989 and whose main functions relate to the regulatory control of the newly privatised water industry. For a further explanation of the water industry see Chapter 13.

General environmental duties and the water industry

Under the Water Act 1989, s. 8, all bodies with responsibilities in relation to water (i.e. the NRA, water and sewerage undertakers, the Director General of Water Services, internal drainage boards, and the Secretary of State and Minister of Agriculture, Fisheries and Food when carrying out water-related functions) are placed under some general environmental duties. These include *furthering* the conservation and enhancement of natural beauty and the conservation of flora, fauna and geological and physiographical features of special interest, and *having regard to* such things as matters of archaeological, architectural and historic interest, the beauty and amenity of an area, the nature conservation interest of an area, and public access to natural and other features.

In addition, the NRA is placed under a duty to *promote* the conservation and enhancement of the natural beauty and amenity of inland and coastal waters and associated lands, the conservation of flora and fauna dependent on an aquatic environment, and the use of such waters and lands for recreational purposes. Further specific duties are laid down in relation to specially protected sites, such as sites of special scientific interest (SSSIs) (see p. 351). A Code of Practice on Conservation, Access and Recreation has been issued jointly by the Secretaries of State and the Minister of Agriculture, Fisheries and Food under the Water Act 1989, s. 10, after consultation with a large range of interested bodies. Contravention does not give rise to any criminal offence or civil right of action, but will be taken into account by relevant bodies in deciding whether to use any powers available to them.

These general duties are couched in fairly positive terms. Whilst they may not give rise to direct legal rights they are of enormous importance in internal decision-making within these bodies and as political levers for environmentally-sensitive decisions. They are certainly stronger than in other legislation and may act as a model for other systems.

Countryside bodies

Within the countryside, the absence of a controlling 'Department of Rural Affairs', such as many other countries possess, is crucial. In the past the dominant force has tended to be MAFF, simply by virtue of the weight of resources available to it. This has traditionally been a very insular Ministry, although under the Agriculture Act 1986, s. 17, the Agriculture Ministers are now required to seek to achieve a balance between the interests of agriculture, the economic and social needs of rural areas, and conservation and recreation.

There are, however, other independent agencies within the Government responsible for specific matters. In England there is a Nature Conservancy Council for England (known as English Nature) and a Countryside Commission, which have responsibilities for nature conservation and for recreation, landscape and amenity respectively. This division of responsibility reflects a split in functions decided upon as long ago as 1949 and some reasons behind this are explained in Chapter 15. The Nature Conservancy Council was organised on a Great Britain basis until 1 April 1991 when, for largely political reasons, it was split into three separate national bodies by the Environmental Protection Act 1990. (In this book, for ease of reference, these are referred to generically as the Nature Conservancy Councils.) In Wales, the nature conservation functions were amalgamated with the amenity functions in a new Countryside Council for Wales. In Scotland, a similar body called Scottish Natural Heritage has been established under the Natural Heritage (Scotland) Act 1991, which also combines the two functions. There is no intention at present to combine the Nature Conservancy Council for England and the Countryside Commission for England. In addition, there is the Forestry Commission, which has some environmental and amenity duties as well as duties relating to the promotion of commercial forestry.

Local authorities

Since the abolition of the metropolitan county councils in 1986, there have been two separate structures for local government in England and Wales. There are three if the system within London is counted separately, although it is similar to the one that applies in the metropolitan areas. In metropolitan areas, there is a one-tier system, the metropolitan district councils. These obviously have responsibility for all matters, although some functions (police, fire, transport and, in some metropolitan areas, waste management) are run by joint boards of the Councils. In non-metropolitan areas, there is a two-tier system of county and district councils. In constitutional terms these two tiers are equal, but they have differing responsibilities. County councils have responsibility for the police, fire services, personal social services, transport, highways, education, libraries, waste management and strategic planning. District councils have responsibility for housing, development control, recreation, and environmental and public health.

This split causes problems for the public, which often finds it difficult to identify which tier is responsible for any particular matter. The problem is particularly acute in the environmental sphere because of the overlapping powers of the two tiers (e.g. in town planning). In April 1991, the Government issued a consultation paper on the future of local government which suggests that the two-tier system will be abolished in some counties, citing the confusion over who is responsible for what as one factor which clouds democratic and financial accountability in these areas.

Any reorganisation is still a few years away. Until then, there are 36 metropolitan district councils, 33 London borough councils (including the City of London), 47 county councils and 373 district councils, all of which undertake a wide variety of tasks in relation to environmental protection. There are 5 main areas to consider:

(a) Town and country planning

The local authority is normally the local planning authority. This means that it is responsible for the making of development plans and for the control of development. The powers also incorporate responsibility for related matters, such as tree preservation orders, listed building protection, conservation areas, hazardous substances consents, the control of derelict land, and the protection of the countryside. As explained above, planning functions are split between county and district councils, with county councils being responsible for strategic planning and for National Parks, minerals and waste disposal matters, whilst district councils have responsibility for other development control decisions. The scope for conflict between the two tiers was lessened slightly by the reduction in the range of county functions in the Local Government, Planning and Land Act 1980.

(b) Waste regulation and disposal

The county council is the waste disposal authority under the Control of Pollution Act 1974. It is also the local planning authority for waste disposal applications. In Wales, these functions are carried out by district councils. In the new system which is being introduced under the Environmental Protection Act 1990, county councils will become waste regulation authorities. Disposal of waste will be carried out by 'arms-length' local authority waste disposal companies, in an attempt to split the current 'poacher-gamekeeper' role of the county councils, and to encourage competition with private firms for waste disposal. (For the exact roles of these various bodies, see Chapter 12.)

(c) Public health matters

Local authorities have always had responsibility for a very wide range of matters under the Public Health Acts. In particular, this involves duties in relation to the control of statutory nuisances, the law on which it has been remodelled in the Environmental Protection Act 1990, Part III (see Chapter 8). Local authorities also have powers as principal litter authorities in relation to new duties and offences laid out in the Environmental Protection Act 1990, Part IV.

(d) The control of noise

Local authorities have primary responsibility for the control of noise from premises. In the past these provisions have been separate from those relating to statutory nuisance, but in the Environmental Protection Act 1990 the two sets of powers are treated together (see Chapter 8).

(e) Air pollution

Local authorities have long had responsibility for the control of smoke, dust, grit and fumes under the Clean Air Acts and related legislation. In the Environmental Protection Act 1990, Part I, they are given more complete powers to control air pollution from plants which are not the responsibility of HMIP under integrated pollution control.

One of the difficulties with this range of powers is that, when faced with a local pollution problem, people are frequently confused as to whether it is the responsibility of the local planning authority, the Environmental Health Department, or the waste disposal authority. The problem is compounded by the range of other agencies with environmental powers and duties. The result is that the majority of complaints are directed in the first instance to the Environmental Health Department, even if that is not the appropriate body.

Decision-making in local authorities

Local authorities are elected bodies. In theory it is the elected councillors who make the ultimate decisions, usually through the appropriate committee. However, in practice, most actual decisions are taken by officers, with the committee rubber stamping them. The councillors are always free to disagree with the recommendation of an officer, but, in so doing, they must be careful to act only on grounds permitted in the relevant legislation, otherwise their decision will be capable of being challenged as *ultra vires*. The constitutional monopoly of the elected councillors has also been removed. The Local Government Act 1972, s. 101, provides that the Local Authority may delegate any of its powers (apart from a few that must be exercised by a resolution of the whole council, such as the adoption of a local plan) to committees, or to specified officers.

This structure makes councils accountable to the electorate. But it also means that the range of considerations taken into account by local authorities is necessarily wider than those which relate simply to environmental protection. Local authorities, because of their elected status, have a democratic right to balance the advantages of conflicting courses of action which is arguably lacking in many other bodies, even if it does occasionally mean that strange decisions are reached.

In addition, all local authorities are subject to rules on the ability of the public to attend meetings and to receive information about the council's activities. Originally, the Public Bodies (Admission to Meetings) Act 1960 gave members of the public a right of admission to meetings of local authorities. This was extended in the Local Government Act 1972, s. 100, to cover all committee meetings. That provision was itself greatly expanded in the Local Government (Access to Information) Act 1985, which added new ss. 100A-100K to the 1972 Act. In essence, a member of the public has a right not only to attend meetings of the council and its committees and sub-committees, but also to have access to agendas, minutes, and background reports. This enables information to be obtained on such things as the grounds for a decision, or whether the councillors have diverged from the recommendation of an officer. This written information must be available at all reasonable hours at the offices of the council, and members of the public may make copies of it.

There are limitations. There is a list of exempt information, and the council may resolve to exclude the public if publicity would be prejudicial to the public interest. This may cover meetings such as those to consider whether to recommend that enforcement action is taken on a particular issue, since it may be rendered useless if prior warning is obtained. However, in practice, many local authorities not only allow access to meetings, but permit objectors to address the meeting.

Unlike the questions of secrecy and access to environmental information covered in Chapter 7, the purpose of these powers is to show openness in decision-making and to give an impression of public accountability in what is accepted to be a political system. These powers should therefore be compared with the restrictions on access to meetings of most of the other regulatory bodies discussed.

Mention of local authorities would not be complete without a reference to their current finances. It is quite clear that with restrictions on spending they are unable to carry out properly many of the tasks entrusted to them in the environmental area, thus calling into question the effective enforcement of parts of environmental law.

The future: an environmental protection agency?

In 1989 the House of Commons Select Committee on the Environment, in its Report on Toxic Waste, recommended that an Environmental Protection Commission should be established with responsibility for the whole range of pollution control matters. This recommendation was rejected by the Government, a stance that was reiterated in the White Paper *This Common Inheritance* (Cm. 1200, 1990). One reason given was that there have been many changes in relation to environmental protection in recent years, and that such a major change may have to wait until things have settled down. The White Paper did suggest, however, that consideration would be given to the establishment of an umbrella body overseeing the work of HMIP and the NRA. It also proposed that HMIP should become a separate executive agency within the Government (i.e., a 'Next Steps' agency) 'as soon as possible', although it would still remain part of the DoE. (Similar status has also been recommended for the Planning Inspectorate.) An independent HMIP Advisory Committee was also proposed.

However, in an important reversal of policy in July 1991, the Prime Minister, John Major, announced the Government's intention to introduce a unified environmental protection agency, merging HMIP, the NRA and the Drinking Water Inspectorate. No details have been provided on the degree of independence such an agency would possess under these proposals, or on the time scale for its introduction, but, given that all the political parties are now committed to such a body, it will be a major surprise if one is not established in the next few years.

FOUR

The European Community and the environment

Notwithstanding its economic basis, the EC is a major and increasing source of British environmental protection law. It also has a central and profound influence on the direction of environmental policy, both at a Community level and within each Member State. As a result, every subject covered by this book is affected, either directly or indirectly, by the activities of the EC.

There are four main ways in which the EC plays a role in shaping British environmental law and policy:

(a) Some pieces of EC legislation lay down rules and standards that are directly enforceable in Member States without any need for further implementation. In these cases EC law is British law. This is rare in the environmental field.

(b) Other pieces of EC legislation are addressed to Member States and require changes in British law or administrative practice. This is normally the situation in relation to environmental legislation, because of the predominant use of Directives, which are not usually directly effective within Member States (see p. 43). British law is therefore not necessarily the same as EC law until the EC law has been implemented. In such cases the precise role of the EC in initiating the change is often forgotten, since the domestic legislation resulting from the EC requirements will constitute the law which is applied in practice. An important point to note is that EC law and British law often differ in such circumstances, because EC law frequently consists of aims and goals rather than precise legal rules, and allows for some discretion in the Member States as to how and when to implement it.

(c) The third role is somewhat wider and rests upon the constitutional position that Britain now occupies as a Member State of the EC. The EC not only passes environmental laws, it has an environmental policy. This policy and the general economic and environmental principles which underpin it exert an important influence on British policy-making and on British attitudes towards environmental law and its enforcement. The direction in which environmental protection will go therefore depends as much on wider European attitudes as it does on engrained British ideas, although of course British ideas will in turn help to mould the general EC view and to affect the attitudes of the other Member States.

(d) Finally, the economic policies of the EC have a profound effect on the direction of both EC and domestic environmental law. Environmental protection cannot be isolated from economic policy and the current push for the substantial completion of the single internal market by the end of 1992 will have significant spin-off effects on the environment. Indeed, many 'green' commentators would argue that the economic policies of the EC, based as they are on economic growth and on economies of scale in industrial and agricultural production, are themselves antithetical to the achievement of the aims of a clean environment and conservation of natural resources.

The specific pieces of EC law and policy that have an influence on British law will be integrated into the relevant chapters of the rest of the book. This chapter will concentrate on more general matters, such as the place of environmental policy within the EC, the history and principles of that policy, the institutions of the EC and their law-making and enforcement powers, and the way in which the policies and laws are implemented in Britain.

The nature of the EC

The EC is more than just a free trade agreement between twelve fairly similar Western European states. It has institutions and law-making powers of its own, making it a form of supranational state in which the Member States have limited their sovereign rights, albeit within limited fields (although for political reasons the extent of this is often denied).

The activities over which the EC has powers are set out in the Treaties which establish the EC, which are effectively the EC's constitution. In fact there are three Treaties and three linked Communities, the European Economic Community (EEC), the European Coal and Steel Community (ECSC) and the European Atomic Energy Community (Euratom). It is the EEC, established by the Treaty of Rome and amended by agreement of all the Member States in the Single European Act 1986, which is the central Community and to which environmental policy relates. All future references to Treaty Articles are to the EEC Treaty, as amended.

The institutions of the EC

The four main EC institutions are the Commission, the Council, the Parliament, and the European Court of Justice. Each has powers and duties specified in the Treaty and an obligation to further the aims of the EC. There is also an advisory Economic and Social Committee.

The European Commission

The Commission is the executive of the EC. It consists of 17 independent members appointed by the Member States (two each from the five larger states—

Germany, France, Britain, Italy and Spain—and one each from the others), serviced by a large number of officials. It has responsibility for implementing EC policies and initiates and draws up proposals for legislation for the Council to approve. It also has a major responsibility for policing and enforcing EC law, in which role it has extensive investigatory powers.

It is the Commission which draws up the environment action programmes and drafts proposed EC legislation. By means of information agreements with the Member States, the Commission is informed of proposals for domestic legislation and these often give rise to a Commission proposal for a common policy across the EC. However, the ambivalent nature of the Commission must be appreciated. On the one hand it is often the driving force behind new environmental policies: on the other, it is responsible for enforcing the economic aims of the EC (see its position in the *Danish Bottles* case—p. 53).

Internally the Commission is divided into a number of Directorates. Directorate General XI (DG XI) deals with Environment, Consumer Protection and Nuclear Safety. As a result of the formal adoption of the principle that environmental policies should form a component of the EC's other policies, DG XI has had its hand strengthened in relation to its dealings with other Directorates, such as those with responsibility for transport and energy policy, which have traditionally tended to have greater influence.

The Council of Ministers

The Council is a political body made up of one representative of each Member State. The identity of this representative alters according to the nature of the business. Thus, transport ministers normally agree transport measures, environment ministers normally agree environmental measures and so on. As a body it has a duty to ensure the attainment of the Treaty objectives, but clearly national interests play a central role in the Council's decisions.

As a result the Council's voting procedures are crucial. There are some differences in the procedures to be adopted for different matters, but most legislation has to be passed unanimously by the Council, acting on a proposal from the Commission, and after consultation with Parliament and the Economic and Social Committee. Some legislation can be passed by a qualified majority of the Council, a system of weighted voting in which two large States (including Britain) or up to five small States can be outvoted (see p. 51).

The European Parliament

The European Parliament is mainly a consultative and advisory body, although it does have some supervisory powers over the Commission and the budget. The advent of direct elections in 1979 revitalised the European Parliament and it has been a significant mouthpiece of concern over environmental issues ever since. For example, it set in motion a ban on imports of sealskin products. It also has an important role in ensuring a certain amount of openness in EC decision-making. The deliberations of the Council and the Commission are secret, and debates on proposals for legislation in Parliament are the only open part of the EC's decision-making process.

The Single European Act 1986 increased Parliament's powers over legislation in a significant way. Consultation with Parliament has always been a mandatory requirement, in the absence of which a piece of EC legislation will be void. Parliament now has increased powers, under the 'Cooperation Procedure' set out in Article 149, to reject, or propose amendments to, legislation subject to qualified majority voting. The procedures are complex, but in essence the Council will adopt a 'common position' based on the Commission's proposals. If Parliament rejects this 'common position', the Council may only adopt the measure if it does so unanimously. If Parliament proposes amendments, the Commission must reconsider the matter. It may choose to insert Parliament's amendments and, if it does so, the Council has a choice: it can either agree the amended proposal by a qualified majority, or it can agree some other formula unanimously, or it can allow the proposal to lapse.

This procedure was used in relation to Directive 89/458 on Emissions from Small Cars, when Parliament inserted a stricter test than that wanted by the majority of the Council or originally proposed by the Commission. The Commission agreed with the stricter test and amended the proposal, thus effectively forcing the Council to agree also, or face not having a Directive at all (see Haigh and Baldock, *Environmental Policy and 1992*, 1989).

The European Environmental Bureau, an umbrella organisation of environmental groups, has recently suggested the extension of the 'Cooperation Procedure' to all environmental measures brought under Article 130S, which at present normally requires unanimity in the Council (for Article 130s, see p. 50). This may well be in line with the thinking of some Member States, and would to some limited extent tackle the problem of the secrecy and lack of democratic accountability of EC legislative procedures.

The European Court of Justice

The European Court of Justice consists of 13 judges appointed by common agreement of the Member States. It is assisted by six Advocates-General, one of whom makes reasoned submissions to the Court in each case. It has supreme authority on matters of EC law. This means that it has ultimate power to interpret the meaning of the Treaties and of any legislation made by the other institutions. The Court can thus, if asked, review the legitimacy of the actions of the other institutions, provide answers on matters of EC law to Member States' courts and declare whether Member States are implementing EC law properly.

Article 177 plays a major role here. Under Article 177, any court or tribunal in a Member State can refer any matter of EC law to the European Court of Justice for its interpretation of the law. This procedure aims to ensure uniformity between Member States in their application of the law. It also provides a quick way of obtaining an authoritative ruling. Since the Court is the ultimate arbiter of any law having an EC input, Article 177 references should be made where there is any doubt as to the meaning of EC law, or the compatibility of domestic law with it. However, one drawback is that national courts effectively have a discretion whether to make a reference or not.

In carrying out its functions the European Court of Justice has been exceptionally activist and creative. It has developed several novel principles, including the doctrines of the supremacy of EC law and of direct effects, and has been responsible for extending the scope of the powers of all the institutions (including itself). It has done this by adopting a purposive approach to interpretation in which it looks as much at the spirit as at the letter of the law. On matters of EC law, therefore, the Court's view is central to any discussion of the law. For example, in Cases 206 and 207/88 *Vessoso* and *Zanetti* ([1990] 2 LMELR 133), it ruled that the definition of waste in the Framework Directive on Waste 75/442 included waste which was to be recycled, since it was waste as far as the disposer was concerned irrespective of the intentions of the recipient.

The Court gives one agreed judgment. These are often very brief and formal and for the full reasoning the opinion of the Advocate-General must be read, although sometimes the Court and the Advocate-General do not agree. The European Court of Justice should not be confused with the European Court of Human Rights, which exists to police the European Convention on Human Rights.

The European Environment Agency

The European Environment Agency is a new body provided for in Regulation 1210/90. However, the Regulation will not come into force until the seat of the Agency is decided, a matter which is proving controversial. The Agency has been established with the limited role of gathering information and data on the state of the environment in the EC. A report on the state of the environment must be published every three years. It also has functions relating to the dissemination of that information and the harmonisation of methods of measurement of data throughout the EC. This will include such things as the development of adequate forecasting and cost-benefit techniques. In order to help with these tasks, the European Environment Information and Observation Network will be established, under which Member States must inform the Agency of their main national environmental information networks, which the Agency will then integrate into an EC Network. In recognition of the international nature of environmental pollution, the Agency is open to non-EC members.

The Agency has not been given any enforcement or policing powers in relation to environmental legislation, despite a determined attempt by the European Parliament to introduce such powers by proposing amendments to the Regulation. However, there is a provision in the Regulation that requires the Council to reconsider the scope of the Agency's powers within two years of the Regulation coming into force, in particular specifying a possible role in the monitoring of the implementation of EC environmental legislation. In time, therefore, the Agency may well evolve into a European Environment Inspectorate, as proposed by the European Environment Bureau.

Sources of EC law

EC law is contained in the Treaties, legislation passed by the institutions, international treaties to which the EC is a party, and the judgments and principles of the European Court of Justice.

To understand the relevance of these sources, an explanation of the concepts of the supremacy of EC law and direct effects is required. The doctrine of the supremacy of EC law is that, where there is a conflict between EC law and national law, EC law prevails, even if the national law is later in time; national courts should thus apply EC law rather than national law which does not comply with EC law. This is, however, intimately linked with the idea of direct effects. A law has direct effects if it gives rise to rights and obligations which can be enforced by individuals and companies before national courts. If an EC law is directly effective in this sense, the doctrine of supremacy means that the non-conforming national law can simply be ignored.

Not all EC law is directly effective in this sense. For any provision to be directly effective it must be sufficiently clear and precise to form a cause of action. It must also be unconditional and must not require further definition at the discretion of the Member State. There are also limitations on direct effects related to the source of the EC law. Treaty Articles and Regulations are capable of having direct effects, as long as they fulfil the above tests. For Directives, the Treaty suggested that they would not be capable of having direct effects. However, the European Court of Justice has indulged in some significant judicial legislation and has decided that Directives may have direct effects if the action is against the State or an emanation of the State, but not if against another private body. Since most environmental legislation is in the form of Directives, this is of great importance.

Even if not directly effective, EC law may have some effect in domestic courts. The European Court of Justice held in *Von Colson* [1986] 2 CMLR 430 that domestic legislation must be interpreted so as to comply with EC law if the domestic law was passed to implement it, and the House of Lords has accepted and approved this view in *Litster v Forth Dry Dock & Engineering Co Ltd* [1989] 2 WLR 634.

Treaty provisions

The provisions of the EC Treaties lay down the powers of the EC institutions and the procedures for decision-making. They are of enormous importance in actions before the Court relating to the legality of EC actions. In addition, some Treaty provisions are directly effective (e.g. Article 119 on equal pay), but this is not the case for the Articles concerned with the environment.

Regulations

Regulations are legislative acts of general application. They are normally directly effective, as long as they are sufficiently precise. However, there are few Regulations in the environmental sphere, except those relating to international wildlife protection (which mainly give effect to international treaties), agriculture and the European Environment Agency.

Directives
Directives are addressed to Member States and are binding as to the result
to be achieved. They are well-suited to environmental measures, since they
leave the choice of how to implement them to the Member States, which will
each have different methods for setting environmental laws. Most EC
environmental legislation is in the form of Directives.

Normally implementation is required within a specified time period (often
two years). This will be done by the Member State changing its domestic
law and it will be in breach if it has not *fully and correctly* implemented the
Directive within the time limit. In Britain, once the Directive is implemented
the domestic rule will constitute the relevant law.

A distinction must be drawn here between formal and actual compliance.
Changing the law to comply with EC law constitutes formal compliance.
However, this is no guarantee that the law is complied with in practice since,
for example, a regulatory agency may exercise its discretion not to enforce
the law. Increasingly the Commission is looking for evidence of both formal
and actual compliance, although its lack of resources for monitoring
developments in all the Member States hampers this. The creation of the
European Environment Agency may well help here in the future.

A Directive cannot be relied upon in the courts of a Member State unless
it is directly effective. Originally it was assumed that no Directive could be
directly effective, since discretion was given to the Member States on the method
of their implementation. But, the European Court of Justice has held that
some Directives which are sufficiently precise as to the ends to be achieved
are directly effective once the time limit has expired. However, even then,
Directives have direct effect *only* against a Member State or an emanation
of the State (this is known as vertical direct effect), not against another private
body or person (horizontal direct effect). The reason for this distinction is
that the State itself cannot plead a failure to implement the Directive properly
as a defence—a form of estoppel principle (see the European Court of Justice
decision in *Marshall* v *Southampton and South West Hampshire Area Health
Authority* [1986] 2 WLR 780).

An 'emanation of the State' has been defined widely by the European Court
of Justice in *Foster* v *British Gas plc* [1990] 3 All ER 897, where it was stated
that:

> a body, whatever its legal form, which has been made responsible pursuant
> to a measure adopted by the state, for providing a public service under
> the control of the state, and had for that purpose special powers beyond
> those which resulted from the normal rules applicable in relations between
> individuals, is included among the bodies against which the provisions of
> a Directive capable of having direct effect might be relied upon.

One limitation is that it is up to the national courts to apply this test.

The effect of these cases is that some environmental Directives will be directly
effective in some circumstances. If that is the case, an incompatible domestic
law can be ignored and the Directive applied instead by the national court.

But a significant restriction is that in order for a Directive to be relied upon directly there must be someone with a direct cause of action that can be brought in the British courts, and this is rare in the field of administrative regulation. There have not yet been any cases on this matter, but it is at least arguable that a Directive laying down precise limit values, such as Directive 80/778 on Drinking Water, may be directly effective.

Decisions

Decisions are binding on the individual or group to whom they are addressed, and may also be directly effective. They are again rare in environmental law, being limited mainly to matters of monitoring and information gathering, but precautionary steps in relation to CFCs were taken in the 1980s by means of Decisions. The institutions may also issue Recommendations and Opinions. These are not binding and only have a persuasive effect.

Validity of EC legislation

The validity of Regulations, Directives and Decisions can be challenged within two months under Article 173. This Article sets out grounds which are slightly wider than the English *ultra vires* rules. As a judicial review action it also requires the applicant to have *locus standi*. Member States, the Commission, the Council and Parliament have it, whilst an individual has to show direct and individual concern. Such a requirement virtually restricts individuals to challenging Decisions addressed to them. The only Directive to be challenged successfully under Article 173 is Directive 89/428 on the Titanium Dioxide Industry (see *Commission* v *Council*, European Court of Justice, 11 June 1991).

The decisions of the European Court of Justice give rise to law and this has been a particularly fertile area. The Court has developed the idea of direct effects, extending it to Directives and Decisions, and the concept of supremacy of EC law. In so doing it has borrowed and developed general principles of law from the jurisprudence of the Member States, such as the principles of natural justice, proportionality, certainty, equality and the protection of legitimate expectations. The concept of proportionality is a particularly important one in environmental law and was applied in the *Danish Bottles* case (*Commission* v *Denmark*) [1989] 54 CMLR 619 (see p. 53).

Compliance by Member States with EC law

Under Article 5, Member States are required to 'take all appropriate measures, whether general or particular, to ensure fulfilment of the obligations arising out of this Treaty or resulting from action taken by institutions of the Community'. A further requirement is to 'abstain from any measure which could jeopardise the attainment of the objectives of the Treaty'. Abiding by EC law therefore entails a positive and a negative obligation: implementation of relevant Directives, and not doing anything contrary to EC law. Since environmental law consists mainly of Directives, compliance will be discussed in terms of them.

In order to comply with a Directive, a Member State must implement it fully and within the time limit. Any incompatible law must be repealed. It is irrelevant whether other States have also failed to comply.

It thus appears that there are a number of ways in which there may be non-compliance with a Directive:

(a) failure to implement at all within the time allowed (the case law is clear that there is no real excuse for this, since the Member State will have agreed the time limit in the first place);

(b) failure to implement all the requirements of the Directive;

(c) implementation by adopting an incorrect interpretation of the Directive, the European Court of Justice being the ultimate arbiter of this point;

(d) attempting to implement by mere changes in administrative practice; *Commission* v *Belgium* [1982] CMLR 627 makes it clear that a change in the law is required, because administrative measures may be altered at any time by the administration;

(e) inadequate enforcement of measures that have been implemented.

Each Member State will normally be required to send a 'compliance letter' to the Commission explaining the measures that have been taken to ensure compliance with a Directive. These provisions are often stated in each individual Directive, but have not always been adhered to rigorously in the past. Accordingly, the Commission has recently proposed a draft Directive relating to the harmonisation of provisions on reports on the implementation of environmental Directives (OJ 1990 L214/6). If accepted, this will no doubt increase the Commission's ability to identify non-compliance, as will the creation of the European Environment Agency, though at present it is quite clear that complaints from environmental groups and individuals in Member States are the most significant sources of information on non-implementation.

If a Member State does not implement a Directive properly, or maintains in force a law which is contrary to EC law, there are only a limited number of options. The main responsibility for ensuring compliance rests with the Commission which has a discretion to start infringement proceedings. Its current policy is to start these automatically in cases where any failure to comply is alleged.

These infringement proceedings have various stages. The Commission will write to the State informally, asking it to explain its position. If a satisfactory answer is not received, a formal letter will be sent, and the State's observations will be formally required. If the Commission is still not satisfied that the matter can be settled, it will issue a Reasoned Opinion, explaining what it thinks are the main features of the non-compliance. Most cases are resolved at these preliminary stages, and there are obvious parallels with the graded procedures adopted in practice by most regulatory agencies when dealing with breaches of domestic environmental law.

Under Article 169, the Commission then has a discretion to bring the Member State before the European Court of Justice. Another Member State may join in Article 169 proceedings as a third party to argue for one side or the other (Britain did this to support the Commission in the *Danish Bottles* case). If the Commission does not bring infringement proceedings, another Member State may bring them under Article 170, though this is very rare. An individual has no *locus standi* to bring infringement proceedings, or to compel the Commission to do so.

The European Court of Justice is the sole arbiter of whether there has been compliance in law, and will give a decision on whether the State is in breach of EC law, but it has few powers to enforce its ruling. Nevertheless, States normally do comply as a matter of political necessity. Otherwise the Commission or another Member State can reinstitute the infringement proceedings (again this is rare). The Commission has also recently suggested the possibility of withholding funds provided by the EC for environmental matters in the event of non-compliance.

A directly effective law can be relied upon directly in the courts of Member States without the need for implementation and any incompatible national law can simply be ignored. An individual wishing to rely on a Directive rather than on a contrary national law might try to get a national court to refer the question of its direct effects under Article 177.

The common market

The fundamental basis of the EC has always been economic. The primary aims are set out in Articles 2 and 3 of the Treaty of Rome, which established the EEC in 1957. These are the creation of a 'common market' (i.e. a fully integrated single internal market within the boundaries of the Member States) in 'goods, persons, services and capital', together with the progressive harmonisation of the economic policies of the Member States. In order to achieve these primary aims, internal barriers to trade and competition need to be dismantled, so that there are no internal frontiers to hamper the free movement of goods, persons, services and capital, and no discrimination between people or firms on the grounds of nationality. This policy of free competition may be referred to as the provision of a level playing-field for producers across the EC. Common tariff barriers against the outside world are also to be erected and common policies developed in relation to certain key sectors of the economy, such as agriculture, transport, coal and steel, and energy.

This fundamental economic basis remains. In 1985, the Member States agreed to push for the completion of a fully integrated internal market by the end of 1992, and this requirement was incorporated into the Treaty as Article 8A by the Single European Act 1986. There is little doubt that this has led to fresh impetus towards economic integration, although there is equally little doubt that full integration will have to wait for some time after 1992 in some sectors (e.g. fiscal policy).

It is clear that there is a fundamental conflict between some of these aims and the protection of the environment. This problem has been tackled by the creation of an environmental policy.

The EC's environmental policy

There was no mention of the environment in the original Treaty of Rome. To some extent this was because the primary aims of the EEC were, as explained above, economic, but it was mainly because the potential environmental impact of the expansionist, growth-related economic policies adopted at the time was not perceived. By the early 1970s, however, the need for some form of policy on the protection of the environment was accepted. There were two reasons for this. One was the acceptance of the interrelationship between economic growth and environmental degradation. The other was that the environment was then emerging as a significant political issue. Environmental protection thus fits into the activities of the EC in two overlapping ways: first as an adjunct to economic policy, and secondly as a positive end in itself.

In October 1972, declaring that 'economic expansion is not an end in itself', the Heads of State of the Member States accordingly requested the Commission to draw up an EC environmental policy. It responded by formulating the first Action Programme on the Environment. This has been followed by three further Action Programmes in 1977, 1982 and 1987 (the latter is due to expire in 1992). This was the effective beginning of what is now a very wide-ranging environmental strategy. (Even so, it was not actually the beginning of EC involvement in environmental matters—as long ago as 1967, Directive 67/548 provided specifically for the classification, packaging and labelling of dangerous substances.) Well over 100 items of environmental legislation have now been agreed as part of this policy, ranging across the whole spectrum of matters covered by this book.

The constitutional justification for this policy was not at all clear before 1986, but it was never directly challenged. In 1986, the Single European Act went some way towards reflecting the reality of the situation by amending the Treaty to add a whole new Title relating to the protection of the environment. It also added some express social aims, such as health and safety of workers, consumer protection, and research and technological development, to reflect a similar expansion of activity in those fields. There remains a very live political issue about how far this widening of the goals of the EC has moved it away from a strictly economic union towards political union. Environmental policy is a good indicator of this process. The more that explicit environmental policies are adopted, the more it looks as if the EC is moving towards full political union.

At the time of writing, the future direction of the EC is being discussed at two Inter-Governmental Conferences (on Economic and Monetary Union and on Political Union), which started their work in December 1990, and which will soon produce draft proposals for an amended Treaty. It is clear that most Member States are pushing for an extension of EC powers, including those relating to environmental, health and consumer affairs, and also for changes in EC decision-making procedures so as to encourage common developments in these areas.

The basic economic assumptions about the nature of the EC are also being reassessed. The Treaty itself still suggests the paramountcy of economic aims rooted in the unashamedly pro-growth 1950s, but this no longer fits with the mood of the times. Accordingly, the British Government (amongst others) has proposed an amendment to the EC's fundamental objectives, which are set out in Article 2, to add a new objective of 'promoting throughout the Community sustainable growth which respects the environment'. It is likely that an amendment along these lines will be made.

The constitutional basis of the EC's environmental policy

The constitutional basis for an environmental policy must be considered in two distinct phases: before and after the Single European Act 1986. The history of the development of the EC's environmental policy will be considered first, because it is a good illustration of the way that the institutions have in practice widened the scope of what the EC deals with by a generous reading of the Treaty.

Before 1986 the legal justification for the policy was not entirely clear. In practice, two Articles of the Treaty, Articles 100 and 235 (the former relating to the harmonisation of national laws in order to further the establishment of the common market, the latter relating to the EC's general and residual powers), were used as justification.

Directives relating to pollution control and common standards tended to be justified on the basis of Article 100, whilst those where the content was almost purely environmental, such as Directive 79/409 on Wild Birds, were justified on the basis of Article 235. It was quite common for both Articles to be cited, just in case of a challenge.

In cases that did come to the European Court of Justice, the environmental policy was supported, which is not surprising since it had been formulated with the agreement of all the Member States. In *Commission* v *Italy* [1981] 1 CMLR 331, the Court held quite clearly that environmental matters may fall within Article 100. It stated:

Provisions which are made necessary by considerations relating to the environment and health may be a burden on the undertakings to which they apply, and if there is no harmonisation of national provisions on the matter, competition may be appreciably distorted.

Then, in a case 240/83, on the legitimacy of Directive 75/439 on Waste Oils, the European Court of Justice stated that environmental protection was 'one of the Community's essential objectives', and as such it justified some restrictions on the operation of the common market (see [1985] ECR 531). In a sense this amounted to a rewriting of the Treaty by the European Court of Justice as a matter of political reality.

The Single European Act 1986 introduced explicit environmental law-making powers in Articles 130R, 130S and 130T, as well as amending Article 100. This not only formalised the existing *de facto* position, it also established some clearer constitutional rules on the extent of the law-making powers and on how decisions are to be made.

Articles 100 and 100A

Article 100 enables Directives to be made that seek to harmonise laws and administrative practices of Member States which directly affect the establishment or functioning of the common market. The normal methods of achieving this are to lay down uniform, common standards or to outlaw specified discriminatory practices.

The relationship with the environment here is that a unified internal market depends upon trade and competition not being distorted by Member States applying different rules and standards. The EC therefore tries to harmonise laws in all the Member States so that a producer in one country does not have an unfair advantage over one in another. A law permitting producers in one country to pollute more than an equivalent producer in another country is seen as anti-competitive, since it amounts to a form of disguised subsidy. In this sense environmental policy is little more than incidental to the central economic policy.

By inserting Article 100A, the Single European Act introduced qualified majority voting for many proposals of this nature. However, as a safeguard, it also required that, if action is taken under Article 100A concerning health, safety, environmental or consumer protection, a high level of protection should be taken for those standards (Article 100A(3)). In addition, it added a power for Member States to derogate from the common standards in certain limited ways (Article 100A(4)—see p. 53)

Articles 130R, 130S and 130T

These Articles now provide a specific justification for pure environmental protection laws, even where there is no direct link to the economic aims of the EC. In contrast with Articles 100 and 100A, either Directives or Regulations may be made, though only a few Regulations have yet been made (see, for example, Regulation 1210/90 on the Establishment of the European Environment Agency). A further contrast is that, whilst Articles 100 and 100A required uniform application of standards, under these Articles that is not always required, since the motivating force behind them is the improvement of environmental standards, rather than the creation of the common market.

Article 130R(1) lists as objectives of the EC the preservation, protection and improvement of the quality of the environment, the protection of human health, and the prudent and rational utilisation of resources. Given the importance of environmental or green matters on the political agendas of the Member States, no one can doubt the political wisdom of adopting a positive stance in this way.

Article 130S provides the mechanics for this by setting out the voting procedures in the Council (see below). Article 130T provides for the possibility that stricter measures than those agreed under Article 130S may be employed by Member States (see p. 53).

The international dimension is covered by Article 130R(5). Many pollution, conservation and environmental matters, such as acid rain, the protection of migratory species, or pollution of the North Sea, are international in scope. A supranational body such as the EC is well-placed to tackle them by having a common internal environmental policy with uniform standards. It may also act by putting forward a common platform in dealings with the rest of the world. Article 130R(5) specifically permits the negotiation and conclusion of international agreements, a power which justifies the EC's independent involvement in international treaties and dealings with Eastern Europe.

There are some as yet rather unclear limitations on these powers. Article 130R(4) states that the EC should take environmental measures which can be better attained at an EC level than at a domestic level. This is known as the principle of subsidiarity, and it suggests that the true purpose of EC environmental legislation should be the establishment of common policies and standards rather than any interference in local issues. But there is some disagreement over its exact meaning. Some argue that it is a competency clause, which prevents the EC from interfering in matters which are better attained at a national level. But it specifically does not say that the EC may *only* take decisions which can more effectively be taken at Community level, and an alternative (and preferable) view is that it is only a guideline (see Krämer, *EEC Treaty and Environmental Protection*, 1990, p. 70).

Under Article 130R(3), the institutions are required to take account of available scientific and technical data, environmental conditions in the various regions of the EC and the balanced development of these regions when preparing any proposals. In addition, some form of cost-benefit analysis should be performed before environmental measures are agreed—another example of the close interrelationship between environmental and economic matters.

Article 235

Article 235 is a catch-all power which permits the institutions of the EC to take appropriate measures to attain any of the objectives of the EC that cannot be achieved through other powers. It has frequently been cited in the past as a justification for environmental actions, especially those relating to international action, although there is no longer any great need to do so in the light of Articles 130R and 130S.

Qualified majority voting

Prior to the Single European Act, unanimity in the Council was required for all environmental legislation (i.e. under Articles 100 and 235). In order to move more quickly towards the single internal market, the Single European Act 1986 extended the range of matters over which a qualified majority is sufficient. For measures furthering the single internal market (i.e. those things covered by Article 100, such as the fixing of product and pollution control standards) a qualified majority is all that is required under Article 100A(1). It must be pointed out, however, that this provision is currently timetabled to expire on 31 December 1992, though if the internal market is not complete at that time it may well be extended.

Measures agreed under Article 130S normally require unanimity, but the second subparagraph allows a qualified majority in cases where a unanimous Council has stated a qualified majority will suffice. This has not been much used but, for example, in order to speed up the slow progress of adoption of limit values and quality objectives for 'black list' substances under Directive 76/464 on Dangerous Substances in Water (see p. 302), the Commission has recently proposed that a qualified majority suffice for agreeing these values in relation to 16 specified substances.

Qualified majority voting allows environmental policy to be pushed forward at a faster rate than before, because the possibility of a national veto is reduced. For example, important Directives such as 88/609 on Emissions from Large Combustion Plants (which deals with the causes of acid rain) and 85/337 on Environmental Impact Assessment were delayed for many years by the opposition of one or two Member States. Thus, the procedure under Article 100A was used to avoid the objections of the Danish Government (which wanted stricter standards) to the agreement of Directive 88/76 on Emissions from Large Cars. Because qualified majority voting involves the possibility of a Member State being outvoted, some form of democratic input is required. This is provided by the application of the 'Cooperation Procedure' (see p. 41) in these cases, thereby giving Parliament some influence.

The difference in the voting procedures therefore makes it important whether a Directive is adopted under Article 100A or 130S. This question has recently been tested in the European Court of Justice, which annulled Directive 89/428 on the Titanium Dioxide Industry in June 1991 on the grounds that the wrong Article (and thus the wrong voting procedures) had been used (see *Commission* v *Council* [1991] 197 ENDS Report 15). The Commission in proposing the Directive had argued that it could be adopted under Article 100A, because it related to the harmonisation of rules relating to an industrial process. The Council, however, unanimously agreed that it should be adopted under Article 130S. At the time of writing, the judgment of the court has not been published, but it decided that the Commission's argument was essentially correct, and this must act as an encouragement to the Commission to base future legislation on Article 100A, and thus take advantage of the benefits of qualified majority voting. In a different sphere, the British Government has already threatened to test the legitimacy of using qualified majority voting for the proposed Social Charter. In this regard, there is still a non-binding agreement between the Member States called the Luxembourg Accords which allows Member States a veto on matters of crucial national importance, though whether these will ever be invoked in the event of disagreement over qualified majority voting is questionable.

However, all of this may soon be overtaken by events. Most EC Governments and the Commission support the extension of qualified majority voting procedures to *all* environmental matters. This will also involve a parallel extension of the Cooperation Procedure and the powers of Parliament. Should this be agreed at the Inter-Governmental Conferences, the pace of change in relation to environmental matters may well speed up significantly, although there is opposition from some of the less developed EC countries on the grounds that the imposition of stricter standards would harm their economic development, and affect them unfairly compared to more developed States.

Is uniformity required?

As shown above, there is a difference between Articles 130S and 100A over whether Member States may diverge from the standards laid down. Article 130T allows Member States to apply more stringent environmental measures than those agreed under Article 130S, as long as they do not distort trade between Member States. But, for Directives agreed under Article 100A, uniformity is required throughout the EC: the standards that are set must be common, otherwise the objective of a common market is not achieved. Article 130T cannot be used to justify a derogation from a Directive agreed under Article 100A.

For example, in *R v London Borough Transport Committee, ex parte Freight Transport Association Ltd, The Times,* 4 October 1990, the Court of Appeal held that the Committee's requirement that silencers be fitted to air brakes in certain London streets was illegal because it contravened Directive 70/157 on the approximation of exhaust systems (which was held to be directly effective). The Directive had been agreed under Article 100A and therefore stricter standards were an infringement of the common market.

There is one exception under Article 100A(4). National provisions may be stricter than the Directive if the Directive was adopted by a qualified majority, the national provision is justified by the need to protect the environment, and the Commission verifies this. This exception is intended to cover the situation where a Directive is agreed against the opposition of a Member State that already has a more stringent piece of legislation.

The *Danish Bottles* case

The interests of environmental protection may also be used as a defence in other ways. For example, Article 36 permits national laws which are effectively restrictions on imports (under Article 30), if there is a genuine need to protect, amongst other things, the environment, public health or national treasures.

The very important decision of the European Court of Justice in the *Danish Bottles* case (*Commission v Denmark* [1989] 54 CMLR 619) amplifies this point into a more general rule. The Court concluded that the protection of the environment is one of the EC's so-called 'mandatory requirements'. As such it can justify an interference with the operation of the common market, as long as the method adopted is proportionate to the aim which is being protected. However, it will not justify derogation from a Directive agreed under Article 100A.

The case arose from a Commission challenge to Danish laws which required beer and soft drink containers to be returnable, arguing they were a form of disguised discrimination against foreign manufacturers and hence an impediment to free trade under Article 30. The European Court of Justice held in clear terms that it was permissible to use environmental protection as an excuse for such discrimination. It went on to hold that such a derogation from the free market must be proportionate to the end to be achieved. Since a returnability requirement was clearly more environment-friendly than a recycling one, this requirement was acceptable. But a further licensing requirement, whereby only a limited number of container shapes was permitted, was disproportionate and thus illegal in EC law.

This decision has an obvious impact on the ability of Member States to pass environmental legislation that is stricter than in other Member States and which thus interferes with the common market. But it will also have an impact on the attitude of the Commission, since in order to re-establish the single internal market, it will wish to lay down common standards by proposing EC legislation. The case may thus act as an incentive to move towards common standards based on the stricter environmental protection legislation of the non-conforming State, using Article 100A(3) as a justification. In this regard, an interesting sidenote to the *Danish Bottles* case is that these Danish returnability laws have now led to renewed Commission proposals for a common policy on returnable drinks containers.

The scope of EC environmental policy

The Action Programmes on the Environment have laid down certain basic principles of EC environmental policy. The most important are now set out in Article 130R(2). They are that:

(a) preventative action is to be preferred to remedial measures;
(b) environmental damage should be rectified at source;
(c) the polluter should pay for the costs of the measures taken to protect the environment (the 'polluter pays' principle, see p. 85); and
(d) environmental policies should form a component of the EC's other policies.

These are not directly enforceable obligations, but they will be taken into account in drawing up environmental and other EC legislation. They also influence domestic pronouncements and policies (see, for example, Nicholas Ridley's pamphlet *Policies Against Pollution*, 1989, setting out his view of the Conservative Government's record and principles).

The Action Programmes also plan future action in relation to the environment. The first two Action Programmes were reactive in nature and concentrated on pollution control and on remedial measures. This fitted in with the economic justification of environmental policy under Article 100, but was also designed to tackle the most obvious and pressing problems first. The third and fourth Action Programmes have emphasised preventative measures at the same time as continuing the work on pollution control. For example, a number of Directives have been agreed on product standards and on the design of industrial plant and processes. They also stress the need to integrate environmental protection into other EC policies. Whilst there are not too many clear examples where this has happened as yet, (the designation of environmentally sensitive areas for agricultural grant purposes (Regulation 797/85) is virtually the only direct example), the importance of this principle for the shape of future policy should not be underestimated.

There is no doubt that the amendments made by the Single European Act have aided this shift in emphasis by encouraging more wide-ranging measures. For example, because of Danish objections to the use of Article 235, it was accepted after the passage of the Wild Birds Directive 79/409 that no further legislation would be passed on wildlife unless it related to trade. Such a limitation is now clearly removed. As a further example, the recent Directive 90/313 on Freedom of Access to Environmental Information was made under Article 130S and there is little doubt that it would have been difficult to justify such a measure under Articles 100 or 100A.

The range of environmental Directives

It is not possible in the space available to list all EC Directives that relate to the environment. What follows is a selective list intended to illustrate the major areas of EC involvement. Greater detail on individual Directives is given in the relevant chapters of Part II of this book and in Haigh, *EEC Environmental Law and Britain*, 2nd Revised Edition, 1989, which explains each Directive in turn. Where the number of a Directive is given below, it normally refers to the original piece of legislation, which may subsequently have been amended. In some cases, such as in relation to the use and production of CFCs or emissions from vehicles, no number is given simply because the amount of legislation is very great. In these cases reference should be made to Part II of this book.

EC Directives have been made in relation to the following:

(a) setting quality standards for water (e.g. Surface Waters for Drinking 75/440; Drinking Water 80/778; Bathing Water 76/160; Water Standards for Freshwater Fish 78/659; Shellfish Waters 79/923);

(b) setting emission standards for discharges to water (e.g. Dangerous Substances in Water 76/464; Groundwater 80/68);

(c) setting quality standards for air (e.g. Smoke and Sulphur Dioxide 80/779; Nitrogen Dioxide 85/203; Lead in Air 82/884);

(d) setting emission standards for emissions to the atmosphere (e.g. various Directives on Emissions from Vehicles such as 70/220, 88/76 and 89/548; Emissions from Industrial Plants 84/360; Emissions from Large Combustion Plants 88/609; New and Existing Municipal Waste Incinerators 89/369 and 89/429);

(e) setting noise standards (e.g. Noise in the Workplace 86/188; various Directives on Noise from Vehicles; Noise from Construction Plant 84/532);

(f) controlling emissions of dangerous pollutants (e.g. Dangerous Substances in Water 76/464; Toxic Waste 78/319; Mercury 84/156; Lindane 84/491; Cadmium 83/513; Disposal of PCBs 76/403 and various Directives on CFCs, Lead and Pesticides);

(g) controlling the disposal of waste (e.g. Framework Directive on Waste 75/442; Toxic Waste 78/319; Transfrontier Shipment of Toxic Waste 84/631; Sewage Sludge 86/278);

(h) controlling the storage and use of hazardous materials (e.g. Major Accident Hazards 82/501 (the 'Seveso' Directive); Asbestos 87/217);

(i) controlling dangerous activities (e.g. Transfrontier Shipment of Toxic Waste 84/631);

(j) setting product standards (e.g. Lead in Petrol 88/195; the various Directives on Noise and Emissions from Vehicles; Classification, Packaging and Labelling of Dangerous Substances 79/831);

(k) setting standards for the operation of certain industries (e.g. Emissions from Industrial Plants 84/360; Titanium Dioxide Industry 78/176 and 89/428; Emissions from Large Combustion Plants 88/609);

(l) procedures for the planning of development (e.g. Environmental Impact Assessment 85/337);

(m) protection of wildlife (e.g. Wild Birds 79/409; Trade in Endangered Species Regulation 3626/82);

(n) protection of the countryside (e.g. Environmentally Sensitive Areas 797/85);

(o) the use and release of genetically modified organisms (e.g. 90/219 and 90/220).

There are also Directives and Regulations on ancillary matters, such as the establishment of the European Environment Agency and the Monitoring of the Environment (Regulation 1210/90, which is expected to replace the CORINE programme on the Collation of Information on the State of the Environment 85/338), and that on Freedom of Access to Environmental Information 90/313.

One area where progress has been slow in the past relates to the provision of finance for carrying out environmental policy. The ACE programme (Action by the Community Relating to the Environment), first established under Regulation 1872/84, made limited amounts of money available for a restricted range of projects, mainly concerned with clean technologies and nature conservation. However, there has been a great deal of activity in this area recently. There are now programmes on the Environment and Regional Development (ENVIREG), the Mediterranean Environment (MEDSPA) and nature conservation (ACNAT). A further Commission proposal for a Financial Instrument for the Environment (LIFE), which would incorporate ACE, MEDSPA and ACNAT, appears to signify movement towards an official EC environment fund to match the three existing EC structural funds dealing with economic and social matters. Such a fund is something for which Parliament has long pressed.

Framework Directives

It is difficult to draw any firm conclusions from such a wide range of Directives. As one would expect, they utilise a wide range of techniques, selecting different tools for different jobs. Some of the Directives are framework Directives, i.e. they lay down a framework or structure of controls that may be applied to specific circumstances by further Directives (sometimes called 'daughter Directives') in the future. For example, Directive 76/464 on Dangerous Substances in Water is a framework Directive which enables the principles laid down in it to be applied to particular dangerous substances where limit values are agreed in daughter Directives. Limit values, in this context, refer to the setting of standards that require that a certain minimum (or maximum) standard be reached, but allow Member States to impose more stringent standards if circumstances require. They are thus of great use for creating general uniformity throughout the EC, whilst retaining some flexibility on the ground.

Directive 76/464 is discussed elsewhere in terms of some differences between Britain and other Member States over the types of standard that ought to be adopted. These mainly relate to policy differences where the EC's desire for uniformity conflicts with the British view of the different needs of the receiving environment (see p. 71).

The future of EC environmental policy

There are a number of trends in relation to the future of the EC's environmental policy which may be picked out.

(a) Future policies are increasingly likely to be preventative in nature. The focus of attention in environmental and safety matters is shifting from straight regulation of activities to precautionary measures, such as the fixing of product standards (e.g. on lead content in petrol) or plant design standards (e.g. Directive 84/360 on Emissions from Industrial Plants), or the avoidance of problems through waste reduction and recycling (there are draft Directives on each subject). In particular, the existence of the single internal market demands that emphasis is placed on products and processes so that free competition does not lead to a lessening of standards and to environmental degradation.

(b) Cross-media approaches to pollution control are likely to be encouraged, along the lines of integrated pollution control in this country. Most of the existing Directives have tended to concentrate on one particular sector, whether an industry, a substance or an environmental medium.

(c) The integration of environmental matters into other policies, as required by Article 130R(2), is likely to increase, especially since this is essential for pursuing effective preventative measures. In this respect, the British Government has put forward a proposal for a change to the Treaty for consideration at the Inter-Governmental Conferences to the effect that *all* EC legislative proposals should include a statement on the environmental effects of the measure.

(d) One of the impacts of the single internal market is likely to be a concentration of economic activity in the geographical centre of Europe. The potential effects of this on more marginal areas have already been recognised through the EC's Regional Policy and the environmental effects will require tackling. One particular attempt to do this is the proposed Habitats Directive (see p. 356), although at present this is delayed by doubts as to its form and content.

(e) Ancillary measures, such as freedom of information, the encouragement of public participation in decision-making, and the creation of environmental rights are likely to be stressed, following the lead of Directive 90/313 on Freedom of Access to Environmental Information and Directive 85/337 on Environmental Impact Assessment, which encouraged openness in the planning of environmentally significant developments.

(f) This previous point links to the need for an increased democratisation of the EC's decision-making processes. At present, efforts in this regard are effectively channelled into the granting of greater powers to the European Parliament.

(g) Action on international problems, such as global warming, acid rain, ozone depletion and oil pollution, will continue to be taken, since the EC is well placed to tackle these problems. This book has not dealt in detail with these issues, but the role of the EC has been significant in coordinating a European-wide response and this will continue.

(h) As on the domestic scene, economic and fiscal instruments can be expected to be developed. The Environment Council accepted the idea in principle at its meeting in October 1990.

(i) The Commission has also stated an intention to concentrate on the enforcement of existing legislation. Environmental law is one of the areas where Member States have been weakest in implementing EC legislation (see the Seventh Annual Report on Commission Monitoring of the Application of Community Law, 1989, COM(90) 288 final). Over 200 infringement procedures are pending on environmental matters, and given the limited monitoring that is done of compliance, this is clearly an underestimate of the number of Directives that remain unimplemented. Increased numbers of infringement proceedings may be expected as a result of the policy of bringing them automatically, particularly if the European Environment Agency does gain monitoring powers. Of special importance will be those situations where a Member State has not implemented EC law in practice, despite having formally complied by passing the required laws. A particular difficulty relates to the general inadequacy of the EC's sanctions for non-compliance with legislation (see p. 45), but the future existence of substantial Community environmental funds suggests the possibility of withdrawal of those funds being used a threat for non-compliance.

In the light of all these points, one of the most significant proposals for legislation is the draft Directive on Civil Liability for Damage Caused by Waste (COM (91) 219 final), which aims to prevent harm by encouraging producers to take steps to reduce waste or dispose of it properly. As its title suggests, it seeks to impose a wide civil liability for damage, which will include damage to the environment as such. If adopted, this will impose significant extra costs on the management of waste.

Another potentially significant development relates to proposals for legislation on environmental auditing. Originally the Commission proposed a mandatory scheme in which companies involved in specified industrial activities would have to carry out an annual self-assessment of their environmental performance, coupled with annual environmental statements. External verification would be required for certain activities with a major impact on the environment. However, after opposition from Member States and industrial organisations, a voluntary scheme has now been proposed (see [1991] 192 ENDS Report 13 and [1991] 194 ENDS Report 33).

EC environmental law and Britain

There is no doubt that the EC's environmental policy has had an important influence on British environmental law. It has led directly to new legislation (e.g. the Environmental Assessment Regulations—see p. 206), to new standards being adopted (e.g. consents for discharges to controlled waters and sewers incorporate standards laid down in EC Directives), and to changes in policy (e.g. the Bathing Water Directive 76/160 and the newly agreed Directive on Urban Waste Water Treatment 91/271 have led to important changes in capital spending programmes).

Except for those rare matters which are directly effective, Directives are of no domestic legal effect until implemented, although they may have considerable publicity value. A good example of this is the use made of EC standards on drinking water in the debate over water privatisation. Some Directives require there to be a 'competent authority' with responsibility for the matters in the Directive. When privatisation of the water industry as a whole was first proposed, it was suggested that a private regulator of water pollution may not fulfil the requirements for being a 'competent authority' and this was one reason why the National Rivers Authority was created.

As with all Member States, not all Directives have been implemented properly or on time, although the British record is in fact better than most. At present a number of infringement proceedings have been commenced, most significantly in relation to breaches of Directive 76/160 on Bathing Water and Directive 80/778 on Drinking Water.

Britain has often been in a minority in the EC over a particular measure. A good example is the insistence on a different method of controlling water pollution in Directive 76/464 on Dangerous Substances in Water (p. 71). It is thus significant that the ability to vary or veto measures is now restricted by the qualified majority procedures introduced by the Single European Act 1986.

As far as the legal system is concerned, the British courts have mainly come to terms with the supremacy of EC law. This has not been done directly, but through s. 2 of the European Communities Act 1972, which provides the constitutional basis for the application of EC law in Britain. The result is that the courts will *construe* British legislation to comply with EC law if it was passed to implement it. This construction will be purposive (see *Litster* v *Forth Dry Dock & Engineering Co Ltd* [1989] 2 WLR 634). However, it still appears that if there is a *direct* conflict between EC and national law, the national law would be applied if no intention to implement the EC law could be discerned (see Steiner, *Textbook on EEC Law*, 2nd Edition, p.39 for the relevant cases). The Courts have now held certain environmental Directives to be directly effective. In *R v London Borough Transport Committee, ex parte Freight Transport Association Ltd*, *The Times*, 4 October 1989, a requirement in Directive 70/157 on Noise from Vehicles was held directly effective, and in *Twyford Parish Council v Secretary of State* [1991] 194 ENDS Report 38, the Environmental Impact Assessment Directive was similarly held directly effective. This may well suggest an avenue for future development of the law. For example, it is reported that Friends of the Earth are bringing a test case over the implementation of the Drinking Water Directive 80/778, which will raise the issue of direct effects (see *The Guardian*, 10 April 1991).

FIVE
The regulation of environmental protection

Despite the current vogue for suggesting economic or fiscal mechanisms for combating environmental problems, the system of regulation by public bodies remains the prime tool for environmental protection in this country. This commitment to regulation is reiterated in the White Paper *This Common Inheritance* (1990, Cm. 1200), which states that 'administrative controls will for the foreseeable future remain at the heart of Britain's system of environmental control—just as they are in many other countries in the world', even at the same time as the possibility of using economic mechanisms is suggested as a future, additional, tool.

What does regulation mean in this context? At one level all the word means is the use of rules to control activities. These could be criminal law rules, or civil law rules, or private non-legal rules operated by a body such as a trade association, or maybe even the 'rules' of the free market. In this book, however, the word regulation is used to mean administrative or bureaucratic regulation (i.e. the application of rules and procedures by public bodies so as to achieve a measure of control over activities carried on by individuals and firms).

Other means of controlling activities, such as the criminal law, the civil law and the use of the market, will be considered later in the book, but since these are often subsidiary to administrative regulation, this will be explained first.

Administrative regulation

Administrative regulation is far more than just the setting of rules on what can and cannot be done. It denotes a coherent *system* of control in which the regulating body sets a framework for activities on an on-going basis, with a view to conditioning and policing behaviour as well as laying down straight rules.

The advantages of such a system include the ability to provide uniformity, rationality and fairness between those who are regulated. Some form of public accountability is also produced by having a public body responsible for regulation. In particular, one advantage over the criminal law is that a coherent link can be made with other policies, so as to balance all relevant factors. This is often seen as an important part of the British approach to regulation: that it involves an explicit balancing of environmental factors with such things as economic and social considerations.

British regulatory systems can be said to exhibit a pragmatic and flexible approach. The same mechanism is not used for each situation. In some cases the reason is simply that it is recognised that a control mechanism that works for one problem is unlikely to work for a different one. This is a good illustration of the use of law as a tool or a technique to help to solve particular problems. In other cases, there are historical reasons, since one of the features of having a long history of environmental control is that the administrative structures have built up piecemeal and in response to problems as they arise. For example, many controls have in the past been given to local authorities purely because they happened to be dealing with similar matters already, or because there was no other relevant body around at the time.

The processes of regulatory decision-making

Before looking at the main features of regulation in this country, it is necessary to summarise the main processes or stages in regulatory decision-making. These are:

(a)   the establishment of general policies;
(b)   the setting of standards or specific policies in relation to the environmental issue concerned;
(c)   the application of these standards and policies to individual situations;
(d)   the enforcement of standards and permissions;
(e)   the provision of information about the environment and the regulatory process.

(a)   The establishment of general policies

The process of establishing general policies is not really part of the regulatory system, but a necessary precondition for any system of environmental control. Having said that, one of the most obvious features of the British political system is the absence of formal national policies in many areas. Even where there are local or sectoral plans, there is often no national plan, or, if there is, it is made up of somewhat imprecise and flexible policies laid down in a variety of documents. A good illustration of the flexible nature of policy-making in Britain is provided by the town and country planning system, where the 'national plan' is to be found scattered amongst numerous Circulars, Planning Policy Guidance Notes, Ministerial decisions, White Papers and other assorted policy statements.

Given the essentially political nature of much of environmental law, the general tenor of the policies tends to be decided by Central Government. The presumption in favour of development in town planning is one example, but general decisions on energy and transport policy, such as the favouring of road transport over rail, or the retention of a nuclear power programme, are others. Certain political philosophies may also be imposed by Central Government; good examples are the principle of voluntariness in relation to controlling agricultural activities, or the policy of privatisation. However, because of the decentralised nature of much of pollution control, some general policies are effectively decided by bodies other than the elected Central Government. Other policies stem from general assumptions about the nature of the regulatory system itself—which we later refer to as the 'British approach' to environmental regulation (see p. 73).

A final factor is that the shape of many policies is now decided, or at least affected, by the EC. Arguably some of the most significant impacts on the environment in the next few years will follow from the establishment of the single European market and the countervailing powers adopted by the EC in terms of such things as regional and social policy.

(b) The setting of standards or specific policies in relation to the environmental issue concerned

Obviously any system of control must have some objectives that are set for it, otherwise it runs the risk of ceasing to be rational, uniform or fair. These may be fairly explicit objectives, such as air quality standards with specific maximum concentrations for a range of pollutants, or they may be far more vague, such as a water quality objective to the effect that a river should be capable of supporting fish.

In the past reliance has usually been placed on rather vague standards, such as the test of nuisance at common law, or the idea that best practicable means should be used to reduce gaseous emissions to the atmosphere. In addition, standards were often set in an informal manner, as used to happen with non-statutory water quality objectives. More specific and more formal standards are becoming far more common. In the development control system, policies of this type are set out in development plans and in Central Government Circulars, although there is often overlap between this stage and stage (a) above.

(c) The application of these standards and policies to individual situations

This is often seen as the central part of the regulatory process. There are numerous examples where a permission, authorisation, consent or licence is required from a public body. Whether one is granted, and the nature of any conditions attached, will normally be a discretionary decision, but one that is made by reference to the general standards established at stage (b). The application of standards may also be seen in such processes as court actions for nuisance and the specific application of whether best practicable means are being used.

(d) The enforcement of standards and permissions

In practice, one of the most important areas of environmental law is whether the legal instruments that are available are used, since there is often considerable discretion given to the regulatory body. 'Enforcement' covers a far wider range of matters than the single question whether to prosecute for breaches of the law. In any regulatory system, there is normally a whole range of administrative and other remedies available in addition to prosecution. The question of which remedy to use is also tied up with how the regulator should proceed. There is a wealth of evidence to show that informal methods of enforcement are often preferred, and that regulators normally adopt a 'compliance strategy' towards enforcement, rather than a 'sanctioning strategy' (i.e. one-based on confrontation, see Chapter 6). Questions of inspection and monitoring also arise as part of the enforcement process.

(e) The provision of information about the environment and the regulatory process

A theme which runs through the regulatory process concerns the openness of the system. This includes such questions as the production of official information on the state of the environment, the availability of public registers, and the publication of information about how the regulatory system itself works. Britain's traditionally secretive administrative processes are slowly becoming more open. This is most obvious in relation to stage (c), but is also apparent in the extension of public registers, enabling more information to be available for enforcement purposes. It may also be seen in the increased willingness of the Government to issue Consultation Papers before changes in the law are adopted.

Anticipatory and continuing controls

Regulatory mechanisms may be divided into two general types, anticipatory controls and continuing controls.

Anticipatory controls

These are measures in which controls are imposed on an activity at its commencement in order to forestall potential environmental problems. Usually the objective is to prevent the activity unless certain requirements or conditions are met. The category includes a wide range of licensing-type controls, where permission of some sort is required before an activity may be started or carried on. These are normally complemented by a combination of criminal and administrative sanctions if the activity starts without permission, or if the permission is contravened.

The range of possible anticipatory controls is quite wide. It includes:

(a)   An outright ban (e.g. the intended ban on the use of CFCs in products after 2000, or the prohibition on emissions of dark smoke from chimneys under the Clean Air Act 1956, s. 1). Of course, there is no *necessity* for a public regulatory body to be involved here, but someone will need to police the ban.

(b)   A prohibition on an activity unless a particular body is notified in advance (e.g. the requirement under the Wildlife and Countryside Act 1981, s. 28 that owners and occupiers of a site of special scientific interest notify the relevant Nature Conservancy Council of any intention to carry out a potentially damaging operation, thus forewarning the Council of a possible need to take further protective steps).

(c)   A prohibition on an activity unless it is registered, registration being something that cannot normally be refused by the registering body (e.g. there is a requirement to register offensive trades with the local authority under the Public Health Act 1936, s. 107, although this is being gradually abolished under the Environmental Protection Act 1990 as the system of authorisations under Part I is brought into force).

(d)   A prohibition on an activity until a licence, permission, authorisation or consent (these words are in practice interchangeable) is obtained, where the granting of the permission is at the discretion of the regulating body.

In relation to this last type, there are two distinct categories of permission or consent. Some are one-off permissions which, once granted, create what are in effect permanent rights because it is difficult to vary or revoke them. A good example is the granting of planning permission. Others provide for variation or revocation in the light of future circumstances. Most pollution control consents fall into this category, examples being the requirements to obtain an authorisation from Her Majesty's Inspectorate of Pollution for carrying on a prescribed process, or a consent from the National Rivers Authority for a discharge to controlled waters.

Continuing controls

These are measures where the carrying out of an activity is controlled on a continuing basis. Typically they relate to the way an activity is carried on, so another way of referring to them would be as *operational* controls. An obvious example is the on-going duty to comply with the terms of a consent, licence, authorisation, or permission granted by a pollution control authority, which will normally be combined with a range of other regulatory controls relating to monitoring and enforcement. The distinction between anticipatory controls and continuing controls is thus that one relates to *whether* an activity should be carried on in the first place, whilst the other relates to *how* it is carried on once it has started.

Of course, anticipatory and continuing controls are mutually supportive and most regulatory systems combine the two types of mechanism. Anticipatory controls still require some monitoring to ensure that the prohibited activity is not being carried on. Conversely, most continuing controls rest on the need for some initial permission before an activity may be started; indeed, the threat of withdrawal of the initial permission may well constitute the strongest inducement to comply with continuing regulatory requirements. For example, planning permission is required before a new activity is started, but that permission will often include conditions that require some adherence to defined standards over a period of time, such as permitted working hours or noise limits. Similarly, consents, authorisations and licences obtained from pollution control authorities normally combine the initial need for a consent with an ability to vary the requirements as the situation changes. This mutually supportive position is reinforced by the fact that many activities are subject to the requirements of more than one regulatory system.

Planning and prevention

The town and country planning system is the major system of anticipatory control in environmental law. To a large extent this stems from the very nature of planning control. It involves the preparation of plans, which may then guide future behaviour. The controls are necessarily imposed at the outset, whilst most pollution control mechanisms basically assume a continuing activity. Planning also mainly concerns land use, siting and locational issues that logically pre-date the operational controls.

A further reason results from practice. In these other systems, it is rare for the initial consent to be refused or revoked (although this power does remain as a threat for those who contravene the continuing controls). For example, it appears that no instance has ever been recorded of a certificate of registration being refused under the Alkali Acts, either at the outset or on renewal (see Wood, *Planning Pollution Prevention*, 1989). In other areas of pollution control, the record may be slightly different, but there are still very few examples of a consent from a pollution control authority actually being refused where there is already a planning permission.

One result is that the main burden of deciding whether a particular plant should go ahead normally falls upon the local planning authority. By way of example, a new factory will require planning permission as well as consents for emissions from Her Majesty's Inspectorate of Pollution or the National Rivers Authority, and maybe the sewerage undertaker and local authority (in its capacity as regulator of air pollution) as well. It will be the local planning authority that decides whether to have the factory in that particular place. The pollution control authorities tend to see their task as setting limits on what is acceptable in terms of pollution from the site proposed rather than as stopping the development going ahead at all. Traditionally, these authorities have had little scope for saying, 'this development would be better somewhere else'.

This is perhaps inevitable given the differences in nature between local planning authorities and other regulatory bodies. A local planning authority has a specific remit under the Town and Country Planning Act 1990, s. 70 to consider *all* material factors relating to a development, whilst other bodies often have a more limited range of relevant factors to consider in making their decision. It is also an elected body, where ultimate power resides with elected members, and therefore has greater legitimacy in terms of making a balanced policy decision to refuse a development.

Standards in environmental law

Most environmental controls rely on some form of measurable standard. This standard may be used as a guideline (i.e. an objective) or it may be used as a means of defining what an individual or firm may do. Indeed, one of the distinctive features of environmental regulation is that the regulatory body often has responsibility for defining the standard as well as enforcing its application.

There are a number of different types of standard, but a crude division can be made into those which are set by reference to the *target* which is being protected and those which are set by reference to the *source* of the pollution. Source-related standards may be further divided into emission standards, process standards and product standards. There are other factors that have a significant impact on the nature of a standard, such as whether it is centrally or locally set, uniform or flexible, precise or imprecise.

The following summary is not intended to be an exhaustive list of the various types of standard (from the list of variables above obviously the number of potential types is very great), but is an attempt to introduce a basic vocabulary of terms. It also aims to illustrate some of the more common methods used, together with some thoughts on their relative strengths and weaknesses. In a sense, these are the tools available to the legislator in deciding how a regulatory system is to work.

(a)   Environmental quality standards (target standards)

Some standards concentrate on the effect on a particular target. In many cases, the protected target may be human beings and the standard is accordingly set by reference to the effect on them (e.g. the effect of radiation on workers). However, since this is a book about environmental protection, it will concentrate on situations where the protected target is the environment, or part of it. The phrases 'target standards' and 'environmental quality standards' will therefore be treated as interchangeable.

The effect on the target may be measured in different ways. It may relate to a biological effect, thus channelling all information directly into a consideration of the actual impact of a pollutant (e.g. a standard requiring that a discharge to water is not harmful to fish or aquatic animals). Alternatively, it may relate to the exposure of the target, from which certain biological or other effects may be presumed. In the environmental field, however, it will more usually relate simply to some measurable quality of the receiving environment, such as the level of a particular pollutant. Biological and exposure standards are mainly used where the protected target is human (e.g. in relation to radiation protection).

An environmental quality standard can therefore be defined as a standard where conformity is measured by reference to the effect of a pollutant on the receiving environment. It is unusual for the selected target to be the whole environment. More commonly a particular medium will be chosen as the reference point, such as air or water quality. In order to retain flexibility, there will frequently also be a geographical limitation: the standard may thus be set by reference to a particular river or area, or may be even more specific, such as where air quality or noise levels are fixed within factories or any other enclosed area.

Examples of environmental quality standards include:

(a)   setting air quality standards for the maximum or minimum concentration of any specified substance in air;

(b)   setting water quality standards for the concentration of specified pollutants in 'controlled waters' (see p. 317);

(c)   the nuisance test at common law, under which property owners are entitled to the enjoyment of their property without unreasonable interference from neighbours.

It will be clear that these standards may be set by reference to any number of parameters. For example, a water quality standard could be set specifically for the maximum concentration of zinc, or a whole range of parameters may be used, as is the case for drinking water.

(b)   Emission standards

An emission standard can be defined as a standard where conformity is measured by reference to what is emitted rather than the effect on the receiving environment. Emission standards thus tend to concentrate on wastes produced. For example, the content of a discharge from a pipe or chimney could be controlled by reference to an emission standard.

Examples of emission standards include:

(a)   the maximum content of a particular substance in a liquid discharge from a pipe to a sewer or 'controlled waters';

(b)   the noise level measured as it emanates from a building;

(c)   the maximum content of a particular substance in an emission from a chimney or exhaust pipe.

(c)   Process standards

A standard may be imposed on a process either by stipulating precisely the process which must be carried on, or by setting performance requirements that the process must reach. In the second case there would be a choice as to how to reach these requirements. These standards may relate to the whole of the process or, alternatively, to a part of it, such as the way that a product is made or the way effluent is treated. They may include requirements about the technology that is used, the raw materials, or operational factors such as whether the process is being carried out properly.

Examples of process standards include:

(a)   a requirement that a particular pre-treatment plant for effluent be used;

(b)   a stipulation on the height of a factory chimney;

(c)   a stipulation about the use of a particular grade or quality of fuel;

(d)   a requirement that the Best Available Techniques Not Entailing Excessive Cost (BATNEEC) are used (see p. 231).

It is clear that current practice is to emphasise the use of process standards, and this is illustrated by their use in Part I of the Environmental Protection

Act 1990. They are a good means of preventing harm to the environment arising in the first place.

(d) Product standards

Product standards may be defined as where the characteristics of an item that is being produced are controlled. This may be done with the aim of protecting against damage the product may cause whilst it is being used, or when it is disposed of, or even during its manufacture. Examples include:

(a) a requirement that all new cars are capable of running on unleaded petrol;

(b) a requirement that cars are fitted with catalytic converters;

(c) it may even be thought that requirements on the labelling of goods are a type of product standard.

Interrelationship of standards

Of course, these four categories of standard are not exclusive of each other. An emission standard will often be set so as to achieve an environmental quality standard. Product standards for a car will include many matters relating to the emissions from it, such as lead, carbon dioxide or noise. In addition, the cumulative effect of these emissions will have an impact on the attainment or otherwise of any environmental quality standard.

Taking one particular, toxic pollutant, lead, environmental concentrations may be controlled in a number of ways:

(a) Environmental quality standards may be set, stating that levels of lead should not rise above a certain level in the air, in water, or in the soil.

(b) Emissions of lead may be controlled, so that any emission, whether into air or water or on to land, should not include more than a specified concentration of lead, to be set by reference to some form of permission or consent.

(c) Processes may be regulated to reduce the use of lead, or to reduce by good design possible emissions and escapes of lead into the environment.

(d) Products likely to include lead may be regulated, either to ban its use (e.g. lead fishing weights) or to limit the use of lead (e.g. setting maximum amounts of lead in leaded petrol).

Other characteristics of standards

As stated earlier, a number of other matters are also important in relation to the nature of a standard. The standard may be a precise one, such as one set by reference to a scientifically provable maximum or minimum—often a numerical value. Alternatively, it may be an imprecise one, such as a requirement that Best Practicable Means (BPM) or Best Available Techniques Not Entailing Excessive Cost (BATNEEC) are used, or one applying the common law test of nuisance.

The standard may be a uniform one across the country (or the EC), or it may vary from area to area. Indeed, it may be set on an individual basis. Certain matters demand uniform standards. For example, uniformity is normally desirable for emissions from mobile sources such as cars, otherwise problems are caused at boundaries. For similar reasons, most product standards are set on a uniform basis. It is strongly argued by some that uniformity creates equality, a particularly important consideration in the context of the EC and the common market. Limit values, as used by the EC in a number of Directives, create a special form of uniformity. They require that a certain standard is reached, but allow Member States to impose more stringent standards if circumstances require.

The standard may be set centrally or locally. This distinction tends to reflect the same division as that between uniform and individualised standards, since centrally set standards will usually be uniform whilst locally set ones will vary with the discretion given to the decision-maker. In this context, it must be remembered that few standards are set by legislation. Often this is left to local bodies, although this is changing as EC standards permeate domestic environmental law.

Strengths and weaknesses of different types of standard

Obviously it is not possible to cover all types of standard, but it is possible to see the relative strengths and weaknesses of the more commonly used examples.

Environmental quality standards, by concentrating on what it is that requires protection, are able to deal with inputs to the environment from all sources and via all potential pathways, whilst the other mechanisms, used on their own, tend to permit cumulation of any particular pollutant. For the same reason, environmental quality standards can also cater for potentially harmful combinations of substances on the environment. They can thus enable a policy-maker to identify areas where work is needed, and channel resources effectively. They can also be tailored for particular circumstances, for example by being more stringent in sensitive areas than in others.

However, there are a number of limitations to environmental quality standards. They require constant monitoring of the environment, which may prove to be impractical or expensive. Enforcement poses difficulties, since failure to reach a standard may alert us to the existence of a problem, but does not necessarily tell us the cause or how to remedy it. For example, in order to clean up a river which is chronically contaminated with organic wastes, a regulator would first have to identify the causes of the pollution and then find some method of restricting inputs that was fair and enforceable. A further problem of environmental quality standards is that they may give no incentive to polluters to improve their performance in areas where the standard is already being met.

The very nature of environmental quality standards is that they tend to be set as *objectives* rather than as legal requirements, except in those situations where there is a limited number of sources and targets, such as enclosed work environments. This use as objectives makes them useful at the strategic and planning stages of the regulatory process (see p. 62). For example, development plans often set environmental quality standards, even if they are frequently very imprecise, such as a policy that developments liable to cause a nuisance should not be permitted in a defined area.

The strength of emission standards is that they are relatively easy to control and monitor by sampling at the point of emission. Enforcement is also easier because of the simplicity of the causation requirements where there is a point of discharge. In addition, an emission standard may be tightened progressively to encourage a discharger to improve the process, whilst still retaining choice as to how this is done.

A main drawback of emission standards relates to the difficulty of controlling diffuse (or non-point) emissions, such as fertiliser or pesticide run-off, by these means. There is also the difficulty (shared with process standards and product standards) of organising a system that can cope with an accumulation of similar emissions in one area, such as car exhausts in Los Angeles or similar industrial concerns in one water catchment area. This second difficulty is not an insoluble problem, however. It may be tackled by setting very strict local emission standards, by linking them explicitly to an environmental quality standard, or by applying the 'bubble' approach (i.e. by aggregating together all emissions in a particular area and permitting a total amount of emissions for that area).

Process standards are obviously limited to where there is a process to control and thus tend to apply mainly to the manufacturing industry. Their main strength is that they may be set so as to prevent a problem arising in the first place. They may also help to pool resources for research at a central level. There is a potential disincentive for producers to find more effective ways of reducing pollution, unless the standards are made progressively stricter, or are periodically altered, or are set at levels that force the producer to develop the technology so as to reach the standard (so-called 'technology forcing' rules).

Product standards are similarly limited to where there is a product and have similar strengths and weaknesses as process standards. As stated above, both categories also have difficulty in catering for the cumulative effect of pollutants on their own.

Locally set and centrally set standards: Britain versus the EC?

It has often been noted that Britain and the rest of the EC do not seem to see eye to eye on pollution control. This is sometimes translated into a conflict between a British preference for locally set and variable (i.e. non-uniform) emission standards, set by reference to local environmental quality, and an EC preference for centrally set uniform emission standards. Haigh (in *EEC Environmental Policy and Britain*) points out that any conflict on these grounds has been much exaggerated (see below).

Nevertheless, these two types of standard provide an excellent opportunity for a case study on their relative strengths and weaknesses.

Locally set and variable emission standards set by reference to local environmental quality

Each of the features of this combination of ideas merits some mention. Referring everything to environmental quality can be said to target controls where they are needed—at the protection of the environment. In this way, the impact of non-point emissions and background levels of pollution may be taken into account, as well as discharges from pipes and chimneys. The fact that neither the emission standards nor the environmental quality standards are uniform provides flexibility. This enables more sensitive areas to be protected more strictly, or polluters who are seen as more useful to the community to be treated more leniently. In all cases, a great deal of discretion is granted to decision-makers. It is also argued that, since standards can be varied to take account of local circumstances, the mechanism is economically efficient. For example, greater pollutant loads could be permitted in remote, unpopulated areas or where the self-cleansing properties of the local environment are greater.

Centrally set uniform emission standards

These have obvious advantages. Uniform standards are easily imposed, easily implemented and easily monitored. They are fair between polluters since all are treated the same, and they avoid difficult problems about allocating the right to pollute amongst different polluters. As a result they may be relatively cheap for the regulator to operate, because they involve less administrative discretion than variable standards. They also fit in well with the economic principles of the EC's common market.

On the other hand, they can be said not to allow local conditions to be taken into account, because there is no flexibility (although this can be provided at the enforcement stage). They are meant to be unable to deal with the situation where there is a number of polluters in one area, since there is no jurisdiction to reduce the emission standard to fit local conditions. They are also sometimes said to lead to the possibility of a uniformly polluted country if there is one relevant discharge in every area. These last two criticisms are rather too general, since good use of preventative controls would help in both cases.

Why Britain and the EC differ

It is not difficult to think of reasons why Britain may differ from other Member States within the EC. As an island, Britain has no frontiers. Thus, the argument about fairness has never had the impact that it has in France and Germany, which share the Rhine as a border, and where the inequality of one factory being allowed to discharge more than another on the other bank is obvious. Other factors stem from the 'British approach' to pollution control (see p. 73), such as that Britain has a tradition of discretionary, local decision-making and a system based on pragmatism, in which the effects on the environment are balanced with social, economic and political factors.

But the main argument for the British position probably stems from self-interest. With its rainy climate, fast-running streams, ample coastline and relative remoteness, Britain can claim a comparative advantage when it comes to pollution. Put very crudely, the same discharge is supposed to cause less pollution in Britain than in other countries, because of its lesser effect on the environment. When it comes to setting standards, some people in Britain do not see why stringent uniform standards should apply across the EC if they have no justification in terms of environmental protection in the British context, even if they provide that protection elsewhere.

As stated earlier, the differences have been exaggerated. Even discounting the influence of EC legislation, there are many examples of uniform emission standards applying in Britain, although this is sometimes hidden by being the product of administrative practice rather than legislative action. This is especially the case in relation to dangerous substances, where no amount of discretionary balancing with other factors will make them safe. Also the differences set out above relate mainly to water pollution, which is, appropriately, the area where Britain has arguably the greatest comparative advantage. Even in relation to water pollution, the differences have mainly surfaced over one particular Directive—the framework Directive 76/464 on Dangerous Substances in Water. It was in relation to this Directive that Britain's position led to alternative regimes being adopted for the control of dangerous substances (see p. 302). But, as Haigh points out, it seems that what the other EC Member States saw as cause for concern was not the use of environmental quality objectives to define the context for the setting of variable discharge consents, but the fact that these quality standards were, at the time, informal, unpublished, and set by regional authorities. It is not hard to imagine that other Member States thought they were being told that the British approach to controlling dangerous substances was that 'it all depends on the circumstances'.

As a final point, it should be noted that in any case Directive 76/464 did *not* lay down uniform emission standards. It laid down limit values, and many of the arguments against uniform emission standards do not apply to these, because there is the flexibility to have a stricter standard if desirable.

The 'British approach' to regulation

Since administrative regulation can take many forms, it is important to establish the distinctive features of the British style or approach. In other words, what types of rules and standards are employed? How are they set and by whom? How are they enforced and by whom? What role does the public play in these processes?

In *National Styles of Regulation* (1986), David Vogel identifies a number of characteristics of the British style. The book claims to be 'an examination of British environmental policy as seen through the eyes of a student of American politics', and consists of a comparison of approaches to environmental regulation in Britain and the USA. Vogel writes that Britain's regulatory style is characterised by flexibility and informality, and summarises the system as involving:

An absence of statutory standards, minimal use of prosecution, a flexible enforcement strategy, considerable administrative discretion, decentralised implementation, close cooperation between regulators and the regulated, and restrictions on the ability of non-industry constituents to participate in the regulatory process.

At the risk of producing an unmanageable list, to these points could be added others, such as delegation of decision-making to autonomous quasi-governmental and non-governmental bodies, extensive use of industrial self-regulation, a limited availability of legislative and judicial scrutiny of regulators, a gradualist approach to change, reliance on scientific knowledge for decision-making and habitual reference to economic factors before decisions are made.

Vogel compares this approach with that of the USA, which he characterises as rule-oriented, normally employing rigid and uniform standards, and making little use of industrial self-regulation. In addition, less use is made there of administrative discretion, prosecution is much more common, there is great executive and judicial scrutiny of regulators and technology-forcing rules are favoured. All of these features lead to conflict between regulator and regulated and to an adversary mentality.

Of course many of these differences are not unique to environmental regulation in the two countries, but are a matter of general political culture. They probably stem from different attitudes towards regulation engendered by different population densities and degrees of cultural homogeneity. In Britain the need for a balancing process is all too clear, whilst in the USA the 'frontier mentality' is understandably more prevalent.

At this point a warning should be given. Since the 1960s the situation in the USA has changed dramatically, and what Vogel describes in the 1980s is quite different from what happened then. Similarly, the British approach is currently changing quite rapidly. The informal and flexible basis remains, but the approach has undoubtedly got more open, more centralised, more legalistic and more contentious, especially in the last 10 years or so. The changes in legislation have been substantial, but there have also been more disguised internal changes of practice by regulators. As a result, Vogel's analysis is already beginning to look outdated.

One crucial factor in this change is the attitude of the EC. The British approach has tended to conflict with that adopted by other Member States and has had to be modified to fit in with that (though this has been something of a two-way process). At the same time, the increased profile of environmental issues, particularly international ones requiring common responses, has led to some changes of style out of political necessity. A further factor lies in the political preferences of the current Government, which has after all been in power for twelve years, and has adopted some radical and clear, if controversial, policies in that period. It is clear that such major features of policy as the rejection of long-term planning in favour of market forces, deregulation of unnecessary bureaucratic controls, privatisation of public services, imposition of strict spending controls on public bodies, the general weakening of local authority power, and the use of voluntary controls allowing choice wherever possible have all had an impact on the nature of regulation in this country.

The following sections will explore some of the manifestations and implications of the British approach, and will seek to illustrate just how it is changing and in what direction. However, it must be stressed that this is only a general approach. No-one would suggest that all these symptoms are displayed by each of the various regulatory processes in the country, merely that these are recognisable general features.

The implications of the British approach also vary at the different stages identified earlier, with the result that, for example, general policy-making remains mainly a central national function, rather than being particularly decentralised (although many of these general policies are now in practice agreed at international or EC level). Nevertheless, the general features of the regulatory system can be illustrated by considering a number of key issues.

Decentralisation

Decision-making is decentralised in three ways: by being given to a wide range of bodies, by significant use of delegation, and by geographical decentralisation.

There are numerous bodies exercising environmental responsibilities (see p. 27). Unlike countries with a unified environmental protection agency, Britain has a large number of autonomous or semi-autonomous environmental agencies, such as the National Rivers Authority, Her Majesty's Inspectorate of Pollution, the Nature Conservancy Councils, the Health and Safety Executive, the Nuclear Installations Inspectorate, and the Countryside Commission. Local authorities also have wide-ranging environmental protection powers in relation to such things as air pollution, waste regulation and disposal, noise control, town and country planning and environmental health. There is also decentralisation within Central Government. Although the Department of the Environment is nominally responsible for much of environmental policy, many decisions and policies which have important environmental effects are made by the Department of Energy (e.g. on power stations), or the Department of Transport (e.g. on emissions from vehicles), or the Ministry of Agriculture, Fisheries and Food (e.g. on agricultural support schemes). The diversity is compounded by the tendency to have separate bodies in Wales and Scotland.

Even within the Department of the Environment, matters are often delegated. For example, the list of buildings of historic interest is in practice largely drawn up by English Heritage (the Historic Buildings and Monuments Commission), an independent body, and appeals against refusals of planning permission are normally dealt with by the Planning Inspectorate, although this remains formally part of the Department of the Environment.

Over the years this decentralisation of power has tended to result in a rather incoherent environmental policy, with very little uniformity across the country. Even such a central function as the monitoring of the environment has tended to be done in an uncoordinated way. There have been a number of changes in recent years which have altered matters. For example, the regulation of water pollution was organised on a regional basis until 1989, when the National Rivers Authority was established as a national body covering England and Wales. Her Majesty's Inspectorate of Pollution was created in 1987 to draw together a number of inspectorates at that time operating separately within the Department of the Environment and the Health and Safety Executive. Both these institutional changes have clearly fostered uniformity in decision-making.

Decisions are also commonly made locally. Local authorities have the wide powers referred to above, whilst many of the inspectorates and other agencies operate on a regional basis, granting some discretion to local decision-makers. There is a philosophy underpinning this, of course. The British approach is geared pragmatically towards the protection of the receiving environment, so it is sensible that decisions are taken by people or bodies with a knowledge of local conditions, whether environmental, social or economic.

An important change has been the centralisation of policy decisions in recent years. This has been most marked in relation to matters where there is conflict between central and local government. For example, in the town and country planning system, increased intervention in local decisions by Central Government has been the major issue of the 1980s. It has been manifested mainly through hard-hitting and directory Circulars, which have been applied on appeal so as to alter the policy context of most planning decisions, though there have also been changes to the law and in institutional structure designed to reduce local control, through such creations as urban development corporations. However, centralisation is also a reality in relation to pollution control. Local authorities have lost a significant amount of discretion in relation to air pollution as a result of the Environmental Protection Act 1990.

Centralisation may also be seen at work in the control of public spending. The regional water authorities were severely limited for many years in their ability to make capital expenditure decisions, and the same is true for local authorities. For bodies such as the Countryside Commission which rely on Government grant, the position is even clearer.

Finally there is a very significant element of centralisation involved in the relationship between Britain and the EC. Not only is EC decision-making essentially secret, but there is little input to it by local or regional bodies in Britain. However, the central point is that EC law is binding on Member States. The requirement to conform with it, coupled with the policy goal of uniformity throughout the EC, means that power is taken away from local and non-governmental bodies and given to central bodies. This is clearly true in relation to the first two stages of the regulatory processes identified earlier (the policy-making and objective-setting stages), and it is becoming increasingly true for the third stage (the operational stage of setting individual consents) as well.

Discretion

The amount of discretion is great at all the stages of regulatory decision-making. Parliament rarely sets firm policies and standards in legislation, allowing for these to be defined in delegated legislation or even through administrative guidance. For example, in the town and country planning system the nature of central guidance is nowhere dictated in the legislation, but is set out in

Government Circulars and Planning Policy Guidance Notes, which may be altered at any time.

At the standard-setting and consent-setting levels the discretion is usually given to the relevant regulatory body. As examples, local planning authorities have the ability to grant or refuse planning permission as they think fit (subject mainly to the Secretary of State's control over policy on appeal), the National Rivers Authority has discretion over the setting of standards for discharges to water, and Her Majesty's Inspectorate of Pollution has wide discretion in the definition of Best Practicable Means (BPM) and Best Available Techniques Not Entailing Excessive Cost (BATNEEC).

A similar wide discretion can be seen at the enforcement stage. There are few statutes which lay down duties to enforce the legislation, or which set out statutory factors to take into account, and usually the decision whether to take action is taken by the regulatory body on the basis of practical and political factors which are not mentioned in the legislation. Since many of the most important remedies are administrative remedies which are unavailable to individuals, this discretion is of enormous practical importance. Enforcement is discussed in greater detail in Chapter 6.

Judicial interference is frequently limited by the width of discretions given in legislation. This is best illustrated in the town and country planning legislation, where there is a clear policy of judicial non-intervention in decisions about the weight to be attached to material considerations. A recent reiteration of this policy is shown in *London Residuary Body* v *Lambeth BC* [1990] 2 All ER 309, where the Secretary of State's decision to grant planning permission for office development in London County Hall was held to be unchallengeable by the House of Lords. This was so even though he had accorded overriding weight to the presumption in favour of development where there was nothing else in favour of the development and some grounds against. A different example is the decision in *R* v *Secretary of State for the Environment, ex parte Rose Theatre Trust Ltd* [1990] 1 All ER 754, where a decision by the Secretary of State not to make the site and remains of the Rose Theatre a scheduled ancient monument was held to be unchallengeable because of the width of the discretion given in the legislation.

As a result of all these factors, and also the general British preference for variable rather than uniform standards, the British system of environmental control has become characterised by flexibility and lack of uniformity.

Gradualism and reliance on scientific evidence

The place of these ideas as two of the key tenets of British pollution control is emphasised in Department of the Environment Pollution Paper No. 11, *Environmental Standards—The UK Practice*. This very readable document was published in 1975 and is now somewhat out-of-date, but it has great significance in terms of explaining the British approach to pollution control, since it is effectively a justification of that approach in the face of alternatives being put forward within the EC.

The philosophy of gradualism is that pollution controls should be strengthened gradually as economic circumstances, the goodwill of producers and scientific abilities allow. This links very strongly with the related idea that decisions should be taken on the basis of a reliable scientific base, although it should be recognised that science does not necessarily produce facts in the environmental sphere, but estimates of risks or probabilities. There is accordingly always a political factor involved in whether to accept a risk or not (see below).

One major effect of these two ideas has been that environmental controls have tended to be reactive rather than anticipatory. They have rarely been concerned with laying down a framework in advance, leading to the fragmentation of the system and to its lack of uniformity. A more specific effect is that time is normally given for changes to be made in order to give industry time to adjust capital programmes and work methods. In relation to the requirement that Best Practicable Means be used, it has been normal practice to allow any process to continue for its operational life (often ten years) before declaring it in contravention of the requirement, even though it may have been superseded before then. A similar discretion is provided for in relation to BATNEEC under the Environmental Protection Act 1990, but it is expected that the time allowed for changes will be much shorter.

The extended time scale for implementing the 1990 Act (full implementation is not planned until 1995), apart from being a comment on the complexity of the new requirements, is a further example of the gradualist approach. Interestingly, the timetable for the introduction of Part I of the Act was laid down after an undertaking was given in Parliament to do so, and thus avoid a re-run of the non-implementation of the Control of Pollution Act 1974. At the EC level, this approach is also reflected in the time scale allowed for implementation of Directives, which is normally at least two years, and often five years. A final example is that the British have frequently rejected the use of 'technology-forcing' rules. These represent the setting of a rule which is stricter than currently achievable, though with a time scale for its achievement. The theory is that producers will thus be forced to adapt their current technology to meet the requirements. This concept is much used in the USA, but in Britain the potential cost to industry is more frequently used to argue for a gradual change.

The importance of context

In establishing environmental controls, importance is nearly always attached to economic and other factors. As Pollution Paper No. 11 puts it:

> The tendency in setting standards in the UK is less to seek an absolute scientific base than to use scientific principles and all relevant and reliable evidence, then to try and progressively reduce emissions in a way that is consistent with economic and technological feasibility and with what at any one time is thought to be an acceptable ultimate objective.

It is difficult to separate the reasons for this policy from its effects. One reason is undoubtedly the historical influence that the town and country planning system, with its explicit requirement to balance all material considerations, has had on the development of the law, but a major reason must relate to the definition of pollution and the objectives of environmental controls.

Pollution was defined earlier as a relative concept, in the sense that there is no absolute rule about what amounts to pollution. The same applies to other forms of environmental change, such as urban or agricultural development. It is not possible to eradicate pollution, merely to reduce it. It follows that, at some stage, a choice has to be made about what is, and what is not, permissible. This is ultimately a political question, and involves a balancing of various factors. However, there are two possible objectives of pollution control. One is to aim to reduce pollution to 'acceptable' levels. An alternative is to aim to reduce pollution as far as possible. In Britain the first approach is implicitly adopted in relation to most substances. This explains the inevitability of a political balancing process, and also the preference for variable environmental quality standards. The second approach tends to lead to a reduction in discretion and to greater reliance on uniform standards, because if one producer can reduce to a particular level others should be able to do so as well.

The contextual approach accepts, therefore, that there is always going to be a trade-off between environmental protection and other factors, such as cost. This is fundamental to most British environmental controls. For example, it is reflected in the phrase Best Available Techniques Not Entailing Excessive Cost (BATNEEC) which is the cornerstone of Part I of the Environmental Protection Act 1990. The best available techniques part of the formula suggests that every step should be taken to protect the environment, but the not entailing excessive cost part qualifies it by reference to economic factors. One of the most interesting features of the interpretation of the 1990 Act will be how the balance is struck in practice between the two parts.

This philosophy of balancing environmental protection with material welfare is apparent in most areas of the law. It explains the wide discretions given to decision-makers, the emphasis on decisions being taken by reference to local factors, and the practice of defining some concepts after consultation with the industry involved. For example, the requirement of Best Practicable Means involves balancing technological, economic and local factors. The first two may be set at a national level (through such things as BPM Notes, which are often drawn up with the agreement of the relevant industry), but the third factor reflects the need to adjust the requirements to take account of individual circumstances. The emphasis on balance also explains such fundamental features of British law as the preference for flexible environmental standards rather than uniform ones, and the flexible and cooperative enforcement strategies that are employed by regulatory agencies.

Market mechanisms or the use of economic tools

These rather general phrases are meant to encompass all approaches which seek to use prices or economic incentives and deterrents to achieve environmental objectives. This could be done, for example, by encouraging pricing systems that signal the true environmental costs of products to consumers, thereby making environment-friendly items cheaper than those that pollute or waste natural resources. In a sense, therefore, these economic tools or instruments are the exact opposite of using the free market, since they normally involve an interference or intervention in the free market for the purpose of environmental protection. However, they do involve the use of the market in the sense that they are normally designed to allow consumers and industry to make choices about their actions. By way of contrast, many people would argue that most, though certainly not all, regulatory systems tend to operate so as to remove choice.

There is thus a potential confusion in referring simply to 'using the market' for environmental protection ends, since that runs together the policy of allowing an unrestricted free market to allocate resources on the assumption that that is somehow more efficient, and the separate policy of intervention in the market for protective purposes. As Nicholas Ridley, a devoted free marketeer, wrote in an explanation of the Government's environment policy whilst Secretary of State for the Environment: 'It is an essential part of the free market philosophy that regulation by Government is necessary to secure the public interest in environmental protection' (*Politics Against Pollution: The Conservative Record and Principles*, Centre for Policy Studies, 1989).

Annex A to the White Paper *This Common Inheritance* (Cm 1200, 1990) discusses a range of different ways in which economic instruments may be used to further environmental protection. These build on five general categories identified by the Organisation for Economic Cooperation and Development, namely, charges, subsidies, deposit or refund schemes, the creation of a market in pollution credits and enforcement incentives. It is accepted in the White Paper that charges and subsidies have constituted the main uses of economic instruments so far. It also becomes clear that some of the mechanisms are self-standing whilst others, such as most charging schemes, require a regulatory framework and proper policing, so they must be seen as additional to, rather than separate from, regulatory systems.

The following types of economic tool or instrument may be used.

(a)   Charges for the administrative cost of operating the regulatory system

This now goes under the title of 'cost recovery charging' and has been adopted in relation to a number of regulatory activities. The idea is to recover the regulatory costs that are incurred in granting applications or consents, or in such things as inspecting, monitoring or policing those consents. The current policy is not to charge for the general costs of operating the whole regulatory system, but to limit the charge to the amount which can be referable to each consent or discharge. In the interests of administrative simplicity, the charges are normally arranged in bands, rather than being worked out individually.

For example, in relation to water pollution under the Water Act 1989, a scheme of charging for applications for consent was introduced in October 1990. This was intended to recoup the costs of administering the application procedures for discharge consents. More significantly, annual charges to recover the cost to the National Rivers Authority of policing any discharges to controlled waters were introduced on 1 July 1991 (see the Scheme of Charges in Respect of Applications and Consents for Discharges to Controlled Waters). These are set so as to recoup the costs associated with inspecting and monitoring discharges, not the full cost of monitoring water quality, which will still be paid for by the taxpayer (see p. 314).

Similar schemes have been introduced from 1 April 1991 for applications and authorisations for operating a process subject to integrated pollution control (HMIP Integrated Pollution Control Fees and Charges Scheme (England and Wales) 1991) and for local authority air pollution control (Local Enforcing Authorities Air Pollution Fees and Charges Scheme (England and Wales) 1991). In the Integrated Pollution Control Scheme, the various processes subject to integrated pollution control have been divided into components and a flat rate is payable for each component. This is an attempt to cover the approximate cost to HMIP of granting and monitoring an authorisation.

Cost recovery charging systems may be progressive and thus have a beneficial environmental effect. For example, the charging schemes referred to involve higher charges for discharges which cause more pollution because they cost more to monitor.

Fees for planning applications were introduced in the early 1980s. At present there are standard fees set according to the size and nature of the proposed development and they do not reflect the full cost to the local planning authority of processing the application, much less the cost of policing the system of planning controls. However, it is proposed to increase these fees over the next few years so that more of the full cost of the system is recovered.

There always has been a rather different system of charging for discharges to sewers. This involves a rate for domestic consumers which is linked to property value, and a variable rate for trade dischargers linked to the volume and strength of the discharge as measured by Chemical Oxygen Demand. This produces a relatively unsophisticated method of charging for the cost of sewage treatment according to the demands made upon the system by the discharge. An incidental effect of concentrating on volume is, however, to reduce the level of water used and the level of waste, and thus to encourage both conservation of resources and recycling.

(b)   Charges reflecting the full environmental cost of an activity

The system of charging for sewage discharges shows the potential for use of charging systems which aim to charge for the full environmental cost of an activity. Such systems may be seen as the true environmental or pollution taxes referred to by Pearce, Markandya and Barbier in *Blueprint for a Green Economy*, 1989. The most topical example is the so-called 'carbon tax'. The objective behind this idea is to raise the price of fossil fuels to reflect their true (and hitherto uncosted) environmental effect, thus curtailing their use and reducing the greenhouse effect. Obviously there are distinct problems with such an idea. One is obtaining sufficient information about the discharge or process to make the taxes work properly. This would seem to demand a strong regulatory structure to police the system, although self-monitoring methods may have a large part to play in this respect. Another is the problem of obtaining accurate information about environmental effects on which to base the tax levels.

There is no doubt that this is an idea which is going to be greatly used in the future, and the White Paper includes a promise to consider it for water pollution. However, it must be said that a great deal of work needs to be done on the details of its implementation.

(c) Charges to finance environmental or pollution control measures

A number of examples may be given here. The National Rivers Authority may, under the Water Act 1989, s. 115, pass costs incurred in preventing or remedying water pollution back to the person who caused it. In relation to listed buildings, there are powers for local authorities to carry out repairs and recover the costs from the owner.

Fines levied in court for offences may also be seen as a form of environmental charge. Indeed, given the nature of environmental offences and the low moral blame often attached to them, many people treat fines as administrative penalties rather than as true criminal sanctions. The typically low level of fines means that their economic effect is limited, though levels are rising steadily, for example, the maximum fine for many environmental offences was raised to £20,000 on summary conviction by the Environmental Protection Act 1990. In the Crown Court, Shell (UK) was recently fined £1m for polluting the River Mersey in addition to which it paid a reported £1.4m in clean-up and other costs. However, at present there is no way of ensuring that fines are actually used for the benefit of the environment or that part of it which is damaged.

Civil law remedies may also be seen as achieving the same objectives. Many statutes now include civil liability for damage to people or their property, and the creation of a remedy of breach of statutory duty may act as a potent method of reallocating costs. The drawback at present is that few civil actions recognise fully the costs involved in environmental damage. The law has never developed any concept of environmental rights, with the result that the only possible civil law claimants are people with private rights. Put more simply, animals, birds and plants do not have civil law rights. However, the draft EC Directive on Civil Liability for Damage Caused by Waste (COM (91) 219 final) introduces the concept of 'injury to the environment' and provides that any plaintiff should be entitled to recover for costs incurred in preventing or remedying harm to the environment (in addition to damages for injury to persons or property), as well as obtaining injunctive remedies. This may signal a new development of environmental rights.

(d) Charges levied on polluting materials or processes

Instead of a charge being levied on the results of pollution it could be levied on a process or product. Alternatively a charge may be reduced for environment-friendly activities. The most obvious example is the reduced tax payable on unleaded petrol compared with leaded petrol. This has clearly led to a dramatic rise in the use of unleaded petrol over the last three or four years. A further example is the Environmental Protection Act 1990, s. 52, which introduces the concept of waste recycling credits for authorities or people who retain waste for the purpose of recycling it.

(e) Subsidies and grants

These are commonly used for environmental ends, although their use within the EC is restricted by the rules on illegal state aids. For example, subsidies are available for the construction of facilities for the improvement of the treatment of agricultural water and silage effluent—both particularly potent, and increasingly common, causes of pollution. Care has to be taken that the subsidies achieve the result intended. Some subsidies on forestry and agriculture, for example, have been accused of having detrimental environmental effects because of their inability to select between beneficial and non-beneficial projects.

Compensation payments for environmentally sensitive activities may also be seen in this category. The prevailing policy in relation to countryside protection has tended to be one of voluntariness, whereby farmers and landowners are compensated for agreeing to forgo certain advantages in the interests of the environment. Sometimes this is through the payment of direct compensation and sometimes through the negotiation of management agreements. For example, management agreements may be agreed in relation to the protection of national nature reserves or sites of special scientific interest, and similar methods are being used in other designated areas such as environmentally sensitive areas and nitrate sensitive areas.

(f) The creation of a market in pollution credits

A further instrument is the use of tradeable quotas, or emissions trading. These are methods of creating a market in the right to pollute. For example, a total for emissions of a specified substance may be set for a particular area. Firms may then bid for the right to take up a part of that total. Prospective or new polluters would have to buy the rights of existing holders if there was no spare capacity. By restricting the available emissions, prices would be driven up, providing an incentive to reduce emissions or to develop alternatives.

The idea is most developed in the USA, but the groundwork for its use in the UK is laid in the Environmental Protection Act 1990, s. 3(5), which allows the Secretary of State to establish total emissions of any substance either nationally or for a limited area, and to allocate quotas, with power progressively to reduce the total allowed. This idea is designed for use in relation to the commitment to cut carbon dioxide emissions by specified dates (currently the UK commitment is to stabilise emissions at 1990 levels by 2005, five years behind the rest of the EC), as agreed internationally as a method of combatting global warming. Once again, a regulatory structure would be needed to police the system.

(g) Deposit and refund schemes

Although deposit and refund schemes are clearly severe interferences with a free market, it is also clear that they may have an enormous impact on the amount of waste produced. The current Government favours voluntary mechanisms here, rather than ones imposed by law, and seeks to get them introduced by the industries concerned. By way of example, the British Government intervened in the *Danish Bottles* case (*Commission v Denmark* [1989] 54 CMLR 619) in the European Court of Justice, supporting the EC Commission's argument that a Danish law requiring drinks containers to be returnable was contrary to the free market principles of the EC. The Court of Justice upheld most of the Danish scheme despite its clear anti-competitive effect, on the grounds that the aim of environmental protection justified some interference with the operation of the single internal market within the EC.

Future uses of economic instruments

The above summary is not intended to be an exhaustive list of those mechanisms which might be tried, or even of those which are already in use, but to give an idea of the type of instrument that may be available. As stated before, there is little doubt that market-related instruments will increasingly be used in the future. Indeed, they could currently be said to be 'flavour of the month' as far as environmental regulation is concerned.

One reason for this is undoubtedly that market mechanisms appeal to the political philosophy of the current Government. There is a strong link with the principle of choice, the idea that people should be given a choice of how to act, as long as their actions do not breach some generally accepted limits. This idea is seen most strongly in the realm of town and country planning where the importance attached to market forces is made explicit in much of Central Government policy advice (see for example Circular 22/80). The principle is also seen in relation to such things as the adoption of voluntary methods of protection in the countryside (see p. 348) and the preference for pollution control systems which set objectives whilst leaving producers to work out for themselves how to achieve them. There is also a strong link with the related policy of deregulation pursued throughout the 1980s and explained in White Papers such as *Lifting the Burden* (Cmnd 9571, 1985) and *Building Businesses, Not Barriers* (Cmnd 9794, 1986). Amongst other things, this policy amounts to a rejection of imposed restrictions in favour of agreed ones and a removal of unnecessary state powers.

Within the EC, the Environment Commissioner, Carlo Ripa di Meana, has also recently suggested a shift in EC environmental policy towards the greater use of economic instruments rather than the administrative regulation approach. Appropriately enough, this suggestion was made when proposing an EC-wide system of environment-friendly labelling for consumer goods, recognising that in order for any of these market-based methods to work there needs to be accurate information available to consumers and regulators. It is significant that EC action has been concentrated in this area recently. For example, 1990 saw the agreement of Directive 90/313 on Freedom of Access to Information on the Environment and Regulation 1210/90 on the establishment of the European Environment Agency, which will initially have a role in acquiring and disseminating information about the state of the environment in the EC.

The polluter pays principle

The EC can claim another important contribution to the development of economic instruments; its environmental policy has always included the adoption of the 'polluter pays' principle although it was probably the Organisation for Economic Cooperation and Development (OECD) which first popularised the idea in the early 1970s (see OECD, *The Polluter Pays Principle*, 1975). The principle basically means that the producer of goods or other items should be responsible for the costs of preventing or dealing with any pollution which the process causes. This includes environmental costs as well as direct costs to people or property. It also covers costs incurred in avoiding pollution, and not just those related to remedying any damage. There is a very strong link between the principle and the idea that prevention is better than cure. It will also be clear from the foregoing discussion that these costs should include the full environmental costs, not just those which are immediately tangible.

The relevance of this principle to the discussion of economic instruments is obvious, since a producer will have to pass on any costs in the price of goods to the ultimate consumer. However, this is only a principle, it has no legal force and there is no agreed definition that has anything approaching the precision of a statute. On the contrary, there has frequently been dispute over its exact scope, especially over the limits on payments for damage caused. It is essentially a guide to desirable courses of action, but it is fairly clear that it has rarely been fully satisfied in either EC or UK environmental legislation.

As a result the principle has sometimes seemed to be all things to all people, and has even been used to justify views with which it has little connection, for example the suggestion that producers may pollute as long as they pay for it. That is a complete misunderstanding of the principle's true meaning, and the potential abuse of such an imprecise phrase should be appreciated.

The criminal law as a tool for environmental protection

The criminal law can be used either to provide direct criminal sanctions for environmental harm, or in a subsidiary and complementary role within a regulatory system. It tends to be of greater use in the second way. This is because the main purpose of the criminal law is to punish clearly identified wrongs. Yet, in relation to many environmental matters, it is often impossible to identify wrong without reference to other factors. For example, it is clearly desirable to have industry and many other activities which may cause pollution. The question is not a simple one of whether to have them, but a more difficult one of how much pollution is acceptable (see also the definition of pollution on p. 14). That requires a balancing of the various factors involved against what is reasonable—a discretionary, political process, for which the regulatory system is well-suited. The criminal law is rather inadequate for such a balancing process, and thus tends to be used mainly to deal either with clear acts of environmental vandalism, or to support the regulatory system once it has decided what is and what is not acceptable.

There are a number of examples of offences which stem directly from environmental harm. Under the Environmental Protection Act 1990, s. 87, it is an offence to drop or deposit litter in a public or other specified place. In the Water Act 1989, s. 107, there is a general offence of causing or knowingly permitting any poisonous, noxious or polluting matter to enter controlled waters. It is not always necessary to show actual harm to the environment: in some cases an activity may be prohibited because harm can be assumed to follow or because the risk of harm is too great to take. For example, under the Clean Air Acts 1956 and 1968, it is an offence to emit dark smoke from premises.

However, even in these cases, enforcement is often left to a public body. One reason for this is practical, given the difficulty in some situations of identifying and proving environmental harm. Another reason is that the right of prosecution is often restricted in English law. This is becoming less common, but a good example is the restriction in relation to water pollution. Under the Rivers (Prevention of Pollution) Acts 1951 and 1961, which established a system of consents for discharges to water for the first time and also a general pollution offence in similar terms to the Water Act 1989, s. 107, it was provided that a prosecution could only be brought by a water authority, or with the consent of the Attorney-General. This restriction was removed by the Control of Pollution Act 1974.

A third reason for enforcement being left to public bodies is the lack of available public information relating to pollution. Under the Rivers (Prevention of Pollution) Acts, there was no public register of consents, samples taken of water quality, or samples taken of discharges; indeed it was an offence for water authority officers to disclose such information gained in the course of their duties. Under the Control of Pollution Act 1974 and Water Act 1989, a system of public registers has been established which is starting to remove the secrecy of earlier years. Similar limitations on private prosecution and access to information have been present in most areas of environmental law over the years.

The most frequent use of the criminal law is therefore in a subsidiary capacity to administrative controls (i.e. to the regulatory system). Many criminal offences consist not of committing a direct act of pollution, but instead of ignoring the dictates of the regulatory body. Under the Water Act, s. 107, it is a criminal offence to discharge trade or sewage effluent without, or in breach of, a consent from the National Rivers Authority. In relation to town and country planning, the offence consists not of breaching planning control but of ignoring an enforcement notice. This makes the criminal offence truly subsidiary to the regulatory process, since only the local planning authority may issue an enforcement notice, thus taking the possibility of enforcement away from the public.

All of these matters have an effect in decriminalising the law. The offence is not directly linked to the environmental harm, but to an administrative process. Enforcement is normally by an administrative body and often for breach of an administrative requirement. The message that is given is that these things are truly related to administrative processes rather than the criminal law. In addition, the low sentences that are imposed (often because only low sentences are available), the marked reluctance to prosecute, the limited amount of moral censure that has traditionally been attached to environmental offences, the lowly status of many who are selected for prosecution and the escape of many major industrial polluters from prosecution (all factors which are discussed elsewhere in this book) tend to emphasise the decriminalisation of the laws. Once again, however, there is no doubt that things are changing very rapidly as a result of changes in the perception of the general public.

SIX

The enforcement of environmental law

The British approach to enforcement

Essentially, enforcement is carried out by regulatory bodies. Although there are supplementary powers available to those with private rights under the common law, there are inherent disadvantages in relying upon extra-statutory powers to control the protection of the environment (see Chapter 8).

The identity of the enforcement model exercised by those regulatory bodies is strongly underscored by themes which dominate Part I of this book. For instance, flexibility in both the setting of standards and the methodology of pollution abatement, use of non-statutory 'guidance' to control emission standards, large degrees of open texture within statutory definitions to enable enforcement bodies to utilise highly discretionary powers and the reliance upon self-policing based upon the mutual self-interest of industrialists and enforcement officers are characteristic of the British approach to enforcement.

In enforcing regulations, it is possible to identify two different models which can govern the enforcement process. First, the cooperative model and second, the confrontational approach. The cooperative approach is characterised by the development of a continuing relationship between enforcer and polluter. Thus, mutual respect and trust develop which can be utilised to ensure that there is compliance within a system. The confrontational approach involves the penalising of activities. At its extreme, such an approach can result in the sanctioning of every breach.

The nature of enforcement mechanisms in environmental protection

Regulatory enforcement is concerned with the use of tools or mechanisms to achieve an objective. It is not *only* concerned with punishment but with compliance.

At one end of the enforcement spectrum, powers of prosecution enable regulatory bodies to punish one-off incidents, but the use of the criminal sanction is only one in a variety of mechanisms used to control activities. Formal statutory/regulatory enforcement tools are also available. For instance, the Environmental Protection Act 1990 contains provisions which allow for authorisations to be varied or revoked and activities to be prohibited or to be subject to enforcement procedures without any reference to the criminal courts.

Furthermore, there are 'informal' tools. The word 'informal' here does not necessarily indicate that such controls are not serious. There are steps in all enforcement procedures which can be identified as being the 'last warning' or penultimate step before 'formal' action. These are not formal sanctions in the true sense. For example, the taking of legal samples under the Water Act 1989 or a notice for the requisition of ownership details under the Town and Country Planning Act 1990 are all 'formal' steps which can lead to prosecution although there is no element of punishment explicit in such action.

Further down the severity scale of regulatory enforcement lie such informal mechanisms as threats or an increased number of visits from an enforcement officer. Such tools will be used at an initial stage in the enforcement procedures but must not be seen as sanctions at all.

Finally, there are informal problem-solving mechanisms. The idea that the regulatory bodies can be viewed as consultants or educators underpins the cooperative approach so prevalent in Britain.

Throughout any discussion of the legal context of the practical enforcement of pollution control, it must be borne in mind that those bodies who regulate activities often do so with an 'active' discretion; that is to say a discretion which actually defines the limits of what is permissible in any case. Such an approach is clearly evidenced by the use of non-statutory guidance notes to set emission standards. Moreover, there is further discretion over and above this 'active' discretion; when enforcement bodies decide whether or not to sanction the breach of these standards.

The legal context

The vast majority of pollution offences are defined as offences of strict liability. That is to say there does not need to be proof of any negligence or fault on behalf of the defendant/offender for liability to attach. Indeed, most pollution offences tend to be accidental in the sense that there is no forethought or malice on behalf of the person responsible for the pollution of the environment. However, with offences of strict liability, theoretically every breach should amount to an offence as there is no element of fault, the absence of which can be offered as a defence. Nevertheless, when the figures are examined, the incidence of prosecution for environmental pollution offences is remarkably low. As an example the South-West and Southern Water Authorities brought no prosecutions for water pollution offences in 1988 and 1989. Other authorities were also relatively reluctant to prosecute. This is in contrast to the figures available, in certain areas, showing compliance rates as low as 35% of trade effluent discharges falling below reasonable levels of compliance with their consents. Thus, there is an apparent dichotomy between the theory of strict liability and the exercise of the discretion as to enforcement. How has this situation arisen?

The pollution control system in Britain has all the characteristics of an administrative and bureaucratic regulatory system. Within the wider definition of regulatory systems it falls into the same class as many other analogous systems, including the system of the criminal law.

However, one of the major differences between the regulatory system of pollution control and the criminal regulatory system is that the central aim of the pollution system is to prevent harm to the environment and/or human health rather than to detect and punish harm. Often, under environmental legislation, enforcement agencies utilise regulations to control continuing activity rather than to penalise single offences. The basis of this mechanism of control is the utilisation of an on-going relationship between the enforcers and those who pollute. By encouraging the use of a system to control activities rather than to punish, this relationship is fostered.

This on-going relationship can only exist because of the wide amount of discretion used in interpreting regulations; this allows 'technically' guilty offenders in breach of regulation to avoid liability. The methods that the enforcement authorities use are largely peculiar to the pollution control system. Put simply, the enforcement agencies will normally carry out specific statutory enforcement activities only when there is a belief (on behalf of the individual officer of the agency concerned) that the continuing relationship between the enforcers and the polluters is being ignored. The breakdown is characterised by an increasing unpleasantness and a move away from a cooperative approach for so long as an unauthorised activity is carried on.

There have been three studies carried out examining the activities of enforcement bodies in England. The first and second, *Environment and Enforcement* (Hawkins) and *Policing Pollution* (Richardson, Ogus & Burrows) investigated the enforcement mechanisms utilised under the old-style water authorities. The third, *The Reasonable Arm of the Law* (B Hutter) looked at the role of local authority environmental health officers. By questioning officers at length about their attitudes to enforcement in relation to both 'offenders' and the offence itself, all three studies provide an in-depth study of the themes of environmental enforcement. Further studies carried out in Scotland gave similar findings.

The evidence presented in these three studies demonstrates that the enforcement agencies in question walk a tight-rope between a cooperative approach and the effective enforcement of environmental legislation. *Policing Pollution* indicated that out in the 'real world' of environmental enforcement the final sanction of prosecution for the breach of a regulation was very rarely used. In the study it was shown that officers believed that prosecutions tended to upset offenders to such an extent that any cooperation or continuing relationship built up between the two parties was quickly and effectively demolished. Moreover, officers tended to utilise a quasi-enforcement system based upon 'informal' mechanisms of enforcement as perceived by individual officers rather than as provided for in regulations.

It was shown that prosecution was used only in approximately 10 cases out of every 3,000 breaches of the trade effluent discharge consent system. These statistics raise an obvious question—why is there such a reluctance to prosecute on behalf of the enforcement authorities?

The attitude towards the offence

One of the main reasons for encouraging a cooperative, continuing relationship rather than a confrontational approach is the moral ambivalence surrounding regulatory offences. For a long time pollution offences have generally been regarded as morally neutral. Research has suggested that although the enforcement agencies are enforcing the same standards for all polluters they are not necessarily concerned with the standards themselves, instead they tend to look at the intent behind the act of pollution.

The discretion used in enforcing the strict regulations has been identified as being within a 'doughnut-ring' of decision-making. Enforcement officers use this discretion as identified by the doughnut-ring of decision-making to attach moral blame to a particular incident by changing the level of a particular sanction involved with the moral opprobrium which they feel towards the activity complained of. This is one explanation of the extremely low prosecution rate, as the enforcing authorities are reluctant to use the ultimate sanction of prosecution unless the level of moral blame is at the top end of the scale, which could be equated with gross criminal negligence or actual intent on behalf of the offender. Most accidents are not morally offensive as 'they could happen to anyone'. Secondly, the enforcement agencies tend to have grave doubts about the level of criminal penalties involved for breach of the regulatory system. The fines are notoriously low and therefore are not always seen as an effective sanction when compared to the profits which are often generated from the polluting activities. Additionally, the low level of punishment tends to reinforce the view that it is not only the enforcers who have morally ambivalent views of the offence, but the judiciary as well.

Moreover, the typical attitude to 'white collar crimes' suggests that offences committed as a process of industrial activity are less heinous than normal offences. It is often said that pollution is a natural consequence of industrial activity which creates jobs, therefore, for the balance to be weighted in favour of protecting against harm to the environment, the need to protect has to significantly outweigh the utility of the process in creating jobs.

Traditionally, those who have been polluting have been of a high status in society and those affected by pollution of low status. Pollution was more commonplace in working-class areas of high industrial activity. Indeed, many of those living in the area were working in a factory which was polluting the area. It was often seen as a way of life rather than a matter for complaint.

Finally, commentators have identified the existence of the so-called capture theory in the relationship between the polluters and enforcement agencies. The capture theory testifies to the belief that large corporations who are the traditional polluters have a large degree of control over the enforcers by using the traditional power-relationship model. Put simply, the smaller enforcement agencies are traditionally in awe of the larger powerful corporations who not only are worth many millions of pounds but also have tremendous powers.

Attitudes towards the offender

The attitude towards the offender is not necessarily based upon the actual cause of the pollution incident but what the enforcement agencies believe to be the cause of the pollution incident. Research has shown that where there are problems with trade effluent discharges offenders are far more likely to be prosecuted if they make their relationship with the enforcement agency more difficult. The reverse is also true: if the offender has had a good relationship with the enforcement agency then it is less likely that a prosecution will ensue. This brings an element of 'just deserts' into the enforcement process; moral blame is more likely to attach to an offender where previous warnings have been given of a particular danger. The work of the enforcement agencies is technically and scientifically based rather than based on the sanctions available under the law. They have perceived their relationship with the offender as being one of helping to achieve a particular solution rather than enforcing the regulations by the letter of the law. Cooperation with the polluters to achieve a better quality environment rather than confrontation was always seen to be their objective.

Enforcement agencies have tended to view offenders in three different groups:

(a)   Business firms seen as amoral calculators. The view of the enforcement agencies is that certain businesses are motivated entirely by profit and will disobey the law when they calculate that it is in their interest to do so. The enforcement agencies tend to view this type of operation with considerable disdain and are far more likely to want to prosecute every breach.

(b)   Firms seen as political citizens. The operators of these businesses are perceived as going about their business properly and any breach of the regulation is likely to be on the basis that the operators feel that the regulation is unreasonable and is requiring them to carry out actions which are unnecessary in a purely commercial sense.

(c)   Firms seen as organisationally incompetent. These firms can be characterised as ignorant and beset by organisational difficulties rather than possessing any particular moral attitude. In practice, non-compliance by them is perceived by the enforcement agencies as bad housekeeping derived from a lack of understanding or a lack of responsibility on behalf of the individuals in charge of industrial processes. Enforcement agencies are unwilling to identify such firms as amoral calculators because of their perception of such individuals.

In the last type of case, the enforcement agencies utilise a cooperative approach which gives them the role of educator/consultant rather than policeman. Another underlying reason or justification for this cooperative approach is shown perversely in the enforcement agencies' attitude to those who they view as being amoral calculators. They have said that where an amoral calculator is identified it is quite clear that they will enforce the regulations strongly and severe punishment will result. However, it is argued that the understaffing of the enforcement agencies means that prosecutions in all cases of breach would be impossible and therefore it is imperative that the cooperative approach be taken. It is felt that industry could 'pull out the plug' if a confrontational approach were taken. Indeed one officer was quoted as saying 'if we lose cooperation we lose control'. Thus, the need for cooperation is mutual.

The use of sanctions other than prosecution

As the regulatory system of pollution control is concerned with the continuing prevention of harm, the availability of sanctions other than prosecution could be considered to be an influential factor in deciding whether or not to prosecute.

Many contraventions are of a chronic nature rather than an acute, one-off accident. In such circumstances, the use of non-criminal sanctions may be more appropriate. Variation, enforcement notices etc. allow for a continuation of the cooperational approach as they allow for a remedy without any explicit punishment. As such, they offer an opportunity for a greater flexibility for negotiation and cooperation. However, where there is a one-off pollution incident the use of such sanctions is limited.

Even where non-criminal sanctions are used there is still scope to punish the uncooperative offender as most of the non-criminal sanctions have as their ultimate step the prosecution for breach.

The process of enforcement

Having examined some of the attitudes that the enforcement agencies have towards both the offender and the offence, how do they translate these attitudes into the process of enforcement?

In *Policing Pollution* Genevra Richardson suggested that there is often a set pattern of enforcement which is adopted by enforcement agencies to underpin the cooperational approach. A six-fold process was identified:

(a)   presenting the problem;
(b)   problem solving;
(c)   presence;
(d)   threats;
(e)   taking a legal sample;
(f)   prosecution.

(a)   Presenting the problem

The first stage in the process of enforcement was identified as the setting up of a reasonable image of the enforcers. Put simply, they wished to present themselves as reasonable people making reasonable demands.

This was achieved by appearing authoritative and stating the problems that a company faced. This idea was strongly linked to the view of the firm as a political citizen. By appearing authoritative but reasonable it was hoped that a firm base could be established on which to build a relationship of mutual trust.

(b) Problem solving

After a problem had been presented, the next phase of this quasi-enforcement system involved an investigation to find a reasonable solution. Sometimes, in complicated cases, the attempt to find a solution using the cooperational method obscured the fact that standards were being breached. There was often a perception amongst enforcement bodies that where a problem was complex then it was only to be expected that there would be a failure to attain the required standard.

(c) Presence

Policing Pollution suggested that not all traders responded to these first two steps in the enforcement process. If there was little effort made to cooperate, enforcement officers would become more assertive. This attitude was founded upon a belief that the longer an offender failed to comply, the more likely that it was that the business could be identified as a moral calculator. Consequently, it was less important to follow a strategy of cooperation as a greater degree of moral blame could attach to the offender. In an attempt to increase the severity of the pressure upon an offender, the next 'step' in this quasi-enforcement process was an increase in presence. Put in simple terms, any offender persisting in non-compliance was visited regularly and constant check-ups were made. This was hoped to have the effect that 'big brother was watching' and firms would recognise the futility of continuing to confront the enforcement agencies.

(d) Threats

Although a heightened degree of presence carried with it an implied threat, continuing non-compliance often resulted in explicit threats. Even here, there were grades of threatening behaviour. For example, at one end of the spectrum will be the verbal warning whereas at the other are formal letters on headed notepaper signed by the Chief Inspector/Head of Committee/Chief Executive, etc. Throughout this process, officers could also assure themselves of the reasonableness of their actions in an effort to seek compliance.

(e) Taking a legal sample

The penultimate step prior to prosecution was the taking of a formal legal sample. Such samples form the essential evidence on which a prosecution can be founded. Indeed, in the case of the Water Act 1989, such a sample has to be taken to be admissible. This was seen to be a very serious step and one which was not taken lightly. As a serious step, officers were wary of utilising such powers regularly. As a 'last chance' mechanism, the value of such a procedure would be lost if samples were taken regularly without any consequential prosecution in the case of continuing non-compliance.

(f) The prosecution

Within the system of enforcement for water pollution the final step is prosecution. *Policing Pollution* and *The Reasonable Arm of the Law* indicated that there were no particular objective factors which determined the incidence of prosecution.

Thus, it made little difference that one area was heavily populated and another more rural, or one industrialised and another residential. Even within regions figures varied.

Although these steps of enforcement characterised the water authorities' operations prior to the Water Act 1989, other enforcement agencies have also been identified as using a similar framework. Indeed, in *The Reasonable Arm of the Law*, Bridget Hutter puts it thus:

> 'Enforcing the Law' to an Environmental Health Officer means securing compliance with the law through persuasion and advice, rather than the apprehension and subsequent punishment of offenders. The law is regarded as a means to an end rather than an end in itself and officers consider themselves to be delivering a service both to the local community—by promoting and maintaining a required standard of public health—and, in some respects, to be regulated—by advising them on how best to attain these standards, rather than being members of an 'industrial police force'.

This methodology of compliance rather than sanction is unusual in that, in a heavily regulated system, those outside the enforcement agencies would assume that the regulations are being enforced properly. What effects does this methodology of compliance have?

Lack of public confidence in the enforcement system

The public are often the main source of primary information regarding pollution incidents. Enforcement agencies are often understaffed and overworked. Not all pollution occurs between 9.00 am and 5.00 pm and certainly not when an officer happens to be on site. Many prosecutions for water pollution commence in court with the words:

> Acting upon information received from an anonymous member of the public, an officer attended a pollution incident at . . .

Often third parties are viewed with mistrust by both enforcers and polluters. Complaints from the public can put a cooperational relationship in jeopardy. The enforcers are faced with a dilemma, should they proceed against an activity to the detriment of the trust built up or should they continue to seek the cooperation of an offender but risk the wrath of a disappointed third party?

An argument has been put forward by Keith Hawkins that the enforcement bodies often choose a third way. In *Environment and Enforcement* he suggests that selective enforcement *enhances* the public's view of the enforcers. By choosing 'high profile' cases the agencies could attempt to draw attention to their own effectiveness:

> A policy of fuller enforcement expressed in a swelling prosecution rate cannot be employed as an indicator of efficiency, or in an environment of ambivalence

this risk has been treated as evidence of agency harassment. It is, rather in the careful and sparing selection of cases for prosecution, that the agency is best able to protect its own interest by showing that 'something is being done'.

However, the Tenth Report of the Royal Commission of Environmental Pollution quoted a poll commissioned by the EC which found that 93% of interviewees agreed with the proposition that stronger measures should be taken to protect the environment against pollution. This led later on in the Report to the comment that 'The success of our regulatory authorities needs to be judged on their performance rather than their methods'. This reiterated their finding in the Sixth Report in 1976 that the public lacked confidence in the Industrial Air Pollution Inspectorate because there was a view that the interests of the Inspectorate were too closely linked with those of industry. The point being made stressed the public's misunderstanding of the conciliatory approach. In traditional regulatory systems, there may be a degree of discretion, but this would normally stem from a desire to police effectively by means of not over-loading the system. It is difficult for the public to understand that using a conciliatory approach is, by its very nature, helping to secure compliance.

The close links between industry and their enforcers can be directly attributed to this non-confrontational approach. In an era of increasing environmental awareness the public need to *see* that the law is being used effectively. It is difficult to explain to a member of the public that the cooperational strategy will secure environmental quality improvements where a company is clearly breaking the law. Actual proof of the breach of a regulation would normally result in enforcement and thus the public perceive that the enforcement of statutory regulations in the environmental field is not a worthwhile process.

Differing levels of enforcement

One of the findings of the different research projects carried out in the 1980s was that there were various levels of enforcement in different geographical locations. For instance, in *Policing Pollution*, it was shown that in a three-year period, 48 prosecutions were brought by a 'Northern Water Authority' for the contravention of trade effluent consents. In a 'Southern Water Authority' not a single prosecution was brought over the same period. Indeed, officers within that authority only had 'a very hazy impression of the prescribed route that the decision [about whether to proceed with the prosecution] would take'. Secondly, the figures for the Northern Water Authority for prosecution stemmed mainly (some 90%) from one division of that authority.

This lack of uniformity could be a consequence of the 'doughnut-ring' model of decision-making. Many different factors need to be taken into account when considering whether or not to bring enforcement action, and clearly within one authority more factors would preclude a prosecution than promote it. Put another way, the many different factors, including the personality of the officers themselves, alter the width of the 'doughnut-ring' when deciding whether or not to prosecute. The wider the discretion, the more uncertain a system becomes.

The counterbalance to discretion is certainty, and, depending upon the width of the discretion used, there will be varying degrees of certainty as to whether or not a particular regulation will be enforced. Uncertainty detracts from the power of the regulatory framework. Some officers were disturbed by this lack of uniformity. They favoured a more explicit policy applicable at least throughout the whole authority, if not nationwide. They were evidently anxious to ensure procedural reasonableness and the application of predetermined rules to guide the exercise of their discretion.

The concern expressed stems from the need for a degree of certainty to ensure that both enforcers and industry know where they stand in relation to any breach. Certainty brings fairness of a different sort from that in a system where there is a wide discretion. If all those controlled by the regulatory system know the parameters within which they can work, and that such parameters are applied equitably throughout the system, then clearly there are greater degrees of moral and legal authority. When the enforcement agencies express concern over the uniformity of regulatory enforcement, it is quite clear that the system itself cannot be operating with total efficiency.

Administrative difficulties

Aside from the attitudes that enforcement agencies have towards the offence and the offender, other external factors have had a marked effect upon the efficient enforcement of environmental regulations. These can properly be related to all the usual problems facing administrative and bureaucratic systems.

As was seen in Chapter 3, the traditional model for environmental regulation in Britain has been to set up large administrative bodies charged with both organisational and regulatory responsibilities. Thus, agencies have been both poacher and gamekeeper. This of course can lead to fundamental difficulties in the contradictory nature of these two functions. The two main examples of this dual role came in the control of water pollution under the regional water authorities and the control of the disposal of waste to land through the county-wide waste disposal authorities. Both these authorities carried out activities which were the subject of control which had to be policed by themselves. The water authorities operated sewage treatment plants, and the waste disposal authorities were site operators disposing of waste within their own area. Additionally, these two bodies possessed the regulatory powers for the supervision of private sector activities. The failure to separate the two contradictory roles created great problems. Often the gravest breach of regulations came from the operational arm of the regulatory authorities. For instance, pollution from the water authorities' sewage treatment plants was perhaps the most significant factor in the deterioration of water quality. In the waste disposal sector, the Commons Environment Committee stated:

. . . many local authorities appear to have concentrated on their operational activities to the detriment of their regulatory duties . . . [some waste disposal authorities] regard keeping consignment notes in a box in the corner as adequately discharging their record-keeping responsibilities.

This dual role led to two difficulties in enforcement. Firstly, the private sector argued that it was inequitable for the enforcement agencies to prosecute when their own operations were also in breach. Secondly, it led to a desire to use the conciliatory approach because many officers within the enforcement agency empathised with those in the private sector as to the problems faced in pollution control. Their officers had experienced difficulties within their own agency and thus were far more likely to be sympathetic in enforcing the law generally.

Staffing and funding levels

To maintain a proper level of enforcement, adequate manpower and funding has to be available. If there were only 500 police officers covering the whole of England and Wales we would undoubtedly see a dramatic increase in the levels of crime. Environmental enforcement has, however, been the poor relation in terms both of staff on the ground and funds available to those staff.

The crisis in local government is well documented. Cuts in funding and low morale has led to a smaller complement of staff attempting to deal with a large number of complaints. However, the other enforcement agencies fare little better. It is estimated that HMIP needs approximately 300 inspectors to regulate and advise on the new system of integrated pollution control. In addition, approximately 50 inspectors are required to inspect and enforce the Radioactive Substances Act 1960 and a further 50 to be involved in miscellaneous activities, such as the control of Red List substances in sewers and hazardous waste checks, bringing a total requirement of 400 inspectors to operate the regulatory system effectively. In October 1990, there were 155 inspectors.

Even in the past, the Inspectorate did not meet its targets for enforcement visits or for the number of samples taken. For example, the numbers for site visits with respect to air pollution controls fell from 9,150 in 1987/88 to 7,350 in 1989/90 to a provisional figure of 4,825 in 1990/91. In a situation such as this it is difficult to maintain a confrontational stance. The enforcement agencies expect to rely upon industry cooperating to keep within the emission limits.

This situation is not just peculiar to HMIP. In its second Report (1988–89), the Inspectorate outlined its concern over the ability of the waste disposal authorities to fulfil their obligations under Part II of the Environmental Protection Act 1990. They alleged that there were very few authorities with a full staffing complement, stating that 'Even a 25% increase in staff may not be sufficient for any effective regulation'. Even the 'strongest environmental protection agency in Europe', as the Government has labelled the National Rivers Authority, is about to suffer from a 30% shortfall in Central Government funding. In its corporate plan for 1991/92, the National Rivers Authority identified the need for grants of £119 million, £108 million, and £105 million over the following three years. This compared with Government estimates of funding of £84 million, £72 million, and £73 million over the corresponding period. The plan stated:

Significant amounts of investment are needed to reduce pollution levels, over and above current estimates of expenditure along with increased monitoring and regulatory activity by the authority, in order to achieve the authority's mission to reduce pollution substantially and improve water quality.

Clearly, this lack of funding and manpower ensures that the enforcement agencies have to rely on industry self-policing rather than having a policy of continuous assessment and enforcement from outside bodies.

Changes in attitudes to enforcement

Most of the research referred to so far in this chapter dates back to empirical studies in the mid-1970s to the early 1980s. Perceptions of environmental difficulties have changed dramatically since that time. New environmental quality objectives imposed by the EC have meant that the enforcement agencies are being placed under increasing pressure to take a proactive approach to enforcement and to use prosecution as the short term weapon to bring industry into line in the long term. For instance, the Environmental Protection Act 1990, s. 7, provides for such objectives to be taken into account when authorising processes subject to integrated pollution control and air pollution control. Similarly the Water Act 1989, s. 106, makes water quality objectives a statutory consideration. The evidence of this fundamental change in the control of pollution in Britain can be seen with the introduction of the Air Quality Standard Regulations 1989 (SI 1989 No. 317). This move towards fixed standards and away from individualised flexible enforcement requires the redefinition of the enforcement of environmental protection.

The redefinition of the regulatory role

With the creation of the National Rivers Authority under the Water Act 1989 and the proposed formation of the new system of regulation in the waste disposal industry under the Environmental Protection Act, there has been a move away from the dual-function approach of the 1970s and 1980s. The NRA and the new waste regulation authorities will have almost total regulatory control without the problems of organisational complications to blunt their effectiveness. This, in turn, has allowed the NRA to become the self-styled 'Water Guardian' and to concentrate on the policing side of their role in order to achieve compliance by confrontation. This has been evidenced by an increase in the incidence of prosecution since its creation. In the first year of its life the number of prosecutions for water pollution offences rose by some 15%, with the anticipated number for 1990/91 expected to rise significantly again.

The incidence of prosecution is only one piece of evidence of a changing attitude to enforcement. In the first of a series of new water quality papers, the NRA outlined its new approach to enforcement. In addition to the conciliatory model, there was a new desire to prosecute where a discharger has shown little care in attempting to comply with consent obligations. Although at first glance this may not be far away from the previous attempts at moral judgment in exercising enforcement discretion, it does however demonstrate that the NRA are far more likely to consider accidents as requiring enforcement action even where moral opprobrium is low. Furthermore, the NRA have brought a number of prosecutions against the newly privatised water services companies. Five of the 10 companies were prosecuted within 18 months of the introduction of the Water Act. These figures are all the more remarkable given that the companies were given a prosecution 'holiday' to enable them to upgrade their plants etc. This will have indirect effects upon those who discharge into sewers controlled by the companies. Where levels of prosecutions against the private water companies rise, they in turn will have to enforce trade discharge standards thus increasing the enforcement pressure considerably.

Finally, the waste regulation authorities will not have the same difficulties that face officers under the waste disposal authority of policing sites which are in a better condition than those run by their own authority. The new arm's length local authority waste disposal companies will be subjected to the same degree of control as private operations, and therefore will undoubtedly face different pressures as Part II of the Environmental Protection Act is phased in.

The redefinition of the enforcement agencies' relationship with industry

The traditional image of the enforcement agencies collaborating with industry over a table in a room at the factory with a cup of tea while 'problem-solving' is fast disappearing. Most enforcement agencies were renowned for their ability sympathetically to suggest ways to abate pollution. Indeed, most guidance notes controlling the processes within an industry were drafted with close assistance from those who operated the processes themselves.

HMIP has taken up a different stance when drawing up the guidance notes to govern integrated pollution control and air pollution control. The Inspectorate specifically rejected the Chemical Industry Association's claims that it should be involved throughout the process of drawing up the new guidelines. The dismay expressed by the association emphasised the about-turn in this traditional relationship. It was suggested by some within the association that, in the absence of representations from industry, the system would be unworkable as a large number of appeals against unreasonable authorisations would overload the Inspectorate.

HMIP stressed the advisory capacity of *all* consultees. The then director, Frank Feates, pointed out that he would be happy to take into account the views of the Chemical Industry Association but that these views would not be the overriding consideration. Other bodies would also be entitled to make representations, 'For instance we might also want to take into account the views of Friends of the Earth'.

Furthermore, the Inspectorate has made it clear that they see their new role as having four main strands:

(a)   a preventative approach;

(b)   a positive but structured relationship with operators;
(c)   the provision of information and guidance to industry on an arm's length basis; and
(d)   a systematic targeting of resources on the highest priorities.

These strands include a possible suggestion that those producers supplying high quality pollution technology will be the proper people to advise HMIP as to what constitutes the 'best available technology'. This move indicates that the Inspectorate will take into account a much wider sample of opinions when deciding the framework which they govern. Thus, the 'active' discretion in standard setting and methods of abatement will have a basis in objectivism.

There are other more far-reaching changes, however, which go beyond formal enforcement to more proactive issues, such as the setting of consent levels. In its first water quality paper, *Discharge Consent and Compliance Policy—A Blueprint for the Future*, the NRA makes a number of recommendations stressing the importance of tighter numeric consents with percentile limits for 'environmentally significant discharges'. This confrontational style has also spread into the way in which prosecutions are presented. When the facts of a pollution incident are put before the court, an assessment is made of the damage caused by the pollution in ecological as well as scientific terms. Photographs are often used to display vividly to a court what is meant by the dry, and often incomprehensible, scientific evidence. Attempts are made to explain to the court in lay terms both the short and the long term effects of the pollution caused. These sometimes emotive prosecutions are bound to have a confrontational effect and will undoubtedly undermine any continuing relationship to some extent.

Recent events have cast a shadow upon the idea that the new regulations would mean a new era for enforcement. Belmont Bleaching and Dyeing of Bolton were said to be discharging pentachlorophenol (PCP) into a nearby brook and thus breaching the relevant environmental quality standard. The NRA stated that they would be prosecuting North West Water Services Plc for breaches of the PCP limit in its consent for the nearby sewage works.

Initially, HMIP, who act on behalf of the Secretary of State in determining conditions in consents, were not swayed by the arguments presented to them that such companies as Belmont should be allowed more time to comply with the new EEC standards. However, there was a sudden change of direction and HMIP allowed the company to continue to discharge levels of PCP's far in excess of the Department of Environment Guidance on Emission Standards. What is not known is why such a change occurred in the face of all EEC and Central Government guidance.

The redefinition of the importance of environmental protection

The changes in emphasis in the regulatory system are not solely ones of detail and are more than superficial. Underlying the changes is a fundamental shift in the way that environmental problems are perceived, not only by the public but also by the enforcement agencies themselves. The concept of the environment having rights of its own is increasing in importance, and generally the desire to protect the environment has begun to undermine previous assumptions made as to the 'goodness' of industrial activities which causes pollution. As environmental issues have become more important in the public eye, the desire to ensure that environmental standards are maintained has increased generally. These changes have brought about a retreat from the cooperational approach to a new, more ambivalent standard. That is not to say that the enforcing agencies are ambivalent as to the difficulties faced by industrialists. However, they are now balancing the cooperational and the confrontational approaches in order to achieve environmental quality improvements.

When public interest in the environment increases, the moral opprobrium attaching to pollution increases. Incidents such as the Shell oil leak into the Mersey and the Camelford disaster, where aluminium sulphate leaked into the drinking water supply, have supported the view that the public are now ready to perceive incidents of environmental pollution as something more than mere administrative difficulties. The distinction between this particular branch of white collar crime and other more recognisably 'criminal' activities is becoming blurred.

This change in emphasis has had a consequential effect upon areas of environmental regulation. First, there has been an increase in the fines and penalties for pollution offences. Historically, it was unusual for a prosecution for environmental pollution to be heard anywhere other than the magistrates' court. The level of fines imposed by the magistrates tended to reflect the public opinion of white collar crime being a morally neutral offence. Although many environmental pollution offences are triable either in the magistrates' court or the Crown Court, the option to try the matter in the Crown Court, with the opportunity to impose an unlimited fine and even imprisonment, was not often taken.

It is now becoming more usual for matters to be committed to the Crown Court. Perhaps the most celebrated Crown Court prosecution, of Shell (UK) in February 1990 for an oil spillage into the Mersey, reflects the latent powers of the Crown Court which have not been very much in evidence. In that case the total of the fine and compensation costs amounted to some £2.4 million, which cancelled out approximately 50% of the annual profits derived from the process which caused the pollution. In that particular situation, it was clear that the Crown Court judge not only viewed the offence with the seriousness that it required but also took into account (even subconsciously) the need to make the polluter pay. Moreover, the judge specifically pointed out that the level of fine was 'lenient' taking into account all the mitigating factors. More recently, British Steel were fined £200,000 after oil leaked from a supply pipe into the Severn Estuary. It was said that the size of the fine should serve as a warning to companies that they must protect the environment.

Moreover, the notoriously low levels of fine, which have traditionally undermined the use of prosecutions, have been increased to take into account the need for the magistrates to have wider powers to reflect the seriousness of offences which do not merit being heard in the Crown Court. As a consequence, most of the offences of environmental pollution under the

Environmental Protection Act 1990 have had the maximum fine level in the magistrates' court increased from £2,000 to £20,000. This is also mirrored in the increased penalties in the Planning and Compensation Act 1991. Furthermore, there are explicit references in some Acts to the financial benefit which has accrued or is likely to accrue to an offender (for example see the Planning (Listed Building and Conservation Areas) Act 1990 and *R* v *Chambers and others* 1989, JPL, unreported 229). Finally, the demand for increased fines to take into account the potential profits from pollution was made explicit by the Government in the White Paper, *Crime, Justice and Protecting the Public*, which said:

> Companies which see commercial advantage in creating pollution or neglecting safety precautions cannot be punished effectively by fines at the level given to most offenders.

It then goes on to say that higher levels of fines should be imposed to take into account both the means and the resources of the offenders.

Although there are still difficulties in ensuring that there are sufficient funds and there is sufficient manpower to meet the increasing work in detection, these difficulties are being addressed. In January 1991, staffing levels of HMIP were given an increased priority with a view to expanding the overall staff level from 223 to 310 by 1 April 1992. Central Government has promised an extra £130 million from the overall budget to be spent on environmental protection. Furthermore, in bringing in charging schemes to cover applications for authorisations under the integrated pollution control system and under the Water Act, the levels of funding for the administrative side of the regulatory function can be properly balanced to take into account the complexity of the work required.

More recently, HMIP has taken the unusual step of announcing that it was issuing an improvement notice on a fuel plant near Coventry to reduce particulate emissions. It did so by means of both a press conference and a general press release. This would suggest that as with the NRA, HMIP are clearly intending to bring their actions more into the public eye in order to increase their profile and to assure the general public that they are indeed carrying out their enforcement role properly.

In addition to the criminal sanctions available to the enforcement agencies, there is now a wide range of powers to remedy pollution problems. The Environmental Protection Act 1990, s. 61, allows for a waste regulation authority to enter onto closed landfills and take any steps which they consider to be necessary to avoid pollution of the environment or harm to human health. They are then entitled to recover the costs of their action from the person who at that time is the owner of the land unless those costs are unnecessary. Similar provisions are available under the Water Act 1989 and Part I of the Environmental Protection Act 1990 in relation to integrated pollution control. This provides a dual mechanism of control, and indeed seeks to promote the real purpose of environmental enforcement; that is to say, the securing of environmental quality improvements. These powers can be used either in conjunction with prosecution or on their own, and it is quite clear that, where there are such powers available, those powers could be of a far greater consequence to an industrial operation in terms of financial penalty than any fine imposed by the magistrates.

Public participation in the enforcement process

Having examined closely the way in which regulatory bodies enforce the law, it must be pointed out that there are residual powers providing for direct action to be taken by members of the public. It is likely that the next phase of environmental enforcement will be supplemented by a greater degree of public participation in the enforcement process. Generally, there is a constitutional right to bring private prosecutions for statutory offences. However, in environmental matters, this right has often been specifically limited by the statute concerned (e.g. in air pollution legislation). The Control of Pollution Act 1974 did not have any prohibition on prosecutions for offences of water pollution and Anglers' Associations and others took action themselves against water authorities. This trend has continued under the Environmental Protection Act. Unfortunately, such powers are often overlooked. Indeed, as the Environmental Protection Bill passed through Parliament, the Labour Party proposed an amendment in order to include a clear reference to the public right to prosecute. This was rejected as unnecessary. As the public become aware of their rights, any action on the part of the regulatory bodies may become superfluous.

In order for non-statutory enforcement bodies or individuals to take enforcement action, members of the general public have to have proper access to environmental data. To bring an informed prosecution, information is required so as to properly identify the breaches of any regulation. This, of course, is a major weakness in the environmental regulatory system in Britain, the difficulty of achieving access to environmental information.

SEVEN
Access to environmental information

As we have seen in Chapter 3, the system of the enforcement of pollution control is mostly exercised by statutory enforcement agencies. These enforcement agencies do not however engender public confidence. As restrictions on the right to take action by private prosecution are removed, the general public are able to enforce the law where, for instance, an enforcement agency fails to prosecute for a regulatory breach. These powers of prosecution enable private individuals to take severe action. For example, under the Environmental Protection Act 1990, s. 26, where a prosecution is successful a court can order action to be taken within a certain time-limit to ensure that any breach complained of is remedied. These powers could ensure that the general public have a degree of control over the enforcement of pollution control.

Why then do the public not take more action? There are a variety of reasons including high cost, apathy, ignorance of the powers available and a fear of the legal system. However, even if these difficulties could be overcome, access to information which could form the basis of an enforcement action is limited.

Most environmental offences involve the carrying out of unauthorised activities. This may be via the breach of a condition in an authorisation or it may be an entirely unauthorised action. To assess levels of compliance, the public need to be given access not only to information concerning the details of an authorisation but also to monitoring data which can provide an assessment of the success of the controls.

The enforcement agencies, of course, have specific and wide-ranging powers to enable them to obtain information. Naturally, these powers are not open to all, but the information obtained is crucial in assessing whether or not enforcement action should take place. It is this information which could, if available, be utilised by those outside the statutory enforcement system to bring an action themselves. Moreover, the public have additional rights of enforcement in both resorting to the common law for a private remedy (see Chapter 8) and applying for judicial review, in the case of the abuse of statutory powers by an enforcement body.

Without adequate information, public rights such as these are useless. Although documents containing general information about environmental pollution are freely available, specific information is far more difficult to obtain. For instance, basic information as to who is polluting, where they are polluting, with what they are polluting and how much is being emitted, can be elusive. This chapter examines some of the reasons for this secrecy, in addition to putting forward the possible dangers of keeping environmental information from the general public. However, it will also examine the various methods by which information can be obtained and, as such, it is hoped that it will be a guide to private individuals and pressure groups who are involved in ensuring that environmental regulations are properly enforced. Finally, it includes some of the proposals for change in the access to environmental information, as suggested by the EC, with some tentative comments upon the practical difficulties of allowing freedom of information to the general public.

The development of a general environmental secrecy policy

The roots of environmental secrecy can be traced back to the mid-nineteenth century and the age of industrialisation when, in 1864, the Alkali Inspectorate, which was then empowered to regulate atmospheric pollution, commenced its enforcement activities under the Alkali Act 1863 with a policy of keeping any information regarding the alkali industry private unless publication was demanded by a particular statute or was permitted by the owner. Naturally, the alkali industry itself was concerned to keep the information as quiet as possible in order to ensure that the public did not know of the dangers and consequences of the pollutants emitted into the atmosphere. This, coupled with the beginning of a cooperational approach between enforcers and the polluters, ensured that the Inspectorate was very unlikely to make such information available to members of the public unless specifically required to do so.

Central Government holds important information about the environment. As central policy makers and legislators, its ability to make fundamental changes in the nature of environmental protection heightens the need for proper public accountability. Until very recently, the disclosure of information in these areas, when unauthorised, would have resulted in the commission of a criminal offence under the Official Secrets Act 1911, s. 2. Although Central Government has very little detailed information which would be of help to the public, the unamended Official Secrets Act 1911 gave rise to situations which could only be described as bizarre.

The draconian nature of the restrictions placed upon Central Government organisations led to the reform of the Official Secrets Act in 1989. The new Act narrowly protects a certain limited class of information which does not now include environmental information. However, the time taken to respond to the proposals made by the Franks Committee in 1972 and by a White Paper in 1978 reflects the reluctance of Central Government to take action upon not only general information held by themselves but also more detailed environmental information held by others.

Mechanisms of secrecy

Historically, secrecy has been endemic in environmental legislation. Many statutes contained specific sections explicitly forbidding the disclosure of information relating to environmental discharges. Even if there were no specific sanctions for disclosure, access to information was prohibited unless another statute specifically required that it be made available to the general public.

Water pollution

The Rivers (Prevention of Pollution) Act 1961 restricted the public right of access to information concerning applications, discharge consents, or effluent samples taken by the enforcing authority, unless the person/company making the discharge permitted its disclosure or there was a further statutory requirement to disclose. In *The Secrets File*, Maurice Frankel gives an illustration of the type of situation which arose under this old legislation. In a case where a pigment manufacturer was discharging highly polluting substances into the Humber Estuary he says:

> On three occasions the company has been asked for the results of its monitoring—and it has refused on each occasion. Although the water authority has copies of data it is prevented by law from passing it on; an official releasing the information without the company's consent could, under Section 12 of the Rivers (Prevention of Pollution) Act, be jailed for three months. The water authority also carries out its own monitoring of the effluent discharge; again, it is prevented by law from releasing the results without the company's permission.

Air pollution

The Alkali Inspectorate maintained a policy of secrecy from its inception and, in its very first report in 1864, stressed the importance of keeping information from the public, 'Of course, all information regarding any work must be considered private unless publication is demanded by the Act or permitted by the owner'. This policy was maintained on an informal basis until the introduction of the Health and Safety at Work etc. Act 1974. Under s. 28(7), the Alkali Inspectorate was subject to an unqualified prohibition to ensure that no information was publicised regarding any details of recordings or measurements taken whilst exercising their duties.

Under the Clean Air Acts 1956 and 1968, a local authority's power to publish information could be said to be somewhat wider than that contained under the Health and Safety at Work etc. Act. Under Part IV of the Control of Pollution Act 1974, local authorities were allowed to publish information on emissions to air from premises other than private dwellings if that information was not information that could be required by the Alkali Inspectorate. Unfortunately, this power was restricted in three ways. Firstly, before publicising information a committee had to be created to involve business/industry and local amenity groups to discuss the proposals to make information public. Secondly, the powers under the Act were directory rather than mandatory, that is to say that the local authorities were not under any legal duty to publish the information. Thirdly, there was an appeal mechanism available to those dischargers affected by any disclosure if the collection of the information required would have been too expensive, a trade secret or not in the public interest.

With these hurdles to overcome and no positive incentive, the expenditure required to set the system in motion would prove to be greater than the benefits received. Additionally, with an enforcement regime based upon the cooperational approach, any attempt to impose discretionary powers upon industry would have fractured fragile basis of local authority control. As evidence of this, it was reported in 1982 that in the whole country only eight premises had been made the subject of local authority registers and only five local authorities had cut their way through the administrative jungle in order to set up the registers.

Miscellaneous controls
Other examples of the restrictions on the free availability of information can be found in the legislation covering a variety of environmental issues such as pollution at sea, radioactive substances and hazardous sites. One of the major reasons for such strenuous efforts to keep information away from the public eye stems largely from industrial paranoia about the free availability of information. This paranoia was best characterised in a statement made by the CBI in 1979 entitled 'The Release of Environmental and Technical Information' which stated:

> greater release of data enhances the risk of their misinterpretation and the likelihood of unwarranted alarm or ill-founded 'remedial' actions . . . Data are often highly detailed and technical, requiring interpretation by trained toxicologists; hence the capacity for correct interpretation is limited. This restricts further the amount and type of information which could usefully be released without problems of misinterpretation . . . The threat of legal proceedings would be enhanced by increasing disclosure of data. Applications for injunctions at common law could become more likely, putting industry at greater risk of additional costs and penalties even when it satisfies the requirements of the competent control authorities.

This feeling was amplified when the CBI again attacked existing legislation allowing public access to information on effluent discharges under Part II of the Control of Pollution Act 1974 as 'one of the worst bits of legislation on the statute book'. Against this background of paranoia attempts were made to defend the formal and informal 'cloak of secrecy'.

Commercial confidentiality

Industries' main argument in favour of secrecy was outlined in the evidence submitted by the CBI for the Tenth Report of the Royal Commission on Environmental Pollution. It was suggested that free public access to environmental information could affect the viability of industrial operations:

> General disclosure of data about the content of discharges to the environment causes industry concern because it could involve highly sensitive data which may be of commercial advantage to a competitor. Such data are first and

foremost the property of the discharger and their disclosure should not be expected or demanded without good reason. In practice, industry often discloses information which relates to the quality of the environment, as a responsible neighbour and part of society; but this disclosure cannot be assumed to be a public right nor can refusal to disclose be taken to mean that there is 'something to hide'. On the contrary, it normally means that the firm believes it right to keep to itself its own property of which disclosure could damage it commercially.

Concern stemmed from the belief that competitors will be able to investigate public registers to gain access to secrets. This could be done in one of two ways. Firstly, by checking the data relating to discharges, it would be open to competitors to calculate the composition of effluents in terms of the types or amounts of raw materials used in a process. This would help the assessment of the output of a particular factory and thus give competitors an advantage. Secondly, it was often claimed by industrialists that keeping information relating to applications for environmental authorisations on public registers would allow free access to information governing the composition of complex products. These products would have taken a number of years to research and develop and the costs involved in that process are only recovered if the information is kept confidential.

In reality, these fears have been overstressed. Any commercial operation intent upon finding out about a rival's business can use far more sophisticated methods of commercial espionage than relying on public information. Even complex compounds can be analysed using fairly simple procedures. Additionally, the constituents of a compound are often widely used within an industry, and the idea that information is commercially confidential only truly applies to those outside the industry.

The necessity for protection of intellectual property is well provided for in the patent and trade mark legislation. The need for additional secrecy is often unwarranted. The situations where this protection is not available seem particularly limited.

Evidence from other countries of far freer access to environmental information than in Britain did not suggest that there were many occasions on which the availability of the information led to the breach of commercial confidentiality. When the CBI were asked to give examples, they were able to point to only three cases which justified these concerns in such countries.

The Royal Commission on Environmental Pollution considered the question of trade secrets over a number of reports during the 1970s and 1980s. Their conclusion was always the same, that the reliance upon the concept of confidentiality did not reflect the true nature of the risk involved with greater disclosure. In the Commission's Second Report in 1972 (No. 4894) it was stated that there was:

a need for an increased flow of information to persons of responsibility who can use it for the ultimate benefit of the environment, e.g. MPs, research workers in universities and persons with similar interests in pollution.

In the Commission's Seventh Report in 1979 (No. 7644), this stance was reiterated. Referring to industries' refusal to disclose information on trade secret grounds, it was stated that commercial confidentiality was often a 'reflex action' which did not reflect the commercial risk involved. Finally, the Tenth Report of the Commission in 1984 (No. 9149) concluded that the emphasis given to commercial confidentiality was disproportionate and misconceived. Even so, in oral evidence to the House of Lords Select Committee in 1989, the CBI reiterated their view that:

> there is always a risk that technical information taken out of context can be misinterpreted by non-scientists.

'Green nutters'

The second justification for the maintenance of secrecy often put forward by industry is that open access would lead to mischief-making and an unacceptable level of interference by fanatics. *The Secrets File* gives the example of comments made by an environmental health officer in 1977:

> Action groups, civic societies and pseudo environmental organisations persistently petitioned and pressured local authorities to implement those provisions . . . action groups frequently composed of university research workers, lecturers, people who had failed election through the ballot box and including many cranks, persisted in twisting the truth concerning emissions to atmosphere and their predictions of doom were made to the delight of an ever waiting national press . . .

This sort of view is not just historical. In 1984 the CBI called Part II of the Control of Pollution Act a 'busybody's charter' and during the passage of the Environmental Protection Bill through the House of Commons, Andrew Hunt, MP for Basingstoke, said that widened rights of prosecution available to the public would 'allow the "green nutters" to get on parade and have a field day of litigation against industry on entirely inconsequential grounds'. Further MPs warned of dire consequences. The chemicals industry would 'disappear from this country', there would be an 'endless stream of prosecutions', and environmental groups would use the information and prosecutions merely as a media tool rather than a means of securing environmental improvements.

The underlying factor in this concern does not stem from misinterpretation of the data. Rather it emphasises the conciliatory strategy employed by the statutory enforcement agencies. If the information supplied on the public register raises issues of non-compliance where industrial operations are breaching their consents, then clearly it serves as evidence that there are difficulties in pursuing a non-confrontational enforcement strategy. In answer to the issues raised in the debate, a junior minister put it thus:

> If an individual has the necessary evidence to mount a case, he should be free to do so . . . we must rely on the courts to deliver justice. The commitment of industry to pollution controls is the surest defence against such litigation.

In other words, if the enforcement agencies are not willing or able to prosecute an offender then an individual should, if there is a proper case to be answered, be allowed to act.

It is not altogether clear who these 'fanatics' would be. It has been alleged that 'they' are amateurs and unable to properly analyse the data available. In the words of the CBI expressed earlier in the chapter, 'only trained toxicologists' could interpret this information.

The reality is somewhat at odds with this view. Many environmental pressure groups employ specialists as full-time technicians. Others have members who can interpret data perfectly adequately because of many years of experience. The Royal Commission's Tenth Report said that they had seen a growing professionalism in such groups. This had led to high quality reports which compared favourably to those drawn up by trained toxicologists. It is also interesting to note that the Second Report identifies 'research workers' and 'others' as receiving the ultimate benefit of greater disclosure. In the intervening period, the pressure groups have increased in both number and size. Greenpeace and Friends of the Earth often carry out monitoring exercises supplementing statutory enforcement bodies. Clearly, the definition of 'extremists' depends upon which side of the enforcement fence you are. To industrialists, such groups are causing trouble; on the other hand, the pressure groups see themselves as demonstrating the lack of authority that the enforcement agencies possess.

The House of Lords Select Committee did not consider this a problem. They said:

> The Committee most emphatically do not subscribe to the public need to be 'protected' on the grounds that raw data may be unintelligible or misleading; many members of non-governmental organisations which may wish to utilise the raw data are familiar with the processes of interpretation. There is inevitably the risk that some raw data may be used mischievously to suit a particular purpose, but that must be accepted as part of the price of openness.

Administration costs

In setting up any system of public registration for environmental consents, the CBI pointed out that the administration costs of such an exercise would not be proportionate to the public benefit which would accrue. No doubt this was in the hope of appealing to a political ideology which wanted to cut down on administration and bureaucracy and considered that the creation of a further burden upon an understaffed, over-worked administration would be inadvisable. However, it is clear that such records are required to be kept to maintain the proper running of the system and therefore the additional burden would be minimal.

There is of course another interpretation to be put upon this argument in favour of non-disclosure. The ability of the public to monitor the success or failure of the enforcement agencies in controlling pollution problems could well add to the workload of the agencies in more than a mere administrative fashion. The most likely avenue for complaint once non-compliance is discovered on the register by a member of the public will be the enforcement agencies. The investigation of these complaints over and above the more general monitoring will amount to an increase in the activity of the agency and therefore increase costs. This underlying argument—that secrecy would be cheaper than openness—cannot be doubted, however, whether 'cheaper' means 'more effective' is perhaps more contentious. The House of Lords Select Committee put it simply, 'The fundamental principle to which the Committee adhere is that information should in no circumstances be protected by price'.

The ability of enforcement agencies to maintain registers in a number of different formats, including the more normal paper records but also extending to information on computer, microfiche or photographic record, enables cheaper updating of the information and also cheaper storage and easier access. Whether or not the public interest in the registers is sufficient to justify the expenditure incurred is a different matter.

The Royal Commission's approach

Having had these arguments put to them on a number of occasions, the Royal Commission on Environmental Pollution constantly denied their strength. They considered that the public were entitled to know of the risks that they faced from environmental pollution, that the only way to re-establish public confidence in the enforcement system was to allow them access to the information which would allow them to enforce themselves, and that the public had a 'beneficial interest' in the environment, and therefore they were entitled to know how much it was being polluted. Whilst finding that these concepts held great weight, they rejected the justifications for secrecy and recommended that the public should be:

> . . . entitled to the fullest possible amount of information on all forms of environmental pollution, the onus placed on the polluter to substantiate a claim for exceptional treatment. Accordingly, we recommend that a guiding principle behind all legislative and administrative controls relating to environmental pollution should be a presumption in favour of unrestricted access for the public to information which the pollution control authorities obtain or receive by virtue of their statutory powers, with protection for secrecy only in those circumstances where a genuine case can be substantiated.

This was to form the 'guiding principle' for all legislative and administrative control relating to environmental pollution.

The effect of secrecy upon risk perception

Where information is difficult to obtain, the perception of the risk involved in an activity may well be misconceived. The Royal Commission said that 'Secrecy—particularly the half kept secret—fuels fear'. The reality is that there is no widespread conspiracy to keep the public from finding out about environmental pollution. However, when the public is not allowed to judge for itself the incidence of pollution within the environment, the true picture may never be known. It is necessary to disclose such information to enable informed debate not only about the risks to the public and the environment but also as to what steps might be taken to minimise those risks. In the Eleventh Report the Royal Commission commented further on the assessment of risk:

A proper evaluation of the risk requires access to the relevant information and its interpretation, and the public will not be reassured by interpretations provided by the putative polluter who has an interest. In the absence of public confidence in the role of bodies that are both authoritative and independent, interpretations by the press or pressure groups are often accepted even if they go beyond what an informed expert would regard as justified by the evidence.

There are those, however, who believe in a paternalistic form of government. Thus, it could be argued that where there is legislation in place and enforcement agencies are empowered to take action against pollution, there is no need for members of the public to be involved in such activities. However, in Chapter 6 we have seen that, in terms of prosecution rates and compliance with existing standards, the formal enforcement agencies have had limited success. The need to supplement the official enforcement agencies is still required.

The ability to detect environmental pollution is not solely the responsibility of the enforcement agencies. Many incidents are reported first by members of the public, and the availability of information would enable them to assess whether or not criminal activities are taking place. For legislation to be effective, the public will need to have confidence both in the enforcement agencies and their willingness to take action once they have been notified of any pollution.

Environmental rights

Industry does not have a permit to pollute the environment. Although individuals do have private rights over the environment (e.g. land owners), the environment is not owned by any one individual. The general public has an interest over all elements of the environment and, as a consequence, that interest should be balanced with the competing interests of industry and its right to pollute. Where there are such competing interests, there should be a facility whereby each party has full access to information which allows decisions to be made as to which of the competing interests should out-balance the other. In the words of the Royal Commission 'the public must be considered to have a right, analogous to a beneficial interest, in the condition of the air and water and to be able to obtain information on how far they are being degraded'.

It may well be argued by those in industry that these very people who have a beneficial interest in the environment are also the people who are employed in the factories which compete with that right. The right to pollute is essentially a utilitarian right, which has been expressed by those who defend such a right on the basis that the need to maintain a certain standard of living more than outweighs the need to ensure that there is long term protection of the environment. This view is being challenged more and more. The need to maintain natural resources and to ensure a proper environmental quality requires that the full extent of any particular problem needs to be assessed.

The recommendations of the Royal Commission

The history of the Royal Commission, and particularly of the recommendations regarding confidentiality, have been an interesting study of the way in which industry and government have joined together to block at every available opportunity the introduction of a concept which in industry's view could jeopardise the successful and profitable operations of its members. In total, five Royal Commission Reports address the issue of access to environmental information in one way or another but it was not until the mid-1980s that initial steps were taken to make disclosure more widespread. Furthermore, it is only with the introduction of the Environmental Protection Act that disclosure of environmental information in all sectors of control will become a reality.

The Royal Commission's tune has hardly changed since 1974 when in its Second Report it stated:

> as a rule . . . the legislation which protects secrecy over industrial effluents and wastes no longer safeguards genuine trade secrets . . . it is in the public interest that information about waste should be available not only to the statutory bodies which have a right to demand it but to research workers and others who make use of it to improve the environment . . .

As a consequence, the Control of Pollution Act 1974 introduced a system of access to public registers of information on water for the first time. The implementation of Part II of the Control of Pollution Act was delayed for more than ten years until mid-1985, amidst pressure by the CBI to delay disclosure even further. Other areas either remained secret or, in the case of the Health & Safety at Work etc. Act 1974, regressed from informal non-disclosure agreements to more formal statutory powers. In 1986, the Government moved away somewhat from its previous standpoint when urging the European Parliament to pass a Directive requiring all Member States to allow free access to environmental information. This new-found enthusiasm was short lived. In 1986, Pollution Paper No. 23, an interdepartmental Working Party responded to the Royal Commissions' criticisms in the Tenth Report by embracing the 'guiding principle' but rejecting the recommendations to move towards a uniform regime of public access to all environmental information. Thus the Working Party, charted a different course between appeasing the critics and political pragmatism by supporting minimal changes designed to avoid upsetting the system. When in 1989 the first drafts of the Environmental Protection Bill were published, it showed that there were to be no general obligations of disclosure introduced by the new Act. However, when Chris Patten was appointed Secretary of State for the Environment there was a further change in policy and, by January 1990, it was accepted that the public should have free access to information about industry's compliance with environmental authorisations which had been obtained under statutory powers. Clearly there were to be safeguards, but the underlying concept of free access was agreed.

Water pollution

In many ways the provision of public registers on water pollution have been the model for the introduction of other controls. After much pressure from the Royal Commission, Part II of the Control of Pollution Act 1974 introduced a system of public registration which would contain not only information on the consents granted to a company to allow it to discharge effluent into water, but also the frequency with which the limits of the consent were not complied with. Despite an 11-year gap between the publication of the Act and the implementation of the information requirements, the principles of the register were seen to be a model for other areas of environmental control.

The provisions of Part II of the Control of Pollution Act have been re-enacted in the Water Act 1989, s. 117(1). The public registers contain a wide variety of information. The Act requires that the contents of the register must be available at all reasonable times for inspection by the public free of charge. Copies of the entries can be taken by anybody on payment of a reasonable charge. The information contained on the register is prescribed in detail by the Control of Pollution (Registers) Regulations 1989 (SI 1989 No. 1160).

Where an application for a discharge consent is made, the National Rivers Authority is obliged to enter the details of the application within 28 days. The details contained within the register covers such things as the name of the applicant and any additional information which has been supplied with the application in order to amplify the application. If the application is granted, details of the consent, plus any conditions attached to that consent, also have to be entered within the 28 day limit (s. 117(1)(c)). These must include the name of the person/company to whom consent is given, where the discharge will take place and when it will take effect. If there is any notice served on the holder of the discharge consent, that fact must also be registered on the register (including revocation or variation notices). Furthermore, the register must show the time limit within which no variation or revocation may be made to the consent.

Normally, the way in which the information is kept will show the maximum levels of substances contained in the effluent as laid down by the original consent, alongside a figure of the content of the effluent as taken on the sample date. The particulars contained in the registers should normally show where the sample was taken from, the date and time of day it was taken and whether or not any action was required to be taken on behalf of the NRA. Where the sample was taken by or on behalf of the NRA, the information must be placed on the register within two months of the sampling date. There are facilities for people other than the NRA to take samples (e.g. self-monitored samples). In such a case, the sample information should contain reference to the fact that it was taken by a different person. Such information has to be placed on the register not more than 28 days from the receipt of the information by the NRA.

Perhaps of more interest to members of the local public are situations where a formal legal sample has been taken under the Water Act 1989, s. 147. These are samples which are taken prior to prosecutions. Indeed, there is evidence to suggest that the taking of formal samples as a mechanism in the cooperational strategy for pollution enforcement is often seen to be a last resort. Where a formal sample has been taken this will clearly alert a member of the public to the seriousness of the situation within the plant.

Previously, under the Control of Pollution Act 1974, the time limit for placing information on the register did not start to run until the information was given to the 'registrar' within the water authority. This led to practical difficulties of enforcement. In 1988, Derbyshire County Council prosecuted the North West Water Authority for pollution from a sewage works situated at Whaley Bridge. There was evidence of samples being taken which showed a massive breach of the consent levels set for the works. Previously, there had been breaches of up to four times the consent limit, but the figures which showed that there had been a breach of up to 20 times the consent limit were not put on the public register until some five months after they were taken.

The regulations exempt certain information which it would be contrary to the public interest to make public or which is a trade secret. In such circumstances, the Secretary of State is entitled to issue a certificate (under sch. 12, para. 1(7)) to exclude it.

Any entry in the register only has to be kept there for a period of five years; thereafter it would be maintained on the register only if it is necessary for the exercise of the NRA's pollution control functions.

The register system as set up under the Water Act 1989 has been criticised by a number of bodies. Firstly, it is considered that the 'raw data' showing the results of single samples does not provide lay people with an adequate picture of compliance. There is no information relating to environmental quality standards or a summary of any cumulative effects of the discharge. Moreover, some of the samples taken are defined as 'operational' and thus do not fall within the definition of 'samples to be taken as a result of pollution control'.

Waste disposal

Under COPA 1974, s. 6(4), each waste disposal authority is under a duty to keep a register open to the public containing details of all disposal licences they have issued. That register is open to inspection at reasonable hours, free of charge, and the public are allowed to examine the register and, on payment of a reasonable charge, to copy entries from the register. These registers are kept at the waste disposal authority's principal office and can be examined to find out the following information regarding waste disposal licences (see the Control of Pollution (Licensing of Waste Disposal) Regulations 1976 (SI 1979 No. 732)).

(a) The date of granting of a disposal licence.
(b) The full name and address of the holder of the licence.
(c) The full name and address of the local representative of the holder of the licence.
(d) The location of the site to which the licence relates.
(e) The form of deposit or disposal to which a licence relates.
(f) The types of waste the deposit or disposal of which is authorised by the licence, and any limitation as to the quantity of waste allowed.
(g) The conditions attached to the issue or variation of the licence.

These provisions mean that there are a limited number of things that can be investigated concerning a waste disposal licence under COPA. However, Part II of the Environmental Protection Act 1990 which deals with waste disposal contains far wider provisions with relation to publicity. Although there is no timetable for the implementation of these registers, and indeed there have been many question marks over the proposed viability of establishing such detailed registers, they are expected to be introduced by the end of 1993. Section 64 of the Environmental Protection Act lays down the duty of each waste regulation authority to maintain a register containing certain information. These relate to three main areas, namely:

(a) the application and waste management licence;
(b) enforcement and prosecutions;
(c) remedial action.

Details of applications for a waste management licence must be kept on the register for a minimum of 12 months from the date of rejection or deemed rejection. All details relating to licences in force must be kept and retained for 12 months after they cease to be in force. This will enable members of the public to check up and see whether or not aftercare conditions have been properly complied with and, in the case where a licence has been surrendered, whether or not conditions have been properly complied with.

Information will have to be kept as to any enforcement action taken by the waste regulation authority. This will include information on modification, variation, revocation or suspension notices. It will also contain information relating to appeals made against such notices. More importantly, it will contain information relating to any offences of which holders of licences have been convicted, whether in relation to a licence or not. Furthermore, where the waste regulation authority has issued a certificate of completion under the Environmental Protection Act, s. 39(9), this will be contained in the register itself. This is significant in that members of the public will be able to enforce the EPA's obligations upon the waste regulation authority if a certificate of completion has been issued by them. Reference will also be made in the register where the waste regulation authority have carried out remedial works under EPA, s. 61.

This information will enable the public to gain a full picture of waste disposal sites within their area and whether or not they are being monitored and policed. It should enable far greater research to be done on the long term implications of waste disposal sites and also avoid secrecy in relation to the difficult issue of remedial action.

Exclusions

Under EPA, s. 65, information which would, in the Secretary of State's opinion, be contrary to the interests of national security, is to be excluded. This will allow for a fairly limited body of information to be excluded owing to its sensitive nature. There will be no indication on the register that such information has been excluded, as it has been suggested by the Government that even the acknowledgement that there was such information would be contrary to national security itself.

Under EPA, s. 66, there is the traditional exemption for information which is commercially confidential. However, it is for the Secretary of State to decide whether or not something is commercially confidential, and the Department of the Environment has made it very clear that there will be only a limited number of instances where such an exclusion will apply. There is an additional power under s. 66(7) to allow for an outline description of the process notwithstanding that it is commercially confidential. This is to allow for a general picture to be painted of a waste disposal site where giving details would give rise to problems of confidentiality.

Where an application is made for a waste management licence, it is open to the person applying to ask for the information to be excluded from the register because of its commercial confidentiality (s. 66(2)). The waste regulation authority has 14 days to make a determination, and if they fail to do so then the information is treated as being commercially confidential (s. 66(3)). Where the waste regulation authority are to include the information on the register on the grounds that it is not confidential, they have to allow the applicant an opportunity to make representations on that particular issue and take into account the representations made (s. 66(4)). If, after this somewhat complicated procedure, the authority still decides to publish the information, there is a period of 21 days in which information is not to be published and an appeal is allowed to the Secretary of State (s. 66(5)).

As mentioned earlier, the confidentiality of information depends to a large extent upon whether or not it would prejudice to an unreasonable degree the commercial interests of the person concerned (s. 66(11)). Clearly one of the difficult issues will be whether or not this is to be a subjective or objective test. It is fair to say that, if it were to be subjective, then clearly any applicant for a waste management licence would be happy to say that the information would prejudice them to an unreasonable degree and therefore it could be excluded. On the other hand, if objectivity is sought, the waste regulation authority would be able to balance the effect upon an individual with the necessity to make the information public. The Department of the Environment has recently made it clear that it is for the person claiming the disclosure to substantiate that disclosure would prejudice to an unreasonable degree some person's commercial interest. There is a need to demonstrate that this disclosure of information would negate or significantly diminish the commercial advantage that one operator has over another. Where information is treated as commercially confidential then, under s. 66(8), the information will only be excluded from the register for a period of four years. This allows for the fact that commercial confidentiality has a finite period and after a certain length of time the need to disclose such information to the public will outweigh the harm created to the commercial interests of the individual. There is, however, a right to apply for continuation of the exclusion (s. 66(8)).

Integrated pollution control

The new systems for integrated pollution control and air pollution control introduce a new system of public registration which radically alters the access to information on authorisations. Under the Health and Safety at Work etc. Act 1974, s. 28(7), all information relating to the works covered by that Act were forbidden to be disclosed by the Industrial Air Pollution Inspectorate. This was criticised on many occasions. The Royal Commission said that these restrictions should be removed as they were an obsolete and unnecessary bar on the disclosure of information. The introduction of the new system of integrated pollution control and air pollution control under Part I of the Environmental Protection Act has now seen the removal of those restrictions and far more open access to information of an environmentally sensitive type.

The controls are contained in EPA, ss. 20 to 22, and govern both Part A processes controlled by HMIP and Part B processes controlled by local authorities. Local authorities will hold information relating to processes they control and processes controlled by HMIP. There are further controls contained within the Environmental Protection (Applications, Appeals and Registers) Regulations 1991 (SI 1991 No. 507). The format of the registers closely follows those of the waste management licence registers under Part II of the Act.

The register will contain details of (reg. 15):

(a)   all particulars of any application of an authorisation made to the authority;
(b)   all particulars of any notice to the applicant by the authority under paragraphs 1(3) of sch. 1 to that Act and of any information furnished in response to such a notice;
(c)   all particulars of any representations made by any person required to be consulted under paragraph 2, 6 or 7 of sch. 1 to the 1990 Act pursuant to reg. 4(1) above;
(d)   all particulars of any authorisation granted by the authority;
(e)   all particulars of any variation notice, enforcement notice or prohibition notice issued by the authority;

(f) all particulars of any notice issued by the authority withdrawing a prohibition notice;

(g) all particulars of any notification given to the holder of an authorisation by the authority under s. 10(5) of that Act;

(h) all particulars of any application for the variation of the conditions of an authorisation under s. 11(4)(b) of that Act;

(i) all particulars of any revocation of an authorisation effected by the authority;

(j) all particulars of any notice of appeal under s. 15 of that Act against a decision by the authority, the documents relating to the appeal mentioned in reg. 9(2)(a), (d) and (e) above, any written notification of the Secretary of State's determination of such an appeal and any report accompanying any such written notification;

(k) details of any conviction of any person for any offence under s. 23(1) of that Act which relates to the carrying on of a prescribed process under an authorisation granted by the authority, including the name of the offender, the date of conviction, the penalty imposed and the name of the court;

(l) all particulars of any monitoring information relating to the carrying on of a prescribed process under an authorisation granted by the authority obtained by the authority as a result of its own monitoring or furnished to the authority in writing by virtue of a condition of the authorisation or s. 19(2) of that Act;

(m) in a case where any such monitoring information is omitted from the register by virtue of s. 22 of that Act, a statement by the authority, based on the monitoring information from time to time obtained by or furnished to them, indicating whether or not there has been compliance with any relevant condition of the authorisation;

(n) all particulars of any report published by an enforcing authority relating to an assessment of the environmental consequences of the carrying on of a prescribed process in the locality of premises where the prescribed process is carried on under an authorisation granted by the authority; and

(o) all particulars of any direction (other than a direction under s. 21(2) of the 1990 Act) given to the authority by the Secretary of State under any provision of Part I of that Act.

Again, these registers have to be freely available at all reasonable times for inspection by the public free of charge and copies are allowed to be taken of the documentation on the payment of a reasonable charge (s. 20(7)).

The EPA acknowledges the introduction of more sophisticated methods of information retrieval and allows the registers to be kept in any form which allows for such things as computer retrieval, microfiches or photographic storage.

There are two exceptions to the normal rule that information should be freely available. Firstly, there are safeguards against the disclosure of information which is contrary to the interests of national security. Section 21 allows the Secretary of State to direct, if in his opinion the information falls within the definition of affecting national security, that the information should be excluded from the register (s. 21(2)). This power is also available if a person makes an application to exclude the information on the grounds that it is contrary to national security; they must notify the Secretary of State specifying the information and its apparent nature and then they must notify the enforcing authority of what they have done. There will be no reference to such information on the face of the register because of the chance that any harm might arise out of the disclosure of such sensitive information.

The second exclusion applies to information which is commercially confidential. Section 22 forbids disclosure of information which 'would prejudice to an unreasonable degree the commercial interests' of a person. Unlike s. 21, the determination of what is commercially confidential lies at first with the enforcing authority and then on appeal with the Secretary of State. It is open to a company applying for an authorisation to, at the same time, apply for information related to that authorisation to be treated as commercially confidential. This also applies when there is an application for a variation of an authorisation or information is supplied to the authority which concerns compliance with a condition of the authorisation or which is in response to a formal request by the authority (s. 22(2)). Where a company applies for information to be treated as commercially confidential, the enforcing authority has 14 days to decide whether or not to exclude the information and, if it fails to make a determination after 14 days it is deemed to have excluded the information (s. 22(3)).

The Act also allows for a strange set of circumstances which permit an enforcing authority to notify the company concerned that the information they have supplied might be commercially confidential. In these particular circumstances, the company are then allowed to object to the information being put on the register and to make representations to the authority justifying that objection (s. 22(4)). It is difficult to see when this provision will apply. It is quite clear that any company wishing to protect its own trade secrets will want to do so from the outset and quite how an enforcing authority will know that some information is commercially confidential in any particular circumstances is difficult to understand.

Where the enforcing authority decide that the information supplied is not commercially confidential, they are not allowed to enter the information on the register for 21 days, giving time for an appeal to the Secretary of State to determine whether or not the information is actually confidential (s. 22(5)).

The Secretary of State does have an overriding power to direct that information be included on the registers even though it is commercially confidential if it is in the public interest for it to be so included. This may well apply to particularly sensitive operations which cause great public concern and which have been the subject of a large amount of lobbying by individuals. It is in circumstances where particular concern is expressed to the local authority or to HMIP by community groups or local residents, that the Secretary of State may find a political bonus in releasing the information required. A good example of when this power could be used would be in a situation where there was a large disaster. The Environment Minister, David Trippier, when explaining this particular section said:

After the Chernobyl disaster, commercial confidentiality affected the amount of information that we could release. The lack of public information served only to increase public disquiet.

Naturally the right to overrule commercial confidentiality is a draconian one and will only be used in limited circumstances.

The time limit for the exclusion of information from the register is four years from the original exclusion. This obviously takes into account the fact that the confidentiality of information may well have decreased somewhat over that time period and therefore the exclusion of the information from the register is no longer justified. However, it is open to the applicant to apply to the authority for a further exclusion on the grounds that the information is still commercially confidential.

The practical effects of the commercial confidentiality rules were seen in the first batch of applications for IPC for existing large combustion plants. Of a total of 118 applications received by HMIP, 36 included requests for confidentiality. In an interesting precedent, HMIP refused or turned down all 36 requests. Whether or not the Secretary of State will lay down more substantial guidance in subsequent decisions is yet to be seen.

The Environmental Protection (Applications, Appeals and Registers) Regulations 1991 (SI 1991 No. 507) make detailed provision for the maintenance of the registers. There are a number of areas for concern. Firstly, only data obtained by the enforcement agencies as a result of their own monitoring, or as supplied to them in exercise of their powers of information—gathering under EPA, s. 19, or under a condition of an authorisation, are to be included.

Secondly, in relation to information concerning 'the assessment of the environmental consequences of a prescribed process', there is only a requirement to release 'all particulars of any reports published'. Clearly, the enforcing authority will have a discretion as to whether or not they publish such 'data'. Once again there is evidence to suggest that informal non-disclosure agreements *may* preclude the provision of access to environmental information.

Finally, there is no deadline for the entry of information after it has been received.

Air pollution

In the majority of cases, access to information relating to air pollution will be covered under registers discussed above. However, there are further controls under a number of different statutes. Primarily, smoke pollution is dealt with under the Clean Air Acts. There are no specific directions for disclosure in the Clean Air Act 1956 although under s. 25 local authorities have vague powers to arrange for research and publicity with regard to air pollution. However, this vague power is then nullified by s. 26 which makes it a criminal offence to disclose any information obtained under the Clean Air Act provisions which relates to a trade secret.

EC Directive on environmental information

Widespread attempts have been made to widen access to environmental information. This has been accepted as a major turn around in government policy. There are a number of reasons for this, not least of which is the desire to comply with the EC Directive 90/313 on the Freedom of Access to Information to the Environment. Article 3 of this Directive provides that Member States within the EEC are required to ensure that public authorities, including all national, regional or local agencies possessing information relating to the environment, must make that information available to anyone on request, without that person having to prove an interest. There are various exceptions to this rule which have already been incorporated into British legislation for some time. Information can be excluded where it affects (Article 3(2)):

(a)   the confidentiality of the proceedings of public authorities, international relations or national defence;
(b)   public security;
(c)   matters which are sub judice;
(d)   trade secrets;
(e)   the confidentiality of personal data and/or files;
(f)   material supplied by a third party on an informal basis without being under any statutory duty;
(g)   material which would make it more likely that the environment to which such material related would be damaged.

There is a time limit of two months on any application for information and if the request for information is refused then reasons must be given (Article 3(4)). Interestingly, Article 4 of the Directive lays down that where there has been an unreasonable refusal there can be a judicial review of that decision in accordance with the Member State's legal system. This of course does not create any additional powers other than those available to the British courts under the normal principles of judicial review.

The public's utilisation of registers

Other areas of the world have advanced systems of disclosure. In the United States, for instance, there is an obligation on companies to submit an annual report to the Environmental Protection Agency concerning the release of some 322 prescribed substances. This information forms the basis of the Toxics Release Inventory which is available for inspection by members of the public. The effect of the inventory has been to galvanise the companies included in the inventory into examining ways of minimising the release of those substances prescribed. After pressure from Friends of the Earth, two major chemical companies within Britain have agreed to disclose similar data voluntarily. Friends of the Earth justified this pressure by saying 'People have a right to know about toxic emissions whether they live in Tonbridge or Texas'.

One of the major difficulties underlining the system of freer access to information within Britain is that research has shown that, even where there is information to be easily obtained, public participation in the system is said to be low. In their Fourth Report, the Royal Commission stated:

> certainly experience in the local government field has shown that 'public participation'—often consisting of little more than one way provision of information at meagrely attended public meetings—can be an unrewarding ritual for those charged with the task of organising it. However, the essential requirement is that information should be *available*, not that it should be forcefully fed to the public.

It is clear though that the basis upon which the system is founded is that the public should have a desire to receive information from the register for themselves. The empirical evidence suggests otherwise. A research project carried out on the utilisation of the registers kept under the Control of Pollution Act 1974 and then the Water Act 1989 has shown that there are relatively few people who are particularly interested in the registers. In the period August 1985 to December 1986, when the registers were first opened, a survey showed that there were 75 enquiries made to Severn Trent Water Authority, 85 to Anglian Water and 70 to Yorkshire Water, making up a total of some 230 enquiries to look at the register as compared with the millions of people who were resident in each of those areas. Furthermore, when the figures were broken down, by far and away the majority of enquiries were sellers of septic tank equipment who used the registers as a database from which to sell their wares. Other enquiries came from environmental protection groups who used the registers to check up on information regularly.

The system of registers has received general approval from most parties. The difficulties with the previous system under COPA and the Water Act 1989 have underlined some practical problems however. In evidence submitted to the House of Lords' European Select Committee, Friends of the Earth pointed out that many samples collected were not entered on to the register because they were 'operational' samples rather than samples taken for the purposes of monitoring compliance and legislation. Thus, it was argued that too great a discretion was given to the enforcement agency which allowed for the system to be abused.

Moreover, they argued that the effectiveness of the register was governed by five factors. They suggested that a system of registers should be:

(a)   conveniently located;
(b)   user friendly;
(c)   not excessively expensive;
(d)   interactive;
(e)   adequately resourced.

The Select Committee regarded it as '. . . of paramount importance that any system of registers should both be accessible geographically and "user friendly". These features should be possible with modern data processing techniques'.

It was suggested that a two-tier system be utilised. The first tier would contain basic data in a register form with an indication of any further information available at the second tier. The second tier itself might contain the more complicated information which would explain some of the references on the simpler level.

Even so, the registers as they exist have a low level of interest for the members of the general public.

Figures available from the NRA's Annual Report in 1989/90 disclose a marked increase in the utilisation of the registers. However, as percentages of the overall population of each individual authority, the use of the registers is still remarkably low. Tim Burton, who has carried out detailed research into access to environmental information in water registers, identified three areas of possible explanation for the low level of utilisation of these registers. These were awareness, accessibility and difficulty with interpreting the data itself.

Awareness

Many members of the public are uncertain as to who actually controls the different areas of pollution control. As has been seen in Chapter 3, there is a plethora of environmental enforcement agencies each with their own individual responsibilities. It is often difficult for those closely involved in the field to understand such a complex administrative structure. For the lay person it is sometimes impossible to differentiate between the various local and national agencies. Furthermore, the presence of registers containing public information is perhaps even less well known. Initially, there were delays in the implementation of the Control of Pollution Act 1974 and the 11-year gap between the passing of the Act and the actual introduction of the registers tended to obscure their value. One of the suggested reasons for the increase in the utilisation of the registers after the Water Act 1989 was introduced was the redefinition of the regulatory role and the media attention given to the newly created NRA. However, the information available to members of the public to inform them of the existence of the registers is still particularly low. In Appendix 6 of the NRA Annual Report and Accounts for 1989/90, there is a list of the publicity material published by each regional authority. It is interesting to note that of the ten regional offices, only two, Yorkshire and Anglian, have specific publicity material relating to the public registers. It may be no coincidence then that, when looking at the figures for the utilisation of the registers, both Anglian and Yorkshire have consistently been two out of the top three for numbers of enquiries, only being overtaken by the Thames region which has a far greater level of population. Clearly, a national policy on the publication of materials to make the public more aware is required. National initiatives rather than just publicity on a region-by-region basis would iron out any disparity between different areas.

Access

The policy governing the location of the registers has differed from region to region. The geographical area of each regional authority is very large and that could mean that people would have to travel a long way in order to view the registers. Certain regions use their powers under the regulations to set up duplicate copies of the registers at different regional offices. For instance, Yorkshire NRA set up their registers at York, Bradford, Leeds and Sheffield. However, two regions, Thames and Anglian, only established one register. In the case of Anglian, where the register was set up at their head office in Peterborough, some people who lived within the area of the water authority were almost 150 miles away from the registers. Clearly, there was very little incentive for these people to go and check the registers.

Also in most legislation, the registers are required to be open only for 'reasonable hours'. This term has received a number of interpretations, including a view that 'reasonable' could take into account the fact that there was insufficient staff to keep the registers open for significant periods of the day. It has always been assumed that 'reasonable' is to be viewed from the perspective of the person coming to view the registers. However, most are open only during working hours and there is no effort made to make one evening a week or a month available to people who wish to view the registers but do not have the ability to leave work early. One suggestion is that there should be some form of 'travelling road show' set up by the NRA which could visit towns within the region other than the central office, informing and educating the public of their right to come and view the register. This would facilitate public participation and, in addition, increase public awareness of the separation of the water services companies from the regulatory body.

Additionally, charges can be made for copies taken from the register. Charging differentials between the regions is high. Some regions charged nothing for a small amount of copying whereas others inflicted relatively high charges. When all these facts are taken together a visit to see the register can amount to a rather daunting experience. As two officials from the old Severn Trent Water Authority put it, 'the obstacles to the man in the street are quite formidable'. Moreover, these formidable obstacles make life particularly unpleasant for those people who are not normally used to dealing with officialdom. This will not act as an incentive for them to use the register again. Tim Burton points out:

> If a first time enquirer finds the enquiry an 'unpleasant' experience not only will he be unlikely to return, but he may dissuade other potential enquirers from taking their first step towards utilisation of the registers.

Difficulties with the information on the registers themselves

One of the issues constantly raised about the interpretation of data contained on the register was that the information would be too complicated for the lay person to understand. There can be a distinction drawn here between the 'semi-professional' amenity groups and the person off the street who is looking at the registers for the first time. In the latter case, to enable the proper interpretation of the data there should always be staff readily available to assist enquirers. The provision of expert help to enable the data to be properly understood is essential to ensure that the registers are utilised by 'newcomers' to the regulatory system. If it is intended that the registers should receive a wider recognition, education as to the manner of use of the registers, together with expert advice on interpretation, will enable the private individual to assess the data in an informed manner. Although the registers have been under utilised in the past, reasons for this are being dealt with. The desire of the public to visit these registers will undoubtedly increase as further information becomes available and there is an increased awareness of environmental issues.

There is one final point. The registers will enable individuals to check and see the slow but steady progress towards the improvement of environmental quality standards in Britain. With the issue of the environment being high on the political agenda the pressure on any Government to 'produce the goods' will only be heightened when there is a national 'auditing' facility contained within the system of registers.

Article 7 of the EC Directive 90/313 makes it a duty to provide general information on the environment by means of periodic reports. The Government has promised the first report by the end of 1992.

EIGHT

The common law and the protection of the environment

The development of the law relating to the protection of the environment is not solely governed by the realm of public and administrative law. Although the spread of administrative and bureaucratic controls has accelerated within the last 50 years, traditionally, at first glance anyway, private law has attempted to serve a similar function in controlling damage caused to the environment. This similarity has caused confusion. Private law, essentially the law of tort and contract, served as a mechanism of environmental protection primarily through the control of the use of land rather than the protection of the environment.

Hybrid nature of the common law's role

This protection has its origins in the system of common law developed from the time of the Norman conquest in an attempt to cope with new disputes over use and abuse of land. As the system developed, it incidentally became a mechanism for environmental protection. The hybrid nature of the common law's role in environmental protection can be demonstrated by looking at the characteristics which distinguish it from the more usual methods of public law control.

The common law acts only as a protector of private interest

The primary function of private law actions is to protect interests in land rather than the more nebulous concept of 'environmental rights'. Consequently, the factors governing the decision to take action against polluters are mainly personal. Potential plaintiffs are more concerned about balancing their own interests against the loss suffered, be that financial or the loss of enjoyment of their property. The protection of the environment demands that other factors have to be taken into account. Sometimes it is clear that human interests are contrary to the interests of the environment. For example, it is possible to acquire an easement to pollute a river. It is arguable whether such activity could ever be in the interests of the environment. However, in certain circumstances, the private law seeks to protect the private interests of individuals.

The protection of private rights based upon imprecise standards

We have already seen in Chapter 5 that the public law controls protecting the environment are based primarily upon standards of environmental quality. Such standards specifically regulate activities by attempting to impose definite levels of substances which can be emitted into the environment. These levels are often expressed in numerical limits. These limits allow for relatively simple enforcement as the detection of breach can be effectively monitored and proper assessments can be made of any discharge.

The monitoring of such discharges involves scientific and technical skills. Without those skills, the accumulation of devastating substances can affect the environment on a long term basis. As Chris Rose recounts in *The Dirty Man of Europe*, the River Mersey displays some of these consequences:

> Greenpeace's survey ship, The Beluga, found no fewer than two hundred and fifty substances thought to be halogenated hydrocarbons and their breakdown products in one effluent stream from a Mersey sewage works . . . the Mersey is still intractably polluted with toxic substances such as PCBs and heavy metals. While the water may be clear and species may return, they may be permanently stressed by invisible chemicals which can build up in their bodies.

It is this type of pollution that can only be dealt with effectively by numerical standards and scientific monitoring. Private law mechanisms meet neither criteria. Generally, the common law is based upon imprecise standards unrelated to numerical levels. In attempting to balance competing private interests, the common law looks to the reasonableness of actions rather than restricting conduct to specific levels. Naturally what is reasonable depends upon the circumstances of each case. Maintaining this balance means that no two cases will guarantee the same result.

The main mechanism of control, private nuisance, can broadly be defined as the unreasonable interference with the reasonable use and enjoyment of land. This clearly begs a number of questions. What is a reasonable use? What would be unreasonable? These questions underline the large degree of uncertainty involved in bringing an action in private nuisance. This imprecise nature involves an exercise in assessing a number of different factors. An illustration of the types of uncertainty surrounding private law actions in nuisance and how there can be a detrimental effect to the environment can be found in the so-called locality doctrine in private nuisance.

This doctrine asserts the need to take into account 'the circumstances of the place where the thing complained of actually occurs' (*St Helens Smelting Co v Tipping* (1865) 11 HLC 642). Putting it simply, those who live in the town or close to factories have to expect a dirtier, smellier environment than those who live in the countryside. The flaws in this doctrine are clear. In terms of environmental protection, those areas which require the greatest degree of control are often the same as those to which the most damage has to occur before an action can be founded. The accumulation of polluting substances, be it dust, noise or fumes, actually lowers the degree of nuisance required.

As one commentator puts it 'Those who suffer most from the ravages of pollution are the least worthy of protection' (McLaren (1972) 10 Osgoode Hall Law Journal 505).

The right of action is limited

As the common law seeks to balance competing individual rights, the right to take action is normally vested only in those who are directly harmed. Generally, this means the individual in possession of land which suffers damage. Although there are narrow rights to take group action in public nuisance, the basis of an action in common law still remains the protection of land and its ownership rather than the environment. The concept of 'environmental rights' is as yet undeveloped in the United Kingdom. The idea that there should be an ability to bring an action on behalf of flora and fauna rather as children bring actions through a guardian *ad litem* seems strange. Unfortunately, the private law seeks to compensate one land owner by granting compensation from another. A move away from this system would be difficult. The private law does not properly seek to compensate for environmental damage where there are no rights of ownership to protect or an owner does not wish to pursue an action.

Problems of proof

Whereas, in public law, the proof of the breach of a regulation involves scientific evidence that is more or less irrefutable, there is great difficulty in showing a cause of action in environmental pollution in the common law.

Firstly, there are often problems surrounding the establishment of a causal link between the origins of pollution and the damage. For instance, it is the nature of airborne deposits that they could have originated from a site many miles from the area of damage. Seeking to show that the damage emanates from a particular site in these circumstances is particularly difficult. Moreover, in areas of heavy industrialised activity these difficulties become even more complex. Thus, there could be five factories within a two mile radius, all producing the same acidic emissions into the atmosphere. Trying to differentiate between each emission requires highly technical evidence. The expense of carrying out investigations such as these will often militate against individuals taking action and it may well be that no definite culprit can be identified.

Secondly, there is a large degree of subjectivity involved in assessing the reasonableness of activities. Unfortunately, what would be acceptable to some in terms of environmental damage would not be acceptable to others. Some find the smells of certain fumes offensive whereas others have a high tolerance level. Again, this uncertainty prevents any proper guidelines being laid down as to when activities will incur liability.

Private law as a fault based system

In certain circumstances, the bringing of an action under common law requires there to be some fault on behalf of the person creating the damage. Very few pollution incidents occur because of deliberate actions by careless and unthinking individuals. Mostly accidents arise because of a number of circumstances which would not normally be foreseeable but give rise to damage. The common law does not always seek to redress any damage caused by such accidents.

Reactive controls

Private law controls are only reactive and compensatory rather than preventative. It is only very rarely that private law can be used to prevent environmental damage. Although it is possible in certain circumstances to seek anticipatory injunctions, on the whole the controls tend to be post-damage, that is to say, after the harm is discovered. Private law offers no continuing control nor does it necessarily seek to remedy harm. When compensation is paid there are no rules governing the manner in which the money has to be spent. Damages are often assessed as being the difference in value between the land as it was before an act of damage and the value afterwards. This does not necessarily include clean-up costs although those can form a natural part of any claim.

Controls are not purely environmental

The wide range of activities covered by civil remedies extends far beyond those activities covered under the umbrella of the environment. As an incidental effect, the common law provides for the prevention of pollution or the protection of the public but the protection spreads much wider to the coverage of a whole range of civil rights. The effect of this is to ensure that the system has built up in an unsystematic way and in some ways mirrors the piecemeal nature of the statutory controls.

Is the common law as a protection mechanism dead?

To a certain extent the criticisms of the private law as being too expensive, too long-winded and uncertain have led to its low utilisation as a tool for environmental protection. The roots of its weaknesses can be traced back to the nineteenth century when industrial pollution was in its infancy. With no statutory regulations to control the growth of polluting processes it might be thought that the common law would serve as the primary mechanism for protection. However, McLaren presented very cogent arguments that other factors, including institutional, social and economic matters, outweighed the importance of the environmental benefit to be procured from such control. (See p. 139.)

Civil liability in statutes

In addition to the common law, there are a number of statutes which impose liability by means of private law remedies, rather than the more normal public law methods.

(a) Nuclear Installations Act 1965

The individual problems of nuclear installations are not adequately dealt with by the law of tort. As the incident in Chernobyl demonstrated, the damage caused by nuclear actions can be widespread and not confined to a specific period of time. There are also difficulties of proving a causal link between the injury caused and exposure to radiation. Many diseases that are caused by radiation also occur naturally, and trying to distinguish between these two different situations is frequently fraught with difficulties. Therefore, to avoid these difficulties, the Nuclear Installations Act 1965 introduced absolute civil liability for all damage caused from certain occurrences (ss. 7–10).

(b)   Merchant Shipping (Oil Pollution) Act 1971

In the wake of numerous oil disasters in the mid to late 1960s, international concern led to the introduction of this Act to compensate for damage from oil. It is specific in that it only deals with pollution from oil tankers. The implementation of this statute again deals with the inadequacies of tort in trying to cope with trans-frontier contamination. The intention of the Act is to impose strict liability on owners of ships in relation to physical damage to property and personal injury from oil pollution (s. 1). The financing of the majority of losses stemming from the Act is covered by a compulsory insurance scheme, although there is a further international fund for compensation which pays out in situations where a ship owner cannot afford to pay the damages. There are a number of statutory defences which cover circumstances such as war, intentional acts of damage by third parties, or poor governmental control of navigation or lighting (s. 2).

(c)   Control of Pollution Act 1974, s. 88: Environmental Protection Act 1990, s. 73

The Deposit of Poisonous Wastes Act 1972 was passed as a reaction to the depositing of noxious waste upon land. Section 2 of that Act introduced the concept of civil liability for the unlawful depositing of waste. This was then re-enacted in the Control of Pollution Act 1974, s. 88, which imposed civil liability for damage caused by poisonous, noxious or polluting waste. This is not an exclusive remedy but the standard of proof required under s. 88 was far lower than that required for common law actions. This provision will remain in force when Part II of the Environmental Protection Act 1990 is implemented under s. 73. There are two defences. Section 88(1) provides that where damage was due wholly to the fault of the person who suffered it, or that person knew of the risk of damage but accepted it, no liability will attach.

(d)   Other private law remedies

The most common application of private law remedies as used for environmental protection is that of the law of tort (see below). However, there are other private law mechanisms which are useful in this context. Restrictive covenants, for instance, govern the activities which can be carried out upon land. A good example of this type of restriction can be seen where local planning authorities enter into planning agreements under the Town and Country Planning Act 1990, s. 106. Such agreements are used for a whole variety of purposes either to restrict the class of occupants of premises or to restrict the type of operation that can be carried out from those premises. Other mechanisms are relatively rare. However they have the advantage of having a fairly tight degree of control over the use of land which can only be varied in a few circumstances.

An unusual mechanism which is being used more frequently is the ability to enter into contractual agreements to restrict the use of land. Agreements made in nitrate sensitive areas under the Water Act 1989 are essentially contracts between the Minister of Agriculture, Fisheries and Food and an individual to restrict the use of certain agricultural activities so that the nitrate used in farming will not escape into the watercourses in the area. Under s. 112(2) of the Act, a voluntary arrangement can be agreed whereby certain agricultural practices will not be carried out on the land to prevent pollution and in return compensation will be paid for the restrictions. These types of management agreement are not as wide as the mechanisms under freehold or leasehold covenants as they are not necessarily binding on third parties (unless of course statute makes them so).

The law of tort and environmental protection

This book does not aim to deal specifically with the law of tort as it is more than adequately covered in other textbooks. However, the general principles can, in certain circumstances, be used to protect the environment.

The law of nuisance

As stated earlier, the law of nuisance is concerned with the 'unlawful interference with a person's use or enjoyment of land, or of some right over, or in connection with it'. This definition illustrates one of the primary distinctions between nuisance and other torts in that the protection afforded is directed towards controlling proprietary interests rather than the control of an individual's conduct. As has already been pointed out, the protection of proprietary rights can have an incidental effect of providing a general benefit to the wider community by achieving improvements in environmental quality. There have been occasions where the effect upon the community has been a negative one. In *Bellew* v *Cement Co* [1948] IrR 61, an interlocutory injunction was granted to restrain the noisy blasting at a quarry. This carried on for several months and the effect of this stoppage upon the supply of cement in Ireland was devastating as 80% of the cement used in Ireland was created by materials from the quarry. The effects upon employment and on construction were clearly outweighed by the protection of the private right involved.

The basis for a claim in nuisance is founded upon a balancing exercise centred around the question of reasonableness. As was stated in *Saunders Clark* v *Grosvenor Mansion Company Limited & D'Alles-Sandry* [1900] 2 Ch 373:

> the Court must consider whether the defendant is using his property reasonably or not. If he is using it reasonably, there is nothing which at law can be considered a nuisance; but if he is not using it reasonably . . . then the plaintiff is entitled to relief.

Thus in attempting to assess liability in a nuisance action, a balance is made between the reasonableness of the defendant's activity and its impact upon the plaintiff's proprietary rights.

In assessing the balance, a court will take into account a number of specific factors including the locality of the nuisance, the duration of the nuisance, and any hypersensitivity on the part of the plaintiff.

The locality doctrine

The case of *St Helens Smelting Company* v *Tipping* (1865) 11 HLC 642 illustrates the workings of the doctrine particularly well. In the mid-nineteenth century, St Helens was the centre of the alkali industry. The average life expectancy was well under 25 and it had built up a reputation as one of the dirtiest towns in Britain. The physical impact of the works had left most vegetation in the area dead and adversely affected the health of cattle. Mr Tipping brought an action in private nuisance. The court drew the distinction between actual physical damage to property and a nuisance which would only cause 'personal discomfort'. In the latter situation, the locality of the nuisance would be a material factor in assessing the balancing exercise. In a famous quote in the case of *Sturges* v *Bridgman* (1879) 11 ChD 852, Thesiger LJ stated 'What would be a nuisance in Belgrave Square would not necessarily be so in Bermondsey'.

The unfortunate consequences of this approach have already been outlined. Although there is a distinction drawn between actual damage done to property and interference with the enjoyment of property, in practice there is often an overlap. It has been alleged that the economic affect of nuisance can be just as detrimental to an interest in land. If, for instance, a house is situated by a pig farm, the smells emanating from that may well make the house less attractive to potential buyers, but under the locality doctrine it could be argued that in an agricultural area an owner has to expect such farmyard smells. Other examples can include subjecting buildings to vibration which could result in structural damage.

However, even in the most heavy industrialised areas, there is not an absolute freedom to produce polluting materials. An illustration was given in the case of *Rushmer* v *Polsue and Alfieri* [1906] Ch 234, where Cozens-Hardy LJ said:

It does not follow that because I live, say, in the manufacturing part of Sheffield I cannot complain if a steam-hammer is introduced next door, and so worked as to render sleep at night almost impossible, although previously to its introduction my house was a reasonably comfortable abode, having regard to the local standard; and it would be no answer to say that the steam-hammer is of the most modern approved pattern and is reasonably worked. In short, if a substantial addition is found as a fact in any particular case, it is no answer to say that the neighbourhood is noisy and that the defendant's machinery is of first-class character.

In that case, there was an injunction sought against a printing press being operated in Fleet Street, even though there were many other printing presses in the area and others also operated at night. The House of Lords affirmed the decision of the Court of Appeal and granted the injunction.

When viewing the case law on the locality doctrine, two main strands of judicial thinking can be identified. McLaren in his article on the foundation of the law of private nuisance suggests that there are two contradictory judicial views. The first is based upon property rights and is essentially a natural rights theory. Basically, where there is any interference with property rights which is not trivial then there should be a right of action to take steps to prevent that interference with rights (e.g. *Bellew* v *Cement Company*). The second judicial view takes a more rational approach to the problem of environmental pollution and nuisance claims. This could be described as the view of social utility. In this view there tends to be a balance taken between the social utility of the action complained of as weighed against the environmental harm caused (see *St. Helens Smelting Co* v *Tipping* and *Sturges* v *Bridgman*). A third view could be that in the cases involving physical damage it is much easier to be influenced by the natural rights argument as the extent of the damage is easily quantified. With the uncertainty of the assessment of damages for interference with the reasonable enjoyment of land there is a far greater demand for a counterbalance to be taken.

Sensibility
One of the balancing factors to be taken into account is the amount to which the nuisance can be 'sensed'. The law does not take into account mere trivial unpleasantness.

Unlike other forms of tort, nuisance is not actionable without proof of damage. This materially interfering inconvenience has to be able to be 'sensed' by reasonable members of the public. It has to be seen, smelt or tasted by persons other than the defendant. However, that does not mean to say that where one person senses the nuisance that is sufficient for an action to be founded.

A good example of this rule of *de minimis* can be found in the case of *Attorney-General* v *Gastonia Coaches Limited* [1977] RTR 219. This case involved a nuisance emanating from a company who were operating a large number of coaches from a residential area. The activities on the site included general maintenance as well as the storage of the vehicles overnight. The judge in the case made a distinction between the two different elements of nuisance. Firstly he said that the nuisance from the smell of the fumes from the engines and the noise from the engines as they were revved could amount to a nuisance. However, he also said that the noise emanating from the vehicles as they were cleaned and repaired did not amount to 'serious interference'.

The duration of nuisance
For a nuisance to be actionable it must be something which is more than temporary. Isolated incidents can give rise to a nuisance only where the use which gives rise to the risk of that isolated nuisance is of itself a continuing use. For example, a factory which produces fumes does not necessarily have

to produce those fumes continuously over a period of years for there to be a nuisance. However, where there are isolated incidents occurring regularly then the use of the land for that purpose is of itself a nuisance. The more isolated the occurrence however, the less likelihood that the use being carried out is a nuisance. In *Harrison* v *Southwark and Vauxhall Water Company* [1891] 2 Ch 409, the defendants were a water company who had dug a shaft to pump water from land adjacent to the plaintiffs. As the shaft was being sunk the pumps that were being used created a continuous noise. Mr Harrison brought an action in nuisance to stop the noise. In finding against Mr Harrison the Court held that the works were not actionable because they were temporary and that such temporary works would only be actionable if unreasonable methods were used, unless physical damage was caused. Vaugham Williams J said:

> For instance, a man who pulls down his house for the purpose of building a new one no doubt causes considerable inconvenience to his next door neighbours during the process of demolition; but he is not responsible as for a nuisance if he uses all reasonable skill and care to avoid annoyance to his neighbour by the works of demolition. Nor is he liable to an action, even though the noise and dust and the consequent annoyance be such as would constitute a nuisance if the same . . . had been created in sheer wantonness, or in the execution of works for a purpose involving a permanent continuance of the noise and dust.

Again, judicial thinking seems to have been affected by taking a realistic balance of the number and type of occurrence as against the utility involved in the operation itself.

The hypersensitive plaintiff

The test for assessing a nuisance has two elements. Not only must the use of land which is complained of be unreasonable but also the use of the land to which the nuisance applies must be a reasonable use. If a potential plaintiff is particularly sensitive to one type of nuisance then it will not be actionable unless that nuisance would have affected a 'reasonable' person. In *Robinson* v *Kilvert* (1889) 41 ChD 88, the defendant let out part of his building to the plaintiff to be used as a paper warehouse. The defendant himself kept some of the space in the building for a particular use which required the air within the building to be kept hot and dry. This use had consequently heated the floor of the paper warehouse and damaged the paper kept there. Unfortunately, the paper stored in the upper rooms was of a particularly sensitive nature. Normal paper would not have been affected to such an extent. The defendant argued that the plaintiff had not told him of the intended use of the premises and in the particular circumstances the Court of Appeal held that there was no nuisance:

> A man who carries on an exceptionally delicate trade cannot complain because it is injured by his neighbour doing something which would not injure anything but an exceptionally delicate trade.

The effect of the rule laid down in that case is perhaps not as wide as first imagined. The principle only applies when the nuisance is specifically the result of the hypersensitivity of the plaintiff. If there is an independent cause of action brought because of the inherent unreasonableness of the nuisance, then action can still be taken. In *McKinnon Industries Limited* v *Walker* [1951] 3 DLR 577, the defendants operated a motor car plant which emitted poisonous gases. The plaintiff grew orchids for sale and the gases unfortunately killed off his stock. He brought an action in nuisance. The defendants argued that the growing of orchids was a hypersensitive activity and therefore any damage suffered was not as a result of the reasonable use of land. The Court disagreed and held that the nuisance was independent of the special sensitivity of the plaintiff.

Thus, in pollution cases, there will be very few occasions where this particular factor will be taken into account. Normally, the type of pollution complained of will be itself a cause of action which can cancel out any arguments put forward about hypersensitivity.

Defences to a claim for nuisance

There are a number of defences which attempt to restrict the ambit of the principles of the law of nuisance. However, in practice, they are either so difficult to prove as to be useless, or of dubious merit.

The defence of prescription

Although it is possible in principle to acquire a right to pollute as an easement through 20 years continuous use, there are so many caveats that the practical use of the defence is very restricted. For the defence to apply, the right to pollute must be exercised openly, continuously and not with any specific permission of the person against whom it is so acquired. It must also be the result of a lawful act, so a discharge in breach of a consent would not suffice. For example, in the case of *Sturges* v *Bridgman* (1879) 11 ChD 852, the defendant, a confectioner, had used a noisy pestle and mortar in his premises in Wimpole Street for more than 20 years. There had not been any complaints over that period but a doctor residing at the back of the site built a new consulting room in close proximity to the defendant's operational area. Consequently, the noise became a problem. The Court of Appeal held that the defendant in this case had not acquired a right to pollute by prescription. In the Court's opinion, the nuisance had only commenced after the consulting room had been constructed because previously the activities complained of did not give rise to any interference. When the consulting room was occupied however, such interference commenced. Thus, the period of 20 years did not commence until the construction of the consulting rooms.

No defence to say that the plaintiff came to the nuisance

In *Bliss* v *Hall* (1838) 4 Bing NC 183, the defendant operated a business as a tallow chandler. This business had been operated for at least three years when the plaintiff moved in nearby. Unfortunately, the defendant's business created highly toxic fumes which were blown over the plaintiff's land. The defendant argued that as he had been on the site before the plaintiff, the plaintiff should have realised the state of the premises nearby and should therefore not be able to bring an action in nuisance. Tindal CJ said:

> The Plaintiff came to the house he occupies with all the rights which the common law affords, and one of them is the right to wholesome air. Unless the Defendant shows a prescriptive right to carry on his business in the particular the Plaintiff is entitled to judgement.

When this principle is combined with the principle contained in *Sturges* v *Bridgman*, it is clear that whenever an individual moves into an area there could be the creation of a new 'nuisance history' which negates the prescriptive rights principle because of the need to allow a further 20 years before a prescriptive right attaches.

In practical terms, the principle that it is no defence for a defendant to allege that the plaintiff has come to the nuisance is very important. Many old factories constructed in early Victorian times have now been surrounded by new housing. These potentially antagonistic uses can give rise to conflict. On the one hand, industrialists argue that they have been carrying out polluting activities for a large number of years without complaint and anyone who moved into the area would fully know of any problems. However, in law, the creation of a new right to take action effectively renders their process liable to be brought before the civil courts.

The courts have also held that a planning authority can grant planning permission for a new development even though this is likely to give rise to complaints from the new occupiers as a result of an existing incompatible use (see *R* v *Exeter CC, ex parte JL Thomas and Co. Ltd* [1990] 1 All ER 413).

Statutory authority

There may be occasions where nuisances are caused by statutory or non-statutory bodies exercising their statutory authority. Where a body can point to such authority then this will amount to a defence if an action is brought against them for any consequential nuisance.

For example, in *Smeaton* v *Ilford Corporation* [1954] 1 Ch 450, there were particular problems with the Corporation's sewers. The nuisance complained of arose from the fact of the sewers in the area being overloaded as a consequence of many new houses in the area utilising their right to be connected to the existing sewer system. Unfortunately, the sewers were not able to cope properly with the amount of sewage. Furthermore, the local authority did not have powers to refuse to connect the houses to the existing sewer system. Upjohn J held that the overloaded sewers were not a nuisance, since the local authority had a statutory duty to take sewage and could not refuse the amount that was causing an overflow. There is, of course, a degree of control over such difficulties by restricting the grant of planning permission for development of housing, or restricting housing development without proper provision being made for discharges to sewers.

Although most statutory obligations are expressly contained within the body of the statute itself, it is also clear that a defendant could claim the defence of statutory authority where there is a clear implication that such activities have been authorised by an Act. In *Allen v Gulf Oil Refining Limited* [1981] 1 All ER 353, the Gulf Oil Refining Act 1965 (a private Act of Parliament) gave the defendants power to acquire land for an oil refinery at Milford Haven. The oil refinery emitted smells, noise and vibration and a local resident brought an action against Gulf Oil in nuisance. The plaintiff argued in that case that although the Act gave the defendant the power to acquire land for the construction of the refinery, it did not give any guidelines as to how the refinery should be operated. Therefore, when the defendant sought to rely upon the defence of statutory authority it was suggested that, as the Act did not specifically allow for the operating of the plant in a manner which gave rise to a nuisance, the defence was unavailable. The House of Lords held that the statute implicitly gave the defendant an immunity to every act inevitably flowing from the construction of the refinery. The only possible exception to this would be where the nuisance complained of was of a greater degree than was necessary or where such activities were carried out in a negligent manner.

It should be pointed out that, where private rights are interfered with, it is often the case that statutes themselves provide for compensation. For example, where a new road is being built, statutory compensation is payable where there is injurious affection to the enjoyment of property which is the direct result of the works carried out.

An assessment of nuisance as a tool for environmental protection

The common law principles of nuisance were available to counteract the problems of industrial pollution a long time before industrial growth started to bring about an increase in noxious emissions. However, it was still felt necessary to introduce statutory regulations under the Alkali Acts of 1873 to counteract the problems caused. This was not the only example of statutory intervention. There has been much argument amongst academics as to why, given the availability of common law remedies, it was felt necessary to introduce the supplementary administrative/public law controls.

Essentially, the reasons that have been identified for suggesting that the common law was under-utilised echo many of the weaknesses of the other mechanisms in environmental control. Environmental law was not, and is not, in a legal vacuum. The social and political context of pollution and the law neutralised attempts to deal with the environmental issues of increased industrialisation.

Resort to the law in the nineteenth century was always a rich person's prerogative. Taking an action to law was both lengthy and ultimately outside the reach of the vast majority of the population. Until 1854 an action to prevent a nuisance through an injunction required two actions to be taken, one through the common law, and one through the Chancery Court.

Secondly, as we have seen, to bring an action in nuisance required a proprietary interest. In the mid-nineteenth century it has been estimated that only somewhere in the region of 15% of the population were owner/occupiers. Thus, the vast majority of the population would have great difficulty in even founding an action. When coupled with the level of damages, notoriously low for interference with the enjoyment of land, there was an inevitable reluctance to take action.

Moreover, what has subsequently been identified as a complex system of power relationships ensured that in the social context there was tremendous pressure not to 'cause trouble'. Few workers would wish to proceed against their bosses and it was also clear that there was a certain degree of class solidarity amongst the industrialists themselves. Many factory owners bought up large areas of land surrounding their own sites and constructed low cost, high density housing to house their workers. This, coupled with the fact that it was often the case that the presence of an industry lowered surrounding land prices meant that a factory owner could purchase the right to pollute the surrounding area very cheaply. Furthermore, although society has become inherently more litigious over the last 50 to 100 years, bringing environmental actions was, and has always been, somewhat different to the norm.

One of the few recorded cases, *St Helens Smelting* v *Tipping*, illustrates these points well. Mr Tipping was a rich cotton magnate who owned 1300 acres of land. He could afford to risk the backlash of industrialists because of the well documented conflict between the cotton and the chemical industries. The damages received in his case and also in other nuisance cases were appallingly low. In *Halsey* v *Esso Petroleum Company* [1961] 1 WLR 683, there had been constant noise, dirt and commotion which had caused great difficulties and misery to the plaintiffs for some five years. Finding for the plaintiff, the court awarded the derisory sum of £200 damages.

Although the physical effects of pollution could often be seen, the long term effects of exposure to noxious fumes and hazardous chemicals were not fully understood. In an era where so many preconditions were placed upon the bringing of an action, the ignorance of many of those subjected to a high level of pollution ensured that no action would ever be taken. Practical difficulties of proving the causation of the pollution also indicated the lack of technical knowledge. Without scientific instruments, and without a right to enter onto land and take samples, individuals were restricted in their ability to monitor problems.

The power of industrialists at legislative, local government and magisterial level was too great for the 'man in the street'. Thus, a climate was set in which pollution control received a low priority. Local authorities were most reluctant to use their powers to prosecute for public nuisances, and indeed were often responsible for much pollution themselves. The law of nuisance was just one aspect of a legal regime which included as its other elements political, social, economic and philosophical responses to pollution. The limitations of the civil law in general, which apply more particularly to the law of nuisance, was commented on in the Third Report of the Royal Commission on the Pollution of Rivers in 1867:

It [bringing a common law action] is an expensive remedy. For the same money which is spent over a hard fought litigation against a single manufacturer, a Conservancy Board armed with proper powers, might for years keep safe from all abuse, a long extensive river with hundreds of manufactories situated on its banks.

Public nuisance

Although seemingly a close relative of private nuisance, the law relating to public nuisances contains both similar elements and distinguishing features. Public nuisance can be defined as a nuisance that affects a wide class of the public in general.

An illustration is the case of *R* v *Lloyd* (1802) 4 Esp 200. A number of people living in Cliffords Inn complained of a noise nuisance which was disturbing their work. Although the court did not rule out the possibility that it might have amounted to a private nuisance it was held that the inhabitants of only three chambers did not constitute a wide class of the public in general. The case of *Attorney-General* v *PYA Quarries* [1957] 2 QB 169 demonstrates the width of class required. The defendants operated a quarry. During operations they carried out various blasting activities. These activities caused vibration and noise over a wide area. In attempting to lay down guidelines, Denning LJ declined to give any specific numbers which would be required to show that a particular nuisance was public rather than private. He did however say:

I prefer to look to the reason of the thing and to say that a public nuisance is a nuisance which is so widespread in its range or so indiscriminate in its effect that it would not be reasonable to expect one person to take proceedings on his own responsibility to put a stop to it, but that it should be taken on the responsibility of the community at large.

Aside from the need to show an effect over a wide class of the public, there is a good degree of overlap with the factors that are taken into account when deciding whether or not there is a private nuisance. For an example, in the *PYA Quarries* case above, if there had only been intermittent blasting then it may have arguably fallen foul of the rule in *Harrison* v *Southwark and Vauxhall Water Company*, which would have negated any liability not only in private but also in public nuisance.

The distinction between public and private nuisance

The primary difference between public and private nuisance lies in the remedies sought. A public nuisance is a criminal offence which can be tried either before the magistrates or in the Crown Court. Consequently, it is possible to obtain an injunction to restrain a public nuisance through the Attorney-General on a relator action. The difficulty with this approach is that it is open to the Attorney-General to turn down an application for a relator action. There is a further possibility. Under the Local Government Act 1972, s. 222, local authorities are entitled to take injunction proceedings in the High Court in order to prevent harm to inhabitants of their area.

Aside from these two restricted avenues, the right to take civil action against a public nuisance by private individuals can only arise if they have suffered special damage, (i.e. damage different from everybody else).

Trespass

One of the simplest of the torts, trespass, involves direct interference with personal or proprietary rights without lawful excuse. Trespass to the person has never been properly developed in pollution cases, although in theory making someone inhale toxic fumes gives rise to an action in trespass. The main reason for this restriction lies in the requirement of directness. The interference with the personal or proprietary right must be direct rather than consequential. As an example, in *Reynolds* v *Clarke* (1725) 1 Stra 643, Fortescue J said, 'if a man throws a log into the highway and it hits me I may maintain trespass because it is an immediate wrong; but if, as it lies there, I tumble over it and receive an injury, I must bring an action upon the case because it is only prejudicial in consequence'. In relation to trespass onto land a good illustration would be that throwing stones onto someone's property would be a direct trespass whereas allowing tiles to fall off a badly repaired chimney would not be.

Furthermore, an act of trespass also has to be intentional or negligent. *McDonald* v *Associated Fuels* [1954] 3 DLR 713 illustrates the distinction well. Although this was a Canadian case where an action was successfully brought in negligence, the court also decided that a trespass action would have succeeded. The case involved the supply of sawdust fuel to the plaintiff's house. The delivery method was somewhat unusual in that the defendants parked their truck and blew the sawdust into a bin inside the house by means of a blower unit. Unfortunately, the intake mechanism for the sawdust was too close to the exhaust system of the truck. Consequently, as well as sawdust, carbon monoxide was blown into the house, the occupants were overcome and one of the occupants broke a hip when she collapsed. It is clear here that the trespass itself (i.e. the entrance of the carbon monoxide directly into the house) was not intentional, however, the act which caused the trespass was.

A major disadvantage with an action in trespass is that a causal link between the directness of an act and the inevitability of its consequences has to be established. In *Jones* v *Llanrwst UDC* [1908] All ER 922, faecal matter from sewage had collected in the local authority's drains and was passed untreated into the River Conway. As a consequence, it collected on the gravel banks of a river owned by the plaintiff. The question that the court was asked to answer was whether or not this deposit could amount to a trespass as it was not intended to pass onto the plaintiff's land. The court held that it was a trespass as it was intentional in the sense that the sewage was intentionally passed into the river; it was also direct in the sense that it inevitably came onto the plaintiff's land. Thus, even though it may have appeared that the matter was some way away from the plaintiff's land when it first entered the river, it was still both intentional and direct.

Jones v *Llanrwst UDC* was distinguished in the case of *Esso* v *Southport Corporation* [1956] AC 218, which at first glance would seem to fall on similar facts. A 680 tonne tanker was grounded in the Ribble Estuary. In order to lighten the ship, the master discharged much of the cargo of oil. This was then carried by the wind and the tide onto Southport's beach. The beach was under the ownership of the Corporation and they claimed against the company for the clean up costs involved. The case largely concerned the question of negligence as there was more than a suggestion that the cause of the pollution was bad navigation. That case failed, but views were expressed in the House of Lords on the possibility that the output of the oil onto the beach was a trespass. Lords Radcliffe and Tucker expressed the view that this could not be a trespass and sought to distinguish it from the *Llanrwst* case by looking at questions of inevitability. Unlike the river which inevitably flowed downstream, there was no inevitability about the deposit of the oil onto the foreshore, which depended on the action of the wind, waves and tide.

This principle would make it almost impossible to bring an action in trespass for air pollution. In a situation where air currents and wind could throw the pollution in any particular direction, the element of directness required for trespass would be difficult to show.

One of the main advantages of bringing an action in trespass is that there is no need to show damage. Trespass is actionable *per se*, therefore all that needs to be shown is some interference. Whereas most environmental pollution actions will involve some form of damage, this actionability *per se* enables an injunction to be obtained far more easily than with any other common law mechanism (see **Remedies** below).

Negligence

To attempt a full coverage of the law of negligence in a book on environmental protection would be both foolish and unnecessary. There are many other texts which contain a considered study of the principles. Moreover, the utility of the principles of negligence in bringing action for environmental protection is somewhat limited.

The law of negligence is a fault based system; in order to succeed in negligence there has to be some fault on behalf of the defendant. Thus negligence would only really be utilised where other strict liability remedies under the common law (e.g. nuisance and trespass) are not available. Furthermore, proving negligence owes much to the state of technology at the time; where a polluting factory meets the standard expected of other factories of that type, then any action in negligence will fail.

The law of negligence only controls one-off incidents. Thus, as a control over continuing activities such as polluting emissions into the atmosphere or watercourses, it does not necessarily provide adequate protection. An injunction would rarely be appropriate in a negligence action.

The three main principles of negligence are that the plaintiff must establish that (a) a duty of care is owed by the defendant to the plaintiff; (b) that the defendant has breached that duty; and (c) that there has been foreseeable damage resulting from the breach. These criteria illustrate one major advantage of the use of negligence over other mechanisms of control in the common law. Nowhere in the principles is there mention of the need to have a proprietary interest prior to bringing an action. Thus anyone who has suffered damage from the negligence can bring an action. This widens the class of possible claimants.

Considering how often negligence is used to provide a cause of action in other areas of life, it is perhaps surprising to find how little it has been used to control environmental problems. There have historically been fairly few examples, although in recent years there has been an upsurge in the use of the mechanism. Recent examples include the case of *Tutton* v *A D Walter* [1985] 3 WLR 797, which involved the use of insecticide. Farmers had been advised by the manufacturers and Central Government that using a particular insecticide when oil rape was flowering could lead to the death of insects such as bees. Furthermore, they were told that the insecticide was actually most effective when used after the flowering period. Unfortunately, the defendant sprayed his crop whilst the oil rape was in flower and a number of bees owned by the plaintiff were killed. The court held that the farmer was liable for using the insecticide in a negligent manner.

More importantly perhaps, the case of *Scott-Whitehead* v *National Coal Board* (1987) 53 P&CR 263 showed the court's approach to statutory bodies and the advice they should give concerning environmental matters. The defendants discharged an emission of a chlorinated solution into a river. The river was in drought and therefore there was insufficient water to dilute the strength of the pollutant. Mr Scott-Whitehead was farming down stream and abstracting water to irrigate his crops. The water abstracted from the river contained a high level of pollutant and damage was caused to his crops. The second defendant in this case, the regional water authority, was held to be liable in negligence for not advising the farmer of the potential danger from the condition of the water he was abstracting. Extending the principle in this case, it may well be possible to bring an action against other environmental bodies in negligence if it can be shown that their failure to give adequate warnings of pollution contributed to damage.

The rule in *Rylands* v *Fletcher*

The principle known as 'the rule in *Rylands* v *Fletcher*' was first established in a case reported in 1865 ((1865) H&C 774). It involved the construction of a reservoir on the defendant's land. The contractors failed to block off mine shafts with the result that when the reservoir was filled up, water went into the shafts and flooded a mine belonging to the plaintiff. Although there was no negligence on behalf of the defendant, the House of Lords held that he should be liable. In the lower court, Blackburn J first expounded the principle:

. . . that the person who for his own purposes brings onto his land and collects and keeps there anything likely to do mischief if it escapes, must keep it in at his peril, and, if he does not do so, is *prima facie* answerable for all the damage which is the natural consequence of its escape.

Thus, the principle imposes strict liability (not absolute liability) if something brought onto land or collected there escapes.

The implications as far as environmental protection is concerned are clear. Many acts of pollution are caused by materials and/or substances which are brought onto land escaping from that land. Over the years the rule has been applied to cover water, fire, gases, electricity, oil, chemicals, colliery spoil, poisonous vegetation and even a chair-o-plane at a fairground! The sheer simplicity of the principle would seem to cover many potentially hazardous situations. However, the limitations of the principle are such that it is rarely successful nowadays.

Non-natural user

By far and away the most important restriction upon the principle is that where a substance is kept on land it must have been kept by means of a 'non-natural user'. Originally, this may have meant only that there is no liability if the water (in the case of *Rylands* v *Fletcher*) had been a natural lake or naturally flooded area rather than a man-made reservoir. In time, it came to mean that the use had to be 'some special use bringing with it increased danger to others and must not merely be the ordinary use of the land or such a use as is proper for the general benefit of the community' (*Rickards* v *Lothian* [1913] AC 263).

Thus a slightly different interpretation to the word natural came about. Instead of meaning 'artificial' the courts began to interpret the phrase as meaning an 'abnormal' use of land. Consequently, some rather strange things have been held to be a natural use of land and a flexible test of what is an *especially* or *unduly* hazardous activity has evolved which has attempted to import some element of public utility.

In *Rainham Chemicals* v *Belvedere Fish Guano Company* [1921] 2 AC 465, a factory which manufactured high explosives for the Ministry of Munitions exploded, killing a number of people and damaging the respondent's factory. The House of Lords held it to be a non-natural user and also found that the effects of the explosion amounted to an escape even though it was actually bits of the factory which had escaped rather than the substance stored, i.e. the explosives. However, in a similar case, *Read* v *Lyons* [1947] AC 156, the defendants managed the Elstow Ordnance Factory where they made high explosive shells for the Government. Ms Read was an inspector in the factory in 1942 when there was an explosion in which she was injured. There was no negligence in their activities but she argued that the defendants were manufacturing high explosive shells and they knew them to be dangerous, and therefore the rule in *Rylands* v *Fletcher* ought to be applied. In the House of Lords, Lord MacMillan said:

Every activity in which man engages is fraught with some possible element of danger to others. Experience shows that even from acts apparently innocuous, injury to others may result. The more dangerous the act the greater is the care that must be taken in performing it . . . . one who engages in obviously dangerous operations must be taken to know that if he does not take special precautions, injury to others may very well result. In my opinion it would be impracticable to frame a legal classification of things as things dangerous and things not dangerous, attaching absolute liability in the case of the former but not in the case of the latter . . . . accordingly I am unable to accept the proposition that in law the manufacturer of high-explosive shells is a dangerous operation which imposes on the manufacturer an absolute liability . . . .

This decision may well have had something to do with the fact that in war time it would clearly be a natural use of industrial land to make explosives. However, it is now common for a court to find that an ordinary industrial use is a natural use if it is sited with due care and consideration. To that extent, where a factory is given a planning permission, that would, it is suggested, amount to prima facie evidence that consideration had been given as to its suitability as a use.

Other restrictions on the use of the rule

Further limitations on the principle do not have the same restrictive nature as the non-natural user principle. However, they are still important in seeking to restrict the introduction of a strict liability concept into the common law. Firstly, there is a requirement that the substance escapes from the land where it is kept. Therefore, in *Read* v *Lyons*, the workers in the ammunition factory could have no action under the rule in *Rylands* v *Fletcher*. Furthermore, the principle applies specifically to protect landowners and therefore it is generally accepted that no actions for personal injuries received from the escape of substances from a non-natural user of land can lie. Lord MacMillan said in *Read* v *Lyons*:

Whatever may have been the law of England in early times I am of opinion that as the law now stands an allegation of negligence is in general essential to the relevancy of an action of reparation for personal injuries.

Although there have been a number of restrictions placed upon the rule in *Rylands* v *Fletcher*, this does not necessarily condemn an escape from land of hazardous substances to failure, it merely means that negligence, nuisance or trespass must be shown for liability to accrue. In many circumstances, fault will be able to be shown fairly easily.

Defences

There are a number of defences to an action brought under the rule in *Rylands* v *Fletcher*.

Defence of common benefit

It has been suggested that there is a defence where the plaintiff benefits from the harmful activity. Therefore, where gas, electricity or water supplies have caused damage on the plaintiff property, no liability should accrue. The concept of this defence is perhaps taking the desire to restrict absolute liability too far (see *North Western Utilities Limited* v *London Guarantee and Accident Co Ltd* [1936] AC 108). The thinking behind the development to this principle has been somewhat confused (e.g. the decision in *Anderson* v *Oppenheimer* (1880) 5 QBD 602). Some have seen the use of this defence as an extension of the defence of consent which can be simply stated as in *Attorney-General* v *Cory Brothers & Co* [1921] 1 AC 521—if the plaintiff has allowed the defendant to accumulate the matter or thing which is being complained of then they are unable to sue if it escapes.

Statutory authority

As in the case of private nuisance, it is a defence that a statute allows for certain activities (see *Smeaton* v *Ilford Corporation* [1954] Ch 454).

Act of God

The relevance of this defence is somewhat restricted. As one commentator has put it (*Street on Torts*, 8th ed):

> The defence has received in connection with this tort a prominence out of all proportion to its practical importance. If an escape is caused, through natural causes without human intervention, in 'circumstances which no human foresight can provide against, and which human prudence is not bound to recognise the possibility', there is then said to exist the defence of Act of God.

The only things which fall under this defence would be escapes caused by such things as earthquakes, tornadoes or freak acts of nature.

The usefulness of the rule in *Rylands* v *Fletcher*

Along with the restrictions placed upon the use and the defences available, the strictness of the liability imposed by the rule in *Rylands* v *Fletcher* has been diluted so that an incoherent and sorry-looking remedy is left. In summary, the rule is very much limited in its practical application. Most uses will fall within the category of a natural use. Although recommendations have been made to introduce a new system of strict liability for particularly hazardous activities backed by a compulsory insurance cover, this has not materialised in English legislation. Furthermore, the introduction of the EC draft Directive on Civil Liability for Damage Caused by Waste may yet form a statutory basis for the imposition of strict liability in cases of environmental pollution.

The protection of riparian rights

There is a separate action for interference with the rights of owners of riparian land. Although this action has some similarities with private nuisance, it is in practice used far more frequently owing to the strength of riparian owners' natural rights to water. For further explanation of the law on riparian rights see p. 330.

Civil law remedies

Of course, the use of the common law as a mechanism for environmental protection would be useless unless there were effective remedies once a cause of action had been established. There are three main types of remedies which can be sought, these are compensatory remedies, preventative remedies, and abatement. Monetary damages act as compensation for any damage suffered but also can pay for any clean up costs involved in rectifying pollution. On the other hand, an injunction allows for actions which are creating an environmental problem to be stopped by order of the court. Finally, there are certain limited circumstances where a plaintiff can take individual action and abate the activity causing environmental damage themselves.

The utility of the common law in dealing with environmental pollution depends upon the nature of the problem. An isolated occurrence could cause tremendous environmental damage and, where a problem is not likely to recur, it may well be an adequate remedy to pay for the restoration of the environment to its prior state. However, in cases where the pollution is perhaps of a lower level but more persistent, it may be necessary to prevent an accumulation of potentially hazardous substances which cannot be properly compensated through damages alone. Therefore, an injunction may be the only suitable remedy. There are many instances where the remedies available through the common law will give a far wider range of options to a potential plaintiff than are available through seeking to have statutory bodies act on his behalf.

Damages
The aim of awarding damages at common law is to place the plaintiff as far as possible in the position he would have been in had the wrongful act not occurred. This could be calculated in two ways; on the cost of clean up operations to restore the property to its previous state, or the difference between the value of the property as it was after the pollution had affected it, and before. It is a principle which is far easier stated than it is to fully explain. In *Marquis Granby* v *Bakewell UDC* (1923) 87 JP 105, the defendants operated a gas works which discharged poisonous effluent into a river over which the plaintiff had fishing rights. The effluent killed all the plaintiff's fish and thus he claimed damages against the defendant for the interference with his fishing rights. He received compensation equalling the costs of restocking the river in addition to the loss of a large amount of the food supply for other stocks. The court also took into account the effects of the pollution on higher quality areas of

the river and considered that the damages would be higher where environmental pollution was greater.

Damages for all *future* loss are only available in lieu of an injunction. This remedy is only used sparingly because of the ready availability of the more usual injunction procedure.

Injunctions

The granting of an injunction is a discretionary remedy which can prohibit a defendant from carrying on an activity which is causing pollution. The principles for the granting of an injunction are well established. Normally, either the activity complained of has to be continuing at the date of action, or there has to be a threat that the activity will continue. Even though the activity may have ceased at the time of trial, an injunction can still be sought if it existed when the action was brought.

When exercising its discretion, the court will take a number of factors into consideration. Firstly, it will not grant an injunction if the activity complained of is not of sufficient gravity or duration to justify stopping the defendant's activities. Turner LJ in *Goldsmid* v *Tunbridge Wells Improvement Commissioners* (1866) 1 Ch App 349 said:

> it is not in every case of nuisance that this Court should interfere. I think that it ought not to do so in cases in which the injury is merely temporary or trifling; but I think that it ought to do so in cases in which the injury is permanent and serious: and in determining whether the injury is serious or not, regard must be had to all the consequences which may flow from it.

The court attempts to balance the competing interests of the plaintiff and defendant by assessing the balance of convenience between the parties. Where all things are equal, an attempt will be made to assess the social utility of the activity by comparing its public importance with the interference of the private rights of the plaintiff. Basically, the harm suffered to the plaintiff has to be balanced against the effect the granting of an injunction would have upon the defendant.

There are situations where it is possible to obtain an injunction before the occurrence of the action causing injury or damage. A *quia timet* injunction, as it is known, does not require proof of environmental damage at all. However, there must be sufficient proof of imminent damage and it must be demonstrated that if the activity were to continue the damages accruing would be substantial and of such degree that it would be difficult to rectify.

Injunctions are rarely specific in nature, the court merely sets the standard for the defendant to meet and he can achieve this standard in any way possible. Thus, it may be met either by closing down a particular plant which is causing environmental difficulties or by fitting new arrestment equipment. Even where injunctions are granted it is often on the basis that there is a certain amount of time given for compliance.

Injunctions are seen to be an effective method of dealing with pollution problems and are the most common remedy sought by such interest groups as the Anglers' Association. For example, in their contribution to the Armer Committee on Trade Effluents in 1960, the Anglers' Association stated that they had issued 32 writs and obtained 32 injunctions on long-standing pollution problems in the 1950s.

Abatement

The remedy of abatement tends to be more historical than useful. The remedy involves the removal of a nuisance by the injured party without recourse to legal proceedings. The courts view this remedy unfavourably as it is extra-judicial in nature and therefore open to abuse. An example of the use of abatement can be found in *Lemmon* v *Webb* [1895] AC 1. Any damages subsequent to an abatement action are restricted to damages in respect of harm prior to the abatement.

Statutory nuisance

The law of statutory nuisance represents a bridge between the common law controls of environmental protection and the more characteristic statutory mechanisms. The law on statutory nuisance was consolidated in the Public Health Act 1936 after previous Acts in 1848, 1855, 1860 and 1875. Originally, the purpose of the Act was to attempt to control matters which, although nuisances in the common law sense, affected sanitation levels and thus public health in Victorian times. The law has been updated yet again and consolidated in Part III of the Environmental Protection Act 1990. The main aim of the statutory nuisance provisions is to provide a quick and easy remedy to abate nuisances which the common law is too slow or expensive to deal with.

The control of statutory nuisances

District councils and London borough councils are under a duty to inspect their area for statutory nuisance (EPA, s. 79). The consequence of this is that if an individual within an area complains of a statutory nuisance emanating from within that area then a district council is obliged to investigate this. The EPA implies that the level of such an obligation is only to take such steps as are reasonably practicable. Although the duty imposed is only that inspection be periodic, it is clear that if there is strong evidence to suggest that a statutory nuisance exists within an area, and a local authority refuse to inspect, then it is possible that the remedy of judicial review will lie to any aggrieved applicant. It is important therefore for any individual wishing to complain to a local authority that proper evidence is gathered (e.g. dates, times and length of the nuisance if it has already occurred, or strong evidence to show that the statutory nuisance is about to occur). There are default powers under EPA, sch. 3 para. 4 which allow the Secretary of State to take action if local authorities are not carrying out their duties.

The general control of statutory nuisance is contained in EPA, s. 80. The basis of the section is that where a local authority is satisfied that a statutory nuisance exists, or is likely to occur or recur, then they are under a mandatory duty to serve an abatement notice on the person responsible for the nuisance or, if that person cannot be found, the owner or occupier of the premises on which the statutory nuisance is present.

The categories of statutory nuisance

There are a number of categories of statutory nuisance contained in the Environmental Protection Act 1990, s. 79. These are supplemented by other statutes which declare specific things to be a statutory nuisance and thus controlled under the provisions of the Act (EPA, s. 79(1)(h)). Much of the language used in s. 79 is somewhat antiquated and difficult to reconcile with modern technology. The categories of statutory nuisance are listed in the headings below (pp. 151–153).

Each local authority is under a duty to inspect their area for statutory nuisances (EPA, s. 79(1)). The Act lays down certain activities or states of affairs which if 'prejudicial to health or a nuisance' will amount to a statutory nuisance.

'Prejudicial to health or a nuisance'

The main criterion for the existence of a statutory nuisance is that anything complained of must be either 'prejudicial to health or a nuisance'. These are not be read conjunctively.

'Prejudicial to health' is defined under EPA, s. 79(7), as meaning injurious, or likely to cause injury, to health. In *Coventry City Council v Cartwright* [1975] 1 WLR 845, the Council owned a vacant site within a residential area on which they allowed people to dump all sorts of materials. These included not only normal household refuse but also building and construction materials. Occasionally, the Council would move household materials. A nearby resident complained of a statutory nuisance under the Public Health Act 1936. The Divisional Court held that, where the accumulation complained of was inert rather than putrescible, there was no likelihood of disease or that vermin would be attracted which could spread disease. Although there was a chance that physical injury could be caused to people who walked on the site it was not sufficient to amount to being prejudicial to health.

In defining the word 'nuisance', it is generally accepted that the word contained within the EPA is the same as the concept under the common law. In *National Coal Board v Thorne* [1976] 1 WLR 543, the nuisance complained of amounted to defective guttering and windows within premises. The complainant argued that the physical condition of the building amounted to a nuisance under the Public Health Act. Watkins J said that a 'nuisance coming within the meaning of the Public Health Act 1936 must be either a public or private nuisance as understood by common law'. Thus, when deciding on the point of whether or not a statutory nuisance could arise when it was the inhabitants of premises who were suffering, such a state of affairs could not amount to nuisance because it was not an interference with the use or enjoyment of neighbouring property.

There has to be more than just mere discomfort to the occupier's property unless such a state of affairs would be prejudicial to health.

Any premises in such a state as to be prejudicial to health or a nuisance
Section 79(1)(a) provides that where premises are kept in a state which is prejudicial to health or a nuisance then this will amount to a statutory nuisance. 'Premises' includes land and any vessel not powered by steam-reciprocating machinery. The provision covers the physical state of premises rather than any use to which those premises are put. Therefore, where noise or dust etc. is emitted from those premises from a use, this is not covered. The aim is to prevent situations where there are physical elements which are either prejudicial to health or a nuisance. Such things would cover the lack of proper insulation of council owned flats against noise (see *London Borough of Southwark* v *Ince* (1989) 21 HLR 504) and dwellings which are subject to heavy condensation from poor heating and ventilation (see *Greater London Council* v *The London Borough of Tower Hamlets* (1983) 15 HLR 57).

Smoke emitted from premises so as to be prejudicial to health or a nuisance
Section 79(1)(b) replaces the Clean Air Act 1956, s. 16, which previously made separate provision for the control of smoke from premises. There are exemptions contained within s. 79(3) so that:

(a)   smoke emitted from a chimney of a private dwelling within a smoke control area;
(b)   dark smoke emitted from a chimney of a building, or a chimney serving the furnace of a boiler or industrial plant attached to a building, or for the time being installed on any land;
(c)   smoke emitted from a railway locomotive steam engine;
(d)   dark smoke emitted, otherwise than as mentioned above, from industrial or trade premises

will not be statutory nuisances. (See, however, Chapter 11.)

Fumes or gases emitted from premises so as to be prejudicial to health or a nuisance
Section 79(4) controls fumes or gases emitted from private dwellings. Fumes are defined as 'any airborne solid matter smaller than dust, gases including vapour and moisture precipitating from vapour' (EPA, s. 79(7)). (See also APC controls under EPA, Part I.)

Any dust, steam, smell or other effluvia arising on industrial, trade or business premises and being prejudicial to health or a nuisance
The meanings of dust, steam and smell are fairly well established. However, the term 'effluvia' was defined in *Malton Board of Health* v *Malton Manure Company* (1879) 4 ExD 302. This case involved the production of manure by the defendant company which produced vapours. It could not be conclusively

demonstrated that these vapours were prejudicial to healthy people in the locality, although the Board of Health did demonstrate that it had the effect of making people who were ill more ill. The court held that this effect could amount to effluvia which was prejudicial to health. It is suggested that the meaning of effluvia covers the outflow of harmful or unpleasant substances.

Any accumulation or deposit which is prejudicial to health or a nuisance
To come within s. 79(1)(e), the accumulation or deposit has to be capable of causing disease rather than injury (see *Coventry City Council* v *Cartwright* above). The wide range of accumulations or deposits covered by this section have included sheep dung (*Draper* v *Sperring* (1869) 10 CB 113) and cinders which emitted offensive smells (*Bishop Auckland Local Board* v *Bishop Auckland Iron and Steel Company* (1882) 10 QBD 138).

Any animal kept in such a place or manner as to be prejudicial to health or a nuisance
The keeping of a large number of animals on premises can give rise to a number of different enforcement actions. First, the keeping of a large number of animals may amount to sufficient intensification of a use to give rise to a change of use, which could result in enforcement action under the Town and Country Planning Act 1990 (see *Wallington* v *Secretary of State* [1990] JPL 112). Secondly, there may be common law actions which could be brought for nuisance. Thirdly, there could be action taken by the local authority under by-laws passed under the Public Health Act 1936, s. 81(2), and finally, there could be action taken under the statutory nuisance provisions of s. 79(1)(f).

Noise emitted from premises so as to be prejudicial to health or a nuisance
This provision replaces Part III of the Control of Pollution Act 1974 dealing with noise from premises. There is an exemption for noise from model aircraft.

Any other matter declared by any enactment to be a statutory nuisance
This provision is to include any statutory nuisance provided for under future statutes. It also includes nuisances from mines, shafts and quarries under the Mines and Quarries Act 1954 (EPA, s. 151).

What is required to satisfy the local authority?

In practice, it is the responsibility of the local Environmental Health Officer to decide upon whether or not a statutory nuisance is occurring or likely to occur. As has been stated, the test is whether or not a statutory nuisance is prejudicial to health or a nuisance. An Environmental Health Officer will visit the premises and make a subjective decision as to whether or not the state of the premises or anything on those premises amounts to a nuisance. When reverting to the common law for the definition of nuisance, it is up to the Environmental Health Officer to balance the many different factors used when deciding on whether or not a common law nuisance exists. The most important of these factors are:

(a)   the nature and the location of the nuisance;
(b)   the time and duration of the nuisance; and
(c)   the utility of the activity concerned.

Balancing all these factors together is the only way in which an Environmental Health Officer can make an adjudication between respective neighbours' rights because it is quite clear that a statutory nuisance will only apply to affected neighbours' properties.

Section 80(1) provides that for a local authority to act, the statutory nuisance must exist or be likely to occur or recur. Thus this procedure can be used to prevent a nuisance before it actually occurs, although there has to be evidence that a forthcoming activity is likely to give rise to a statutory nuisance and the standard of evidence required is particularly high. However, where these problems can be overcome, such as in the case of a party where there is more than a suggestion that powerful audio equipment will be used, this may well be the only method of prohibiting certain types of nuisances which have to be stopped before they occur. Where a local authority has delegated enforcement powers to individual officers then they are able to carry out the enforcement procedures on behalf of the local authorities themselves.

Who is the 'person responsible'?

The enforcement of a statutory nuisance is normally taken against the 'person responsible' which is defined in EPA, s. 79(7), as being 'the person to whose act, default or sufferance the nuisance is attributable'. This is a particularly wide definition and can include a local authority (see *Rossall* v *London Borough of Southwark*).

If there are any difficulties in locating the 'person responsible' for the existence of a statutory nuisance, EPA, s. 80(2)(c), states that the definition of the person responsible can be extended to include the owner or occupier of the premises in question.

The abatement notice

Once the local authority through its Environmental Health Officer is satisfied that there are conditions which amount to a nuisance under s. 70(1), they are under a duty to serve an abatement notice which must require any or all of the following:

(a)   the abatement of the nuisance or the prohibiting or restricting of its occurrence or recurrence;
(b)   the execution of works or other steps necessary to comply with the notice.

The notice should specify the time within which compliance with the notice is required. The evidential basis for issuing an abatement notice can be purely scientific and therefore objective (e.g. in relation to noise nuisances in decibel terms), and there is no need for that to be corroborated by evidence of a particular occupier who has suffered interference with the reasonable enjoyment of property (see *Cooke* v *Adatia* [1989] LGR 32).

Where an individual has been served with an abatement notice, the contravention of that notice without reasonable excuse renders that person guilty of an offence under EPA, s. 80(4).

Defences

Where an offence has been committed under s. 80(4) there are a number of defences.

Reasonable excuse

It is a defence to a prosecution for the contravention of an abatement notice to show that there was a reasonable excuse for carrying out the activity which resulted in the contravention. The test laid down for this would seem to be an objective one, i.e. 'would a reasonable man think that the excuse given was consistent with a reasonable standard of conduct?'. It is not sufficient to say that there would be a defence to a private law action in nuisance. Indeed, in *Lambert (A) Flat Management* v *Lomas* [1981] 2 All ER 280, it was said that COPA, s. 58(4) was designed to provide a defence to a criminal charge where an individual had some reasonable excuse, such as some special difficulty in relation to compliance with the abatement notice. It was not an opportunity to challenge the notice; that should only properly arise on an appeal.

Best practicable means

Where an abatement notice is served on trade or business premises and the nuisance complained of is caused in the course of the trade or business, it is a defence under certain heads of EPA, s. 70(1), to show that best practicable means have been used to prevent or counteract the nuisance (s. 80(7)). This does not apply to fumes or gases emitted from premises (s. 79(1)(c)) or the catch-all provision under s. 79(1)(h). Although there is not any complete definition contained within the EPA, certain elements are required to be taken into account under s. 79(9). These include local conditions and circumstances, the current state of technical knowledge, financial implications, and the design, installation, maintenance, manner and periods of operation of plant and machinery.

Special defences

There are specific defences available in relation to noise and nuisances on construction sites and in areas where there are registered noise levels under the Noise Abatement Zone Procedure (see EPA, s. 80(9) and COPA ss. 60, 61 and 65–67).

The right of appeal against an abatement notice

Where an individual is served with an abatement notice there is a right of appeal against the notice to a magistrates' court. One advantage of the appeal system over a defence to a prosecution under contravention proceedings is that it allows for a far greater range of defences and therefore provides a greater scope for disputing the nuisance. An appeal normally lies within 21 days of the service of the notice. The grounds of appeal are set down in regulations made under EPA sch. 3. The Statutory Nuisance (Appeals) Regulations 1990 (SI 1990 No. 2276) and the Statutory Nuisance (Appeals) (Amendment) Regulations 1990 (SI 1990 No. 2483) set out the grounds of appeal against an abatement notice, which include:

(a)   that the abatement notice is not justified in the terms of s. 80;

(b)   that there has been a substantive or procedural error in the service of the notice;

(c)   that the authority have unreasonably refused to accept compliance with alternative requirements or that their requirements are unreasonable or unnecessary;

(d)   that the period for compliance is unreasonable;

(e)   that the best practicable means were used to counteract the effect of nuisance from trade/business premises.

Furthermore, the regulations allow for the suspension of an abatement notice pending the court's decision, unless the local authority override the suspension in the abatement notice with a statement to the effect that notice is to have effect regardless, and that:

(a)   the nuisance is prejudicial to health;

(b)   suspension would render the notice of no practical effect (e.g. where nuisances are to cease before the action can be heard in court); or

(c)   any expenditure incurred before an appeal would be disproportionate to the public benefit.

Individual actions by any person

It is often the case that a local authority's Environmental Health Department are overworked and understaffed and have neither the manpower nor sometimes the inclination to deal with disputes regarding statutory nuisances. Section 82 of the Act allows a complaint to be made to a local magistrates' court by any person who is aggrieved by the existence of a statutory nuisance. This procedure allows for any person within an area to bring a much more economic and expeditious proceeding than a private law action. One particular limitation upon this procedure is that the nuisance must be in existence and therefore it cannot be used to anticipate problems. Therefore, a person has no right of action under this section to stop a nuisance which is likely to occur in the future (e.g. loud parties). If the person can satisfy the magistrates that there is an existing nuisance, or that there is likely to be a recurring nuisance, they are under a duty to issue an abatement notice requiring the defendant to abate the nuisance within a specified time, and to execute any works necessary for that purpose and/or prohibiting a recurrence of the nuisance, and requiring the defendant, within a specified time, to carry out any works necessary to prevent the recurrence. The magistrates may fine a defendant at a level not exceeding level 5 on the standard scale (currently £2,000) (s. 82(2)). There is a notice procedure, which differs slightly from that which governs local authority actions, in that s. 80(6) provides that where an individual is bringing an action they must give not less than three days' notice in relation to a noise nuisance and, in relation to other statutory nuisances, 21 days' notice, before the bringing of proceedings under s. 80(2).

Sentencing powers for contravention of an abatement notice

Section 80(5) and (6) of the EPA provide for penalties for a person who is guilty of an offence of contravening an abatement notice. The matter is triable only in the magistrates' court and, if found guilty, an offender is liable to a fine not exceeding level 5 on the standard scale (currently £2,000). If the offence continues after the conviction they are liable to a further fine not exceeding one-tenth of that level for each day on which the offence continues. The previous levels of fine included under the Public Health Act and Control of Pollution Act indicated that for major industrial uses there were no real disincentives to carry out works to improve premises, indeed, it was often cost effective to pay off fines at a low level in order to ensure that a particular activity could be carried on rather than abated. Section 80(6) closes this particular loophole by imposing a maximum fine level of £20,000 on industrial, trade or business premises.

The use of injunctions and proceedings in the High Court

In many cases the provisions of s. 80 would not provide an adequate remedy in terms of either gravity or speed. Under s. 81(5), a local authority may take action in the High Court for the purpose of securing the abatement, prohibition or restriction of any statutory nuisance where they are of the opinion that proceedings for an offence of contravening an abatement notice would not provide a sufficient remedy. The usual method for doing this would be by seeking an injunction in the High Court. In *Hammersmith London Borough Council* v *Magnum Automated Forecourts Ltd* [1978] 1 WLR 50, the Court of Appeal decided that this was an additional power to that contained under the statutory noise nuisance provisions contained within COPA. Thus, the right to take proceedings in the High Court could be used after an abatement notice had been served, but before the prosecution for contravention had been heard, in order to expedite the cessation of the nuisance.

The scope for injunctions has widened considerably with the decision in *Lloyds Bank* v *Guardian Assurance* (1987) 35 Build LR 34, which stated that the jurisdiction of the High Court was not affected by any proceedings under

Part III of the Control of Pollution Act. The real effect of this decision has been to suggest that it will not be open to any individual to apply for an injunction under the common law which is in stricter terms than any abatement notice which has already been served under COPA or the EPA. However, it is open to the local authority to tighten up on a weak abatement notice by applying for an injunction in the High Court under s. 81(5). In such proceedings it will be a defence to prove that noise was authorised by a construction site consent under COPA, s. 61. As to injunctions brought by a local authority other than by means of s. 81(5), see s. 222 of the Local Government Act 1972.

PART II SECTORAL COVERAGE OF ENVIRONMENTAL LAW

NINE

Town and country planning

The British system of town and country planning is undoubtedly one of the most sophisticated systems of land use control in the world. It is virtually unique in incorporating controls over the use of land as well as over the design and form of the built environment. Accordingly, it plays a central role in environmental law because of its enormous importance in relation to locational and siting issues. It is, as stated earlier (see p. 66), perhaps the pre-eminent example in this country of an anticipatory system of control. However, town and country planning is not just about environmental protection. It has a wider role in organising economic development, and in balancing economic, political, social and environmental factors to do with development in a democratic context. This wider role is outside environmental law in the sense in which the term is used in this book, so this chapter is restricted to summarising those parts of planning law which have the greatest importance for environmental protection.

This chapter is written in the firm belief that planning law can be reduced to a number of central principles, and that once the structure of the system is understood, many of the details become self-explanatory. As a result, many matters of detail are omitted, but there are many excellent specialist books and encyclopedias which readers are urged to consult (see Bibliography).

In particular, it should be noted that, for reasons of space, the specific provisions on listed buildings and conservation areas, the protection of trees via tree preservation orders, the system of consents for hazardous substances and various protective designations relating to the countryside are not covered in this chapter.

Pieces of planning law relevant to other chapters within Part II of the book are summarised at the appropriate places.

The main features of town and country planning

These are as follows:

(a)   The local planning authority draws up a development plan, which sets out the strategy for development in the area. This involves a measure of public participation. Development plans are permissive (i.e. they do not guarantee what is going to happen, but act as guides to future development) and must be taken into account in any decision.

(b) All 'development', which is widely construed and includes changes of use as well as physical development, requires planning permission from the local planning authority before it may be carried out.

(c) Procedures are laid down for applications for planning permission. These involve consultation with other public bodies and some limited public involvement.

(d) The local planning authority decides on grounds of planning policy whether to grant permission or refuse it, taking into account the development plans, Central Government policies and any other material considerations.

(e) Unlike most other systems of town planning, which rely heavily on zoning of areas within which certain generalised rules will apply, in this country each case must be considered on its merits.

(f) If permission is granted, it may be subject to conditions; indeed, this is the normal position. If permission is refused, no compensation is normally payable—the right to develop land was effectively nationalised in the Town and Country Planning Act 1947.

(g) The applicant has a right of appeal to the Secretary of State against any refusal or conditions. This is a complete rehearing of the whole matter, including the policy issues, and thus enables the Secretary of State to exercise a stranglehold on policy by having the final say on it.

(h) There is no right of appeal for third parties and no right to appeal against a grant of planning permission.

(i) There is a further right of appeal from the decision of the Secretary of State to the High Court on what are essentially the same grounds as for judicial review. The courts thus exercise a supervisory jurisdiction over the procedures and the decisions taken. However, the courts will not intervene on grounds of fact or policy.

(j) Enforcement of the law is through another discretionary procedure in which the local planning authority may serve an enforcement notice requiring specified steps to be taken. It is an offence to fail to comply with an enforcement notice. Once again, a right of appeal to the Secretary of State is provided and, as this may involve consideration of policy issues, it is in most cases deemed a retrospective application for planning permission.

(k) Planning permission effectively gives a right to develop. Unlike most systems of pollution control, there is no power to vary a planning permission in the future (unless compensation is paid).

Town and country planning as a tool of environmental policy

There are thus three main areas with relevance to environmental law:

(a) The system of development plans, which ensures that environmental protection is considered at the level of policy-making. These plans often set the basic ground rules for action on the environment in any particular area, although they must be read in conjunction with the policy guidance emanating from Central Government.

(b) The development control process, in which planning permission is required from the local planning authority for acts of development. This is a good example of a 'mixed economy' solution to environmental control (i.e. the initiative for development is normally taken by private developers, but permission to go ahead is required from a public authority). This ensures a strict anticipatory control over many activities before they start and normally involves liaison with the relevant pollution control and environmental agencies.

(c) The power to impose conditions relating to environmental protection on a grant of planning permission. These are capable of creating some form of continuing control over activities.

The traditional conflictual model of a regulatory body regulating the applicant by granting or refusing permission is currently breaking down. Modern town planning may be seen as a negotiative process in which consultation between the prospective developer and the local planning authority in advance of the application is the norm, and in which proposals are both made and considered in the light of local and national policies. The local planning authority and the developer often have a community of interest in carrying out a particular development; the developer gets its proposal granted and the local authority obtains the revitalisation of the economy of an area, or the creation of jobs, or some other economic benefit. (Indeed, developments by local authorities and developers in partnership with each other are now quite common.) In addition, agreements between developers and local authorities in which 'planning gain' is bargained for are increasingly used to supplement the regulatory controls (see p. 196).

It should also be borne in mind that the impact of planning control is in many ways incomplete or inadequate. Planning permission is not required for all environmentally harmful activities, for example for mobile pollutants such as cars, or in relation to most agricultural activities. There are difficulties where some form of continuing control is required, because of the limitations on planning conditions, or where positive management is required, since it is mainly a preventative system. The system also tends to get circumvented in various ways where nationally important development is desired by Central Government.

A further point is that the planning decision is a political one, and thus environmental issues may be subordinated to other needs. As the Royal Commission on Environmental Pollution commented in its Fifth Report in relation to pollution prevention, 'Our concern is not that pollution is not always given top priority; it is that it is often dealt with inadequately, and sometimes forgotten altogether in the planning process' (Cmnd. 6371, 1976).

Nevertheless, the planning system is of central importance in many areas of environmental law, especially when used in conjunction with other regulatory controls. This is seen clearly in relation to waste disposal, where planning permission for a waste disposal site is required before a waste disposal or waste management licence can be granted. In other areas, planning control is arguably of greatest importance where the enforcement of pollution control is inadequate, since non-enforcement at the operational end puts increased pressure on initial siting and design issues.

Town and country planning and some themes of this book

This brief summary of the town and country planning system shows how it illustrates a number of the major themes of this book. For instance, it is a good example of a sophisticated anticipatory regulatory mechanism and it emphasises prevention of harm. That also means that the predominant method of control is through negative, restrictive measures, rather than through positive mechanisms. Local decision-making dominates, although there has been an all too obvious shift of power towards Central Government in recent years (see p. 166). It is a highly discretionary system, in which decisions are made on a case-by-case basis and it is a democratic system in which ultimate political control rests with elected members rather than with officers (on appeal responsibility rests with an elected Secretary of State), although in practice most decisions are actually taken by officers. It is a fairly open and public system. Of course, this last point sets up one of the great conflicts of the system: the more open it is, the slower decisions tend to be.

Enforcement is under-emphasised, being almost exclusively the responsibility of the local planning authority and dependent on political and tactical factors.

But the most important point is that this is a highly political system of decision-making. Local planning authorities and the Secretary of State make discretionary decisions by balancing economic, political, environmental and social factors. It is therefore just as important to understand the prevailing policy in relation to a particular issue as it is to understand the relevant law.

The role of the law and the courts requires some explanation here. The planning system is one where the law exercises a supervisory, or review, function. It is there to define the various concepts used in the planning system (such as what development is, or what types of conditions are legitimate), to ensure that the correct procedures are used and to ensure that discretionary decisions are taken in the proper manner. The law is therefore ultimately about procedures, i.e. about ensuring that decisions are made correctly rather than that the correct decisions are made.

The planning legislation

As Lord Scarman stated in *Pioneer Aggregates (UK)* v *Secretary of State* [1984] 3 WLR 32, 'Planning control is the creature of Statute . . . . Parliament has provided a comprehensive code of planning control'. This comprehensive code was originally created in the Town and Country Planning Act 1947, when a uniform and mandatory country-wide system of development control was introduced. One of the most remarkable things about planning is that, whilst there have been numerous detailed additions and amendments to the law, the basic structure of much of this system (apart from that relating to development plans) has remained unchanged since then, although the way in which it is operated has in practice changed quite radically.

The legislation is now consolidated in the Town and Country Planning Act 1990, which came into force on 24 August 1990. Unless otherwise stated, wherever a section number is given in this chapter without reference to a particular Act, it refers to that Act.

However, the 1990 Act has already been amended by the Planning and Compensation Act 1991. The 1991 Act, which received the Royal Assent in July 1991, makes substantial alterations to the law, especially in relation to development plans (see p. 168), enforcement (see p. 200) and planning agreements (to be called 'planning obligations' in the future, see p. 196). But the greatest potential impact is on the crucial question of the relationship between development plans and other material considerations, particularly Central Government policy guidance (see p. 190). This is because of a remarkable last minute addition to the Act which imposes what appears to be a new, statutory presumption in favour of following the provisions of the development plan. The precise implications of this new presumption are unclear, but it is suggested that it marks an important shift in emphasis from 'developer-led' planning towards 'plan-led' planning.

At the time of writing, the Planning and Compensation Act 1991 awaits being brought into force by commencement order. This is expected to be a piecemeal process, with some provisions coming into force in September 1991, whilst others depend on the prior promulgation of subordinate legislation. This chapter will accordingly attempt the difficult task of explaining both the existing law and the new law, drawing attention to any significant changes.

It should also be noted that much of the detail of the law on town and country planning is in subordinate legislation. Of particular importance is the Town and Country Planning (General Development) Order 1988 (SI 1988 No. 1813), which fulfills two rather separate functions: it grants automatic planning permission for a large number of activities, and it provides many of the procedures relating to an application for permission. One effect of the Planning and Compensation Act 1991 is that the General Development Order will require substantial amendment.

What is town and country planning?

One respected town planner has described town planning simply as 'How much of what is put where'. This reflects the fact that planning is a *process* through which decisions are made, rather than anything with an absolutely definitive subject matter. As befits a political system, the question of what planning covers has over the years largely been left to those who make planning decisions. The result has been an expansion of the idea, beyond straightforward amenity, public health and land use issues towards taking into account the economic and social impact of decisions.

This widening of the scope of planning has received the support of the courts. In exercising their supervisory jurisdiction they have often had to ask the question 'What is planning?' in order to decide whether a power has been used legitimately. In so doing they have proved willing to decide that most things are within the scope of planning. The most commonly used legal test is given by Lord Scarman in *Great Portland Estates Ltd* v *Westminster CC* [1984] 3 All ER 744, who suggested that town planning covers anything that 'relates to the character of the use of land'.

However, this accommodating legal attitude is not shared by all and in recent years there have been fundamental divisions over the legitimate role and scope of planning. Until the 1970s, town and country planning was a relatively uncontroversial topic in party political terms, with the exception of the questions of compensation for refusal of permission and taxation of profits resulting from a grant of permission. There was a degree of consensus over what planning should consist of and over the preferred policies. This has now broken down, with the result that there is open conflict over both the proper role of planning and over the content of the policies that should be adopted.

Obviously there is universal agreement that planning includes land use and amenity issues, such as the location and design of new developments. The key question is how far socio-economic issues are a legitimate part of it. Some see planning as one means by which a particular form of social development may be produced. Others wish to see planning restricted as much as possible on the grounds that it interferes unduly with the free market. The second view is effectively the one that has been espoused by the current Government, with its firm beliefs in deregulation, a minimalist approach to restrictions on commercial activity, the power of the market as a distributor of resources, and the consequent need for speed and certainty in any system of control.

Planning policy

Notwithstanding the retention of the basic structure of the system outlined above, town planning has changed radically since the 1970s. Only some of these changes have been to the law. Most have been brought about by administrative means, particularly by the concerted application of strong Central Government policy. This was summarised by Grant in the first updating supplement to *Urban Planning Law* (1986) as follows:

> One of the most distinctive trends of the past five years has been the emergence of Government policy as a dominant force in development control. It has been brought about by a series of hard-hitting Circulars based on the Government's deregulatory and pro-development ideology, coupled to a new willingness to use the appeals process as a means of reinforcing the policies.

The pro-development ideology is arguably the most important aspect, as the Government has sought to increase the role of the free market in generating development. Landmarks in this regard have been the publication of Circular 22/80, with an overt encouragement of small businesses and private housing, and Circular 14/85 with its presumption in favour of development. Now reproduced in Planning Policy Guidance Note 1, paragraph 15, this states 'There is always a presumption in favour of allowing applications for development, having regard to all material considerations, unless that development would cause demonstrable harm to interests of acknowledged importance'. Circular

1/85 also plays an important role, emphasising that conditions should not be attached unless they can be justified on clear grounds. Their role has been described as 'anodyne expedients by which objections to offensive developments can be assuaged' (Miller & Wood, *Planning and Pollution*, 1983).

Not only are these Circulars pro-development in terms of policy, they afford such great weight to this that local planning authorities ignore them at their peril. The result is that in the 1980s these explicitly directory Circulars grew to have far greater importance than local policies such as development plans. As shown below, these were downgraded in importance in the 1980s, though they seem to be enjoying a resurgence at present (see p. 172). The reason for this is straightforward; in a developer-led system, developers value the certainty that is provided by a framework of clear policies, rather than the uncertainty provided by a wholly market-based approach.

The appeals process has been used to support this shift in power from local government to Central Government. Pearce in The Changing Role of Planning Appeals (*Development and Planning*, Ed. Cross and Whitehead, 1989) shows some dramatic changes here. In the early to mid-1970s the success rate of appeals against refusal of permission was in the region of 20%. This had grown to 32% by 1984 and 40% in 1986/7, at which level it has stayed. Not surprisingly, the number of appeals also rose sharply, from around 8,000 in the mid-1970s to almost 30,000 each year at present. This means that a quarter of all refusals are appealed. A similar story is apparent in relation to appeals against enforcement notices.

In keeping with the policy of doctrinal neutrality on the content of planning policies, the courts have not interfered with these changes, except to preserve the rationality of the decision-making process by insisting that adequate reasons are given for decisions. In this respect it should be recognised that the planning system has always been pro-development to some extent. This stems from the prominence of property-based ideas within it and is evident in its very structure. For example, third parties and objectors are not given particularly wide rights within the system. Specifically, there is a right to appeal against the refusal of permission, but no right to appeal against a grant of permission (as there is in many other countries, such as Eire). The result is that permission will be granted if *either* the local planning authority or the Secretary of State is in favour of it.

There has also always been some sort of presumption in favour of granting permission; the difference is that this has changed in substance from the basic public law requirement that reasons be given for a decision affecting someone's right to develop to a *policy* in favour of development that may have a great weight attached to it by the decision-maker (see p. 190 for a discussion of the court's attitude to the presumption in favour of development). Similarly there have always been restrictions on the scope of conditions, with the courts adopting the attitude that conditions that take away private property rights without compensation are *ultra vires* (see p. 193). Finally, the statistics on planning permission show that, of the current 500,000 applications made each year, 80% are granted (September 1990 quarter), a figure which is, if anything, lower than previous years (e.g. it was 86% in 1978/79 before the changes of the 1980s were introduced).

Deregulation

A separate, though related, strand of the changes in the 1980s has been the theme of deregulation. This is well illustrated by the titles of three White Papers setting out Government policy—*Lifting the Burden* (Cmnd. 9571, 1985), *Building Businesses, Not Barriers* (Cmnd. 9794, 1986) and *Releasing Enterprise* (Cm. 512). A major emphasis has been the reduction of red tape and delays. Significant relaxations were made in the General Development Order in 1981, 1985 and 1988 and in the Use Classes Order in 1987 so as to cut out the need for planning permission in many situations, with the objective of encouraging the development of small businesses. Along with the other changes to development plans referred to at p. 173, the procedures for development plans were streamlined, so that they may be adopted more quickly, leading to a consequent reduction in public opportunities for participation in the process. Regular encouragement has been given by Circulars to speed up the process of dealing with planning applications. The politically suspect metropolitan county councils were abolished in the Local Government Act 1985, and this led to the introduction of a new system of unitary development plans in those areas.

The uniformity of the system has also been altered. Enterprise zones were introduced in the Local Government, Planning and Land Act 1980 and simplified planning zones in the Housing and Planning Act 1986. Both mechanisms operate so as to remove most or all planning controls in designated areas, though designation and the controls that are retained remain with the local authority. In contrast, urban development areas, also introduced in the Local Government, Planning and Land Act 1980, are designated (or imposed) solely by the Secretary of State and are put under the management of centrally appointed urban development corporations, with local planning authorities losing all their powers (see p. 186). A final point worth mentioning is that an increasing number of environmentally significant developments avoid the planning system entirely by using the more limited Private Bill procedures.

A change of direction?
In summary it can be said that in the 1980s the planning system became far more centralised. This was true in two senses: more decisions were taken at a central level and central policy pervaded every decision even at a local level. One effect was to shift power from local government to Central Government; another to increase the areas of conflict between the two levels. But, interestingly, at the same time the system has become in a way less centralised. This is because the changes in policy were designed to increase the role of the market at the expense of the State, and to make the system more developer-led.

However, it is becoming clear that in the 1990s these trends are slowly being reversed as the Government steers a slightly different course to that charted in the 1980s. There are signs that greater regard is being paid to local decisions (as represented by development plans) and this impression of a shift in the balance between Central Government and local government is reinforced by the new presumption in favour of following the development plan mentioned above (see p. 163).

Local planning authorities

Initial responsibility for most planning decisions rests with local authorities, which in this context are generically called local planning authorities. In metropolitan areas all planning functions are carried out by the metropolitan district council. In non-metropolitan areas planning functions are split between county and district councils by Schedule 1.

County councils (called county planning authorities) are responsible for:

(a)   structure plans;
(b)   local plans relating to certain county subjects, such as minerals planning and waste disposal;
(c)   county matters in development control (including minerals developments and any related works or buildings, waste disposal applications, and applications relating to land in National Parks);
(d)   certain development control decisions where they are able to grant themselves planning permission;
(e)   county councils are also consulted by the district planning authority over certain large-scale developments, principally those which affect the structure plan or county matters, but also highway matters in their capacity as highways authorities.

District councils (called district planning authorities) are responsible for all other local plans and for *all* development control decisions, *except* those relating to county matters.

There are a number of special areas where different rules apply:

(a)   In National Parks, all planning decisions are taken by the National Park Authority, which will either be a joint board established for that purpose (this is the case in the Peak District and Lake District), or a committee of the county council. In each case the board or committee consists of representatives of the county and district councils within the National Park, with one third of the members appointed directly by the Secretary of State.
(b)   In the Broads, the similarly constituted Broads Authority takes all decisions (Norfolk and Suffolk Broads Act 1988).
(c)   In urban development areas the urban development corporation normally becomes the local planning authority. This was also the case with new town development corporations, but these have now virtually been phased out. (In enterprise zones and simplified planning zones the local planning authority stays the same).

Forward planning: development plans

Local planning authorities are responsible for producing development plans on a continuing basis, which then guide or influence development in the areas covered. In this country, all development plans are permissive, i.e. they lay down policies, aims, objectives and goals rather than state what is definitely going to happen in an area. They have no immediate effect other than as a statement of what the local planning authority considers is desirable. But they do have a great and growing importance in the decision whether or not to grant planning permission (see p. 190).

There is *no* national plan. The nearest equivalent is the Central Government policy set out in Planning Policy Guidance Notes and Government Circulars. There are also no formal regional plans, although groupings of local planning authorities do produce general regional strategies, and there is formal regional planning guidance issued by Central Government, often based on advice from these regional groupings.

For most areas the existing system is to have two tiers of plan—structure plans and local plans, collectively referred to as the development plan. However, in metropolitan areas, unitary development plans are taking over this function. They were first required by the Local Government Act 1985 (a consequence of the abolition of the metropolitan county councils), and though they are still in the course of being made, will replace structure plans and local plans in those areas in the next few years. In National Parks, there are separate plans (currently management plans rather than solely land use plans), which must also be considered in relation to any developments in a National Park.

The Planning and Compensation Act 1991 and development plans

The Planning and Compensation Act 1991 has made a number of significant changes to the law on development plans. The provisions have not yet come into force and require subordinate legislation before they do so. Accordingly, this section of the chapter on development plans is written on the basis of the old law, with summaries of the provisions of the Planning and Compensation Act 1991 at the relevant places. In this way a historical background can be provided in relation to the shape of existing plans, whilst still giving an understanding of how plans will be made in the future.

Structure plans
A structure plan is a statement of general strategic policies, usually for the area of a county, set out in the form of a written statement supplemented by representative diagrams and a written memorandum (which is not a formal part of the plan). It will contain major strategic policies, especially on house-building targets, industrial and retail location and transportation matters, and will be relevant to the process of filling out these policies in the local plan and to major development control decisions.

There is a specific duty to include 'measures for the improvement of the physical environment' and many structure plans now include policies on such things as air pollution. These will set out general objectives for the area and act as a framework for land use decisions (see Wood, *Planning Pollution Prevention*, 1989, Ch.5). On the other hand, the Royal Society for the Protection of Birds has published a report critical of the generally inadequate treatment of nature conservation in structure plans (*RSPB Planscan*, 1990).

All areas now have a structure plan, so consideration of the detailed procedures for making one is unnecessary. They are set out in ss. 31–35 and the Town and Country Planning (Structure and Local Plans) Regulations 1982 (SI 1982 No. 555) which allow for limited public involvement as follows. The county planning authority produces and publicises reasoned proposals and allows at least six weeks for representations. The final proposals are sent to the Secretary of State and put on public display. At least a further six weeks are allowed for objections to be sent to the Secretary of State, who may then hold an examination in public (a limited form of public inquiry at which there is no right to present a case unless invited to do so).

The key point is that a structure plan requires the approval of the Secretary of State, who can approve, amend, reject, or return it for re-submission, giving brief reasons for the decision. This requirement means that the Secretary of State has the final say on the scope and content of the plan and its policies, and this power has often been used to ensure that policies acceptable to Central Government are adopted rather than those originally proposed by the local planning authority.

There is no set time scale for the modification of a structure plan. However, there is a continuing duty for a county planning authority to keep under review matters affecting the development and planning of their area, and a 15 year planning horizon is envisaged by Planning Policy Guidance Note 15. Modifications may be proposed by the county planning authority or directed by the Secretary of State and must go through similar procedures to the original structure plan, except that an examination in public can be dispensed with for modifications (which happens in over half the cases).

A challenge to a structure plan or its modifications can be made within six weeks of the decision under s. 287 but, given the Secretary of State's wide and subjective powers of approval and alteration, unless the decision is perverse, totally unreasoned or internally contradictory, a successful challenge is most unlikely (see *E. Bradley & Sons* v *Secretary of State for the Environment* [1983] 47 P&CR 375).

As stated above, the nature of structure plans is changing. The Planning and Compensation Act 1991 replaces ss. 31–35 with new ss. 31–35C. These redefine the nature of structure plans, though the precise way in which this will be done will be provided for in regulations. Planning Policy Guidance Note 15 sets out the general policy, which is to restrict the scope of structure plans to topics undeniably connected with land use. County planning authorities are encouraged to prepare revised structure plans on a county-wide basis, which should be in conformity with the regional planning guidance produced by the Secretary of State. In addition they should concentrate on the key structure plan topics listed, i.e. new houses, green belts, the rural economy, major employment-generating development, strategic transport issues, minerals matters, waste disposal, land reclamation, tourism, leisure and recreation. The impact of the proposals on the environment should also be covered: indeed the specific duty to include measures for the improvement of the physical environment is retained in s. 31.

The 1991 Act also streamlines the procedures for the modification of structure plans by removing one of the stages at which representations may be made. In addition, the requirement for the Secretary of State to approve them is removed, though there remains a power to call them in and the examination in public procedure also remains.

Local plans

Local plans are more detailed, consisting of written policies and specific land use allocations, so their relevance to individual development control decisions is much greater. There are three types of local plan:

(a)   district plans, including proposals for regulatory controls within a defined area; the district planning authority makes these;

(b)   subject plans, covering proposals for particularly sensitive subjects in an area (e.g. green belt, minerals development, tourism); either county planning authorities or district planning authorities may make these;

(c)   action area plans, dealing with proposals for the comprehensive redevelopment of small areas.

In addition, urban development areas and the few remaining new towns may have their own plans; automatic planning permission is granted by Special Development Order for the matters in such a plan.

There is no duty to include environmental measures in a local plan. Under s. 36(1), the local planning authority is given a discretion to do so, and policies vary from the detailed to the non-existent. It seems that no subject plan directly concerned with pollution control or nature conservation has yet been made, though Humberside CC has an Intensive Livestock Units Subject Plan.

Each local planning authority is required to maintain a public register of all plans in operation in its area and to have copies available for public inspection and purchase (Town and Country Planning (Structure and Local Plans) Regulations 1982 (SI 1982 No. 555)).

Despite their importance for development control, until the passage of the Planning and Compensation Act 1991 there was no requirement for everywhere to have a local plan, and less than half the country currently has one. According to the White Paper, *This Common Inheritance* (Cm. 1200, 1990), 55 of the 333 district planning authorities have no local plan at all. One reason for this is undoubtedly that the making of local plans was actively discouraged by the Government throughout the 1980s, both in Circular guidance (e.g. Circular 22/84) and through the appeals system. However, there has been a distinct U-turn in policy on this point and the making of local plans has been encouraged in the 1990s. Many are in the course of being made, and they become mandatory for the whole country under the Planning and Compensation Act 1991, sch. 4.

The procedures for making a local plan are set out in ss. 36–52. They provide for greater individual involvement than structure plans and hence lead to an increased possibility of a successful legal challenge.

(a) The local planning authority publishes proposals and invites and considers representations. It then puts a draft on public display and invites formal objections, allowing at least six weeks for these to be made (s. 39).

(b) If an objection is made and not withdrawn, the local planning authority must hold a public local inquiry before an inspector. Objectors must be given at least six weeks notice and have a right to appear at the inquiry (s. 42).

(c) The local planning authority must consider the inspector's recommendations and can adopt the local plan formally by resolution (s. 43). The Secretary of State's approval is not required, unless the right to call in the local plan for approval is exercised—a very rare occurrence (ss. 44 and 45).

Modifications to a local plan go through the same procedure, except that there is an expedited procedure under s. 40 where 'it appears to [the local planning authority] that the issues involved are not of sufficient importance to warrant the full procedure'. This expedited procedure requires only that there is publicity of the proposed change and an opportunity provided for representations to be made.

The local plan is required to be in 'general conformity' with the structure plan (s. 46). However, if there is a conflict between the local plan and the structure plan, it is the local plan which prevails, unless the structure plan specifically lists the local plan as not conforming with it (s. 48). Local plans may be challenged within six weeks of their adoption (s. 287).

The Planning and Compensation Act 1991 remodels much of ss. 36–52. Apart from the requirement that local plans become mandatory, the main changes are that the procedures for making a local plan are streamlined (making the existing expedited procedures unnecessary) and that the process for deciding whether a local plan is in general conformity with the structure plan is altered, further reducing the power of the county planning authority. The existing discretion to include measures for the improvement of the physical environment is converted into a duty.

Unitary development plans

The Local Government Act 1985 introduced unitary development plans to replace structure and local plans in metropolitan areas. This is being done gradually; no unitary development plan has yet been made, but all metropolitan authorities have now been directed to start the procedures for making one. Existing plans remain in force until the Secretary of State brings the new plan into force and existing local plans may be incorporated into it.

The unitary development plan will consist of two parts: Part I will in general correspond to the structure plan and Part II to the local plan. The procedures for them are set out in ss. 12–28. Essentially they allow for a mixture of the current procedures used for structure plans and local plans, combining central supervision over strategic and regional matters with a commitment to some public involvement in more detailed matters. There is a provision for all or part of the plan to be called in for central approval, though it is not expected that this will be usual, even for Part I. The Planning and Compensation Act 1991, sch. 4, redrafts and streamlines the procedures for unitary development plans in a similar fashion to those for structure and local plans. In addition, it imposes a duty to include environmental matters in both Parts I and II, not just in Part I as at present.

Development plans and development control

Statutory plans *must* be taken into account in any development control decision. Section 70(2) states that, when making a decision whether to grant planning permission, the local planning authority 'shall have regard to the provisions of the development plan, so far as material to the application, and to any other material considerations'.

This important issue will be covered at p. 188, but it should be noted that, after a period in the 1980s in which it appeared that plans were being downgraded in importance compared to Central Government policy, the Government is now placing increasing emphasis on development plans as the framework within which individual planning decisions should be considered. A particular consideration is the need to provide certain guidance for developers on future policy, since, in a developer-led system, developers value clear policies, as opposed to the uncertainty provided by a wholly market-based approach. To illustrate this, Planning Policy Guidance Note 15 states, 'Where there are clear, up-to-date, policies in the Development Plan which are relevant to the proposal under consideration and are consistent with national and regional policies, they will carry considerable weight'. This is reinforced by the new s. 54A, added by the Planning and Compensation Act 1991, s. 26, which states:

> where, in making any determination under the planning Acts, regard is to be had to the development plan, the determination shall be made in accordance with the development plan unless material considerations indicate otherwise.

Non-statutory plans and guidance

Local planning authorities frequently have other policies and drafts that have not gone through the statutory procedures. In practice, a large range of such 'non-statutory' material, ranging from draft local plans to design briefs and technical specifications, is used by local planning authorities in making decisions. But there are obvious problems in this practice, because it may be seen as subverting the statutory public participation requirements, and thus the democratic legitimacy of the planning process.

In *Great Portland Estates Ltd* v *Westminster CC* [1984] 3 All ER 744, a distinction was drawn between different types of non-statutory guidance. It requires that all matters of *policy* should be included in the statutory plan and that only supplementary matters of detail, or those which relate to the implementation of these policies, should be put in non-statutory guidance. However, as long as this non-statutory material is not illegal (i.e. it must relate to the character of the use of land), it is a material consideration under s. 70(2) and must be considered alongside the statutory development plan, although perhaps not always accorded the same weight. The weight attached to it will depend on the circumstances in which it was produced.

The history and future of development plans

The system of development plans has been one area within planning law where there seems to have been a constant state of change. The original development plans established under the 1947 Act were basically detailed, spatial, land use maps, drawn up by local authorities for all areas, but requiring Central Government approval. Delay was endemic both in making the plans and keeping them up-to-date, and public involvement was not properly catered for, with the result that the current two-tier system was introduced in the Town and Country Planning Act 1968. Increased public participation rights were engrafted in the Town and Country Planning Act 1971.

Before these plans had much of a chance to prove themselves, they became unpopular with a Government unconvinced by the need for strong forward planning and antipathetic to the power of local authorities. Structure plans in particular were downgraded by comparison with local plans by the Local Government, Planning and Land Act 1980 and plans of all types were accorded ever-decreasing weight in decisions compared to Central Government policies. Numerous proposals for reform were produced; the major themes of which were the need for plans to be restricted to land use matters, for less detail to be included in them, and for procedures to be speeded up.

The White Paper *The Future of Development Plans* (Cm.569, Jan. 1989) proposed the replacement of structure plans and local plans with a system that was clearer, quicker, and more responsive to changes in policy and which covered a smaller number of less detailed matters. Structure plans were to be replaced by statements of county planning policies, covering a more restricted range of subjects and not requiring approval by the Secretary of State. They would have to conform to regional planning guidance. Local plans were to be replaced by district development plans, which were to be similar to existing local plans, but less detailed. Procedures for both new mechanisms were to be quicker than for existing plans.

It is a sign of a possible new era in planning control that these proposals have now been dropped, and that instead the changes in the Planning and Compensation Act 1991 have been enacted. At the risk of repeating what has already been stated, these are as follows. Schedule 4 remodels much of Part II of the Town and Country Planning Act 1990. Structure plans are retained, although they will cover a more restricted range of topics than before, which are to be set out in regulations. The requirement that the Secretary of State approves structure plan modifications is removed, although there remains a power to call them in and the examination in public procedure remains. District-wide local plans are to become mandatory, with the Secretary of State having wide powers to direct the timetable for their being drawn up. Development plans for the area of a National Park are also to be mandatory. The county planning authority will be under a duty to draw up a local minerals plan and a waste local plan. This latter plan will contain waste policies and will complement the waste disposal plan required by the Environmental Protection Act 1990, s. 50, which has limited public involvement. There is clearly going to be a great deal of plan-making activity in the near future. In relation to all these types of plan (and also the unitary development plans) the procedures are streamlined, though the main elements of public participation and consultation are retained.

Development control: definition of development

It is in relation to the system of development control that the town and country planning system has its greatest impact on environmental law. Planning permission is required for the carrying out of any development (s. 57(1)). The general approach has been to define development very widely so that virtually everything is included initially, and then to exempt by reference to well-defined categories. This has the effect of shifting the focus in most practical situations from what is included to what is excluded (see the Use Classes Order and the General Development Order in particular).

Development is defined in s. 55(1), which provides:

Development . . . . means the carrying out of building, engineering, mining or other operations in, on, over or under land, or the making of any material change in the use of any buildings or other land.

This definition has effectively remained unchanged since 1947, so past decisions of the courts, which are the ultimate interpreters of the meaning of the Act, are relevant. Decisions of the Secretary of State on appeal are also of importance in understanding the definition, although these are not binding as legal authority.

The courts have decided that the existence of development is a question of 'fact and degree' in each particular case. It is for the local planning authority (or the Secretary of State on appeal) to apply the relevant law to the facts of each case to decide whether there has been development. The courts limit themselves to supervising and reviewing these decisions, i.e. a decision by a local planning authority that a particular state of affairs amounts to development will only be overturned by the courts if the authority has used an incorrect test, or the correct test incorrectly, or has reached a perverse decision.

There are two limbs to the definition—operational development and change of use development. It is important to make this distinction because:

(a)   enforcement action can only be taken against development that has taken place;
(b)   an enforcement notice should specify which limb of development has taken place;

(c)   the limitation period for serving an enforcement notice is different for the two categories (four years and ten years respectively).

There are four types of operational development:

(a)   building operations;
(b)   engineering operations;
(c)   mining operations; and
(d)   other operations.

Building operations

These are defined very widely in s. 336. 'Building' 'includes any structure or erection, and any part of a building, as so defined, but does not include plant or machinery comprised in a building'. 'Building operations' include rebuilding operations, structural alterations of or additions to buildings, and other operations normally undertaken by a person carrying on business as a builder.

Any significant works are included, such as rebuilding works, works of alteration, the building of an extension, and the erection of such things as shop canopies, window grilles, shutters, walls, flagpoles, fences, advertising hoardings, large sculptures, street furniture and many other things. In one celebrated example, the erection of a model shark emerging from the roof of a house was held to amount to a building operation. It is normally considered that very minor alterations, such as the installation of ordinary TV aerials, are not significant enough to amount to development.

Exceptions include:

(a)   Maintenance, improvement or alterations to a building affecting only its interior, or not materially affecting the external appearance, are not development (s. 55(2)(a)).

(b)   Large numbers of minor and public operations are exempted from the need for planning permission by the General Development Order (see p. 180).

(c)   Moveable structures (e.g. caravans) are not normally buildings, unless attached to the land or made permanent in some way (see *Barvis* v *SSE* [1971] 22 P&CR 710).

Demolition raises some interesting points. Until recently the predominant view was that simple demolition of a building was not development, unless it involved such a large amount of removal of materials that it constituted an engineering operation (*Coleshill Investments* v *MHLG* [1969] 2 All ER 525). However, in *Cambridge CC* v *Secretary of State* [1991] JPL 428, David Widdicombe QC decided in the High Court that demolition of part of a building by the removal of roofing materials prior to total demolition, so that the land could be landscaped and turned into a car park, was operational development. He stated that these activities were part of the overall operational development of constructing a car park and thus constituted development requiring planning permission. This decision left open the question whether a simple act of demolition which is not preparatory to any further development amounted to development; it has always been thought that the difficulties of enforcement demand that it should not be.

Nevertheless, the Government has now amended s. 55 in the Planning and Compensation Act 1991, s. 13, so that demolition is included within the definition of building operations. However, the effect of this is mitigated by a new s. 55(2)(g), which excludes from control any description of building specified by the Secretary of State. The intention is to exclude all buildings other than houses. Even then, it is further intended to grant automatic permission in the General Development Order for most houses, perhaps leaving only the demolition of terraced and semi-detached houses subject to planning control. Exactly how these extremely complex provisions will work in practice remains to be seen. Whatever the situation for ordinary buildings or structures, demolition of a listed building or of any building in a conservation area is subject to control (see Planning (Listed Buildings and Conservation Areas) Act 1990).

Engineering operations
These include road building, laying out of access to roads, drainage works, land reclamation, and earthmoving works. There are many exceptions for public works in s. 55 and the General Development Order.

Mining operations
These include all forms of extractive operation, such as mining, quarrying and the removal of materials from mineral deposits and waste tips. There are additional powers over minerals development. County planning authorities are designated mineral planning authorities and given wide powers to review operations and to impose conditions relating to aftercare, restoration of sites and discontinuance of activities.

Other operations
This is a little discussed catch-all category. It appears designed to ensure that matters such as waste disposal and drilling are covered.

An operation has commenced as soon as it has an impact on the land. This includes digging trenches and laying out the lines of roads (s. 56 and *Malvern Hills DC* v *Secretary of State* [1983] 81 LGR 13). The time of commencement is important because every planning permission contains a condition requiring commencement of the work within a stated time, otherwise the permission lapses. If no time is stipulated by the local planning authority, the period is five years from the grant of permission (s. 91). It should also be noted that enforcement action must wait until commencement of the operation (hence the importance of *Cambridge CC* v *Secretary of State* in deciding that partial demolition is development), but that the four-year limitation period for serving enforcement notices commences at the substantial completion of the operation.

Material change of use

The power to control changes in the use of land is virtually unique to British town and country planning, and makes it peculiarly able to exercise detailed control over land use. In the debates on the 1947 Act, Lord Reid, then a Conservative MP but later a Law Lord, is reported to have said of material change of use 'Nobody knows what that means'. Very little guidance is given in the Act on the meaning of this rather vague phrase, but over the years the judges have filled in any gaps by the creation of a number of important explanatory concepts. Nevertheless, this remains a somewhat flexible phrase, and flexibility is aided by the fact that the decision whether development has taken place in any particular case is a matter for the local planning authority, applying the law to the facts.

It is the *change* that is development, not the use itself. Accordingly, a use which has been carried on since before 1948 cannot be the subject of control. The change must be *material* in the sense that it has:

(a)   a physical impact on the land;
(b)   a substantial impact; and
(c)   an impact that is relevant to town and country planning.

For example, in *Snook* v *Secretary of State* [1977] 33 P&CR 1, a change from builder's storeyard to demolition person's storeyard was held not to be a material change because the change in nature did not have planning effects.

Some uses are *ancillary* or *incidental* to the main use of a property, such as keeping pets in a house. They are ignored for planning purposes. However, if the ancillary use extends beyond a normal degree, as it may do if extensive breeding of dogs takes place, it cannot be ignored and a change has occurred. There are then two *concurrent* uses (residential and dog breeding). In *Wallington* v *Secretary of State* [1990] JPL 112, a material change of use was found where 41 dogs were kept in a dwelling house and an enforcement notice limiting the number to six on noise grounds was upheld. Similarly, a factory will be treated as one use of a site, even though a number of different activities, such as manufacturing, storage, offices and distribution, are carried on.

The unit of land to be considered when ascertaining whether there has been a change of use is called the *planning unit*. This is normally the unit of occupation prior to the change and it is unusual to aggregate together more than one unit of occupation, or to subdivide one, unless 'two or more physically distinct areas are occupied for substantially different and unrelated purposes' (see *Burdle* v *Secretary of State* [1972] 3 All ER 240). Thus a factory is normally treated as one unit, allowing some internal shifting of activities between manufacturing, storage, office space and car parking. Two factories on separate sites in the same ownership would be treated as two units.

Intensification of an existing use of a site often causes problems. It is not development unless it results in the use becoming different in character or concept. For example, the *Wallington* case illustrates a change in character, whilst a factory which doubles its output, or begins 24 hour working, would not require planning permission.

Certain matters are stated in the Act to be material changes. These are: splitting a single dwelling-house into separate dwellings (s. 55(3)(a)); the deposit of waste (s. 55(3)(b)); and the display of adverts (s. 55(5)). Conversely, certain matters are stated *not* to be material changes, though in some cases the application of the judicially invented tests would have reached the same conclusions. These include (s. 55(2)(d) and (e)):

(d)   the use of any buildings or other land within the curtilage of a dwelling-house for any purpose incidental to the enjoyment of the dwellinghouse as such;

(e)   the use of any land for the purpose of agriculture or forestry (including afforestation) and the use for any of those purposes of any building occupied together with land so used.

Use Classes Order

Any change within one of the 16 Classes set out in the Schedule to the Town and Country Planning (Use Classes) Order 1987 (SI 1987 No. 764) is not development, thus removing planning barriers that might obstruct a change from one use to another with a similar environmental impact. It is significantly more liberal than previous Orders, part of the deregulatory strategy pursued by the Government in the 1980s aimed at encouraging changes in business structure. It should also be noted that the General Development Order (see p. 180) grants automatic permission for certain innocuous changes in Part 3 of Schedule 2.

It is not possible in a book of this kind to explain all 16 Classes, but some of them are very wide. For example, Class A1 includes most shops, Class A2 all shop-front financial and professional services where the services are provided principally to visiting members of the public, and Class A3 most food and drink premises. Class B1—the general business class—is very important, since it includes both use as offices and use for any industrial process which can be carried out in a residential area without significant detriment to its environmental amenity. Special industrial uses, which include most uses which will have major environmental effects on the locality, are listed in Classes B3–B7, although it is proposed to remove these Classes, with the effect that a change to such uses would always require planning permission. Class B2 is a general industrial Class, including all industrial uses not in the other Classes, and permits a large range of industrial changes.

In line with general principle, ancillary and incidental uses are ignored for the purposes of the Order. In addition, a subdivision of a unit (other than a dwelling-house) into two or more units all within the same Class (such as subdivision of a factory unit) is not development. However, it is possible for a planning permission to contain a condition restricting the future operation of the Use Classes Order in relation to that site (*City of London Corpn* v *Secretary of State* [1971] 23 P&CR 169), although this type of condition is not favoured by the Government (see Circular 13/87).

Many unusual uses will not be in any Class, and neither are concurrent uses where the components are in different Classes. The following uses are specifically stated *not* to be in any Class—theatres, amusement arcades, funfairs, launderettes, petrol stations, taxi businesses, car-hire businesses, scrapyards, mineral storeyards, car-breaking yards, and uses involving a notifiable quantity of a hazardous substance—so a change to these uses always requires planning permission.

In addition to the exemptions provided by the Use Classes Order, certain changes of use in breach of the law are immune from enforcement action. Prior to the passage of the Planning and Compensation Act 1991 these were changes that took place before 1 January 1964; under the 1991 Act immunity is conferred ten years after any breach occurred. It should also be noted that s. 57 states that the resumption of a previous, lawful use after a temporary planning permission has expired, or after the service of an enforcement notice, does not require planning permission. The Planning and Compensation Act 1991 makes it clear, in a new s. 191(2), that a use which is immune from enforcement is a lawful use for these purposes, thus reversing the House of Lords decision in *Young* v *Secretary of State* [1983] 47 P & CR 165.

Existing uses

Normally there is a right to carry on the existing use of a site, unless it is in breach of planning control. This is roughly equivalent to a property right attaching to the land and has a distinct value. Obviously, when the occupier of land voluntarily changes the use, the existing use right switches from the old to the new use.

Existing use rights have been described as 'hardy beasts with a great capacity for survival' (Lord Scarman in *Pioneer Aggregates* v *Secretary of State* [1984] 3 WLR 32), but they may be abandoned by a lengthy period of disuse (*Hartley* v *MHLG* [1970] 1 QB 413). It is also possible to lose the benefit of the existing use of a site by carrying out works or changes which effect a *radical change* to the site (*Jennings Motors* v *Secretary of State* [1982] 1 All ER 471). This applies whether planning permission is obtained or not. If there is a planning permission, any limitations in it will be operative; if there is no permission, then *any* use of the site will be in breach of planning control. Otherwise an existing use right can only be removed by a discontinuance order (s. 102), or an order revoking planning permission (ss. 97–100). In both cases compensation is payable.

It is not possible to abandon a planning permission, since it is a public right attaching to the land not the occupier. This is illustrated by *Pioneer Aggregates* v *Secretary of State* [1984] 3 WLR 32, where a perpetual permission for quarrying was granted in 1950. Quarrying ceased in 1966 and, when it was recommenced in 1980, the local planning authority argued that the use had been abandoned. The House of Lords decided that the planning permission still applied to permit quarrying and any removal of that right would entail payment of compensation.

This position distinguishes planning control from most other areas of environmental control. There is no ability to vary a planning permission once it has been granted, even where circumstances have changed radically in a way that was not foreseen at the time the permission was granted. This emphasises that a grant of planning permission is an irrevocable event, effectively creating rights for the landowner in a way that a consent from a pollution control agency does not.

General Development Order

The Town and Country Planning (General Development) Order 1988 (SI 1988 No. 1813) grants automatic planning permission for 28 classes of development, listed and defined in Schedule 2. Once again, there has been some relaxation in the 1980s in order to remove what were seen as unnecessary restrictions on development.

Three general types of activity are exempted from control in this way:

(a) minor developments;
(b) developments carried out by a whole range of public services; and
(c) favoured activities, especially agriculture and forestry.

There are some general restrictions in the Order. An application must always be made for development involving a notifiable quantity of specified hazardous substances (or a threefold increase of these substances), or for developments involving the formation or widening of an access to a trunk or classified road. Automatic rights may also be restricted by a condition imposed on an earlier grant of planning permission (*City of London Corpn* v *Secretary of State* [1971] 23 P&CR 169).

Under Article 4 of the Order, a local planning authority may restrict automatic rights by serving a direction withdrawing the automatic planning permission, in which case permission must be sought in the ordinary way. The direction may be general to a type of development or specific to a site. Directions under Article 4 normally require the approval of the Secretary of State, must be made before the development is started and involve the payment of compensation to owners and occupiers, because they amount effectively to the taking away of a right to develop.

Certain automatic rights are more restricted in National Parks, Areas of Outstanding Natural Beauty and conservation areas (e.g. on extensions to buildings).

It is not possible in a book of this kind to explain all 28 Parts to Schedule 2, but the following explanation gives a flavour of the wide range of matters that are covered. For example, Part 1 covers 'the enlargement, improvement or other alteration of a dwelling-house', subject to very technical limitations on the size, height, forwardmost projection, proximity to a boundary and total coverage of the curtilage. These rights only apply to dwellings, not to offices, and there are further provisions relating to ancillary buildings and developments, such as porches, sheds, garages, animal shelters, stables, swimming pools, oil tanks, hardstanding for cars, and satellite antennae. The limitations have been altered many times, most recently in the 1980s in an attempt to reduce the number of trivial applications. Part 8 covers 'the extension or alteration of an industrial building or a warehouse', again with size, height and other limitations relating to loss of parking and external appearance of the site. Part 4 permits temporary buildings and works, and temporary uses of any type (apart from caravan sites) for up to 28 days in one year (except markets and motor racing, where 14 days only are allowed). Part 6 permits most agricultural operations on agricultural land and Part 7 most forestry operations, both with generous size and height limits, although in National Parks and other designated areas (mainly adjoining National Parks) local planning authorities are given extra powers over the siting and design of otherwise exempted agricultural and forestry buildings. It is proposed to extend these powers to the whole country.

The remaining Parts include a wide range of works carried out by public bodies, many of which will have potentially large environmental effects. They include repairs to services, developments by drainage authorities, many developments on operational land by statutory undertakers (e.g. in connection with railways, waterways, harbours, water, gas, electricity, lighthouses and the Post Office), and ancillary mining activities at existing mines.

Is planning permission required?

The procedure for ascertaining whether planning permission is required is another area where the Planning and Compensation Act 1991 has altered the law, although in many respects the new procedures are likely to be simpler than the old ones. Under s. 64 a developer could apply to the district planning authority for a determination whether permission was required. County matters were passed to the county planning authority. The application had to be made before the development had taken place and could not relate to a hypothetical situation. The application had to be in writing and state the nature of the proposal. No fee was payable and no publicity to third parties required. Every application for planning permission was treated as an implicit application under s. 64 (*Wells* v *Minister of Housing and Local Government* [1967] 1 WLR 1000). Thereafter the procedure was similar to that for an application for planning permission, i.e. the local planning authority had eight weeks to reach a decision, the applicant could appeal to the Secretary of State against an adverse decision, or a failure to decide within eight weeks, and the decision had to be registered on the public register.

Section 64 has now been repealed. Under the Planning and Compensation Act 1991, a new s. 192 provides for a certificate of lawfulness of proposed use or development. Any person may apply to the district planning authority for one, and it must be granted if the authority is satisfied that the use or operation would be lawful if subsisting or carried out at the time of the application. The exact procedures for applying for such a certificate, or for the related certificate of lawfulness of existing use or development, will be provided for in a redrafted General Development Order.

Applying for planning permission

Anyone can apply for planning permission. It is not necessary to be the owner or occupier of the property, or even a prospective occupier. An application may even be used as a form of publicity stunt. For example, Friends of the Earth once submitted an application for an oversize replica of the Leaning Tower of Pisa in order to draw attention to the inadequacy of the UK Atomic Energy Authority's application for a nuclear reprocessing plant at Dounreay.

There are several types of permission the applicant may seek:

(a)   Full permission.

(b)   Retrospective permission (allowed under s. 63(2)).

(c)   An application for the renewal of a planning permission.

(d)   Outline permission (see s. 92 and General Development Order, Art. 7). This can be sought for building operations only. Matters of 'siting, design, external appearance, means of access, landscaping of the site' (reserved matters) need not be submitted. Subsequent approval of these is needed within three years of the permission, or any other period stipulated by the local planning authority (s. 92(2)) otherwise the outline permission will lapse. An outline planning permission is legally a full permission in that any conditions, apart from those relating to reserved matters, must be imposed at this stage, the normal publicity arrangements apply, and revocation entails the payment of compensation.

(e)   Approval of reserved matters (General Development Order, Art. 8). Any number of such applications can be made within the three-year period. As this is not a full planning application, no further publicity is required and no new conditions can be added. (It may also be necessary to apply to the local planning authority for other approvals, e.g. where a condition in the planning permission requires future approval of a landscaping plan.)

(f)   Under s. 73 (a provision first introduced in the Housing and Planning Act 1986), an applicant can ask for a condition to be discharged without putting the rest of the planning permission at risk. The local planning authority (and the Secretary of State on appeal) is limited to considering the condition in question. This procedure is very important in providing a measure of continuing control over planning permissions. It enables a landowner to get an outdated or unwanted condition removed, but in so doing it jeopardises the local planning authority's original discretionary decision. This is because it enables applications for removal of conditions even where the application might never have been granted in the first place had the condition not been attached.

Steps for the applicant to take

The applicant must notify the owners of all the land and must publicise the application in a prescribed form if the application concerns a rather random list of anti-social activities called 'bad neighbour' development, listed in the General Development Order, Art. 11. In each case a certificate should be submitted stating this has been done. It is an offence knowingly to issue a false or misleading certificate. At present these provisions are in ss. 65–68, but the Planning and Compensation Act 1991 redrafts these sections so that the detailed procedures will be included in an amended General Development Order. It is not intended to change the substance of the requirements.

In *Main v Swansea CC* [1985] 49 P&CR 26, the Court of Appeal decided that failure to carry out the procedures does not necessarily render a subsequent grant of planning permission void: it all depends on whether anyone with *locus standi* has been prejudiced as a result. This applies to most procedures under the Act. In any case, *R v Rotherham MBC, ex parte Rankin* [1990] JEL 503 shows that an action to quash a permission must be brought without delay.

Fees are payable for all applications for planning permission and deemed applications in connection with an appeal against an enforcement notice. There are fixed charges for different types of application. The categories are set out in the Town and Country Planning (Fees for Applications and Deemed Applications) Regulations 1989 (SI 1989 No. 193). The Local Planning Authority need not consider an application until the requisite fee has been paid.

The current rates (they are periodically increased) are set out in the 1990 Amendment Regulations (SI 1990 No. 2473). For example, the rate is £92 for each house, each 0.1 hectare of other developments, and for a material change of use, and £46 for extensions. At present the fees do not cover the full administrative cost to the local planning authority of processing applications but, in line with Government policy, the level can be expected to rise so as to do so in the next few years.

Steps for the local planning authority to take

On receipt of an application, the local planning authority will consult with a wide range of public bodies as required for specified situations by the General Development Order, Art. 18. These include highways authorities, other local authorities, parish and community councils, the National Rivers Authority, British Coal, the Ministry of Agriculture, Fisheries and Food, and the relevant Nature Conservancy Councils. Interestingly there is no duty to consult Her Majesty's Inspectorate of Pollution. There is a Code of Conduct governing this consultation procedure and those consulted have procedural rights in the event of an appeal. Any representations that are made are material considerations which must be taken into account by the local planning authority before it decides the application. However, it must not slavishly follow the advice of another public body, otherwise the decision will be challengeable for fettering of discretion.

The local planning authority must also publicise any application which does not conform to the development plan, unless it intends to refuse it. The publicity requirements are set out in the Town and Country Planning (Development Plans) Direction 1981, which is published as an Appendix to Circular 2/81, and which will have to be amended to reflect the new duty in s. 54A.

Surprisingly, there are no further statutory publicity requirements, except where consent is required for works to a listed building or in a conservation area. Most local planning authorities, however, include provision for publicity in a wider range of cases in their Standing Orders and they are encouraged to do this by Circular advice. For example, neighbours and others likely to be affected will often be informed. If the local planning authority has a policy of publicising applications to a greater extent than required by the legislation, the Local Government Ombudsman is likely to find it to be maladministration not to follow that policy (see [1983] JPL 613). However, this does not get the planning permission quashed and may result only in compensation or an apology.

The courts have recently begun to develop extra safeguards here through the concepts of legitimate expectations and fairness, and there have been cases in which decisions have been quashed for failing to notify neighbours who should have been notified (for a discussion of these cases, see Hinds [1988] JPL 742).

Decisions by the local planning authority

The local planning authority may (a) grant planning permission, (b) grant permission subject to conditions, (c) refuse permission, or (d) grant permission for part of the application only, as long as what is granted is not different in substance from the original, or an effective denial of rights to would-be objectors (see *Bernard Wheatcroft Ltd* v *Secretary of State* [1981] 257 EG 934). The decision must be in writing and must include reasons for the decision and for the imposition of any conditions. These are normally brief and it seems that a failure to provide reasons does not make the decision void. In the event of a grievance, the correct (and cheaper) course would be to appeal to the Secretary of State. The decision should be made within eight weeks of receipt by the local planning authority and payment of the fee, otherwise the applicant can appeal to the Secretary of State as if the application had been refused (General Development Order, Art. 23). The applicant can agree to a longer time scale.

Section 69 requires the local planning authority to keep public registers of all planning applications and decisions. (There is a further public register of details of enforcement notices and stop notices kept under s. 188.) The General Development Order, Arts. 27 and 28 set out the form these registers must take. They are an invaluable source of information on the planning history of a site.

Planning permission attaches to the land, not to the applicant (s. 75(1)). Exceptionally, a condition may limit the person who can take advantage of the planning permission, though such conditions are discouraged by the Secretary of State (see Circular 1/85). A permission cannot be abandoned, since it is a public document (*Pioneer Aggregates* v *Secretary of State* [1984] 3 WLR 32). However, it is possible for a permission to become spent, either through lapse of time, occurrence of a condition subsequent, or occurrence of a situation which renders carrying it out impossible (*Pilkington* v *Secretary of State* [1973] 1 WLR 1527). In any other case where a planning permission is taken away, compensation is payable (ss. 97–100).

Alternative and special procedures

The following are ways that ordinary planning procedures may be circumvented, mainly for public developments:

(a)   Local authorities are effectively allowed to grant themselves planning permission (s. 316 and the Town and Country Planning (General) Regulations 1976 (SI 1976 No. 1419)). They can do this for any land within their area which they own or intend to develop, though, if they intend to carry out the work themselves, the permission is a personal, non-transferable one. The procedures are simple: the local planning authority passes a resolution to seek planning permission, after which it must publicise the application. Having taken any representations into account as material considerations, it may then pass a second resolution granting permission. The resultant planning permission is deemed to have been granted by the Secretary of State, so there is no right of appeal: it can be challenged only by judicial review. In view of the possibility of a conflict of interest, the courts have interpreted the procedural requirements of the General Regulations very strictly *(Steeples v Derbyshire CC* [1984] 3 All ER 468). It is not, however, impermissible for a local planning authority to follow a well-defined policy, provided it considers other possibilities and does not fetter its discretion. Such a course is not contrary to natural justice *(R v Amber Valley DC, ex parte Jackson* [1985] 1 WLR 298). The Planning and Compensation Act 1991 provides a redrafted form of s. 316. How far the new procedures applicable to local authority applications will differ from the existing ones will depend upon the wording of a new set of General Regulations which have yet to be made.

(b)   Developments authorised by a Government Department under other authorisation procedures do not require planning permission (s. 90). This prevents a duplication of effort, but it does result in the decision being taken centrally rather than locally. For example, this option was available in relation to the application for the construction of Sizewell B, since permission for nuclear power stations is also required from the Department of Energy under the Electricity Act 1989.

(c)   Permission may be granted by a Special Development Order made under s. 59. This process has been used for granting blanket permissions in new towns, urban development areas and enterprise zones. The Windscale Thermal Oxide Reprocessing Plant was also permitted by Special Development Order (see SI 1978 No. 523). In that case the Order followed a public inquiry and a Parliamentary debate, but neither is strictly required.

(d)   Increasing use is being made of Private or Hybrid Acts of Parliament which avoid any of the planning procedures and effectively give the decision to a small Parliamentary Joint Committee, with limited public scrutiny. The Channel Tunnel Act 1987 is an example of such an Act with very important environmental effects.

(e)   Under s. 294, Crown land (i.e. all land owned by the Crown, the Duchies of Lancaster and Cornwall, Government Departments, but not nationalised industries) is effectively excluded from the Act by the provision of immunity against service of an enforcement notice. Planning permission can be obtained prior to disposal to private hands and action can be taken against private individuals occupying Crown land. In Circular 18/84, it is stated that the Crown bodies have agreed to abide informally by the same procedures and requirements as apply to private developers, but this system is not legally enforceable. One exception is that Crown immunity has been removed from health authorities and NHS trusts by the National Health Service and Community Care Act 1990.

Special areas

One of the features of the 1947 Act was that it applied a uniform system of control nationwide. Exceptions were made for developments in the areas of the new towns, but it was not until the 1980s that further exceptions were made as part of the Government's strategy of deregulation, with the proclaimed aim of effecting regeneration of the inner cities.

Urban development areas

Urban development areas were introduced in the Local Government, Planning and Land Act 1980. Not only are ordinary planning rules virtually scrapped in these areas, but the local planning authority is replaced by an unelected body. Under s. 134 of the 1980 Act, the Secretary of State may designate an area an urban development area and appoint an urban development corporation, which has general powers to redevelop land, together with wide powers of acquisition, management and resale. It may submit to the Secretary of State proposals for the development of land in its area (s. 148), which establishes a form of master plan. The Secretary of State may then make a Special Development Order, which grants automatic permission for development in accordance with the approved master plan and normally designates the corporation the local planning authority for all planning purposes (1990 Act, s. 7). The local planning authority accordingly loses all planning powers, although there is provision for consultation between it and the corporation. 11 urban development areas have been designated.

Enterprise zones

Enterprise zones were also introduced by the Local Government, Planning and Land Act 1980. The order establishing an enterprise zone, which is made by the Secretary of State after some limited publicity, grants automatic planning permission for categories of development specified in the enterprise zone scheme (1990 Act, s. 88). However, the local authority draws up the scheme to cover those matters it wishes to permit. Thus, while enterprise zones are formally designated by the Secretary of State, local authorities decide what is to be permitted. They also remain the local planning authority for other development not covered by the scheme.

    An enterprise zone normally lasts for 10 years and involves fiscal and administrative advantages for those in it, as well as the planning exemptions. Few new zones are now expected to be made (there are over 20), but development commenced before the expiry of the scheme retains the benefit of the automatic permission.

Simplified planning zones

These were introduced in the Housing and Planning Act 1986. As with an enterprise zone scheme, a simplified planning zone scheme grants automatic planning permission for the matters specified in it, but there are no non-planning effects (1990 Act, s. 82).

Every district planning authority has a duty to consider whether to impose a simplified planning zone in part of its area. It must prepare a scheme if satisfied it is expedient to do so. Anybody may request the making of a scheme and the Secretary of State may direct the making of one. The procedures for making one are set out in the 1990 Act, sch. 7. They are currently similar to those for adoption of a local plan, but the Planning and Compensation Act 1991 streamlines them significantly. There is no requirement that the scheme be approved by the Secretary of State, though it may be called in for approval. A simplified planning zone lasts for 10 years, but development commenced before the expiry of the scheme retains the benefit of the automatic permission. Only a handful have been made.

National Parks, Areas of Outstanding Natural Beauty, conservation areas, sites of special scientific interest, and designated green belt cannot be the subject of a scheme. County matters are also excluded, as are matters covered by the need for an environmental assessment.

The Secretary of State's powers

Under s. 77, the Secretary of State has an unfettered power to call in any planning application for determination. This immediately transfers jurisdiction from the local planning authority to the Secretary of State. This power is sparingly used, usually only for matters of national or regional importance or of local controversy. There is a right to a public inquiry unless waived by the parties and the Secretary of State and one is normally held. The procedures are virtually the same as for appeals, suitably amended to provide for the fact that this is a first determination. There is no formal power to request the Secretary of State to call in an application: objectors should write to the Secretary of State putting their case for this to happen.

The Secretary of State also has power to make directions relating to an application; this is normally used only for certain classes of case (e.g. applications for large shopping centres must be referred to the Secretary of State—see Circular 22/86), but may also be used to prevent a precipitate decision by a local authority in an individual case.

Summary of rights of third parties

Third parties or objectors have few specific rights under the legislation. Statutory publicity is limited, although actual practice and the Ombudsman decisions have meant that rights to know of applications are now wider than before (see p. 184). Any representations made to the local planning authority must be considered as a material consideration.

Since third parties have no right to appeal against a planning decision, they must apply for judicial review of any adverse decision. This entails having *locus standi*, acting without delay, and being able to afford the large costs involved, and has very little chance of success. Only local planning authority decisions can be subject to judicial review: decisions of the Secretary of State are immune to challenge except under s. 288 (see p. 199). If an appeal is brought by the applicant, third parties have wider procedural rights at that stage.

The local planning authority's discretion

Under s. 70(2), in deciding whether or not to grant permission, the local planning authority 'shall have regard to the provisions of the development plan, so far as material to the application, and to any other material considerations'. The Secretary of State is subject to the same requirements in relation to decisions on a s. 78 appeal, or which are called in under s. 77.

It is central to an understanding of planning law to appreciate the scope of s. 70(2):

(a)   It gives the local planning authority a very wide *discretion* whether or not to grant permission.

(b)   This discretion will be exercised on grounds of *policy*.

It should be noted that policy means 'planning policy'. Despite the fact that ultimate responsibility for local authority decisions rests with elected members, decisions may not be 'political' in the sense of being based on party political or personal factors. For example, a decision by elected members that an industrial development should be refused simply because the residents were opposed to it would be *ultra vires*, unless there were valid planning objections.

The discretion is controlled in two ways:

(a)   through judicial review of the legality of decisions; and

(b)   for decisions of the local planning authority, through the appeal system.

There is no doubt that the second way is more important, firstly because of the limited scope of the courts' supervisory jurisdiction, and secondly because of the willingness of the Secretary of State to use the appeals process to impose Central Government policy. In practice, the Secretary of State exercises a stranglehold over the content of the policies that are applied, and has the final say on policy in any case because of the applicant's unlimited right of appeal (see p. 197).

If a local planning authority refuses planning permission, its decision may thus be challenged either on legal grounds (for example, that the objections are not planning objections), or on policy grounds (for example, that too much weight was attached to the objections).

Judicial control of the discretion

The courts control and restrict the discretion through the application of ordinary principles of public law (see in general *E.C. Gransden* v *Secretary of State* [1986] JPL 519 and *Wycombe DC* v *Secretary of State* [1988] JPL 111). Failure to take something that is relevant into account (or, alternatively, taking into account something that is not relevant) means that the resultant decision is *ultra vires* and may be quashed, although the courts retain a discretion whether to do so. Whether something is relevant is a legal matter for the courts to decide.

As long as the policies that are applied are lawful (i.e. relevant to town planning), the courts do not interfere with their content. This is effectively a principle of non-intervention in policy matters. Accordingly, the *weight* given to any policy is a matter for the decision-maker, unless the decision is perverse. However, it is impermissible to have an absolute policy, or to apply it rigidly, since this would constitute an unlawful fettering of discretion (*Stringer* v *MHLG* [1970] 1 WLR 1281). The courts thus see their role as ensuring that decisions are made rationally in the light of all the town planning considerations. This is ensured by the requirement that *reasons* must be given for decisions: something that has attracted a great deal of attention in recent cases.

The application of policy

The decision whether to grant permission will be made by reference to:

(a)   the facts of the case;
(b)   development plans;
(c)   other local policies;
(d)   Central Government policies, especially as set out in Circulars and Planning Policy Guidance Notes (policy used to be published in Circulars, but Planning Policy Guidance Notes are now taking over this role although the process of replacement is not complete, so reference still needs to be made to both types of document);
(e)   representations received; and
(f)   any other material considerations (see below).

As stated above, the weight given to each of these factors is a matter for the decision-maker, but, in practice, development plans and Central Government policies are the most important. The reason for this has little to do with the law, because the courts have always refused to lay down a rigid hierarchy of the relative importance of the different considerations, but is to do with the way that the policies are applied on appeal.

Nevertheless, the legal position must be considered. The policies laid down in a development plan must always be taken into account, but the courts have made it clear that the plan is only one consideration, albeit an important one, in deciding whether to grant planning permission (*Enfield LBC* v *Secretary of State* [1975] JPL 155). Thus, unlike the situation in many other countries, a plan does not have to be followed; it is a statement of aims or objectives only (though this may be changing—see below). Circulars and Planning Policy

Guidance Notes are also material considerations and must therefore be considered where relevant (*J.A. Pye Ltd* v *West Oxfordshire DC* [1982] 47 P&CR 125). However, it is now normally assumed that a Circular has been considered unless the reasoning is inconsistent with it, or it has obviously been ignored or misunderstood. The correct interpretation of a policy in a development plan or Circular is a legal matter for the courts to decide. Misunderstanding a policy is accordingly as bad as ignoring it.

It is left to the decision-maker in each case to weigh up the competing issues. This shifts the emphasis of legal control on to the reasons given for the decision. As long as adequate reasons are given the courts will not interfere. In practice this means that Central Government policies will normally be applied on appeal. But it is clear from recent decisions that, if there is an up-to-date appeal plan with clear policies, that is likely to be followed instead.

This judicial reluctance to get involved in policy matters is crucial in the light of the development of Central Government policy in the 1980s. There was a complete overhaul of existing guidance, and the whole political shape of the planning system was altered by the publication of explicitly directory Circulars (such as 22/80 and 14/85) laying down very strong pro-development policies (see p. 164). For example, there is now a policy presumption that development should be permitted 'unless the development would cause demonstrable harm to interests of acknowledged importance' (originally in Circular 14/85, now in Planning Policy Guidance Note 1). This presumption is not restricted in terms of the subject matter of the application, with the result that it applies as much to industrial development as it does to housing development. However, it does not apply where certain restraint policies are applied, such as where inappropriate development is proposed in the Green Belt (see Planning Policy Guidance Note 2), and it would be rebutted by a strong local policy, such as a policy against industrial development in a defined area.

The relevance of the presumption was addressed by the House of Lords in *London Residuary Body* v *Lambeth BC* [1990] 2 All ER 309, which decided that the policy presumption must be taken into account and has the weight attached to it by the decision-maker. As a matter of interpretation, it is not limited to resolving a deadlock where the factors in favour of permission equal those against, as suggested by the Court of Appeal. This decision, by confirming the principle of non-intervention in the contents of policies, allows the Government freedom to accord the presumption a very high value (as it did in this case by granting permission for the redevelopment of County Hall as offices).

The new presumption in favour of the development plan

However, this current state of affairs may well change as a result of the insertion of s. 54A by the Planning and Compensation Act 1991. This states:

> Where, in making any determination under the planning Acts, regard is to be had to the development plan, the determination shall be made in

accordance with the development plan unless material considerations indicate otherwise.

This new section appears to introduce a presumption in favour of following the provisions of the development plan, because it replaces the existing duty to 'have regard to' the development plan with a duty to act 'in accordance with' it.

At the time of writing, it is unclear exactly how this duty will be applied in practice. To some extent, it will depend on the interpretation of the courts, which have always been keen to emphasise the discretionary basis of the planning system and that no one factor should automatically override all others, as explained above. It is not inconceivable that the courts will simply hold that the relative weights to be attached to the plan and to other material considerations are matters for the decision-maker. This non-interventionism cuts both ways, depending on the way that decision-makers act: it could allow them always to choose to follow the plan, and thus change the whole course of recent town and country planning history, or it could allow them effectively to neutralise the section by always choosing to find an excuse to ignore the development plan in favour of other material considerations (such as Central Government policy).

It therefore seems that the impact of s. 54A will depend on the interpretation placed upon it by Central Government. If the Government really is intending that there should be a change in the direction of planning so that it becomes more 'plan-led' and less 'market-' or 'developer-led', this will soon become clear in its policy guidance and appeal decisions. In any case, guidance will have to be given on the relationship between the section and the presumption in favour of planning permission, since the two are clearly incompatible. Guidance will also be needed on the importance to be attached to such things as the age of the plan, the strength of policies within the plan, and how far they are consistent with national and regional policy.

Other material considerations

Various matters are always material considerations and thus always have to be taken into account—e.g. plans, Circulars, Planning Policy Guidance Notes, the results of consultations, and any representations made by third parties or objectors. In addition, certain issues are clearly nearly always material on the facts—e.g. the effect on the amenity of an area, safety considerations, potential pollution problems, the effect on the local economy, transport and highways considerations, the balance of land use in an area, and the need for the proposed development. To be material they have to be material to planning and material to the application. 'Planning' has been given a wide meaning here and covers anything that relates to 'the character of the use of the land' (*Great Portland Estates* v *Westminster CC* [1984] 3 All ER 744).

This may be illustrated by the range of matters that have been held to be material in certain circumstances: the effect on private rights (*Stringer* v *MHLG* [1970] 1 WLR 1281); the existing use of the site (*Clyde & Co* v *Secretary of State* [1977] JPL 521); the personal circumstances of the occupier (*Tameside*

MBC v *Secretary of State* [1984] JPL 180); the precedent effect of a decision (*Collis Radio Ltd* v *Secretary of State* [1975] 29 P&CR 390); whether the application is premature in the light of an emerging development plan (*Arlington Securities Ltd* v *Secretary of State* [1989] JPL 166); the achievement of a separate planning objective of the local planning authority—in this case the protection of the Royal Opera House by allowing it to raise funds by carrying out the development permitted (*R* v *Westminster CC, ex parte Monahan* [1988] JPL 557); the availability of alternative sites, which has great implications for objectors seeking to put forward the argument that another site elsewhere is more suitable for the development (see *Greater London Council* v *Secretary of State* [1986] JPL 193).

In relation to environmental matters, it is clear that planning permission may be refused on a number of grounds. An industrial development may be refused because of possible pollution or safety problems (e.g. it is possible to prevent a plant handling dangerous substances, or a waste disposal site from being sited near to a sensitive watercourse). A housing estate may be refused because of the inadequacy of the existing sewerage provision. A new workplace may be refused because of the effect of noise on neighbouring properties. It is not just the potential harm the proposed development may cause that is relevant. Any development may be refused because it would be within a *cordon sanitaire* around an existing installation. For example, *Stringer* v *MHLG* [1970] 1 WLR 1281 concerned an area around Jodrell Bank that was subject to a policy of restraint on development to prevent interference with the radio telescope.

However, it must be remembered that these are only some of the matters that must be taken into account. The final decision involves a balancing of all the factors. A clear example of the discretion given to the local planning authority to decide that other factors outweigh environmental ones is *R* v *Exeter CC, ex parte J L Thomas & Co Ltd* [1990] 1 All ER 413. Permission was granted for a housing estate close to an existing animal waste processing plant, despite arguments put forward by the owners of the plant that this might mean that it could be closed down by the future occupants of the houses, exercising their rights in private nuisance. The court held that such a decision was unchallengeable, as long as the local planning authority had considered this factor: it had no *duty* to refuse permission on these grounds.

Conditions

Section 70(1) permits the local planning authority (and the Secretary of State on appeal) to impose such conditions 'as it thinks fit'. This wide discretionary power is limited by statutory guidance in ss. 72 and 75, judicial control over what is permissible, and Central Government policy.

Statutory guidance is limited and relatively unimportant. Section 72 states that conditions attached to other land under the control of the applicant, conditions requiring commencement of the development within a specified time, and temporary permissions are permissible. Section 75(3) enables new buildings to be used for the purpose for which they were designed, unless the permission expressly limits the use.

Legal tests for the validity of conditions

Over the years the courts have developed four tests of validity for conditions. In contrast with the decisions on material considerations, these have produced some rather restrictive results, possibly because the cases were mainly decided earlier, when a more overt policy of protection of private property rights was applied. A condition is *ultra vires* if it is:

(a)   not related to planning purposes;
(b)   not related to the development permitted;
(c)   perverse ('so unreasonable that no reasonable authority could impose it'); or
(d)   hopelessly uncertain.

(a)   Conditions not related to planning purposes
In applying this test, the courts have had to define the limits of 'planning'. They have done this by concluding that certain matters of a social planning nature do not relate to town and country planning. For example, in *R* v *Hillingdon BC ex parte Royco Homes* [1974] 2 QB 720, a condition requiring that houses be occupied by people on the local authority housing list, who should then be granted 10 years security of tenure, was held to be *ultra vires*. However, the dividing line is unclear. An occupancy condition restricting occupation of a rural dwelling to agricultural workers and dependants will be valid (*Fawcett Properties Ltd* v *Bucks CC* [1961] AC 636), as will a personal permission, although in each case the Secretary of State disapproves of the use of such conditions (see Circular 1/85).

(b)   Conditions not related to the development permitted
Such a condition must be geographically and functionally linked to the site to which the application relates. Thus conditions relating to other land controlled by the applicant are valid only if the other land is close by (*Pyx Granite Ltd* v *MHLG* [1958] 1 QB 554). Equally, a condition requiring works to be carried out on land which is neither included in the application nor under the control of the applicant is *ultra vires* (*Ladbrokes Ltd* v *Secretary of State* [1981] JPL 427). Thus, a requirement to screen a site by planting trees on neighbouring land would be *ultra vires*, unless that land was under the control of the applicant.

(c)   Conditions that are perverse
This test has normally been used as a means of preventing the use of conditions which undermine private property rights by requiring the dedication of land to the public without compensation. In *Hall* v *Shoreham UDC* [1964] 1 WLR 240, a condition was attached to a permission for industrial development which required an access road to be built at the developer's expense and dedicated to the public. This was held to be *ultra vires*, even though the Court of Appeal

was clear that the condition was beneficial in planning terms, since it created a useable access to otherwise inaccessible land. In *Bradford MBC* v *Secretary of State* [1986] JPL 598 this position was supported. The Court of Appeal stated that a condition requiring donation of land to the public for a road-widening scheme would be *ultra vires* even if the developer suggested it or agreed to it, since *vires* cannot be conferred by consent.

This restriction is bizarre, since it is surely the whole *raison d'etre* of development control to take away existing rights without compensation. It ignores the community of interest between the developer and the local planning authority; in the *Bradford* case, the developer included the donation of the land in the application since it was clear that permission would not be granted unless the road was widened. It also prevents any great use of planning conditions to secure 'planning gain' for the local community. In *M J Shanley Ltd* v *Secretary of State* [1982] JPL 380, a condition requiring 40 acres of the developer's land to be landscaped and dedicated as public open space, in return for permission to carry out housing development on adjoining land, was stated to be *ultra vires*.

It is interesting, however, that the courts have accepted the validity of conditions restricting existing use rights, or the right to take future advantage of the Use Classes Order or General Development Order (*City of London Corpn* v *Secretary of State* [1971] 23 P&CR 169). They have also accepted negative conditions subjecting development to a condition precedent, even though the condition would be invalid if put in terms of a positive obligation (*Grampian RC* v *Aberdeen DC* [1984] 47 P&CR 633), but only as long as 'there is some evidence of a reasonable prospect of the obstacle being removed' (*Jones* v *Secretary of State* [1990] JPL 907).

(d)   Conditions which are hopelessly uncertain
In this category it is clear that a mere ambiguity will not render the condition invalid. In *Alderson* v *Secretary of State* [1984] 49 P&CR 307, a condition requiring occupation by people who worked locally was valid because it was sufficiently certain to be understandable to the applicant.

If a condition is *ultra vires*, it may be challenged in the courts. This may result in the whole planning permission being declared void, unless the condition can be severed. Alternatives are to appeal against the condition to the Secretary of State, or to apply for a discharge of the condition under s. 73.

Conditions and policy

On appeal the Secretary of State can add, omit or amend any conditions as part of the total rehearing of the issues. This can be done on legal, factual or policy grounds, so an understanding of the Secretary of State's policy on conditions is essential.

Circular 1/85 requires conditions to be (a) necessary, (b) relevant to planning, (c) relevant to the development permitted, (d) enforceable, (e) precise, and (f) reasonable. In addition, it lays down some very important general policy tests: 'As a matter of policy, a condition ought not to be imposed unless there is a definite need for it'; 'a condition should not be retained unless there are sound and clear cut reasons for doing so'; a condition 'requires special and precise justification' if planning permission would not be refused if the condition were omitted. The local planning authority should also consider whether the imposition of any conditions may render an otherwise objectionable development acceptable, so as to save the application from being refused.

These are not legal requirements, but a local planning authority ignores these tests at its peril because of the applicant's right of appeal. It also appears from *Times Investments Ltd* v *Secretary of State* [1990] JPL 433 that a failure to have regard to these policies (i.e. not to demonstrate the harm that would be caused by omitting a particular condition) may render the decision *ultra vires* for failure to have regard to a material consideration. Once again, therefore, the Secretary of State's guidance imposes significant restrictions on the decisions that may be reached. Circular 1/85 notes types of condition that would normally be *ultra vires* and those that require exceptional justification. Appendix A includes a list of model conditions and Appendix B a list of unacceptable ones.

Planning conditions and pollution control

One particular issue relates to the use of planning conditions to achieve continuing pollution control objectives. Government policy (supported by the pollution control authorities and the Royal Commission on Environmental Pollution in its Fifth Report) has consistently been that planning conditions should not be used to deal with problems which are the subject of controls under separate environmental legislation. This prevents an unnecessary duplication of controls, or conflict over the correct conditions to impose. For example, conditions should not be used to impose acceptable levels on emissions or discharges to air or water, since those matters are best dealt with by the relevant pollution control authority. However, the widespread practice of imposing conditions on noise levels from premises illustrates that it is not the imposition of conditions relating to pollution as such which is discouraged, but the use of such conditions where there is an alternative system of preventative control.

This restriction may create a problem for the local planning authority, since it is clear that pollution conditions may not be enforced as rigorously as it may wish (see Chapter 6). Its main alternative, if it felt a risk was too great to take, would be to refuse permission altogether (after liaising with the relevant pollution control authority). However it is not *illegal* to impose conditions which duplicate controls. In allowing an appeal against an enforcement notice served on the Ferro-Alloys and Metals Smelter in Glossop, the Secretary of State attached conditions incorporating the requirements of an improvement notice served by Her Majesty's Inspectorate of Pollution into the permission (see [1990] 2 Land Management and Environmental Law Report 176). The effect was that the requirements of the improvement notice would continue to apply even if it was later withdrawn by Her Majesty's Inspectorate of Pollution. Given the potential advantages to the local authority in having direct enforcement remedies available through planning law, this may well presage a greater use of such conditions in the future.

Planning agreements

Under s. 106, the local planning authority (but not the Secretary of State) may enter into a planning agreement with anyone 'for the purpose of restricting or regulating the development or use' of land. Similar powers are given under other legislation (e.g. Local Government (Miscellaneous Provisions) Act 1982 s. 33, and various Local Acts). Such an agreement may include any terms that relate to planning purposes, although the exact boundary of what is permitted remains unclear.

A s. 106 agreement is enforceable as a contract (*Avon CC v Millard* [1985] 50 P&CR 275, which shows that an injunction may be available for breach), and under s. 106(3) the local planning authority is able to enforce restrictive covenants in the agreement against successors in title. Variation and extinguishment of agreements is currently possible either through further agreement or the Law of Property Act 1925, s. 84.

A s. 106 agreement does not replace the need to seek planning permission in the normal way, but it will enable a local planning authority to supplement a permission by achieving objectives which cannot be achieved by planning conditions. The exact legal extent of this is not entirely clear, but in *R v Gillingham BC, ex parte Parham Ltd* [1988] JPL 336 it was decided that a s. 106 agreement must still relate to planning purposes and must not be perverse, although it need not relate to the development permitted (see the legal tests for the validity of conditions at p. 193). It is clear, however, that the existence of a valid agreement is a material consideration which should be taken into account under s. 70(2).

These agreements are very common in relation to the provision of some form of 'planning gain'. They illustrate the negotiative nature of modern town planning and show that the concept of regulation in which a regulator imposes restrictions on a developer is rather outdated. But they also give rise to some concern. There is no need for approval of agreements by the Secretary of State, there are no provisions for publicity, and there is limited potential for a successful challenge by a third party. As a result, there is a danger that an agreement may be seen either in terms of the local planning authority 'selling' planning permission or the developer offering a bribe in return for permission.

Somewhat unclear policy guidance on what is permissible by way of planning gain is currently provided in Circular 22/83. This suggests that an agreement should not require a developer to provide more than that which is linked to the development in issue. This appears to mean, for example, that a developer may be asked to provide extra sewerage which is needed for the works applied for, but not sewerage for the whole general area. But this limitation seems unenforceable, since neither the developer nor the local authority will wish to challenge an agreement they have themselves reached, and other objectors may well lack either knowledge of the agreement or *locus standi*.

Section 106 is completely rewritten in the Planning and Compensation Act 1991, although the old provisions continue to apply to existing agreements. The changes are potentially quite dramatic. The idea of planning agreements is replaced by that of 'planning obligations', a phrase which includes both agreements and unilateral undertakings. This indicates that developers will in future be able to give binding unilateral undertakings, a change that was strongly criticised by the Opposition parties in Parliament as a 'developer's charter' (the Government expressed the opinion that unilateral undertakings would be very much the exception, but it is unclear how this will be ensured).

In addition, there are new provisions on the modification or discharge of planning obligations. This may be done by agreement, but there will also be a right to apply to the local planning authority for modification or discharge after five years, with an appeal against refusal to the Secretary of State. The new section also clarifies a number of other points. The new powers include a clear right to undertake positive as well as negative obligations, a point that was previously unclear. Where there is a breach of an obligation, the local planning authority is given a right to enter land and carry out operations and to recover its costs in so doing. The Crown is also given a right to enter into planning obligations.

The new s. 106 sets out the various powers far more fully than the old section. However, given the way that practice proved more important than law in relation to the operation of the old section, it is clearly too early to say how the new powers will operate in practice. It is unlikely that the new section will come into force until new Circular guidance to replace Circular 22/83 is published.

Planning appeals

Section 78 provides a statutory right of appeal to the Secretary of State against refusals of permission or the imposition of any conditions, and where the local planning authority has failed to determine an application within eight weeks. Only the applicant can appeal.

An appeal amounts to a total rehearing of the application. The Secretary of State can make any decision originally open to the local planning authority, i.e. allow or refuse permission or attach any conditions. This is true even where the appeal is against a conditional grant of permission (but not where it is against an application for discharge of conditions under s. 73, since there the local planning authority itself would have been limited to a consideration of the relevant condition). An appeal is thus not primarily a contest, but a forum in which all relevant information may be produced and tested so that the Inspector may make a rational decision. However, it is clear that, over the years, appeals have come to resemble the confrontational model of court proceedings far more than was originally intended.

There is also a right to seek judicial review of local planning authority decisions, though an applicant would normally be advised to appeal to the Secretary of State, because the appeal will encompass policy matters and is cheaper. A decision to grant planning permission can only be challenged through judicial review. Such action requires the person initiating the challenge to have *locus standi*, which is fairly easily satisfied for those with some interest in the case (see *R* v *Sheffield CC, ex parte Mansfield* [1978] 37 P&CR 1). Alternatively, the Attorney-General can be requested to bring a relator action on behalf of the applicant.

The number of appeals has increased rapidly in the last few years, with around 30,000 the current annual total. The overall success rate is about 40%, a significant increase on the 1970s. There is clear evidence that the appeals process has been politicised, with the opportunity being taken to impose Central Government policy unless there are strong and clear local policies applicable (e.g. in a local plan), or a clear restraint policy, such as the Green Belt, applies.

Procedure on appeals

Either party (or the Secretary of State) has a right to opt for a public hearing. Normally this will be a public inquiry under ss. 320 and 321, but increasing use is now being made of informal hearings. Otherwise the appeal will be decided by written representations, and currently over 90% of all appeals are decided in this way. The Town and Country Planning (Written Representations Procedure) Regulations 1987, SI 1987 No. 701 introduce statutory rules for such procedures for the first time and lay down time-limits for the various stages involved. Third parties have some limited rights to make representations on written appeals.

Apart from a very small number of matters of national importance, the decision is normally taken by an Inspector. In the remaining cases, the Inspector's report goes to the Secretary of State, who then makes the final decision in the light of the recommendations.

If a public inquiry is to be held, there are two similar sets of rules: the Town and Country Planning (Inquiries Procedure) Rules 1988, SI 1988 No. 944 and the Town and Country Planning (Determination by Inspectors) (Inquiries Procedure) Rules, SI 1988 No. 945 (see Circular 10/88). They are an attempt to solve previous criticisms about the delays and costs involved in a public inquiry by introducing formal rules on pre-inquiry exchanges of information and laying down timetables for the various stages. However, there is no remedy to ensure these time scales are kept, except an award of costs.

The inquiry must be public and anyone is entitled to attend. In general, the procedure to be followed is at the discretion of the Inspector, but the rules give the appellant and the local planning authority full participation rights, including access to evidence, calling of witnesses, and the right to cross-examine. A right to appear and present a case is also conferred on other people who have served a statement of case. However, since the rules are supplemented by the rules of natural justice, as indeed are the written representation procedures, an Inspector normally permits anyone with anything new and relevant to say to put their case properly. The Inspector is entitled to make a site inspection at any time, but this is not the place for hearing submissions.

Reasons must be given for the decision. Again, this duty has been supplemented by the courts, which require the reasons to be adequate, intelligible and not self-contradictory. The conclusions should follow from the evidence and all the main points raised at the inquiry should be dealt with (*Givaudan v MHLG* [1966] 3 All ER 696).

At present, costs can only be awarded where there is a public inquiry, although since 1987 both Inspectors and the Secretary of State may award them (s. 322 will allow awards of costs in other cases when it is brought into force). Costs are not awarded automatically to the winner of a planning appeal. They are only awarded against a party who has been guilty of 'unreasonable behaviour', which is defined in Circular 2/87. However, there has been an increase in the number of successful claims in the last few years. The majority of awards are against the local planning authority, rather than the appellant, and very limited use has been made of the power to make awards against third parties. 'Unreasonable behaviour' for the appellant includes making an appeal that has no reasonable chance of success (e.g. an appeal against a refusal prompted by a clear planning policy such as the Green Belt—see the award in the *Bricket Wood* case [1989] JPL 629), and uncooperative behaviour. For the local planning authority, unreasonable refusal of the application is the main ground for an award, which puts great emphasis on the reasons for refusal and the statement of case submitted before the inquiry (see Walker [1988] JPL 598).

A number of cases are now heard by a less formal procedure, 'a hearing', but only if the appellant and the local planning authority both agree. Hearings are not normally offered by the Secretary of State where third party evidence is expected, or there are disputed matters of fact, or complex matters of law or policy. The details are laid out in a Code of Conduct published as part of Circular 10/88, which stresses pre-hearing exchange of information.

Challenging the decision of the Secretary of State

The Secretary of State's decision can only be challenged under s. 288, owing to s. 284 which ousts all other challenges. Section 288 thus provides a statutory appeal: this must be distinguished from judicial review under Order 53 (see Chapter 2). About 150 cases under s. 288 are brought each year. These are the main source of decisions on planning law.

The s. 288 grounds approximate to judicial review grounds. A decision can be challenged either if it is not within the powers of the Act, or if substantial prejudice has been caused by a failure to comply with the relevant procedures (e.g. the Inquiries Rules). These will cover bad faith, perverse decisions, failure to take account of relevant factors, taking into account irrelevant factors, mistakes of law, acting on no evidence, giving inadequate reasons, or a want of natural justice.

Under s. 288, the High Court is limited to quashing the decision of the Secretary of State and remitting the case. It cannot make the decision for the Secretary of State, but can make some fairly explicit directions as to the relevant law. Thus, even if an appeal under s. 288 is successful, there is no guarantee that the re-determination will be any more beneficial. The High Court also has a discretion whether to quash a decision and will refuse to do so if it considers that the defect made no difference to the eventual decision.

Any 'person aggrieved' by the decision can use s. 288. This includes all parties who appeared at the inquiry or made representations, as well as the appellant, the local planning authority, and owners and occupiers of the site (*see Turner v Secretary of State* [1973] 28 P&CR 123). The time-limit for a s. 288 appeal is six weeks from the Secretary of State's decision, after which the decision is unchallengeable, no matter what the grounds of complaint (*Smith v East Elloe RDC* [1956] AC 736).

Enforcement of planning law

Planning law has a well-developed system of enforcement, which has just undergone some quite radical changes in the Planning and Compensation Act 1991. Most of these changes stem from the recommendations of the Carnwath Report (*Enforcing Planning Law*, 1989), but it is clear that the system of enforcement has in reality been a weak point of the planning system for many years. It has a number of features which differentiate it from most other enforcement mechanisms in environmental law. In particular, it is a two-stage procedure, in which an enforcement notice is first issued and then may be followed up with a prosecution if it is ignored.

Enforcement notices

The major tool for enforcement against breaches of planning control is the enforcement notice. This is an entirely discretionary procedure under which a local planning authority may serve an enforcement notice in respect of unauthorised development, requiring the owner or occupier to take specified steps to remedy a breach. Unlike most pollution control legislation, a breach of planning law is not in itself a criminal offence; the offence consists of failing to comply with an enforcement notice. There are additional powers relating to stop notices and to injunctions, though these have not been greatly used. There are also new powers on contravention notices and breach of condition notices.

A number of limitations of the enforcement notice procedure should be noted:

(a)   The legislation empowers no one other than the local planning authority to serve an enforcement notice (except the Secretary of State, who has a reserve power in s. 182 that appears never to have been used).

(b)   The local planning authority is given a wide and virtually unchallengeable discretion whether to serve an enforcement notice and over its content. One may be issued where the authority consider it 'expedient' to do so, having regard to the development plan and to any other material considerations (s. 172).

(c)   This makes the exercise of the discretion dependent on policy factors. Government policy advice, such as in Circular 22/80, is that enforcement action should only be taken where it is necessary. The local planning authority will take into account effectively the same things as it would when deciding whether to grant planning permissions (after all, failing to enforce against a breach is almost tantamount to granting unconditional permission).

(d)   The whole process of serving an enforcement notice is very lengthy and excessively technical.

(e)   There is an appeal to the Secretary of State: not only does this delay matters, since the appeal suspends the operation of the notice, there is a very high success rate on appeal (averaging around 40% in recent years), mainly owing to the deregulatory policies of the Government.

In a survey carried out in 1983, Jowell and Millichap found that enforcement of the law was given a very low profile in many local planning authorities (see [1986] JPL 482). A significant number of authorities did not have anyone responsible for enforcement. Monitoring of compliance with conditions and agreements was ad hoc and not guaranteed. The most common method of discovery of a breach was from a complaint from a member of the public rather than from investigation. When it came to taking action, informal methods of solving the problem were favoured, such as warning letters and requests for details of ownership of the land (an easily recognised threat of more formal enforcement action). Even if an enforcement notice was served, there was no guarantee that it would itself be enforced if ignored. 40% of metropolitan authorities and 32% of non-metropolitan authorities had not prosecuted once in the two years preceding the survey, low fines being given as a significant reason for failing to do so. Even more starkly, 65% of authorities had not used a stop notice in the previous two years, with fear of compensation being cited as the main reason for reluctance here.

Further surveys have illustrated that enforcement action is more likely to be taken where economic circumstances permit it. For example, enforcement is more common in South East England than in depressed urban areas.

Immunity from enforcement
The following situations provide immunity from the service of an enforcement notice:

(a)   Where four years have elapsed from the substantial completion of an operational development (s. 171B(1)).

(b)   Where four years have elapsed from a change of use *to* a dwelling house (s. 171B(2)).

(c)   Where ten years have elapsed from any other breach of planning control (s. 171B(3)). This is a change introduced by the Planning and Compensation Act 1991; prior to that Act there was only immunity for changes of use if the breach took place before 1 January 1964. All cases where there is a breach of a condition attached to a planning permission are now covered by the ten-year period of immunity, thus mitigating the effect of *Harvey* v *Secretary of State for Wales* [1990] JPL 420, which decided, on the original wording of the 1990 Act, that conditions attaching to an operational permission were subject to the four-year rule. This created some potential difficulties for the enforcement of continuing conditions, such as occupancy conditions or those relating to the operation of a site. However, *Harvey* still applies to any breach which took place before the Planning and Compensation Act 1991 comes into force.

(d) Where there is a certificate of lawfulness of existing use or development, a certificate of lawfulness of proposed use or development, or an established use certificate relating to the alleged breach (see ss. 191–194).

(e) Development by, or on behalf of, the Crown on Crown land (s. 294), though it is possible for a special enforcement notice to be served on a private individual who is occupying Crown land (s. 294(3)), a power that is primarily available for the control of trespassers.

Procedure for issuing an enforcement notice

An enforcement notice is first issued by the local planning authority (normally the district planning authority, though the county planning authority has some powers over county matters). It must then be served on all owners and occupiers of the relevant premises, including licensees. The enforcement notice must specify the alleged breach, the steps required to remedy it (these may include any steps to alleviate an injury to amenity), the reasons for issuing the enforcement notice, and the relevant land. It also has to specify the date on which it takes effect, which must be at least 28 days from the date of service, and a further period after that which is for compliance with its requirements.

At the end of the period for compliance, the owner of the land (or in some cases a person with control of or an interest in the land) commits a criminal offence if its requirements have not been met (s. 179, as amended by the Planning and Compensation Act 1991). It should be noted that compliance with an enforcement notice does not discharge it; it attaches permanently to the land (s. 181). However, an enforcement notice is a local land charge, so future purchasers of the land should find out about its existence. Each district and metropolitan planning authority must keep a public register of enforcement notices and stop notices (s. 188).

The maximum penalty for these offences is £20,000 on summary conviction, or an unlimited fine for conviction on indictment. In determining the amount of any fine, the court must have regard to any financial benefit accruing to the convicted person. There is no provision for imprisonment. The local planning authority also has a power to enter the land and remedy a breach at the owner's expense (s. 178).

Appeals

Any person with an interest in the relevant land (or an occupier with a written licence) may appeal against the enforcement notice to the Secretary of State. The appeal must be in writing and must be received by the Secretary of State before the enforcement notice takes effect. Thus the period in which an appeal must be lodged could be as short as 28 days.

An appeal will suspend the operation of the enforcement notice until the appeal is finally determined. In *R v Kuxhaus* [1988] 2 All ER 705, it was held that this could mean until a subsequent court action had been heard; in that case the number of successive appeals meant that the enforcement notice was suspended for over six years. The effect of that decision has now been reversed by the Planning and Compensation Act 1991. Nevertheless, the enforcement notice is still suspended until after the Secretary of State's decision, and it is quite clear that a determined and experienced operator may delay the final operation of an enforcement notice for a considerable period.

There are seven grounds of appeal set out in s. 174(2):

(a) planning permission ought to be granted for the development, or the relevant condition ought to be discharged;

(b) the alleged breach has not in fact taken place;

(c) the matters alleged in the enforcement notice do not in law constitute a breach of planning control;

(d) the matters alleged in the enforcement notice are immune from enforcement action;

(e) failures to carry out the correct procedures in serving the enforcement notice;

(f) the steps required to remedy the breach are excessive;

(g) the time allowed for compliance with the enforcement notice is unreasonably short.

These grounds are very wide, and cover both policy and legal grounds. Ground (a) is effectively an application for planning permission from the Secretary of State, hence a fee is payable for making an enforcement notice appeal (this is refundable if the appeal is allowed on grounds (b)–(e) or the enforcement notice is withdrawn).

Ground (f) is also important. A local planning authority may not 'over-enforce', i.e. put the recipient of an enforcement notice in a worse position than before the breach took place. This relates mainly to ancillary uses; the local planning authority may not require a developer to cease a use which would always have been ancillary (see *Mansi* v *Elstree RDC* [1964] 16 P&CR 153).

The procedure for enforcement appeals is very similar to that for planning appeals. They are governed by the Town and Country Planning (Enforcement Notices and Appeals) Regulations 1981 (SI 1981 No. 1742) and the Town and Country Planning (Enforcement) (Inquiries) Regulations 1981 (SI 1981 No. 1743). A choice of procedure is provided between a public inquiry, an informal hearing and a written representation procedure, and most cases are decided by Inspectors. Intelligible reasons must be given for the decision.

The Secretary of State may (a) uphold an enforcement notice and refuse the appeal; (b) quash it (often this involves granting retrospective planning permission); (c) vary its terms; or (d) amend it. In the last two cases any error in the enforcement notice may be corrected if it would not cause injustice to the appellant or the local planning authority.

Challenging the validity of an enforcement notice

The service of an enforcement notice is the first step towards the creation of a possible criminal offence, so the procedures set out in the legislation must be strictly observed. However, there is the possibility that the Secretary of State can amend an enforcement notice on appeal. In the past, the courts have tended to adopt very technical reasoning in this area, and have suggested that many procedural shortcomings render an enforcement notice invalid and not capable of correction, but recent decisions suggest that this attitude is changing. In *R* v *Tower Hamlets LBC, ex parte Ahern (London) Ltd* [1989] JPL 757, it is made clear that, as long as the enforcement notice tells the recipient what must be done and why, most technicalities may be corrected by the Secretary of State on appeal, if that can be done without prejudice to either party. This point is reinforced by the redrafting of s. 173, on the contents of an enforcement notice, in the Planning and Compensation Act 1991.

Appeal is made the exclusive remedy for the matters laid out in grounds (a) to (g): it is not possible to seek judicial review of an enforcement notice on these grounds (s. 285). However, some may be challenged in the High Court through judicial review as nullities (and therefore void). This may be the case if the notice is hopelessly ambiguous as to what is required, or if essential procedural requirements are not met (see *Miller-Mead* v *MHLG* [1963] 2 QB 196). The validity of an enforcement notice may not be challenged in a prosecution for breach (*R* v *Smith* [1985] JPL 183).

There is a further right of appeal on a point of law to the High Court against the decision of the Secretary of State (s. 289). It has no jurisdiction to quash an enforcement notice; if the judge thinks the Secretary of State was wrong in law the matter will be remitted to the Secretary of State.

Stop notices

One of the problems with enforcement notices is that immediate action to remedy the breach cannot be ensured. Accordingly, under s. 183, the local planning authority is given power to serve a stop notice on anyone carrying on an unlawful activity. This makes it an offence to continue any activity which is specified in the notice once it has come into force, which may be between 3 and 28 days from service. The penalties are the same as for breach of an enforcement notice.

There are limits on the application of stop notices. A stop notice is parasitic on an enforcement notice; that is it must be served together with or after one has been served, and will automatically cease to have effect if the enforcement notice is withdrawn or successfully appealed. It may not be served to stop use as a dwelling-house, or where an activity has been carried on for more than four years. Most importantly, compensation is payable by the local planning authority if the enforcement notice or the stop notice is withdrawn, or if an enforcement notice appeal is allowed on any other ground than ground (a)— the policy ground. This threat of compensation has meant that service of a stop notice has been quite a rare occurrence, but the availability of compensation has now been limited by the Planning and Compensation Act 1991 so that it is not payable if the activity stopped is in breach of planning control.

There is no appeal against service of a stop notice. Accordingly, it is permissible to challenge the validity of a stop notice when prosecuted for ignoring it (*R* v *Jenner* [1983] 2 All ER 46).

Injunctions

Under s. 222 of the Local Government Act 1972, a local planning authority has always had a power to seek an injunction against any breach of the law where it is considered 'expedient for the promotion or protection of the interests of the inhabitants of their area'. This power has been interpreted fairly widely in the House of Lords in *Stoke on Trent CC* v *B & Q Retail Ltd* [1984] AC 754, with the result that an injunction may be sought not only where there has been a deliberate and flagrant flouting of the law but where the normal enforcement procedures prove inadequate to deal with the problem. For example, in *Westminster CC* v *Jones* [1981] JPL 750, a chemist's shop in a residential area was converted to an amusement arcade. The owner ignored an enforcement notice and appealed against it, thus delaying the enforcement process, but the court granted an injunction in the light of the damage to amenity in the area and the deliberate nature of Jones's actions. A new s. 187B provides a specific power for the local planning authority to seek an injunction if it considers it necessary or expedient to restrain an actual or potential breach of planning control, thus removing the need to rely on the Local Government Act 1972.

An injunction is a discretionary remedy and will not be granted by a court unless the circumstances warrant such a strong solution. The penalty for breach of an injunction is potentially far higher than for breach of an enforcement notice, since the developer is in contempt of court and imprisonment is a possibility. It seems, however, that there is no requirement that other enforcement methods have been exhausted first.

New enforcement powers

The Planning and Compensation Act 1991 has introduced three new enforcement powers as follows:

(a)   The local planning authority may serve a planning contravention notice on any owner, occupier, or other person who is using or carrying out operations on land, seeking information from them relating to its use or occupation (s. 171C). It will be a summary offence to ignore such a notice, or knowingly to provide incorrect information (s. 171D). The idea behind the procedure is to obtain information relating to suspected breaches and to enable the breach to be remedied without recourse to more formal enforcement procedures. Clearly, the issuing of such a notice will warn the recipient that the local planning authority will take further action if necessary.

(b)   A breach of condition notice is introduced (s. 187A). This provides for a simple summary procedure whereby a local planning authority may serve written notice on a person responsible for non-compliance with a condition, or having control over the relevant land, requiring compliance in a period of not less than 28 days. It will be an offence not to comply with such a notice, the maximum fine being £400. As with enforcement notices, it is made clear that a continuation of the non-compliance constitutes a further offence.

(c)   Local planning authorities are provided with wide powers to enter land at any reasonable time to ascertain whether there has been a breach of planning control and what remedial steps may be required (ss. 196A, 196B and 196C).

Enforcement where there is no breach of planning law

There are some courses of action available to the local planning authority where there is no breach of the planning legislation. Normally these require the payment of compensation for the loss of any rights which have been taken away, so they are little used. But they are of importance as reserve powers where there is something creating an environmental problem that may not be removed or controlled in any other way.

Under s. 102 a local planning authority may serve a discontinuance order, which may require that any use be discontinued or that any buildings or works be removed or altered. Under s. 97 a local planning authority may revoke or modify a planning permission that has already been granted. In both these cases there are provisions for a public local inquiry to be held and compensation to be paid. The Secretary of State must also confirm these orders before they have effect and has reserve powers to make either type. Indeed, in March 1991, the Secretary of State took the exceptional step of making an order revoking a planning permission which Poole DC had granted to itself for housing on land designated a site of special scientific interest (SSSI) on Canford Heath in Dorset.

The local planning authority may also conclude a planning agreement under s. 106 in order to remove an existing building or use, although obviously the owner will require something of benefit in return.

Environmental assessment

With the exception of one Directive, 85/337 on Environmental Impact Assessment, the EC has had little impact on the town and country planning system, although it has now published a Green Paper on the Urban Environment (COM(90) 218 final).

Directive 85/337 requires that certain major projects are subject to a process in which the likely environmental effects must be considered before permission is granted for them. As a result, environmental factors are considered as an integral part of the decision-making process, rather than as 'objections' to be thought about after a tentative decision has already been made. Accordingly, developers have to consider the environmental impact of their projects as part of the process of planning them.

In implementing the Directive, the Government has chosen not to go any further than actually required by it. An exception is that it is now recommended that environmental assessment be necessary for Private Bills. These were excluded from the scope of the Directive because the legislative process was supposed to provide all the necessary information on which to base an informed decision—a point which is clearly wrong in relation to British Private Bill procedures. Where planning permission was already required, extra requirements have been built into the existing procedures by the Town and Country Planning (Assessment of Environmental Effects) Regulations 1988 (SI 1988 No. 1199). Numerous other regulations have been made to cover situations where planning permission is not normally required (e.g. on afforestation, agricultural developments, land drainage, marine fish farming, power stations and public works covered by the General Development Order). Since these regulations are mostly faithful to the wording of the Directive, and because the Directive has now been held to be directly effective (see *Twyford Parish Council* v *Secretary of State* [1991] 194 ENDS Report 38), environmental assessment will be considered in terms of the Directive.

The process effectively has three stages:

(a) The developer must submit an Environmental Statement to the 'competent authority'. This Statement should identify the potential environmental effects (i.e. direct and indirect effects on human beings, flora and fauna, soil, water, air, climate and landscape; the interaction between these factors; and the effects on material assets and the cultural heritage) and the steps that are envisaged to avoid, reduce or remedy these effects. It may also include further information, including the alternatives that have been considered. The local planning authority is the 'competent authority' in cases where planning permission is required, but in other cases appropriate public bodies with responsibilities in the relevant area have been designated, such as the Forestry Commission and Government Departments.

(b) The 'competent authority' must then consult with various public bodies, including the National Rivers Authority, Her Majesty's Inspectorate of Pollution, the Nature Conservancy Councils and the Countryside Commission. There must also be an opportunity for the public to express an opinion. The developer's Environmental Statement must be made publicly available and copies must be sent to the consultees.

(c) The 'competent authority' must prepare an environmental assessment of the proposal before deciding whether it may go ahead. This should take into account the views of the public and consultees.

Environmental assessment is *mandatory* for a very small number of major developments (see Annex I to the Directive). These are oil refineries; large thermal power stations; nuclear power stations and nuclear reactors; installations for the storage or disposal of radioactive waste; iron and steel works; installations extracting or processing asbestos; integrated chemical installations; motorways, express roads, airports, and long distance railways; trading ports and inland waterways; and waste disposal installations for the incineration, chemical treatment or landfill of toxic and dangerous wastes.

Other projects require an environmental assessment where they are 'likely to have significant effects on the environment by virtue of their nature, size or location' (Article 2 of the Directive). A broad range of projects is covered by this requirement, including most industrial and waste treatment processes, extractive operations, agricultural and forestry developments, and infrastructure projects. Guidance is given in the various regulations and in Circular 15/88 on what amounts to 'significant effects'. It clearly encompasses fairly small projects if they are in sensitive areas. But, it appears from *R v Swale BC, ex parte Royal Society for the Protection of Birds* [1991] JPL 39 that the 'competent authority' has a wide discretion on whether something is likely to have significant effects, since in that case it was treated as a matter of 'fact and degree' for the local planning authority to decide.

Extensive procedures have been established to determine whether a project requires an environmental assessment. For example, under the main Regulations, the developer may volunteer an Environmental Statement; the developer may request the local planning authority to determine whether one is required; the local planning authority may require one to be submitted; or the Secretary of State may direct that one is required. There is an appeal to the Secretary of State in any case where the local planning authority requires one.

Experience with environmental assessment has so far been mixed. It is estimated that about 380 Statements have been submitted, but there have been some doubts about their adequacy in terms of quality (see Wathern, *Environmental Impact Assessment and the Water Industry* [1991] 2 Water Law 27). Concern has been expressed that no standards laying down what is required of an environmental assessment have been published. But, in the light of the cases considered below, it seems unlikely that the courts will intervene readily where an argument is put forward that the Environmental Statement is inadequate.

The courts appear to have adopted a non-interventionist stance in relation to the procedures. In *R v Poole BC, ex parte Beebee* [1991] JPL 643, it was stated that the purpose of environmental assessment is to draw all relevant factors to the attention of the local planning authority to enable it to make an informed decision. If that is done, a decision will not be quashed simply because the local planning authority fail to consider whether an environmental assessment is required. In *Twyford Parish Council v Secretary of State* [1991] 194 ENDS Report 38, it was decided that the requirements of the Directive did not apply to a project that was already in the pipeline when it came into force on 3 July 1988—in that case the proposed M3 by-passing Winchester. The same case also decided that applicants seeking to get a decision quashed on the grounds that no environmental assessment had been undertaken would have to show they were prejudiced by the failure.

However, it seems that environmental assessment will play an increasingly large role in decisions in the future. An inevitable result of linking the process to ordinary planning procedures is that some form of socio-economic balancing process will be carried out. This may well encourage prospective developers to incorporate an Environmental Statement in their application for planning permission so as to increase their chances of success. A further factor is that the EC Commission is currently reviewing the operation of the Directive, and this may well lead to an extension of its requirements.

TEN
Integrated pollution control

The historical development of the regulatory system of pollution control has been on the whole pragmatic, reacting to environmental problems in a piecemeal fashion. Consequently, there has been a fragmented approach characterised by the control of specific media by diverse administrative and enforcement agencies. Many examples of the reactive nature of environmental law can be seen throughout this book. The Clean Air Acts, the Alkali Acts, and the Deposit of Poisonous Wastes Act all related to specific problems at a particular time that had given rise to public concern. The ad hoc nature of these controls resulted in a haphazard approach characterised by legislation with loopholes enabling certain offenders to avoid liability.

The end result is that the British system of pollution control is characterised by a division in the means of control; there is separate control for emissions into the atmosphere, environmental problems on land, and emissions into the aqueous environment.

Pollution of the atmosphere

Traditionally, the role of environmental law was targeted towards the protection of public health. Although the secondary purpose of such controls was that the environment was protected from harm, this was not the main purpose of the legislation. In the 1830s standards of sanitation in the major cities created a great deal of concern within those enlightened individuals who took an interest in the poorer classes. Consequently, between the years 1840 to 1875, attempts were made to deal with the problem by the setting up of special local boards of commissioners which were the predecessors of today's local authorities. These boards were made responsible for the enforcement of minimal sanitation standards.

At approximately the same time, industry started to utilise newly available materials and there was the formation of new industrial sectors, such as alkali works, which started to produce highly noxious and polluting chemicals as a by-product of their processes. Even in this instance, the problem was not viewed in purely environmental terms and the main thrust of the control mechanism was based on technological answers to scientific problems. Thus the Alkali Inspectorate was created in 1863 to fulfil a technical and advisory role in the combating of pollution. However, the legislation was neither properly enforced nor did it provide a full answer to all the difficulties that could arise from emissions into the atmosphere. Consequently, although noxious fumes were controlled, there was no prohibition on the emission of smoke into the atmosphere, which brought about problems of lower-level pollution with the production of smog. Thus, as the law sought to deal with one problem another problem arose elsewhere.

As new environmental issues emerged, different legislation was brought in which often resulted in separate enforcement bodies for overlapping emissions. For example, in relation to the Alkali Act and noxious fumes, the Alkali Inspectorate was separated from the control of smoke by local authorities under the Clean Air Acts. Other different bodies were created to deal with a variety of subject matters such as the control of health and safety within factories, the control of nuclear installations and the control of mines and quarries. The control of emissions to the atmosphere was built up by means of a haphazard jigsaw of administrative controls enforced by a number of different bodies. As will be seen, air pollution was not the only area of confusion. One of the main flaws in the reactive methodology of environmental protection was that, to a certain extent, enforcement agencies had overlapping controls, notwithstanding that their aims of enforcement were different. (See Chapter 11.)

The Robens Committee was set up in the early 1970s to report on health and safety at work and to answer specifically some of the criticisms that had been levelled at the many different authorities administering different sectors. In 1972, the Committee recommended that a new unified body should be set up to deal with all aspects of health, safety and welfare at work. Traditionally, there had been some confusion as to the role of the Alkali Inspectorate and whether or not its aim was to protect the environment or to safeguard the health of workers. The Robens Committee recommended that a new Health and Safety Executive should be established to include the Alkali Inspectorate. This was duly formed in 1974, in the first real attempt at unifying a number of different inspectorates under one organisational umbrella.

Environmentalists viewed this as a retrogressive step. The HSE was a factory-based control agency and sought specifically to protect the interests of workers rather than dealing with environmental protection on a broader basis. Secondly, basing protection within a factory environment did not necessarily take into account the many environmental difficulties suffered as a result of emissions, although admittedly other sectors were under statutory control through other mechanisms.

Pollution on land

The Control of Pollution Act 1974 created new bodies which were to be known as waste disposal authorities and have responsibility for control over the disposal of waste to land. These authorities were primarily the responsibility of county authorities in the area. Clearly, this protection was not part of the factory-based approach but, unfortunately, in practice there was little or no coordination between the HSE and those controlling waste disposal, even though there is clearly a connection between the production of waste in factories controlled by the HSE and the disposal of waste on sites controlled by waste disposal authorities. (See Chapter 12.)

Control of water pollution

Notwithstanding the separation of responsibilities for the control of pollution within factories and on land, there was a further complication with the separation of the control of emissions into water. The River Boards Act 1948 created a number of river boards to control land drainage, fisheries and the prevention of river pollution. Then, under the Water Resources Act 1963, 27 river authorities were created to take over responsibility from the river boards; they themselves were finally superseded with the creation of the regional water authorities under the Water Act 1973. (See Chapter 13.)

The regional water authorities had sole responsibility for regulating all matters concerned with water. Thus, they had control over prevention of river pollution, the supply of water, the control of sewage, water conservation, fisheries and water recreation. The Water Act 1989 attempted to overcome the inherent difficulties by separating the operational side of the authorities from the regulatory side. In dividing the poacher from the gamekeeper, a further two bodies entered the administrative jungle of environmental protection.

The administrative jungle and the mechanisms of protection

Although attempts were made by the Department of the Environment to rationalise environmental control, the plethora of enforcement agencies, including such bodies as the HSE, local authorities, the water authorities, the successor to the Alkali Inspectorate and the waste disposal authorities, created a complicated web of fragmented control. Unfortunately there was no unified concept of environmental protection; a theoretical and unrealistic sectoral approach had fundamental flaws which constantly served to undermine the authority of the law.

In addition to the jungle of administrative bodies, environmental control was also hampered by the vast number of powers and procedures available to each individual enforcement agency. Where powers to control pollution were available to a number of bodies, overlapping controls often meant that a particular incident or process could be controlled by as many as four different authorities. For example, a factory which was subject to control under the Alkali Etc. Works Regulation Act 1906, which produced dark smoke and discharged trade effluent into the nearby river could be controlled by the Alkali Inspectorate, the local environmental health department, and the water authority. This often created difficult situations, when a particular problem could be approached by these different enforcement bodies with different enforcement powers. In many cases there was an element of too many cooks spoiling the broth.

The controls available to each enforcement agency also varied tremendously. The traditional basis for environmental pollution control has always been seen as discretionary and technical in a scientific sense. Historically, the main basis of this control has been by the operation of the principle of 'best practicable means' (BPM). This principle was first applied in 1842 in an attempt to control smoke nuisances in Leeds, and was further utilised in the Alkali Acts to control *all* noxious emissions from alkali works by 1874. The concept of BPM has since formed the basis of emission control for all media. Although explicit in the Alkali Acts and other statutes (e.g. Public Health Act 1936 in relation to statutory nuisances) the *principle* of BPM governed other areas of control implicitly. Even where no statutory reference to the phrase could be found, consideration was given to BPM to guide standard setting and enforcement.

The phrase 'best practicable means' incorporates both a scientific approach ('means') and also a discretionary approach ('best' and 'practicable'). There were really three main aims of the BPM legislation. Firstly, there was a prohibition on any emission which could constitute a recognised health hazard. Secondly, emissions had to be reduced to the lowest level, always balancing that requirement with local conditions and circumstances, the current state of pollution control technology, the effects of the substances emitted, the financial effect upon a company using such equipment and, finally, what means were to be used to control the emissions. Thirdly, where there were harmful emissions, the aim was that such emissions were as far as possible diluted and dispersed.

The statutory guidance as to what constituted BPM was sparse so as not to fetter the discretion of the regulatory bodies. Certain guidelines were contained within the various statutory controls to which they applied (e.g. the Control of Pollution Act 1974, s. 72), but effectively, the concept utilised a presumptive control mechanism. Thus, where the individualised emission levels were complied with, it was presumed that there were no better practicable means in controlling emissions. In practice, the Alkali Inspectorate used the concept of BPM to balance any cost implications with the statutory objective of controlling noxious or offensive gases. The 1981 report of the Alkali Inspectorate put it thus:

> The expression 'BPM' takes into account economics and all of its financial implications and we interpret this not just in the narrow sense of a works dipping into its own pocket, but including the wider effect on the community. In the long run it is not the owners of the works who pay for clean air but the public, and it is our duty to see that money is wisely spent on the public's behalf. The country's industries and world's current financial situation have to be weighed against the benefits for which we strive and careful thought has to be given to decisions which could seriously impair competitiveness in the national and international markets. Never do we lose sight of our ultimate goal—that all scheduled works should operate harmlessly and inoffensively and that this state shall be attained at the earliest possible moment.

Notwithstanding this 'ultimate goal' there was no clearly defined environmental quality standard. The use of presumptive standards contained in guidance notes issued on a year to year basis attempted to impose some limits on emissions to the atmosphere. However, it was clear that these limits were to be applied flexibly and on an individualised basis to ensure that in each particular case the emission controls were 'practicable'.

The flexibility that 'BPM' gave to the Inspectorate meant that there could be a cooperative rather than a confrontational approach to industry. It was only when all the possible avenues of cooperation had been exhausted that breaches of the presumptive standards would result in enforcement action (for some possible explanations of this, see Chapter 6).

Although not explicit within the water industry, similar considerations applied to the control of emissions into water. However, there was one distinguishing feature. EC environmental policy sought to introduce into the legislation of Member States the concept of water quality standards or objectives. These directives covered such areas as the quality of drinking water, bathing water, and the quality of ground water. Previously there had been no legally binding limits, although both the National Water Council and the Secretary of State had had secondary roles in setting administrative standards of quality. In order to implement Directives (e.g. 80/778 and 75/440 on Drinking Water and Surface Water for Drinking), the water authorities utilised their powers in setting limits for emission levels on discharge consents. There was still a certain amount of balancing required between the financial implications of the cost of pollution abatement equipment and the requirement to bring water quality up to certain standards.

Overall, as Britain entered the 1980s, there was a fragmented, individualised, sectoral approach which did not reflect the growing trend within Europe for an integrated approach to the environment with specific quality objectives. As the fundamental change away from the 'British approach' gathered pace, the consequences of the traditional basis of pollution control became clear.

Consequences of the fragmented approach

(a)   Failure to view the environment as a whole

One of the main concerns of those who criticised the sectoral approach to pollution control in Britain was that there was a failure to deal with the environment as a whole. Each individual medium was seen as a separate area of control and no consideration was given to the possible consequences of imposing control on one sector in relation to others. For instance, where strict controls are placed upon the levels of effluent discharge into water, a simple alteration to the production process may shift the effluent to another sector, such as by incineration (air) or landfill.

The environment as a concept is a series of interdependent sectors. When individual bodies control separate sectors then there can be a reluctance to deal with a problem on a unified basis. Administratively, the idea of two separate bodies with overlapping responsibilities creates tremendous logistical difficulties, misunderstandings arise, inter-departmental communication has its own problems, which can all lead to inefficient control.

(b) The discretionary decision-making process

The different regulatory bodies possessed wide discretionary powers with which to enforce their statutory duties. Discretion can lead to uncertainty within a control system. Certain bodies may take a more rigorous view of enforcement whereas others may be happier to pursue a conciliatory approach. When a number of statutory bodies control the same process, the use of these different criteria can lead to an imbalance in the protection of the environment as a whole. Where an enforcement body shows a tendency to pursue rigorous levels of enforcement, emissions in that sector may be kept at an artificially low level. However, this might be counterbalanced by an increase of emission levels to another medium in relation to which the alternative enforcement bodies exercise their discretion leniently.

(c) The development of a cooperational approach to enforcement

The lack of definitive standards in many areas has seen the development of the cooperative approach by many enforcement agencies. It has been argued that such an approach has resulted in compliance with standards rather than being a wholesale enforcement holiday. However, other consequences have also been identified in Chapter 6.

(d) Overlapping controls

One of the consequences of failing to deal with the environment as a whole is that each individual enforcement agency has a prescribed area of responsibility. Where, however, there are overlaps in that responsibility, an uncoordinated approach can bring about ineffective enforcement of the regulations in question.

For example, where there has been a spillage of toluene within a factory site there can be as many as five different agencies who could take individual action against the company involved. If the toluene has gone into a watercourse, the water authority could take action. Where there is a statutory nuisance arising from smells and fumes, the local environmental health officer could take action. As toluene is a hazardous substance under the COSHH Regulations, the Factory Inspectorate could take action. The water services company could also prosecute for the breach of a discharge consent into sewers, the National Rivers Authority could prosecute for pollution of controlled waters and the Fire Service could take action for the breach of any storage licence conditions. Where such complex administrative mechanisms are required to cope with a simple single incident there is a chance that the proper mechanism is not utilised. The nature of the bureaucratic system of control is such that where administrative controls overlap, any failure of communication between the enforcement agencies renders proper enforcement more difficult.

(e) Lack of public accountability

Finally, where there are so many enforcement agencies, there is often a problem with a lack of public accountability. The trained lawyer can have a difficulty in ascertaining which body is responsible for a particular activity. The person in the street has very little chance of knowing who to turn to. Normally, the local environmental health officer is the first person to receive complaints, not necessarily because the local authority are the proper controlling body for a particular process, but because the public identify the Environmental Health Department of a local authority as being the 'right place' to which to complain. Other more obscure agencies are not fully recognised by members of the public. Where there is obscurity then the accountability of these bodies is also obscured. For an administrative and bureaucratic system to work effectively, the public need to recognise who controls what and how they do so.

Time for a change

The consequences of this fragmented approach were recognised when, in an attempt to address them, the Secretary of State for the Environment asked the Royal Commission on Environmental Pollution in their Fifth Report in 1976 to 'review the efficacy of the methods of the control of air pollution from domestic and industrial sources and to consider the relation between relevant authorities'. After receiving many representations, the Royal Commission identified many of the problems which have already been outlined above. They pointed out specifically that, by treating the disposal of waste to air, land and water as three separate issues, there was a danger that the 'allocation of available resources to each of the media will not reflect an overall view of where the problems are most severe' and also that such an approach would result in the 'haphazard disposal' of emissions to one particular sector without taking into account which of the media a particular pollutant would be best disposed into. As a background to the considerations of the Commission, the proposals of the Robens Committee were being implemented and thus, instead of taking a unified approach to the environment, there was a move away from environmental protection to a more factory-based approach with the creation of the Health and Safety Executive.

Before attempting to deal with the procedural aspects of a unified environmental protection system, there had to be an administrative body in place which could effectively utilise the procedures given to it. Thus, the Commission proposed two changes. First, the Commission recommended that there should be a single unified body to ensure that any regulatory system imposed could be enforced effectively and the full environmental consequences of an operation could be assessed. Secondly, in order to assess the full environmental effect of a process rather than just assessing its impact in terms of different media, it recommended that the new concept of the 'best practicable environmental option' (BPEO) be utilised.

Best practicable environmental option

The concept of best practicable environmental option was intended to adopt some of the more positive benefits of the previous BPM tests whilst maintaining a strategic environmental assessment of an industrial process. When the Royal Commission on Environmental Pollution examined the historical use of the BPM test they identified two main areas which suggested that the test had some environmental utility. First, the test allowed the enforcement agency to set emission standards relating to specific prescribed substances and specific prescribed processes. Secondly, they acknowledged that the scientific and technical background that a properly trained Inspectorate could bring to the system of control would provide a good technological advantage and would imply that any enforcement agency was seen as more than just an environmental policeman but also as an adviser/consultant. The concept of best practicable environmental option sought to keep the more legalistic standard-setting idea, whilst maintaining the scientific and technological approach to pollution abatement.

The basis of BPEO was the extension of the BPM concept so as to introduce consideration of the environment as a whole when setting emission standards and industrial processes. In 1988, in their Twelfth Report, the Commission suggested a definition for BPEO as being:

> . . . the outcome of a systematic consultative and decision-making procedure which emphasises the protection of the environment across land, air and water. The BPEO procedure establishes, for a given set of objectives, the options that provides the most benefit or least damage to the environment as a whole, at acceptable cost, in the long as well as the short term.

Thus, although the BPEO concept was thought to be an extension of the BPM test it was much more than that. It was to form the *philosophical* basis for a more practical test.

These recommendations were ignored by Central Government for some time, mainly for political reasons. In 1982, the Department of the Environment's Pollution Paper No. 18 investigated the role of a unified administrative body without taking specific action. However in 1983, William Waldegrave, a new Minister in the Department of the Environment, pressed for a unified agency to implement the Royal Commission's recommendation. Tim O'Riordan and Albert Weale ([1989] PA 277) point out a number of motivating factors for this sudden re-emergence. Amongst the factors identified was the need to implement the idea of BPEO. In the period since their Fifth Report the Royal Commission had not kept quiet about the concept. In particular, the Tenth Report, *Tackling Pollution—Experiences and Prospects*, was particularly scathing in its criticism of Government in action. However, with the administrative set-up in the 1980s there was no one regulatory body to oversee the new system. The weaknesses of the fragmented, reactive approach finally received official recognition. Mr Waldegrave told the House of Lords Select Committee on the European Communities:

> I have been struck by how often we appear to be dealing with subjects not really on the basis of an objective assessment of environmental priorities but as a result of the changing fashions in pressure from outside.

The difficulties of quasi-governmental organisations being influenced by party political pressures tended to detract from the main priority of environmental protection. Thus, a feeling grew in the Conservative Government and elsewhere that a free-standing body was necessary.

The EC's role in change

At about the same time as the Royal Commission on Environmental Pollution's Fifth Report, the EC were formally adopting their First Action Programme for the environment. The approach for this Action Programme was fundamentally different to that of Britain as it adopted a continental approach which contained few elements of British tradition. The continental approach was to take a proactive rather than a reactive stance. Thus, its driving principle was one of anticipation of environmental pollution problems rather than trying to deal with problems as they arose on a piecemeal basis.

From the date of implementation of the First Action Programme, a number of Directives were introduced which emphasised these differences in approach. Directive 76/464 on Pollution caused by Dangerous Substances discharged into the Aquatic Environment was introduced to eliminate or reduce the pollution of water by dangerous substances. This was to be implemented by means of emission standards on authorisations to sewers *and* controlled waters. Similar Directives were later introduced for Air Pollution (84/360) and Emissions for Large Combustion Plants (86/609).

Increasingly, the flexibility of standard setting in Britain did not reflect this move towards European style emission standards defined with reference to 'permissable maximum concentrations of substances' and 'quality objectives'. Other countries within the EC were already developing new and different ideas.

Vorsorgeprinzip: anticipation through foresight

In the 1970s, as environmental issues started to percolate through the political systems of the Member States of the EC, the methodology of pollution control in other Member States was starting to develop significantly. In West Germany, for instance, environmental control evolved around the somewhat different mechanism of the *vorsorgeprinzip*. This was a stated principle which was to be adhered to when considering the environmental impact of a process and which operated on two bases. First, that the environment should be able to restore itself notwithstanding the effect of industrial activity, and secondly, that environmental controls on emission standards should be set as high as they could, taking into account available technology. These two bases work in tandem to create an overall scheme which takes into account available technology but does not sacrifice environmental quality by putting standards at the margins of environmental deterioration. However, even with the principle of *vorsorgeprinzip* there was also some need to take into account an economic factor. Thus, the principle of proportionality, which takes into account the balance between the environmental improvement achieved and the cost needed to attain that improvement, was also a factor.

The natural consequence of this three-pronged approach was translated into EC policy in the Directive on Atmospheric Emissions from Industrial Plants

(84/360). This required that 'all appropriate preventative measures against air pollution be taken, including the application of best available technology, provided that the application of such measures does not entail excessive cost'. The introduction of this new system—'the best available technique not entailing excessive cost' or BATNEEC—was to play an important part in the development of an integrated pollution control system in Britain.

Some saw this new principle as being not very far removed from the old principle of BPM but the method of its utilisation within the British legislation, when coupled with environmental quality objectives, ensured that there was to be a fundamental restructuring of pollution control within Britain.

HMIP—a unified body

Although the Royal Commission on Environmental Pollution made strong recommendations that a unified body be created to deal with environmental problems, this was specifically rejected by the Government of the day and ignored for approximately ten years until its Tenth Report raised the issue again when considering the concept of BPEO. Whilst considering the *vorsorgeprinzip* from Germany and the concept of BPEO, the Commission accepted the benefits of such a system but pointed out that for BPEO to operate effectively it would require a single agency to deal with the day-to-day running of environmental matters.

Finally, after an investigation of the efficiency of the Health and Safety Executive, a recommendation was made to create a unified Inspectorate which could not only overcome some of the historical problems surrounding environmental protection but also implement the new system of integrated pollution control.

The introduction of integrated pollution control

Any new system of control needed to take into account the requirements of assessing the environment as a whole. With a new administrative agency, Her Majesty's Inspectorate of Pollution, ready to deal with an integrated approach, all that was required was the setting up of the legislation to break down the boundaries between the different sectors. Many of the elements of the new system of integrated pollution control contained some similarity to previous environmental legislation (e.g. Health and Safety at Work etc. Act 1974, the Alkali Etc. Works Regulation Act 1906). However, there are a number of new concepts which have been introduced to enable Britain to fulfil its obligations under the EEC Treaty and also to take a proactive approach to environmental protection.

Thus, the EPA introduced a new system of integrated pollution control to improve pollution control arising from industrial processes. Part I of the Act establishes two separate systems: first, IPC controlled by HMIP; and secondly, APC controlled by the Local Authority Environmental Health Department (see Chapter 11). Both systems contain the same principle mechanisms but differ in two aspects. IPC tends to control the more polluting processes and the mechanism is specifically to prevent or minimise pollution of any environmental medium whereas APC solely controls atmospheric release of the less polluting processes.

The new system of integrated pollution control works on the principle that to carry out a scheduled process without an authorisation from HMIP will of itself amount to a criminal offence. Secondly, when granting an authorisation, various statutory objectives are required to be met before such an authorisation can be granted. Finally, the scope of control has been widened considerably. When assessing an application for an authorisation in relation to the more polluting (and potentially more damaging) processes, account has to be taken of emission to all three media when calculating the effect of a process upon the environment as a whole.

Organisation and administration of the system of integrated pollution control

The legislation controlling integrated pollution control is contained in Part I of the Environmental Protection Act 1990 (EPA). The EPA is something of a lawyers' paradise in that it is only a framework which requires regulations to be passed to fill out various areas of the primary legislation. The reasons for this have more to do with the need for flexibility in controlling environmental matters than any desire to avoid responsibility within the main Act. It is possible to pass new regulations quickly and this allows for new research into environmental problems to be taken into account when assessing what particular matters ought to fall under the control of the framework legislation.

Thus, the EPA itself forms only a small part of the controlling legislation. There are further statutory controls under the Environmental Protection (Prescribed Processes and Substances) Regulations 1991 (SI 1991 No. 472), the Environmental Protection (Applications, Appeals and Registers) Regulations 1991 (SI 1991 No. 507) and the Environmental Protection (Authorisation of Processes) (Determination Periods) Order 1991 (SI 1991 No. 513). Furthermore, there will be a new system of guidance notes issued by HMIP, giving descriptions of processes which will be covered under the new regime. These notes will be similar in effect to the previous best practicable means notes, but they now have statutory backing.

The system of integrated pollution control is to be administered centrally by HMIP (EPA, s. 4(2)). It is referred to in the Act as 'the enforcing authority'. A similar system, which relates solely to the control of emissions into the atmosphere from less polluting processes, will be controlled by local authorities under the air pollution control regime (see Chapter 11).

A timetable for the implementation of the new system is set out in Annex A to this chapter.

The Department of the Environment has stated that the main objectives of integrated pollution control (IPC) are two-fold:

(a)   to prevent or minimise the release of prescribed substances and to render harmless any such substances which are released;

(b)   to develop an approach to pollution control that considers discharges from industrial processes to all media in the context of the effect on the environment as a whole.

Additionally, the system aims to improve the administrative structure of pollution control by clarifying the functions and responsibilities of HMIP and other statutory bodies and by providing 'one-stop shopping' for those carrying out the most environmentally damaging processes. It is also hoped that the system will improve public accountability by making the relevant enforcement body easily identifiable, removing doubts as to who is doing what, and by making it possible to obtain information quickly and simply. Finally, it is hoped that the system will allow a certain degree of flexibility in allowing alterations to be made to the scientific methods of abatement where new information is received, both in respect of abatement technology and in respect of the effect of pollutants. Account will also be taken of new emission standards, whether imposed by the EC or on a more international scale (EPA, s. 7).

The requirement for authorisation

The integrated pollution control system will apply to any process carried out in England and Wales which has been prescribed as being subject to such control by the Secretary of State (EPA, s. 2(1)). The Secretary of State has exercised this power under the Environmental Protection (Prescribed Processes and Substances) Regulations 1991 (SI 1991 No. 472). These Regulations include a list of processes and substances which will be controlled either under the integrated pollution control system or the air pollution control system. Accordingly the regulations split processes and substances into two parts, Part A and Part B. Part A processes are prescribed for integrated pollution control (IPC). Part B processes are prescribed for local authority air pollution control (APC) which, although governed by similar principles, has different detailed guidance (see Chapter 11).

Some 5,000 processes are regulated in respect of the solid, liquid and gaseous wastes under IPC whereas 27,000 are subject to control purely in respect of the emissions to the atmosphere by Local Authority Environmental Health Department. Whether a process is controlled under new systems depends on whether it is a process contained in the Schedule of Prescribed Processes in addition to whether or not it is likely to release certain prescribed substances into specific media.

Prescribed processes

Schedule 1 to the Regulations contains a list of the prescribed processes. This list is split into six main chapters outlining various areas of industry. These areas are:

(a)   the fuel and power industry;
(b)   the waste disposal industry;

(c)   the minerals industry;
(d)   the chemical industry;
(e)   the metal industry; and
(f)   miscellaneous industry.

Within these six different headings the processes are further split into those processes likely to cause greater pollution, contained in Part A, and those more suitable for Part B control. Each individual industry grouping also has subsections.

Fuel and power industry
Gasification processes, carbonisation processes, combustion processes and petroleum processes.

Chemical industry
Petrochemical processes, organic processes, chemical pesticide processes, pharmaceutical processes, acid manufacturing processes, halogen processes, chemical fertilizer processes, bulk chemical storage processes and inorganic chemical processes.

Minerals industry
Cement processes, asbestos processes, fibre processes and ceramic processes.

Metal Industry
Iron and steel processes, smelting processes and non-ferrous processes.

Waste disposal industry
Incinerating processes, chemical recovery processes and waste derived fuel processes.

Miscellaneous industry
Paper manufacturing processes, di-isocyanate processes, tar and bitumen processes, uranium processes, coating processes, coating manufacturing processes, timber processes, animal and plant treatment processes.

All in all, approximately 105 processes covering some 5,000 different installations are covered under Part A of the Regulations. Essentially, the list of processes widens out the previous list regulated under the Health and Safety at Work etc. Act 1974 by including processes which give rise to significant quantities of special waste and processes which give rise to the emission into sewers or controlled waters of Red List substances which have a particularly environmentally damaging effect.

Meaning of process

Industrial processes are often made up of many individual component parts but, in terms of the integrated pollution control system, a process is defined in relation to the operator and the location. So, where there are a number of processes falling within the same class in sch. 1, only one authorisation will be required if there is only one person operating the process. Where there is an overlap between the control of Part A processes and Part B processes, then the Part A processes will take precedence. Thus, where a small element of the process is subject to APC and one element is subject to IPC, HMIP will govern the whole of the process and only one authorisation will be required. Where the processes fall into different categories under sch. 1, different authorisations will be required. Thus, a process involving bulk chemical storage and chemical recovery requires two authorisations. However, it could be possible that one process is within Part A and another process is within Part B of a different class. In that particular situation, individual responsibility would fall to different controlling authorities.

The authorisations themselves cover all operations relating to the main process itself. Therefore, where the production of waste from the main operation is incidental to the overall operation of a plant, that would not necessarily fall within the waste disposal class under sch. 1.

Release of prescribed substances

Alongside the regulations controlling individual processes there are also controls over the release of prescribed substances alone. Often, the release of prescribed substances will be an integral part of the process controlled. However, specific obligations fall upon operators to deal with the listed substances in a particular way. The list of substances is split into three to take into account releases to air, water and land.

Schedules 4, 5 and 6 of the Regulations lay down the substances controlled.

Schedule 4—Releases into the air
The substances listed under sch. 4 are subject to control not only under IPC but also under APC. They are:

Oxides of sulphur and other sulphur compounds.
Oxides of nitrogen and other nitrogen compounds.
Oxides of carbon.
Organic compounds and partial oxidation products.
Metals, metalloids and their compounds.
Asbestos (suspended particulate matter and fibres), glass fibres and mineral fibres.
Halogens and their compounds.
Phosphorus and its compounds and particulate matter.

Schedule 5—Releases into water
This list reflects the Red List, which governs the input of substances which are a danger. The following are listed:

Mercury and its compounds.

Cadmium and its compounds.
All isomers of hexachlorocyclohexane.
All isomers of DDT.
Pentachlorophenol and its compounds.
Hexachlorobenzene.
Hexachlorobutadiene.
Aldrin.
Dieldrin.
Endrin.
Polychlorinated biphenyls (PCB's).
Dichlorvos.
1, 2-Dichloroethane.
All isomers of trichlorobenzene.
Atrazine.
Simazine.
Tributyltin.
Triphenyltin.
Trifluralin.
Fenitrothion.
Azinphos-methyl.
Malathion.
Endosulfan.

Schedule 6—Release to land
The following substances are listed in sch. 6:

Organic solvents.
Azides.
Halogens and their covalent compounds.
Metal carbonyls.
Organo metallic compounds.
Oxidising agents.
Polychlorinated dibenzofuran and any congener thereof.
Polychlorinated dibenzo-p-dioxin and any other congener thereof.
Polyhalogenated biphenyls, terphenyls and naphthalenes.
Phosphorus.
Pesticides.
Alkali metals and their oxides and alkaline earth materials and their oxides.

Exceptions

As in many similar environmental control Regulations there are exceptions
to the general rule that processes in Part A are to be controlled under the
IPC system. Regulation 4 and sch. 2 give a list of criteria for exemptions.
A process is exempted if:

(a)   it cannot result in emissions to air of a substance contained in sch. 4 or, if there are substances, the release of those substances will not cause any harm as they are in such trivial amounts;

(b)   it cannot result in any discharges to water of any substance listed in sch. 5 beyond background concentration;

(c)   it cannot result in any substance listed in sch. 6 being released into land or if such substances are released that they are released in such trivial amounts that the release cannot do any harm.

Other processes excluded include those carried out in:

(a)   working museums demonstrating an industrial process of historic interest or a school (reg. 4(3)).

(b)   certain engines powering aircraft, ships, trains and cars (reg. 4(4)).

(c)   those processes carried out as domestic activities in connection with a private dwelling.

Notwithstanding these exceptions, if the process gives rise to an offensive smell noticeable outside the premises where the process is carried on then they will be subject to control under Part I.

Overlapping controls

The deposit of controlled waste

Section 28(1) of the EPA provides that no condition may be attached to an authorisation which regulates the final disposal by deposit in or on land of controlled waste. However, there is a greater degree of uncertainty over the overlapping responsibilities where waste is treated or kept. It is open to the Secretary of State to draw up Regulations excluding the deposit, treatment or keeping of waste from the need for a waste management licence under Part II of the Act (s. 33(3)). When deciding what to exclude, the Secretary of State must take into account whether other statutory controls (such as IPC) are adequate. Thus, there is a power to designate a particular process for control by HMIP or the WRA. For example, the DoE recently said that operators of industrial waste treatment plants were to be excluded from IPC. However, other waste disposal activities such as waste incineration can be brought within HMIP's control if the licensing system is not appropriate.

The pollution of controlled waters

Where an authorisation covers the discharge of substances to water, the control of such a process remains with HMIP. Section 108 of the Water Act 1989 (as amended by sch. 15, para. 29 of the EPA), provides that any discharges made in compliance with that authorisation would not amount to an offence under s. 107. In other words, there is no need to obtain a discharge consent from the NRA. There are a number of caveats over this recentralisation of control to HMIP. First, the NRA have the power to certify that in its opinion the release of substances into controlled waters from any process will result in, or contribute to, a failure to achieve any water quality objective enforced under the Water Act 1989 (s. 28(3)(a)). In such circumstances, HMIP are not allowed to grant an authorisation. Secondly, the NRA are entitled to notify HMIP in writing as to appropriate conditions to appear in the authorisation (s. 28(3)(b)), and finally, the NRA can write to HMIP requiring them to issue a variation notice (s. 28(4)).

The discharge of effluent into sewers

Section 74 and sch. 9 of the Water Act 1989 have been amended so that they do not apply in relation to trade effluent produced by a prescribed process. There is some degree of overlap in these controls however, as operations involving processes which discharge trade effluent to sewers will require consent under the Public Health (Drainage of Trade Premises) Act 1937 as well as an authorisation under IPC rules. It is difficult to see how one will relate to another as clearly it would be difficult, if not impossible, for them to contradict each other.

Statutory nuisance

Where a local authority wish to initiate their statutory nuisance powers in relation to a prescribed process they must first get the Secretary of State to consent (s. 10). This power applies only in relation to smoke emitted from premises, dust, steam, smell or other effluvia arising on industrial, trade or business premises, or any accumulation or deposit.

Transitional controls

As the IPC/APC systems are being phased in over a five-year period, some clever parliamentary drafting covers the transitional arrangements. In appropriate cases, the Clean Air Acts, Health & Safety at Work etc. Act 1974 and the Alkali Etc. Works Regulation Act 1906 are being progressively repealed. As an authorisation is granted, refused or determined on appeal, controls under the appropriate Act will cease (EPA, sch. 15).

Applications for authorisation

When IPC governs a prescribed process or substance an authorisation has to be obtained from HMIP before that process can be carried out or that substance emitted (EPA, s. 6(1)). To carry out a process without authorisation is a criminal offence (s. 23(1)). Thus, the first step in the integrated pollution control procedure is to apply for an authorisation.

The Environmental Protection (Applications, Appeals and Registers) Regulations 1991 (SI 1991 No. 507) lay down the procedure for an application. Regulation 2 provides for details to be provided in an application on a form prescribed by HMIP. Clearly, certain authorisations can be very complicated and a great deal of information is required. This information includes:

(a)   The name, address and telephone number of the applicant.

(b)   A map of the area within which the process is to be located, with indications of the exact location of the process, the name of the local authority, and the address of the location of the prescribed process.

(c)   A proper description of the process, including such information as relates to the concept of BATNEEC (as to which, see p. 231). This is wider than the information required under the BPM tests and the techniques employed must be described fully.

(d)   Where there is a prescribed substance involved in the process, information regarding the quantity and nature of the releases and also whether or not raw materials are used in the process itself.

(e)   Where techniques are used to prevent or minimise the release of prescribed substances, or such substances are rendered harmless, a full description of the methods used. There should be information as to how waste will be discharged.

(f)   A detailed assessment of the environmental implications of the process. This has to be carried out specifically in relation to the BPEO. It does not have to be a definitive description of the environmental effects but mainly an assessment of the environmental impact on a local, regional or global basis and, alongside this, there has to be a justification of the process used in an attempt to balance the harm caused by a process with the techniques used.

(g)   Information regarding the monitoring of the released substances.

Where any other additional conditions are imposed by HMIP then they may ask the applicant to furnish such information as is necessary. If that information is not forthcoming, EPA, sch. 1, para. 1(3) allows HMIP to give specific notice in writing of the requirement to the operator to give any information within a specified period so that an application can properly be determined.

It is not yet known to what extent HMIP, or for that matter the local authorities, will require details in relation to the more technical aspects of a process. Seemingly, there is far greater forethought required in submitting an application than was necessary under the old system. The Regulations suggest that some fairly serious calculations and strategic planning will be required from those industries controlled by Part 1 to ensure that they properly comply with their statutory obligations.

Authorisation fees and charges

Aside from the shift in emphasis to a more strategic approach to environmental protection, there has also been a move towards a simplified version of the polluter pays principle. One of the Government's concerns in introducing the EPA was that any regulatory body should be able to find sufficient funds to cover their administrative costs in deciding any authorisations. Previously, it had been seen as a weakness of the Control of Pollution Act that there was really no provision to charge adequate fees to cover expenses for the processing of applications for environmental authorisations. Therefore, to a certain extent the polluting industries were able to rely upon a free centrally funded body to process their applications.

The scheme for fees and charges is made by the Secretary of State with the approval of the Treasury (s. 8). In order to meet the regulatory costs the Secretary of State must, so far as practicable, ensure that all fees and charges payable cover the expenditure incurred by those enforcing the Regulations. The details of the scheme were issued in a paper from the HMIP *Pollution Regulation: Cost Recovery Charges*. The scheme operates on three levels: an application fee, an annual charge, and a variation fee. The fees are in proportion to the administrative work required in dealing with the process and are therefore set by reference to the number of components which a process contains. The term 'components' only refers to the charging scheme and not to the number of authorisations required. So, for instance, where there are three boilers involved in a process, there is a requirement for one authorisation, but the fee for processing that authorisation may be multiplied by three.

Application fees
In 1991, the fees, where fixed fees apply, are £1,800 per component or, where a process has been subject to HMIP control under previous legislation, £1,200 per component. In some instances, the complexity of a process will require a great deal of strategic planning, where there is a time-limit between the implementation of a process and the commencement of an application for an authorisation. In these cases, the applicant can use a stay applications procedure which will be subjected to specific charges related to the time spent in dealing with the application.

Annual charges
To cover the costs of monitoring a particular process, there will be an annual charge of £500 per component, except in certain exempted cases. This annual charge becomes payable from the initial date of the grant of the authorisation. The charge is to be levied on 1 April every year.

In certain cases, there is an overlap between the charging scheme operated by HMIP and the charging scheme operated by the NRA (see Chapter 13). It is for HMIP to include this additional expense within their annual charge so that the process operator receives one annual bill. HMIP will then pass the relevant amount to the NRA.

Variation fee
Where a change is to be made to the design, operation, or emissions of a process, either because of an application by an operator or a variation notice made by HMIP, a charge can be made where such a variation would be 'substantial'. Where such a change is to be substantial, this would inevitably involve a reconsideration of the factors taken into account on an original application, therefore, to that extent a substantial variation can be seen as a new authorisation involving separate costs. The fee for variation is £600 per component and is again subject to various exemptions.

Non-payment of charges
Where no fee is paid when there is an application for an authorisation the
enforcing authority do not need to consider the application until the fee is
paid (ss. 6 and 11). Where the annual fee has not been paid the enforcing
authority have the power to revoke the authorisation by notice in writing (s. 8(8)).

Public participation and other consultation procedures

The right of the public to be notified of environmentally harmful processes
has been virtually non-existent in the past. This has been altered under the
Environmental Protection (Applications, Appeals and Registers) Regulations
1991 (SI 1991 No. 507). Regulation 5 obliges the operator of a process to
advertise all applications for authorisation or variation of an authorisation
involving a substantial change. This advert has to be published in a local
newspaper circulating in the area in which the process is to be operated, and
must contain details including:

(a)   the name and address of the applicant and the premises where the process
is carried on;
(b)   a description of the process;
(c)   the availability of information on the registers and where those registers
can be inspected;
(d)   an invitation for representations to be made within 28 days to HMIP.

This advertisement has to appear between 14 and 42 days after the application
was made or the day on which the variation notice was served upon the applicant.

Other consultees are given the right to make representations under regulation
4. The list of consultees reflects the many implications that a process may
have upon different areas of not only the environment but also the workplace.
The bodies entitled to be consulted include:

(a)   the Health and Safety Executive, specifically in relation to the health
and safety at work of people involved in the process;
(b)   the National Rivers Authority in relation to any process which may
result in the release of any substance into controlled waters;
(c)   water services companies or any other sewerage undertaker, in relation
to the release of any substance into a sewer;
(d)   the Minister of Agriculture, Fisheries and Food;
(e)   the relevant Nature Conservancy Council, in relation to the release of
a substance which may affect a site of special scientific interest;
(f)   a Harbour Authority, in relation to the release of any substance into
a harbour.

These statutory consultees are entitled to notification within 14 days of receipt
of an application for authorisation or variation. (EPA, sch. 1). They are then
allowed to make representations within 28 days, and any representations made
have to be taken into account as a consideration when deciding an application.

Where an application does not contain commercially confidential information, the Environmental Protection (Authorisation of Processes) (Determination Periods) Order 1991 (SI 1991 No. 513) provides that there is a four-month period for determining applications, beginning with the date of receipt (see also EPA, sch. 1, paras. 5(1) and (3)). This time limit can be extended on agreement between the applicant and the enforcing authority.

Call-in procedure

As in a planning application, the Secretary of State has the ability to call in an application for an authorisation thus ousting the jurisdiction of the enforcing authority (EPA, sch. 3, para. 3(1)). This power can be exercised at the discretion of the Secretary of State. However it is probable that this power will only be used for particularly sensitive applications, applications of local or national importance, or applications which arouse a great deal of public interest.

When an application is called in, the Secretary of State has no power to grant the authorisation, but instead must direct the enforcing authority as to whether to grant the application and, if so, as to the conditions which are to be attached (sch. 1, para. 3(5)). The manner by which the Secretary of State decides such an issue may be by public local inquiry or by means of informal hearings.

Commercial confidentiality and national security

The EPA seeks to allow free public access to information regarding an application for an authorisation in normal circumstances. However, there are exceptions to this on the grounds of commercial confidentiality and in relation to issues affecting national security. Where an applicant believes that any information contained within an application should be restricted then an application may be made under ss. 21 and 22 to exclude such information from the Public Registers. This application is included along with the information relating to the authorisation, and HMIP (in the case of IPC) have to determine whether or not such information is commercially confidential (s. 22(2)(a)).

In the case of information relating to national security, the only criterion is that the Secretary of State has to be of opinion that the inclusion in the register of that information would be contrary to the interests of national security. On commercial confidentiality grounds, the enforcing authority have 14 days in which to determine whether the information is commercially confidential and, if they fail to make a determination, it is deemed to be treated as such (s. 22(3)). Where the enforcing authority determine that the information is not commercially confidential, it must not enter such information on the register for 21 days so as to allow an applicant to appeal to the Secretary of State against the decision (s. 22(5)). Pending any appeal, the information is also excluded from the register.

The determination of an application

Once the enforcing authority has received all representations made then they are entitled to grant the authorisation, subject to any conditions required, or refuse it (s. 6(3)). HMIP are under a duty to refuse an authorisation if an applicant would be unable to carry on the process in compliance with any conditions which would be included in an authorisation (EPA, s. 6(4)). Other grounds for refusal are if information required under the Environmental Protection (Applications, Appeals and Registers) Regulations 1991 (SI 1991 No. 507) was not supplied or the proper fee had not accompanied the application (s. 8(8)). There is a residual power open to the Secretary of State under s. 6(5) to direct the enforcing authority to either grant or refuse the authorisation.

In considering whether or not to grant an authorisation, there are a number of statutory objectives which have to be taken into account (s. 7). This has introduced a new concept into environmental control within Britain of taking a proactive environmental quality approach to emissions to the environment as a whole. The statutory objectives have to be achieved in every authorisation and most of the conditions in an authorisation will relate to them. These objectives are contained in s. 7(2) and are:

(a)   ensuring that, in carrying on a prescribed process, the best available techniques not entailing excessive cost (BATNEEC) will be used:

(i)   for preventing the release of substances prescribed for any environmental medium into that medium or, where that is not practicable by such means, for reducing the release of such substances to a minimum and for rendering harmless any such substances which are so released; and

(ii)   for rendering harmless any other substances which might cause harm if released into any environmental medium;

(b)   compliance with any directions by the Secretary of State given for the implementation of any obligations of the United Kingdom under the Community Treaties or international law relating to environmental protection;

(c)   compliance with any limits or requirements and achievement of any quality standards or quality objectives prescribed by the Secretary of State under any of the relevant enactments;

(d)   compliance with any requirements applicable to the grant of authorisations specified by or under a statutory plan made by the Secretary of State under s. 3(5) [of the Act].

Section 7(1) provides for three different types of conditions which may be included in an authorisation:

(a)   Conditions to meet the statutory objectives as laid down in s. 7(2).
(b)   Conditions imposed by the Secretary of State under s. 7(3).
(c)   Any other appropriate conditions.

Clearly, what is 'appropriate' will be subject to the Central Government Guidance. However, there is no doubt that such conditions will need to be relevant to environmental protection, concise, reasonable and certain. (See Planning Conditions.)

There is also a general implied condition that a process will be carried on using BATNEEC. Additionally, s. 7(7) specifically provides in relation to IPC processes involving the release of substances into more than one environmental medium, that BATNEEC will be used for minimising the pollution which may be caused to the environment taken as a whole by the releases, having regard to the best practicable environmental option (BPEO) available as respects the substances which may be released. Thus, the dual concepts of BATNEEC and BPEO are incorporated into the statutory objectives of Part I as far as *IPC* is concerned.

BATNEEC

All of the processes controlled by HMIP under IPC are subject to the requirement of BATNEEC. BATNEEC is to be applied specifically to each individual process taking into account various individual problems on a case by case basis. The concept of BATNEEC is somewhat wider than the traditional BPM model in that it includes not only the technical means and technology of pollution abatement but also the number, qualifications, training and supervision of persons employed in the process in addition to the design, construction, lay-out and maintenance of the buildings in which it is carried on (s. 7(10)). Thus, the umbrella of the control mechanisms covers a whole range of subjects which need to be taken into account on a strategic level.

'Best available techniques'

By way of further guidance as to the meaning of the phrase, the Department of the Environment's guide to integrated pollution states that 'available' should be taken to mean procurable by the operator of the process in question; this does not imply that the technique is in general use, but it does require general accessibility. It includes a technique which has been developed (or proven) at a scale which allows its implementation in the relevant industrial context with the necessary business confidence. It does not imply that sources outside Britain are 'unavailable'. Nor does it imply a competitive supply market; if there is a monopoly supplier, the technique counts as being available provided that the operator can procure it.

All this would suggest that the use of easily available abatement equipment would not necessarily satisfy the criteria. Efforts may need to be made to investigate other avenues of technology. 'Best' is defined in relation to the effectiveness of the techniques in minimising, preventing or rendering harmless noxious emissions. 'Best' is not an absolute term and it has been indicated that there may well be a number of different techniques which qualify under this particular category.

The statutory terms are deliberately vague in an attempt to import some flexibility into the decision-making process. There is, however, supplementary guidance contained in the IPC notes (see below).

The Department of the Environment are keenly aware that people within industry are particulary concerned that the meaning of BATNEEC should have a clearer definition than that contained in the Act. Overall, the onus is on an applicant to supply a system which properly and effectively deals with emissions so that they minimise the harm caused to the environment as a whole. It need not be the most up-to-date equipment, but it certainly requires an attempt to demonstrate that the particular system used is effective and that there are no more effective methods of dealing with the waste products of an industrial process.

'Not entailing excessive cost'

However, as pointed out earlier, there is always the need to balance one part of the BATNEEC requirement against the other. Thus, if the cost of a particular process is excessive then, even though it might be the 'best available technique', it need not necessarily become a condition of any authorisation that that process be used. There are, however, different considerations to take into account, depending whether a process is an existing process or a new process.

Clearly, where there is an existing process to update, account needs to be taken of the financial consequences of introducing new equipment. Therefore, it is anticipated that the introduction of new plant and equipment will be phased-in over a number of years. Thus, the cost of upgrading environmental plant will be spread over a number of years so that the two balancing factors of 'best available techniques' and 'not entailing excessive cost' can be taken into account.

Although it is clear that some account has to be taken of economic factors, what is yet to be determined is the extent to which the costs will be allowed to tip the balance. There has been comment made that those who cannot afford to equip their factories with up-to-date plant and machinery should not be allowed to carry out operations which could contaminate the environment. It is this unknown factor which could mean that the concept of BATNEEC will be much harsher than that of the traditional best practicable means. Certainly, with new processes, applicants will be required to show that there has been a cost/benefit analysis to show that whatever they are claiming to be excessive in a financial and economic sense is excessive by objective criteria in relation to the pollution caused.

Best practicable environmental option

Section 7(7) of the EPA specifically introduces the BPEO context. Where a process is controlled by HMIP and substances are released into more than one medium, then BATNEEC is to be used to minimise pollution caused to the environment as a whole, having regard to the best practicable environmental option. Thus, BPEO still has its place in strategic environmental pollution control but now clearly placed 'second fiddle' to the BATNEEC context.

Recently, HMIP have made available their internal guidance notes which form part of the Inspectorate's Manual on IPC. This has made it clear that when issuing authorisations they will be viewing an application in terms of a process standard rather than purely looking at the emission levels. Operators will have to demonstrate the options that they have considered when selecting the best available technique. However, they have pointed out that in a situation where the best technique is not put forward that the applicant must be able to justify the technique on the grounds that the selection of another option would involve entailing excessive cost. The note stresses the onus is on the operator to:

describe excessive cost in absolute terms without reference to the cost of the product. The applicant must be able to demonstrate that the increased cost of the product produced by the best available technique is grossly disproportionate to any environmental benefit likely to accrue from that method of production. The extra cost must represent a significant fraction of the cost of the finished product.

Additionally, HMIP may be able to relax the BATNEEC requirements where substances are released and are required to be rendered harmless. The note goes on to say that the process standard for new processes will be different to that for existing plant. Geographical effects, such as the volume of water carrying away effluent, could affect whether or not something is BATNEEC is one place whereas in another it would not be.

However, the Guidance is different for the prevention or minimisation of releases of prescribed substances. In those circumstances no account is to be taken of the absolute value of any local environmental effects of the releases.

There are, however, to be different considerations when dealing with existing plant. It is stressed that existing processes will have to be upgraded to the BATNEEC standards applicable to new plant within four years of the original date of authorisation. There may be allowable derogations from this period but HMIP have stated that this may not be allowed for more than four years. The tone of the new Guidance is that HMIP will certainly be looking towards the upgrading of existing plant with as much severity as the implementation of new plant.

Integrated pollution control notes

In addition to the sparse definition contained within the Act, an inspector determining an application for an authorisation must take into account the particular guidance note applicable to the class of process which is subject to the authorisation. The notes are supposed to provide a coherent system in which decisions can be made in relation to conditions to be imposed upon authorisations. Thus, all parties to an authorisation will know of the ground rules. The introduction of an element of certainty into the system increases both public accountability and also procedural fairness. As general guidance, the guidance note serves as a framework within which the details can be supplemented by scientific and technological advice from HMIP. This advice, in the form of notes, will take over from the BPM notes. The notes will:

(a) give the rationale behind the designation of the process for IPC;

(b)   state the environmental quality standards which are relevant to the process;

(c)   state HMIP's views as to the achievable standards;

(d)   describe a number of ways by which those standards can be reached;

(e)   give guidance as to what would amount to a substantial change and therefore require authorisation under the variation procedures.

The details contained within the guidance notes act as standards which new processes will have to meet. On the other hand, existing processes will be given an appropriate timescale within which to achieve these standards. To ensure that each note represents the 'state of the art' they are to be reviewed at least every four years.

There are to be over 200 integrated pollution control notes and these obviously require a significant review of the existing guidance. Thus, in respect of applications made before any guidance is issued, there will have to be consultation with HMIP as to the standards required. It is to be hoped that this transitional period is kept as short as possible but, in the meantime, there are five industry sector guidance notes which are intended to provide a proper background to considering applications until the full guidance notes can be brought in. These are Fuel and Power (IPR 1); Metal (IPR 2); Minerals (IPR 3) Chemicals (IPR 4); and Waste Disposal (IPR 5).

Implementation of the IPC system

Integrated pollution control was introduced for new processes, substantial variations of existing processes, and large combustion plants on 1 April 1991. Other existing processes are to be introduced over a five-year period ending on 31 January 1996. (Annex A, *Integrated Pollution Control—A Practical Guide*).

The introduction of a timetable for the implementation of IPC was a direct result of concern expressed over the ineffective implementation of the Control of Pollution Act. Various amendments were proposed to the Environmental Protection Bill requiring implementation within a certain time period. In order to counter such suggestions the official timetable for the implementation of the system was introduced.

Transfer of authorisations

An authorisation is personal to an applicant/operator. However, it is possible to transfer an authorisation from one operator to another. Therefore, if a business has been sold, it is possible to transfer an existing authorisation to the new owner of a factory.

Section 9 of the EPA provides that the person to whom the authorisation is transferred must notify HMIP of the transfer within 21 days. This will allow HMIP to take into account any new considerations arising out of the transfer and provides an opportunity for variation notices to be served. Failure to notify HMIP of the transfer of an authorisation is an offence (EPA, s. 23).

Enforcement powers

The model of enforcement throughout the EPA reflects traditional powers. There are however some changes from the existing law to take into account the new basis upon which the IPC system is controlled and the range of powers available to HMIP is very strong.

Variation notices

The ability to vary an authorisation is not strictly an enforcement power when compared with, for example, enforcement and prohibition notices. However the effect of a variation may be such that an operator would view it as having no practical distinction from an enforcement notice. The distinctive character of a variation notice relates more to the proactive approach rather than the punitive approach. Where new pollution abatement systems are introduced, or there is an understanding of new environmental dangers, then a variation notice can be served to bring operators 'up-to-date' (s. 11). Indeed, the Chief Inspector of HMIP is under a statutory duty to follow developments in pollution abatement technology and techniques (EPA, s. 4(9)).

Where HMIP consider that the conditions to which the authorisation originally applied have changed, they are under a duty under s. 10 of the Act to vary that authorisation. The variation notice specifies what type of variation is required and the date on which the variations have to take effect (s. 10(3)).

It is also open to the applicant to apply for a variation where plant is upgraded or replaced (EPA, s. 11). Thus, s. 11 provides that an operator wishing to make a 'relevant change' can notify HMIP and ask for a determination as to:

(a)   whether the proposed change would involve a breach of any condition of the authorisation;

(b)   if it would not involve such a breach, whether the authority would be likely to vary the conditions of the authorisation as a result of the change;

(c)   if it would involve such a breach, whether the authority would consider varying the conditions of the authorisation so that the change may be made; and

(d)   whether the change would involve a substantial change in the manner in which the process is being carried on.

A relevant change in a prescribed process is defined as a 'change in the manner of carrying on the process which is capable of altering the substances released from the process or of affecting the amount or any other characteristic of any substance so released' (s. 11(11)). Where the change would amount to a substantial change in the manner in which the process is being carried on, this is to be treated as a fresh application and various consultation procedures must be gone through.

These powers allow a degree of flexibility into the system so that changes which do not affect the authorisation can be made without a great deal of administrative intervention. On the other hand, where there is a change in the circumstances surrounding the authorisation, clearly HMIP ought to be able to intervene directly and request certain amendments.

The procedure mentioned above is only a preliminary procedure. Where HMIP decides that a formal variation is required, such an application has to be made. The only other alternative for an operator is to request a variation of the conditions of an authorisation.

There are further powers of variation contained in s. 11(5) and (6). The Department of the Environment envisages that these particular sections will be used during the construction of a plant where a variation in the authorisation is required but no 'relevant change' as defined in s. 11(11) of the Act is to take place. On the other hand, s. 11(6) allows for a variation of the conditions of an authorisation to take account of a relevant change.

The procedure governing a variation under s. 11 is contained in the Environmental Protection (Applications, Appeals and Registers) Regulations 1991 (SI 1991 No. 507). Regulation 3 states that when an application is made by an operator it must be in writing and include the name, address and telephone number of the operator and the address of the premises where the prescribed process is carried on. The request also has to include a description of the change, any change to the overall techniques used in the process, and any further information which the operator wants the inspector to take into account.

Revocation notices

Section 12 of the EPA gives HMIP the power to revoke an authorisation at any time by giving notice in writing (s. 12(1)). This power is absolute, although it will be subject as in any administrative decision to the sanctions of judicial review if the decision is so unreasonable that no reasonable authority could have reached it. Notwithstanding the absolute nature of this power, HMIP are able to revoke an authorisation where they have reason to believe that a prescribed process in respect of which there is an authorisation has not been carried on for a period of 12 months (s. 12(2)). Thus, where authorisations are seen to be redundant, the power to revoke will be exercised to ensure that there is no question of restarting the process. When a revocation notice is served, there is a minimum period of 28 days before it can take effect (s. 12(3)). There is also a residual power open to the Secretary of State to direct HMIP as to whether or not they should revoke the authorisation.

This is a serious power but it will probably only be used to deal with the situations where there is a blatant and flagrant abuse of the authorisation granted to an operator of a process.

Enforcement notices

Where there is a breach of a condition (contained within an authorisation), or an imminent breach of a condition, then HMIP is entitled to serve an enforcement notice under s. 13. The enforcement notice must contain similar information to that required by the planning regime in that it has to contain details of the facts which give rise to the opinion that there will be a contravention of the condition, or that there is likely to be a contravention of the condition, and also it must specify the steps that have to be taken to remedy the problem or anticipated problem within a certain stated period.

Prohibition notices

If HMIP is of the opinion that the carrying on of an authorised process in a particular manner involves an imminent risk of serious pollution they are under a mandatory duty to serve a prohibition notice, whether or not the operator is contravening the authorisation (s. 14(1)). The prohibition notice has to include details of the authority's assessment of the risk involved in the process, as well as specifying the steps that must be taken to remove it and the period within which they must be taken. The meaning of imminent risk to the environment is open to all manner of interpretation. Section 1(2) defines the environment as 'all, or any, of the following media, namely, the air, water and land' whereas pollution of the environment means 'pollution of the environment due to the release (into any environmental medium) from any process of substances which are capable of causing harm to man or any other living organisms supported by the environment'. It will be a matter for the subjective judgment of the inspectors as to what amounts to an imminent risk and what also amounts to serious pollution.

The prohibition notice empowers HMIP to prohibit an authorisation either as a whole or, if it is felt that the risk could be avoided by withdrawing part, then prohibiting that part only. Additionally, there is power under s. 14 to impose new conditions on the original authorisation and thus avoid imminent risk of serious pollution of the environment.

In attempting to explain the difference between prohibition notices and enforcement notices when the Environmental Protection Bill passed through the House of Lords, Lord Reay explained that a prohibition notice would cover:

> circumstances in which a process is being operated in a perfectly reasonable manner and within the conditions of the authorisation, but where some event external to the process requires quick and decisive action. For example, an accident at one process could release substances which could react with those normally allowed to be released at a nearby process, so causing serious pollution. In those circumstances, it would be right to close down temporarily the second process even though it was operating within its authorisation.

Therefore, when considering the wide nature of the prohibition notice, it has to be borne in mind that such a draconian power cannot be used too widely. The width of this power can be seen in s. 14(3) where it is stated that until the notice is withdrawn, an authorisation will cease to have any effect.

Powers of inspectors

These particular methods of enforcement will only be used as a final resort. Attempts also have to be made to ascertain whether or not such enforcement is appropriate. Therefore, the Act provides inspectors with a very wide range of powers to enable them to carry out their functions. Under s. 17, an inspector may:

(a)   enter premises—normally this must be at any reasonable time, but where there is an imminent risk of serious pollution, entry can be made at any time;

(b)   examine and investigate any process contained in any premises;

(c)   direct that any premises and items contained on those premises remain undisturbed;

(d)   take measurements, photographs and make recordings;

(e)   take samples of air, water, articles or substances on or in the vicinity of the premises;

(f)   require any articles or substances to be dismantled or subjected to any process or test;

(g)   take possession and detain any article or substance;

(h)   require persons to answer questions if he reasonably believes them to be able to give relevant information and, once they have supplied answers, to sign a declaration as to the truth of those answers;

(i)   require the production of any records;

(j)   require any assistance or facilities necessary to carry out any of the duties mentioned above;

(k)   seize and render harmless any article or substance which is believed to be the cause of imminent danger.

These powers cover virtually every conceivable situation in which an inspector may wish to exercise control over an industrial process.

Offences and remedies

Section 23 of the EPA gives a long list of offences under Part I. It is a criminal offence to:

(a)   operate a prescribed process without an authorisation;

(b)   contravene the conditions of an authorisation;

(c)   fail to give notice of transfer of an authorisation;

(d)   fail to comply with an enforcement or prohibition notice;

(e)   without reasonable excuse, fail to comply with a requirement imposed by an inspector under the powers in s. 17; or

(f)   intentionally make a false entry in any record required to be kept as a condition of an authorisation.

All offences are triable either way, with the more serious offences having a maximum fine level in the magistrates' court of £20,000. In the Crown Court all offences are subject to a maximum term of imprisonment of 2 years and/ or an unlimited fine (s. 23(2)). The Act also gives rights of audience to inspectors to present prosecutions even though they are not legally qualified (s. 23(5)).

In any trial relating to the breach of the implied condition relating to the use of BATNEEC, the onus of proof falls upon the operator of the process to show that there was no better available technique not entailing excessive cost which could be employed for that particular process (s. 25(1)).

It is open to any court in sentencing an offender for failure to comply with an enforcement or prohibition notice to order that the effects of the offence be remedied (s. 26). This allows for clean-up and compensation costs to come directly out of the offender's pocket. In many instances, these costs will far outstrip any reasonable fine that could be imposed. Perhaps even more importantly, where a process has been operated without any authorisation or has not been in compliance with a condition of an authorisation, the Chief Inspector can arrange for reasonable steps to be taken towards remedying any harm caused as a consequence and recover the costs of taking such steps from any person committing the offence (s. 27(1)). Before doing so however, the Chief Inspector must obtain the Secretary of State's approval in writing. Thus, even where a court is not willing to impose the high financial burden of clean-up costs on an offender, it will be open to the Inspectorate to remedy such harm. There are further remedies available to HMIP in the High Court, under s. 24, where there has been a failure to comply with an enforcement or prohibition notice. This allows HMIP to seek injunctions where the effective enforcement of the criminal law is not securing adequate compliance.

Corporate liability

In an age where the concept of individual responsibility for corporate actions is being accepted by both the courts and the general public, s. 157 of the EPA provides that where an offence is committed by a company and it can be shown that a director, manager, or similar person in the company either consented, connived or was negligent, then criminal liability can attach individually as well as on a corporate basis. Furthermore, where an offence is committed owing to the act or default of an independent third party, proceedings can be brought against either or both under s. 158. These provisions would cover corporate officers who acknowledged that there was a risk of environmental contamination from certain activities and took that risk in the full knowledge of the consequences. Furthermore, where an act of environmental damage is caused by a breach of Part I owing to the activities of an independent contractor and notwithstanding the absence of fault on behalf of the operator of the process, both parties can be prosecuted.

Crown immunity

As in other legislation, the Crown will be immune from criminal proceedings by virtue of s. 159. However, where the Crown operates processes subject to IPC it will not be exempt from the general control mechanisms under Part I. Thus, there is a need to apply for authorisations and the same statutory objectives will apply as in the case of non-Crown bodies.

There is, under s. 159(2), a subsidiary power which allows for the Crown to be taken to the High Court and any breach of any authorisation to be declared unlawful. It is difficult to envisage a situation where this would be useful except in a case where the proof of civil liability depended to a certain extent upon the ability to show unlawful action on behalf of the Crown.

Appeals

Section 15 of the EPA governs appeals. It provides that there is a right of appeal against:

(a)   revocation, variation, enforcement and prohibition notices;
(b)   the refusal to grant or vary an authorisation;
(c)   the imposition of unreasonable conditions.

Furthermore, s. 22 gives an applicant a right of appeal where HMIP have notified the operator that information contained within an authorisation or an application for an authorisation is not commercially confidential.

The detailed appeals procedure is contained in the Environmental Protection (Applications, Appeals and Registers) Regulations 1991 (SI 1991 No. 507). Generally, the time limit for appeals is similar to that in the planning system, being six months from a refusal, or a deemed refusal, to grant an authorisation. Where there is an appeal against an enforcement, prohibition or s. 2(2) variation notice, the time limit is two months from the date of the notice. Where HMIP are seeking by notice to revoke an authorisation, the appeal must be submitted before the notice takes effect. Finally, where there is an appeal concerning commercial confidentiality, it must be submitted within 21 days from the refusal.

Pending the hearing of the appeal, a revocation notice will not have effect. However, in all other cases, although there is an appeal, there is no suspension of the notice. Thus, an operator cannot gain an economic advantage where there is a rush order, by appealing against a notice so as to stop the enforcement process, continuing to pollute until the order is completed, and then stopping the process before the appeal is heard.

An appeal must be made in writing to the Secretary of State (Regulation 9). The appeal has to be accompanied by any relevant information, including any application, authorisation, correspondence, or decision and a statement as to how the appellant wishes the appeal to be determined.

Modes of appeal

An appeal can be heard in one of two ways: either by way of written representations or by a hearing. There has been an attempt by the Department of the Environment to ensure that hearings do not take on a quasi-legal nature, as has happened in the planning system. Thus, the system has very few rules. The Department of the Environment Guidance states:

the procedure at a hearing will be left to the Appeals Inspector. He may hear the parties in what ever order he thinks most suitable for the clarification of issues. He may, for instance, review the case based on the papers already provided and then outline what he considers to be the main issues and indicate those matters which require further explanation or clarification. This will not preclude the appellant or the enforcing authority from referring to other aspects which they consider to be relevant. The approach that will be encouraged will be one of informality, for example, hearings may often take the form of a round table discussion, rather than a formal presentation of evidence.

This air of informality is supposedly to alter the hearing system from being adversarial and (often in the case of planning appeals) inquisitorial. There is to a certain extent a degree of public participation in that Regulation 13 states that notice has to be given at least 28 days before the date of the hearing of the date, time and place for the holding of the hearing. The Department does however concede that in more controversial proposals it may be necessary to adopt a formal procedure. Presumably, where issues are likely to be of great consequence to members of the public, there needs to be some element of the adversarial approach to ensure that there is adequate accountability. Otherwise, public confidence in an appeals system, which to the untrained eye and ear would appear to be a meeting of highly trained, highly specialised people discussing hypothetical problems around a table, would be seriously undermined.

The written representations appeal procedure will contain an exchange of views on paper as to the suitability of any proposals. The procedure will vary little from the planning system.

It is only for the Secretary of State to decide an appeal under the EPA. The inspector who heard the appeal is required to report to the Secretary of State as to any conclusions and recommendations. The Secretary of State in making the decision has to take into account these recommendations but does not have to follow them. The Secretary of State then issues the decision to all interested parties.

ANNEX A

Timetable for Implementing Integrated Pollution Control

Class No. of process	Process	Comes within IPC	Application for authorisation to be submitted between	Chief Inspector's Guidance Note issued
	Fuel & Power Industry			
1.3	Combustion (>50MWth): boilers and furnaces	1.4.91	1.4.91 & 30.4.91	1.4.91
1.1	Gasification	1.4.92	1.4.92 & 30.6.92	1.10.91
1.2	Carbonisation	1.4.92	1.4.92 & 30.6.92	1.10.91
1.3	Combustion (remainder)	1.4.92	1.4.92 & 30.6.92	1.10.91
1.4	Petroleum	1.4.92	1.4.92 & 30.6.92	1.10.91

Class No. of process	Process	Comes within IPC	Application for authorisation to be submitted between	Chief Inspector's Guidance Note issued
Waste Disposal Industry				
5.1	Incineration	1.8.92	1.8.92 & 31.10.92	1.2.92
5.2	Chemical recovery	1.8.92	1.8.92 & 31.10.92	1.2.92
5.3	Waste derived fuel	1.8.92	1.8.92 & 31.10.92	1.2.92
Mineral Industry				
3.1	Cement	1.12.92	1.12.92 & 28.2.93	1.6.92
3.2	Asbestos	1.12.92	1.12.92 & 28.2.93	1.6.92
3.3	Fibre	1.12.92	1.12.92 & 28.2.93	1.6.92
3.4	Glass	1.12.92	1.12.92 & 28.2.93	1.6.92
3.6	Ceramic	1.12.92	1.12.92 & 28.2.93	1.6.92
Chemical Industry				
4.1	Petrochemical	1.5.93	1.5.93 & 31.7.93	1.11.92
4.2	Organic	1.5.93	1.5.93 & 31.7.93	1.11.92
4.7	Chemical pesticide	1.5.93	1.5.93 & 31.7.93	1.11.92
4.8	Pharmaceutical	1.5.93	1.5.93 & 31.7.93	1.11.92
4.3	Acid manufacturing	1.11.93	1.11.93 & 31.1.94	1.5.93
4.4	Halogen	1.11.93	1.11.93 & 31.1.94	1.5.93
4.6	Chemical fertiliser	1.11.93	1.11.93 & 31.1.94	1.5.93
4.9	Bulk chemical storage	1.11.93	1.11.93 & 31.1.94	1.5.93
4.5	Inorganic chemical	1.5.94	1.5.94 & 31.7.94	1.11.93
Metal Industry				
2.1	Iron and steel	1.1.95	1.1.95 & 31.3.95	1.7.94
2.3	Smelting	1.1.95	1.1.95 & 31.3.95	1.7.94
2.2	Non-ferrous	1.5.95	1.5.95 & 31.7.95	1.11.94
Other Industry				
6.1	Paper manufacturing	1.11.95	1.11.95 & 31.1.96	1.5.95
6.2	Di-isocyanate	1.11.95	1.11.95 & 31.1.96	1.5.95
6.3	Tar and bitumen	1.11.95	1.11.95 & 31.1.96	1.5.95
6.4	Uranium	1.11.95	1.11.95 & 31.1.96	1.5.95
6.5	Coating	1.11.95	1.11.95 & 31.1.96	1.5.95
6.6	Coating manufacturing	1.11.95	1.11.95 & 31.1.96	1.5.95
6.7	Timber	1.11.95	1.11.95 & 31.1.96	1.5.95
6.9	Animal & plant treatment	1.11.95	1.11.95 & 31.1.96	1.5.95

ELEVEN
Atmospheric pollution

The air that we breathe is one of the main foundations for human life. It is made up of a fine balance of a number of different elements. Interfering with this balance can have far-reaching effects, often not fully recognised until some time after contamination. The range of problems affecting the atmosphere stretches across the full range of human activities, from highly toxic fumes emitted from a complicated industrial process to such seemingly mundane activities as lighting a fire, driving a car or using spray-on deodorant. The history of atmospheric pollution dates back to early times. The prohibitions on certain activities producing smoke are probably the first instances of environment pollution legislation in Great Britain.

Because such a wide range of activities affects the atmosphere, the range of environmental issues is also wide. On the one hand, there have always been difficulties with polluting activities affecting the locality in which they were situated. International difficulties have arisen with the creation of acid rain. In recent years we have seen a realisation amongst the international community that individual nations' actions can combine to create truly global difficulties. The destruction of the ozone layer and subsequently the issue of global warning have brought home the truly awesome consequences of the combined effect of certain industrial activities.

Local atmospheric pollution

The pollution of the local atmosphere from emissions has traditionally been easy to identify. Such problems date back to the early uses of coal in domestic fires. The production of fumes and particulates from fires caused pulmonary infections and related lung diseases. Notwithstanding this effect, coal continued to be used. In 1661, John Evelyn published his famous work on air pollution in city areas, *Fumi Fugium*, which not only outlined the problems that atmospheric pollution from smoke caused, but also, more importantly, tried to suggest methods by which the problems could be resolved.

With the advent of more complicated processes in the late eighteenth century, the problems of atmospheric pollution grew more severe. The industrial revolution increased the use of coal to drive new machinery and, more importantly, produced very acidic emissions as a consequence of the 'alkali works'. These works used the leblanc process to produce soda, but the by-product of the chemical process used meant that hydrochloric gas was emitted into the atmosphere which, when mixed with water, created a new phenomenon—acid rain.

The consequences of these new processes were that areas of the country were rendered desolate by this very highly acidic moist air burning trees, shrubs and hedges. One of the centres for the alkali industry, St Helens in Lancashire, was reported as not having a single tree with any foliage on it. Even amongst the people working in such factories, concern was expressed. This concern led to the setting-up of a Royal Commission to look into the problem of alkali pollution and subsequently the recommendations for the first Alkali Act passed in 1863. Under this Act, a new Alkali Inspector was appointed who regulated such alkali processes. Although the Act did not attempt to deal with smoke, it did introduce new stricter controls over the production of acidic emissions. It made the first attempts at restricting the composition of emissions with the introduction of primitive emission standard requirements. Under the Act, there was a requirement that 95% of all noxious emissions should be arrested within the plant, so that only 5% of the previously emitted fumes were allowed into the atmosphere.

Even though there were strict emission standards on the volume of noxious gases produced, there were also the first signs of a proactive approach from the newly created Alkali Inspectorate in that they would encourage manufacturers to reduce the emissions to less than 5% in order to protect the environment.

The initial effect of the legislation was a dramatic reduction in the production of acidic emissions from almost 14,000 tonnes to about 45 tonnes. This improvement, however, was only temporary. Within a short time the inadequacy of the legislation was brought home. The imposition of individualised emission standards could not take into account the cumulative effect of a large concentration of such operations. As the Act had only set a reduction for acidic emissions in terms of a percentage for each plant, the overall concentration of such emissions rose as the number of factories increased.

The introduction of the Alkali Act of 1874 attempted to redress the balance by introducing the concept of best practicable means (BPM). The application of BPM was used to widen the scope of the previous emission limits to include all noxious or offensive gases. In essence, the application of BPM relied upon these presumptive limits. The limits saw the introduction of the first proper emission standards in British legislation by specifying actual amounts of certain substances per cubic metre of emitted gas. If these emission limits were being met, then it was presumed that any legislation was being complied with and that the best practicable means were being used. Interestingly, the emission limits set for hydrogen chloride in the 1874 Act, 0.2 grains per cubic foot, still stands today. The use of the concept of best practicable means ensured that there was to be a conciliatory and cooperational approach as the Alkali Inspectorate sought a method of enforcement which would not place 'an undue burden on manufacturing industry'.

Neither of these Acts, nor the consolidation Act of 1906, dealt specifically with the control of smoke from either industrial or commercial premises. Attempts were made to control the emission of smoke through such Acts as the Public Health Act 1875, the Public Health (Smoke Abatement) Act 1926 and the Public Health Act 1936 but these generally dealt with smoke nuisances. These powers could not rid industrial cities of the problems of smoke pollution. The physical evidence of this pollution could be seen on blackened buildings, and by the frequency of smog, which was prevalent from Victorian times. Such smog was caused by fog forming in winter months and combining with smoke particles to produce a compound of gases which could cut visibility to very low levels. Of more concern, however, was the effect that these smogs had upon the dispersion of pollution. With a heavy concentration of smog hanging over a city the air was very still and convection was low. With the onset of these calm conditions, the dispersal of emissions was much more difficult. Such a lethal cocktail was bound to produce tragic effects, but these were fairly minimal until December 1952 when a smog descended upon London which did not clear for five days. Nothing unusual was noticed until prize cattle at the Smithfield Show started to suffer from respiratory problems. The smog got everywhere, even inside the Sadlers Wells Theatre which resulted in the stoppage of a performance because of the difficulty of seeing the stage. When the smog had lifted it was estimated that nearly 4,000 people had lost their lives as a consequence of the smoke and other emissions.

The Government immediately responded by setting up the Beaver Committee to report on the difficulties surrounding smoke pollution. The recommendation of the Committee was to introduce legislation to eliminate particulate emissions such as smoke, dust and grit so that such conditions would not arise again. With the introduction of the Clean Air Act 1956, later supplemented by the Clean Air Act 1968, controls were introduced for the first time to restrict the production of smoke, grit and dust from all commercial and industrial activities not covered by the Alkali Acts but also, more importantly, domestic fires as well. The Acts introduced such concepts as smoke control areas and the complete prohibition on 'dark smoke' from chimneys.

During the 1970s, the problems of the emission of smoke, dirt, dust and grit lessened and coupled with the new approach to industrial processes a gradual improvement took place in the quality of the atmosphere in the UK. There was a move away from the use of coal as fuel to smokeless substances such as coke and gas. Additionally, the gap left behind with the introduction of clean air zones was met by an increase in the use of electricity for power and heat. The main generator of electricity in Britain, the Central Electricity Generating Board, changed its practices in a direct reaction to the difficulties encountered with local pollution by replacing the short chimneys traditionally used in power stations with larger and taller chimneys. The basis of this change was to disperse pollution at a higher level and therefore hopefully dilute any substances over longer distances. The consequence would be a reduction in the concentrations of pollutants in the nearby locality. Unfortunately, this reduction in the levels of local pollution only shifted the problems to a different location. Whilst the pollution of the atmosphere declined nationally, the concern internationally rose. The change of policy from short to tall stacks for chimneys saw the creation of the first environmental problem which could properly be identified across national boundaries—the problem of acid rain.

International difficulties: acid rain

The production of energy from power stations produces, amongst other things, sulphur dioxide, nitrous oxide and nitrogen dioxide. The sulphur dioxide created from power stations amounts to some 80% of all such emissions into the atmosphere. In 1953 the Beaver Report had recommended that such plants should be fitted with desulphurisation equipment but that was rejected specifically at the time as being impracticable for the particular process. Instead, the change of use from short chimneys to a dilution and dispersal method from tall chimneys was introduced. It was thought that the dispersal of such emissions into the upper levels of the atmosphere would render such substances harmless before they could contaminate an area. This applied to the areas around the emission plants but, further afield, the evidence suggested that it had little effect. As was stated in *The Dirty Man of Europe*:

> In smoothly flowing medium speed winds, plumes from power stations travel in a concentrated stream for hundreds of miles. Tall stacks (Drax Power Station is 259 metres tall) can take emissions above a layer of air trapped near the ground into smooth air streams. On a steady south westerly, a plume from Eggborough Power Station, labelled with 'sodium hexafluoride' was tracked all the way across the North Sea to Denmark . . . . . in clear skies sulphur was being slowly oxidised and deposited. Once it entered low mountain cloud, production of acid increased 14 fold and fall out increased over 200%. The total removal rate shot up to 27% an hour, depositing the sulphur in a concentrated drizzle.

The combination of sulphur dioxide and other acids from power stations and traffic combined with the atmosphere to produce not only acid rain, but also acid deposits in the atmosphere made of ammonium sulphate particles.

The effects of the production of such substances into the atmosphere has increased the acidity of rain fall in some areas to over 40 times the natural level. This has had a terrible effect upon areas of not only England, Scotland and Wales but also other countries within Europe where the prevailing winds have carried such emissions. The Scandinavian countries in particular have received a large percentage of the 'export' of Britain's production of sulphur dioxide and acid rain. Vegetation suffers from the increased acidity, trees and shrubs die and, in Southern Norway, it has been shown that there has been a steady increase in the acidity of lakes so that some lakes and rivers are on the borderline between supporting life and not. The specific effects of certain pollutants can range from speckled areas on leaves brought about by acidic deposits through to complete death. These problems require a cooperative approach to be taken between nations. There has been a long running dispute between Britain and the Scandinavian countries as to the cause of the acidic deposits on their countries. The EEC has made some steps towards introducing a desulphurisation programme, however it remains to be seen whether or not this is to be successful.

Global issues: ozone depletion and global warming

The Department of the Environment's White Paper *This Common Inheritance*, published in September 1990, put the international problem of global warming to the top of the environmental agenda.

Global warming is one of the biggest environmental challenges now facing the world. It calls for action by all the world's nations, as no single nation can solve the problem on its own.

The greenhouse effect, as it has come to be known, has arisen because the production of various 'greenhouse' gases have increased in the past century with progressive industrialisation. In the lower atmosphere the production of emissions from power stations, car exhausts and industrial plants have increased by almost 100%. These emissions absorb radiated heat and create a higher ambient temperature level which has led to speculation that there could be shrinking global icecaps and rising water levels.

Additionally, the amount of ozone in the upper atmosphere screens the earth from harmful UV-B radiation. This screen has deteriorated and there have been studies showing a 'hole' above Antarctica. This depletion of ozone has been linked to the use of chlorofluorocarbons (CFCs). The creation of greenhouse gases and the depletion of the ozone layer are worldwide problems which require international cooperation to solve. The use of international law as a mechanism for environmental protection is relatively unusual and there are some limitations to its usefulness. However, the nature of the problems facing the world in terms of these two issues have led to significant steps being taken to prevent any further harm.

The control of smoke under the Clean Air Acts

As we have seen, the control of smoke, dust and dirt from industrial and domestic fires was largely ineffective in dealing with the problems associated with such emissions in the early part of the twentieth century. Although the Public Health (Smoke Abatement) Act 1926 attempted to control certain categories of industrial smoke, domestic smoke was prohibited only if it amounted to a 'nuisance'. The Clean Air Act 1956, later amended and supplemented by the Clean Air Act 1968 provides a comprehensive control mechanism for the protection of the environment from smoke, dust and fumes.

These Acts constitute a separate and distinct area of control. Essentially, they control smoke, dust and grit from all fires and furnaces.

The enforcement agency under the Clean Air Acts is the local authority (1956 Act, s. 29). In practice, enforcement is undertaken by officers from the

Environmental Health Department of the local authorities. These are technically qualified people with the ability to understand difficult scientific issues.

Control of smoke from chimneys

Section 1 of the 1956 Act prohibits the emission of 'dark smoke' from the chimney of any building. Any occupier who breaches s. 1 will be guilty of a criminal offence. The section applies to all types of buildings from domestic houses to industrial premises and crematoria. The mechanism of control specifically applies to chimneys from buildings. Although the definition of the word building covers such structures as a greenhouse, *Clifford* v *Holt* [1899] 1 Ch 698, it would have to be a part of a recognised structure.

The prohibition applies only to 'dark smoke', therefore other types of emissions are covered either elsewhere in the Act or under different statutes. In attempting to determine whether smoke is 'dark', enforcement officers are forced to make a visual assessment of the shade of the smoke emission by comparing the darkness of the smoke with a uniform chart known as a Ringlemann chart. The chart contains five shades of grey by cross hatching black lines on a white background so that it runs from clear (number 0) to black (number 4). The chart is rectangular in shape measuring some 581 mm x 127 mm. The chart is used in accordance with certain guidelines laid down in British Standard 2742. The chart is held up by the operator and compared to the smoke from a distance of at least 15 metres and then comparisons are made between the colour of the smoke and the colour on the chart. If the colour of the smoke is as dark as or darker than shade 2 on the Ringlemann Scale it then qualifies as dark smoke (1956 Act, s. 34(1)). Where, however, an operator is experienced, s. 34(2) allows for an assessment to be made independent of the Ringelmann chart, often by the use of a smaller, more portable smoke chart (129 mm x 69 mm). Some officers rely purely on their experience to assess whether or not the smoke is darker than shade 2.

The prohibition also only covers smoke emitted from chimneys. The definition of a chimney can be found in s. 34(1) and is wide enough to cover all structures of openings through which smoke is emitted. Thus, smoke from outdoor fires or, for instance, burning straw or stubble is not covered by s. 1.

Strict liability

As in other environmental legislation, liability is strict therefore prima facie *any* dark smoke emitted from a chimney would give rise to liability under s. 1. The 1956 Act makes it clear that it is not necessarily the person who causes the emission of dark smoke who will be liable, it is the occupier of the building from which the chimney emits the smoke. Probably the only incident in which it is likely that an occupier will not be liable would be where the chain of causation has been broken by the activities of a trespasser (see *Southern Water Authority* v *Pegrum* [1989] CLR 442).

Exemptions and defences

The practical effect of this liability upon industry could have been that furnaces would not have been able to function properly, but the 1956 Act s. 1(2) and (3) provide firstly exemptions to the general prohibition and secondly statutory defences against a criminal charge.

Section 1(2) provides for certain exemptions to be decided by the Secretary of State. These exemptions are restricted by the duration of emissions. The Dark Smoke (Permitted Periods) Regulations 1958 (SI 1958 No. 498) allows three main exemptions for smoke from chimneys. Firstly, there are time-limits imposed of anything between 10 and 40 minutes during any period of eight hours for emission of dark smoke depending on both the number of furnaces used and whether or not soot is blowing. Secondly, there is a limit of four minutes of continuous emissions of dark smoke where the cause is not owed to burning soot. Finally, there is a limit of two minutes in each period of 30 minutes where smoke is black (that is, smoke is as dark or darker than shade 4 on the Ringelmann Chart).

Section 1(3) lays down three statutory defences. These defences are not absolute and require certain qualifying steps to be taken to ensure that the defences apply. The section provides that it is a defence to a charge under s. 1(1) that the emission was:

(a)   solely due to the lighting of a coal furnace, and that all practicable steps were taken to minimise or prevent emissions;
(b)   solely due to the mechanical failure of plant, and that the contravention of s. 1(1) could not reasonably have been foreseen or provided against nor prevented after the failure;
(c)   solely due to the unavoidable use of unsuitable fuel with the best available fuel being used and suitable fuel not being available;
(d)   any combination of (a), (b) and (c).

Enforcement and offences

Local authorities can take action against dark smoke emitted from outside the area which they control if it affects their area (1956 Act, s. 29(2)). An important prerequisite of bringing a prosecution is that the enforcement authority are under a duty to notify occupiers of the offences 'as soon as may be'. There then has to be written confirmation of this notification within four days of the enforcement officer becoming aware of the offence itself. If neither of these actions is taken then it would be open to a defendant in any proceedings to show that he has not received notification and that amounts to a defence to a prosecution (s. 30(2)). The offence is only triable in the magistrates' court. There are different maximum levels of fine for emissions from private dwellings (level 3 on the standard scale) or for any other case (level 5 on the standard scale).

Emissions of dark smoke from industrial plants

Although the Clean Air Act of 1956 had many wide-ranging effects, it did not control all emissions of dark smoke from trade or industrial premises. Therefore, in 1968, a further Act was passed to extend the prohibition of the emission of dark smoke from trade or industrial premises other than from a chimney of a building. The 1968 Act extends the 1956 Act in a number of ways. The Act applies to premises rather than buildings. This would include the grounds of factories and areas which are not buildings such as demolition sites (*Sheffield CC* v *ADH Demolition* (1984) 82 LGR 177).

Under the 1968 Act, s. 1(3), it is open to the Secretary of State to pass regulations giving exemptions to the burning of prescribed matter which emits dark smoke in the open. The Clean Air (Emission of Dark Smoke) (Exemption) Regulations 1969 (SI 1969 No. 1263) exempts certain materials such as timber, explosives, tar, and waste from animal or poultry carcasses. Section 1(5) provides that industrial trade premises includes premises not used for industrial trade purposes but on which substances or matter is burnt in connection with industrial or trade processes. Thus, open areas without any connection to industrial activities would fall within it. Section 1(1)(a) was inserted after the introduction of the Control of Smoke Pollution Act 1989. This reverses the burden of proof required when attempting to show the causation of dark smoke. On trade or business premises, where circumstances are such that the burning of material would be likely to give rise to an emission of dark smoke then such an emission can be taken as proved unless the occupier or person accused of the offence can show that no dark smoke was actually emitted. Where fires have been extinguished but dark smoke has already been emitted there has often been difficulty in proving from where the dark smoke has emanated. Section 1(1)(a) allows Environmental Health Officers to act against smoke pollution even though there is no smoke emanating from the premises. The 1968 Act further widens the 1956 Act by attaching liability not only to the occupier of premises but also to any person who causes or permits an emission.

There is a statutory defence under s. 1(4) that the emission of dark smoke was 'inadvertent'. Interestingly, this would suggest that although the offence has an absolute liability, some degree of blameworthiness is necessary for an action to be successful. If the emission was inadvertent, it is also necessary to show that all practicable steps have been taken to prevent or minimise the emission of dark smoke. Practicability is defined in the 1956 Act, s. 34.

Again the offence is only triable in the magistrates' court and the maximum fine is set at level 4 on the standard scale.

The control of grit, dust and fumes

The Acts do not only cover smoke. Emissions from furnaces can also contain particulate matter and the Acts extend to cover such particulate matters, ranging from the largest (being grit as defined in the Clean Air (Emission of Grit and Dust from Furnaces) Regulations 1971 (SI 1971 No. 162)) through dust and small solid particles between 1 to 75 µm in diameter (as defined in BS3405) to fumes (which are defined as any airborne solid matter smaller than dust) (Clean Air Act 1968, s. 13). There are proactive measures for preventing smoke, dust, grit and fumes being emitted from furnaces. The 1956 Act, s. 3 provides that furnaces over a certain energy value (excluding domestic boilers) should, as far as practicable, be smokeless when using a fuel for which it was designed. This control is implemented by s. 3(3), under which anyone wishing to install a furnace has to notify the local authority before doing so. Where the local authority are notified and authorisation has been given, then the furnace is deemed to comply with the provision. This, however, does not exempt the furnace from being subject to the prohibition on dark smoke under the 1956 Act, s. 1. Where a furnace is operated without such an approval then the person who installed the furnace will be guilty of an offence (s. 3(1)).

This proactive approach is further strengthened by the requirement for grit and dust arrestment plant to be fitted to furnaces. This power was extended under the Clean Air Act 1968, ss. 3 and 4, which control all furnaces partly installed or for which there is an agreement to install after 1 October 1969. Again, details of the type of arrestment plant must be given to the local authority. Prior to 1 October 1969, the only furnaces covered were those in buildings burning pulverised fuel or solid waste or fuel at a rate of 1 tonne or more an hour. After that date, the 1968 Act extended the powers to include furnaces in which solid, liquid or gaseous matter is burnt as well as reducing the rate of the use of solid matter to a minimum 100 pounds per hour. The statutory requirements are fleshed out by the Clean Air (Emission of Grit and Dust from Furnaces) Regulations 1971 (SI 1971 No. 162) which contain information as to the quantities of grit and dust which may be emitted by reference to either the heat put out by the furnace or the heat taken in by the furnace.

Exemptions
There are exemptions to the requirement to supply details of plant to the local authority under s. 3; the 1968 Act, s. 4 gives two main areas of exemption. Firstly, the Secretary of State can exempt certain furnaces by way of the Clean Air (Arrestment Plant) (Exemption) Regulations 1969 (SI 1969 No. 1262), which exclude mobile or transportable furnaces, and certain other furnaces. Secondly, the local authority has a power to exempt a specific furnace if they are satisfied that the emissions from the furnace will not be prejudicial to health or a nuisance. Application for this exemption has to be made by the person installing the furnace. The local authority have eight weeks in which to give a written decision and if no decision is forthcoming in that period then exemption is deemed to have been granted. Where there is a refusal of an application, there is a right of appeal within 28 days from the date of the decision.

Monitoring provisions
To enable the local authority to enforce their responsibilities effectively, the 1956 Act, s. 7, as amended by the 1968 Act, s. 5, allows the Secretary of State to make regulations which allow the local authority to monitor the emission of grit and dust from furnaces. These provisions do not apply to fumes unless they are controlled specifically under other legislation.

A measurement can be carried out only in very particular circumstances when the provisions regulating the measurement of grit and dust are contained in the Clean Air (Measurement of Grit and Dust) Regulations 1971 (SI 1971 No. 616). Under these regulations, the local authority have to give the occupier of premises not less than six weeks' notice in writing requiring him to make adaptations to any chimney serving a furnace to allow for plant and machinery to be installed to monitor the dust and grit from the furnace. Thereafter the local authority must give at least 28 days' notice in writing requiring a test to be carried out in accordance with the procedure specified in an otherwise obscure book, *The Measurement of Solids in Flue Gases* by P G W Hawksley, S Badzioch and J H Blackett. Then, after giving at least 48 hours' notice in writing of the date and time of the tests, the occupier must send to the local authority within 14 days the report of the results of the test including the date, the number of furnaces and the results in terms of pounds of grit and dust emitted per hour.

These provisions apply only to a number of specific types of furnace including those that burn pulverised fuel or any other solid matter at a rate of 45 kilograms or more per hour.

The control of height of chimneys

As one of the main mechanisms for the control of environmental pollution into the atmosphere was to increase the height of chimneys to disperse the pollutant over a wider area, there is specific legislation to control the height of chimneys. The argument used by many scientists has been that the higher the chimney the higher the emission point and thus the more diluted any emissions will be when they eventually come back down to the ground.

Under the 1968 Act, s. 6, an application for chimney height approval is required to enable the local authority to assess the height required, taking into account the geographical features and the constitution of the emissions, so as to avoid localised pollution. If approval is not obtained, it will only be an offence under the 1968 Act if the chimney is used once it has been constructed. The application form is prescribed by the Clean Air (Height of Chimneys) (Prescribed Form) Regulations 1969 (SI 1969 No. 412). An application must be made in the following circumstances:

(a)   where a new chimney is erected;

(b)   where the combustion space of a furnace serving an existing chimney is enlarged by adding a new furnace to an existing number of furnaces all serving the same chimney;

(c)   where a furnace is removed, or replaced, but only where a furnace burns pulverised fuel, or burns solid matter at a rate of 100 pounds or more per hour, or burns more than 1.25 million BTU per hour of any liquid or gas.

In addition to these controls, planning permissions must also be applied for.

When deciding whether or not to grant chimney height approval, the local authority must be satisfied that the chimney height will be sufficient to prevent, so far as is practicable, the smoke, grit, dust, gases or fumes emitted from the chimney from being prejudicial to health or a nuisance when taking into account (s. 6(4)):

(a) the purpose of the chimney;
(b) the position and descriptions of buildings near it;
(c) the levels of the neighbouring ground;
(d) any other matters requiring consideration in the circumstances.

If the local authority decide to grant approval, they can grant it with or without conditions but these must only relate to the rate and quality of emissions from the chimney (s. 6(5)). If the local authority turn down an application, they have to notify the applicant of their decision in writing with their reasons and an indication as to what they think the lowest acceptable height would be. The applicant may appeal to the Secretary of State within 28 days (s. 6(7)).

As in other areas of control in the Clean Air Acts, the Secretary of State has the power to exempt certain boilers or plants from this control for chimney height approval. These exemptions can be found in the Clean Air (Heights of Chimneys) (Exemption) Regulations 1969 (SI 1969 No. 411). The Regulations specifically relate to the need for approval to construct a chimney under s. 10 and include mostly temporary or mobile boilers or plants.

The guidelines on assessing chimney heights are contained in the Third Memorandum on Chimney Heights published by HMSO. This provides specific mathematical calculations which will supposedly take into account background levels of pollution. Where pollution levels are higher there is a requirement that a chimney should be higher as well. The memorandum indicates that the chimney height required should vary according, among other factors, to the type of area concerned. It identifies the following types of area:

(a) an undeveloped area where development is unlikely;
(b) a partially developed area with scattered houses;
(c) a built-up residential area;
(d) an urban area of mixed industrial and residential development;
(e) a large city or an urban area of mixed heavy industrial and dense residential development.

By assessing the level of pollution in the atmosphere in these generalised ways, it is hoped to achieve an idea of the required height for a particular chimney. In a large city or urban area it will be a requirement that chimneys should be at their highest. More particularly, where environmental quality standards as set down by the EEC, and implemented under the Air Quality Standards Regulations 1989 (SI 1989 No. 317), are not being met then there will be a requirement that chimneys do not exacerbate the problem.

Miscellaneous controls

Aside from chimneys serving a furnace, s. 10 of the 1956 Act applies similar restrictions on chimneys serving a non-combustion process. There is a much simpler procedure for obtaining approval by submitting building regulation plans. The local authority are entitled to reject the plans if the chimney is not adequate to prevent emissions from becoming prejudicial to health or a nuisance. There is a right of appeal against refusal.

The Building Regulations 1976 (SI 1976 No. 1676) apply not only to non-combustible furnace chimneys but also to those controlled by s. 6. Building regulation approval is therefore required for all chimneys.

Smoke control areas

One of the main successes of the 1956 Act was the introduction of the concept of smoke control areas. In order to improve conditions over wide areas and to control non-dark smoke, s. 11 allows local authorities to designate areas which will be smoke control areas. As there are difficulties in defining areas in relation to land, two or more authorities are entitled to join together and declare that a larger area than their own area is to be a smoke control area (s. 31(3)(b)).

The effect of designating a smoke control area is to make it an offence for occupiers of premises to allow any smoke emissions from a chimney.

At the time of implementation of the 1956 Act, there was very little smokeless fuel available so, in order to ensure the practicable enforcement of these provisions, the 1956 Act exempts both authorised fuel and certain fireplaces from control. The Smoke Control Areas (Authorised Fuels) Regulations 1991 (SI 1991 No. 1282), consolidate 17 different Regulations made since 1956. These regulations include all the types of material which can be burnt without emitting smoke. Fireplaces are exempted under various Smoke Control (Exempted Fireplaces) Orders. Therefore, either authorised fuel can be used *per se* or unauthorised fuel can be used on exempted fireplaces and the use of either could amount to a defence to a prosecution under s. 11. The burden of proof for showing that such exemptions apply falls upon the occupier.

The local authority are entitled under s. 11(3) to exempt specified buildings, classes of building or fireplaces from the Smoke Control Area. They may make different provision for different parts of the area or limit their operation to specified classes of buildings in the area, such as factories rather than houses.

The process for making an order designating a smoke control area is contained in the 1956 Act, sch. 1. There is a requirement for general publicity which enables the public to make objections. This publicity is effected by placing advertisements in the London Gazette in addition to notices being posted around the area (sch. 1, para. 1). If there are any objections to the order they must be taken into account as material considerations in deciding whether or not to ratify the order. Where an order is made, its operation is delayed for a minimum of six months whilst the authority bring the effect of the order to the notice of the people within the area.

Department of the Environment Circular 11/81 suggests that there should be sufficient supplies of authorised fuel in the area and the operation of the order should be implemented at some time between 1 July and 1 November to ensure that there are adequate provisions of fuel stocks. On the other hand, the 1968 Act, s. 10 forbids local authorities postponing the implementation of the order by more than 12 months.

Where a smoke control order is ratified, the imposition of new fuels and/ or fireplaces could mean that a tremendous inconvenience is placed upon the residents of the area. Therefore, there is a facility within the 1956 Act to require the local authority to make certain payments to occupiers. Where fireplaces have been adapted under ss. 12 and 13, the local authority are required to pay at least 70% of the reasonable costs of those adaptations and it has a discretion to repay all or any part of the remaining 30%. This is not available in respect of a new dwelling begun after 16 August 1964 as the main purpose of the provision was to alleviate any financial difficulties suffered by residents with outdated fireplace equipment.

The control of noxious emissions to the atmosphere other than smoke, dust, grit and fumes

Although the control of smoke has remained relatively unaffected by the Environmental Protection Act, the control of more noxious pollutants is controlled under the air pollution control (APC) system contained in Part I of that Act.

The framework of control under the APC regime is similar to that under integrated pollution control (IPC), as to which see Chapter 10. It is not intended to reproduce all the statutory provisions of IPC although it is important to note that the main distinguishing feature of APC is the processes and substances controlled. The Environmental Protection (Prescribed Processes and Substances) Regulations 1991 (SI 1991 No. 472) designate the processes and substances contained in Part B of the regulations to be controlled by the local authority. These include the less polluting processes and cover such things as:

(a)   lower grade combustion processes;
(b)   smaller iron and steel furnaces;
(c)   low grade incineration of waste and various coating processes;
(d)   animal and vegetable treatment processes.

As to prescribed substances, sch. 4 to the regulations controls the substances to be released into the atmosphere which are the only substances subject to local authority control (see p. 222).

There are transitional arrangements relating to applications for APC authorisations, see the Table below.

**IMPLEMENTATION OF PART I OF ENVIRONMENTAL
PROTECTION ACT 1990 NEW AND EXISTING PART B
PROCESSES TO BE CONTROLLED BY LOCAL AUTHORITIES:
AIR POLLUTION ONLY**

Processes	Application for authorisation to be made	
	Not before	Not later than
Combustion processes, glass manufacture and production, ceramic production, waste incineration, timber processes and maggot breeding.	**1 April 1991**	30 September 1991
Iron and steel, non-ferrous metals, cement, concrete lime-slaking, asbestos and other mineral processes.	**1 October 1991**	31 March 1992
Recovery of oil or organic solvents, di-isocyanate and coating processes, the manufacture of dye-stuffs, printing ink and coating materials, rubber processes and processes for the treatment and processing of animal or vegetable matter (other than maggot breeding).	**1 April 1992**	30 September 1992

The need for an authorisation
The carrying out of a prescribed process or the emitting of prescribed substances subject to Air Pollution Control without an authorisation would be a criminal offence (EPA, s. 6). APC was introduced on 1 April 1991 for all new processes and existing processes which are substantially modified. Authorisation is to be given by the local authority and must be granted before applications for existing processes are made under the timetable contained in Table 1.

Applications
Applications are to be in a form specified under regulations and generally the requirements are similar to those for an IPC application (see the Environmental Protection (Applications, Appeals and Registers) Regulations 1991 (SI 1991 No. 507) in Chapter 10). There is also a charge to pay under the APC charging scheme. This, however, will be a reduced charge reflecting the less complicated nature of the process. The charge will be based upon the process itself rather than the components of a process as under the IPC regime. In the case of small appliances, an even lower charge will apply. There are provisions for reducing charges even further where HMIP have previously controlled a process under the Alkali Acts and that process has been transferred to air pollution control under Part I of the EPA.

The IPC statutory consultation periods apply and there must be publication in a local newspaper of any application as well as consultation with the normal statutory consultees.

The time period for considering an application is four months, although under the Environmental Protection (Authorisation of Processes) (Determination Periods) Order 1991 (SI 1991 No. 513) such a period can be extended to one year when deciding applications for existing processes.

Granting an application

When granting an application for an authorisation, the local authority must have regard to the statutory objectives contained within the EPA, s. 7. Thus, conditions will be inserted into an authorisation relating to the minimisation of pollution and the rendering harmless of emissions from a process. There will also be provisions for particular emission standards to be imposed for certain substances. Naturally, there will be a requirement that any operator of a process under the control of local authorities will be required to use the best available technique not entailing excessive costs.

Air pollution guidance notes

Unlike the IPC guidance note system, central notes issued by the Department of the Environment have already been issued. There are 25 guidance notes containing information relating to emission limits, requirements for emission monitoring and reporting and record keeping of monitoring data, as well as miscellaneous matters including the use of equipment to abate pollution, the handling of certain materials and the construction of chimneys and other emission points. Significantly, the guidance notes cover situations where existing operations have to be upgraded to meet new quality objectives. The guidance notes state that on the granting of a first authorisation for an existing process, there will be a need to specify interim conditions which will be in force until the best available technique can be employed. The notes go on to specify a specific timetable for upgrading plant to higher standards and these can be seen in Table 2 below.

TIMETABLE FOR UPGRADING PLANT TO HIGHER STANDARD

Process	Upgrading
Cement packing	1 April 1996
Heavy clay and refractory goods	30 September 2001
Glass (excluding lead glass)	1 October 2001
Lead glass	1 October 2001
Non-ferrous metal from scrap	1 April 1994
Animal by-products	31 March 1997
Clinical waste incineration	1 October 1995
Chemical treatment of timber	1 October 1996
Manufacture of timber products	1 October 1996
Maggot breeding	1 April 1993
Fur breeding	1 April 1994
Crematoria	1 April 1998
Incineration processes	1 October 1995
Manufacture of practiceboard and fireboard	1 October 1996

Although these deadlines are not mandatory, it is expected that all existing processes will have been upgraded by that time.

Enforcement provisions

Sections 11 to 14 enable local authorities to enforce the APC system. The provisions include:

(a)   variation notices to take into account changes in circumstances (s. 11);
(b)   enforcement notices requiring certain steps to be taken (s. 13);
(c)   revocation notices to be issued in situations where a process has not been carried out for twelve months (s. 12);
(d)   prohibition notices in situations where there is a serious risk of imminent pollution (s. 14).

There is also a right to appeal under s. 15 and Environmental Health Officers have similar powers to pollution inspectors when dealing with the obtaining of information.

Public registers

Under ss. 20 to 22 of the EPA, there is a duty on local authorities to keep registers and information relating to applications and authorisations, convictions, and monitoring data. They must also hold registers in relation to the IPC system.

Overlap with other controls

Where an authorisation is required under both parts of the regulations, i.e. there are components of a process subject to IPC control and the related components subject to Part B, HMIP will have full control.

The Secretary of State also has power to transfer processes under APC control to HMIP (this is intended to smooth the administrative functions of the system in that, where a process is substantially controlled by HMIP but there are a number of processes which are controlled under APC, it would make administrative sense to amalgamate the two controls under HMIP). It is also thought that such a power could be used where the Secretary of State is of the opinion that the local authority are not conducting their duties properly.

Where matters which could amount to a statutory nuisance are more properly controlled under APC, the Secretary of State's consent is required before a local authority can institute summary proceedings (s. 79(10)). It is important to note that this is not a complete prohibition on the bringing of an action in statutory nuisances. Indeed, where an operator of a process is guilty of an offence under s. 22, it is undoubtedly for a local authority to fulfil its statutory duty under s. 79 to ensure that statutory nuisances within their area are abated.

Other Acts controlling processes to which Part B applies will be progressively repealed as the APC system is gradually brought in. Thus, the Alkali Etc., Works Regulation Act 1906, the Health and Safety at Work etc. Act 1974 and the Health and Safety (Emissions into the Atmosphere) Regulations 1983 (SI 1983 No. 943) will be repealed for each individual group of processes when the APC regulations are brought in by means of the grant or refusal of an application for an authorisation or, if appropriate, any decision on appeal for such an authorisation.

The control of emissions from motor vehicles

Emissions from cars, lorries and motorbikes make a significant contribution to atmospheric pollution. It is estimated that transport contributes approximately 20% of all carbon dioxide emitted in addition to other potentially hazardous gases including nitrogen oxide and hydrocarbon compounds.

The control of emissions from motor vehicles is a good example of market based mechanisms being used to partially control environmental pollution. Such measures as the differential in price between leaded and unleaded petrol and the reduction in the tax advantages of owning a company car are fiscal measures to improve the quality of the atmospheric environment. However, the usual methods of regulatory control still prevail.

Pollution from vehicle emissions can be controlled by the use of product standards regulating the emission equipment installed in cars. Thus, in the UK the emission of pollutants is controlled by the Road Traffic Act 1988 and regulations relating to the construction of use of vehicles and type approval. These regulations have been altered regularly to take into account EEC Directives such as the Luxembourg Agreement (Directive 88/76), which imposed new limits on carbon monoxide, hydrocarbons and nitrogen oxide for new vehicles from the beginning of the 1990s. These emission limits differ in relation to the engine size of vehicles. In the case of the smallest engine size there was a great deal of disagreement amongst car manufacturers about the implementation of such stringent conditions. The UK has agreed to implement the new limits although the timetable for implementation has slipped by a minimum of two years.

All cars are required to be capable of running on unleaded petrol and new models had to comply from 1 October 1989, whereas existing models were controlled from 1 October 1990 (see the Road Vehicles (Construction and Use) (Amendment No. 6) Regulations 1988) (SI 1988 No. 1524). Other regulations implement various EC Directives including Directives 83/351, 88/76, 88/77, 88/436 and 89/458. Finally, Road Vehicles (Construction and Use) (Amendment No. 2) Regulations 1990 (SI 1990 No. 1131) introduce new requirements on exhaust emissions for various classes of vehicles.

Control by the European Community

Aside from measures taken to control emissions from transport, the EC has long been a champion of transfrontier controls. Although the community did not ratify the Geneva Convention on Long Range Transboundary Air Pollution 1979, the influence of EC Directives in changing the nature of the control of air pollution within the UK has been all pervasive.

Historically, the UK had a system of non-statutory, individualised emission standards. However, when the EC introduced fixed emission standards for sulphur dioxide and suspended particulates (80/79), lead (82/884) and nitrogen dioxide (85/203), it was the first time that environmental quality standards as such were specifically laid down in the control of atmospheric pollution. Moreover, measures have been adopted to regulate the problems causing acid rain. One of the main sources of the constituents of acid rain is the emission from power stations. Thus, the large combustion plants Directive (88/609) aims specifically to reduce emissions of sulphur dioxide and nitrogen oxide from power stations as these substances make up the majority of the constituents of acid rain.

The Air Quality Standards Regulations 1989

As the UK was under a duty to implement these EC Directives, steps had to be taken to move away from the informal, flexible legal structures relied upon under the Alkali Acts. Therefore, in 1989, mandatory air quality standards were introduced under the Air Quality Standards Regulations 1989 (SI 1989 No. 317). Unfortunately, conditions in certain areas were so polluted that the UK Government applied for a derogation from the implementation of the Directive for areas of Northern England, Scotland and the West Midlands until 1 April 1993.

Notwithstanding this derogation, the regulations provide for percentage limits to be placed on the amount of certain prescribed gases so as to improve the quality of air within the UK.

Control over global warming

As mentioned at the beginning of this chapter, some environmental issues relating to atmospheric pollution are so large that they require proper international cooperation in order to prove effective. One such measure relates to global warming and is contained within the Montreal Protocol which aims to control the production and use of chlorofluorocarbons (CFC's). This protocol 'The agreement on substances which deplete the ozone layer' was signed in Montreal in September 1987. Sixty Governments throughout the world were signatories and it was to have the effect of reducing the consumption of CFCs by 50% before the year 2000. Unfortunately, the revision of scientific predictions of the effect of CFCs and other greenhouse gases meant that the protocol had to be revised in June 1990 to bring about a 100% reduction in the level of CFCs, halons and carbontetrachloride by the year 2000, with the production of methylchloroform to be reduced by the year 2005. As has been stressed, the ratification of this protocol is not necessarily the most effective method of environmental protection, although in international issues such agreements are the only real way in which cooperation can be achieved.

TWELVE
Waste management

The production of waste is a natural consequence of life in an industrialised society. In the past, both the volume and the types of waste produced were easily dealt with in small country rubbish dumps. This, of course, was in the days before plastic packaging, aluminium cans and other composite materials which make up a large amount of domestic waste in Britain. Furthermore, the amount of domestic waste disposed of in Britain represents only a small fraction of the total amount of waste produced. In the Second Report of the House of Commons' Environment Committee on toxic waste, it was shown that in 1989 Britain produced approximately 2,500m tonnes of waste of which only 1.5m tonnes was domestic and trade waste. Other types of waste included liquid industrial effluent, agricultural waste, waste from mines and quarries, sewage sludge, waste from power stations, hazardous industrial waste and special waste.

These vast amounts of waste are a direct result of living with a 'production economy' in that the consumer boom of the post World War II era has demanded the production of more and more products with less and less durability. As consumption increased so did the volume of waste. The idea of built-in obsolescence in consumer goods means that there is an ever increasing demand and the consumer will replace goods more readily with new items. An article investigating the disposability of certain consumer goods found that a large percentage of household machines disposed of on waste disposal sites did not have anything wrong with them. These included machines which were still available on sale at the time of disposal (Hunkin, *New Scientist*, 24 December 1988). The production of consumer goods often involves the use of toxic substances as either raw materials or by-products thus, in addition to domestic waste, there are large quantities of industrial waste which give rise to their own problems.

Most of the waste disposed of in Britain is deposited in large holes in the ground such as old quarries. The difficulties of burying waste are numerous. Often, substances break down after a number of years to produce contaminating liquids or hazardous gases. In 1989, the House of Commons Environment Committee reported on the issue of toxic waste which was swiftly followed in 1990 by their first report on contaminated land. The evidence submitted to the Committee painted a horrifying picture of the extent to which there may be problems with the state of contaminated land in Britain. Estimates of the area of land contaminated by waste range from a very conservative 10,000 hectares to a possible 100,000 hectares.

Britain has already experienced the dangers of waste disposal sites. In 1986 methane produced from a landfill site at Loscoe exploded causing death. Other examples throughout the world have shown the danger of ignoring the problem of the proper disposal of toxic waste. For instance, the clean up of waste sites in the United States has been estimated as likely to cost more than $100 billion.

Although a large percentage of waste is disposed of into holes on land, there is a small percentage which is incinerated or dumped at sea. All of these methods of disposal have their own particular problems. This chapter looks at some of the controls over the disposal of waste from its creation through to final deposit.

The law of waste disposal is in a state of transition. Presently, the Control of Pollution Act regulates the disposal of waste, although Part II of the Environmental Protection Act seeks to replace those controls. The new concepts that it introduces will fundamentally change the way in which waste is dealt with in Britain. Unfortunately, it would be impossible to understand the control of waste disposal without looking at both Acts. The Environmental Protection Act has to be seen in the context of the many problems that arose under the Control of Pollution Act. These problems may continue to arise until the EPA is implemented.

History

Historically, the disposal of waste was not seen to be a significant issue until a public outcry concerning the deposit of hazardous waste in the West Midlands in the early 1970s led to the introduction of the Deposit of Poisonous Wastes Act in 1972. This Act was a classic example of the reactive nature of environmental legislation in Britain as it approached the deposit of waste from a narrow viewpoint. It was not until the introduction of the Control of Pollution Act in 1974 that there was a comprehensive system of waste management. To its credit, Britain at that stage led the way in legislating against the dumping of waste. It seems strange now to record that the Deposit of Poisonous Wastes Act 1972 was one of the first ever controls over the deposit of hazardous waste in the world.

Its successor, the Control of Pollution Act 1974 (COPA), provided the model for other countries and in particular the European Communities Framework Directive on Waste Management 75/442. Prior to the introduction of the COPA, waste disposal was primarily controlled by reference to the land use characteristics of disposal under the Town and Country Planning Acts.

Waste disposal and planning law

The disposal of waste on landfill sites illustrates the overlap between the use of land and the protection of the environment. The provision of an adequate waste disposal system presents difficult questions of a land use nature. Therefore, planning law and the policy framework that it operates within work closely with the controls which specifically protect the environment. The methods of control under planning law are twofold: development plans and development control.

The law relating to the planning control of waste disposal sites will remain unchanged with the introduction of the Environmental Protection Act.

Development plans

Structure plans

The role of structure plans in dealing with matters of a strategic land use nature is covered elsewhere in this book (see Chapter 9). In terms of waste disposal, structure plans can deal with difficult issues as to the balance to be taken between the use of land for the disposal of waste and other uses. It is particularly important to deal with waste disposal issues at this strategic level as the production of vast quantities of waste in built up areas requires land to be set aside for disposal even though the particular nature of the use is not welcome.

Circular 22/84 makes it clear that waste disposal policies should be considered at structure plan level and states:

> Structure and Local Plans provide an opportunity for the requirements and constraints of waste disposal strategies to be considered in the context of other policies for the development and other use of land, for example, those dealing with minerals.

Therefore, the context of dealing with waste disposal matters in tandem with other policies can be of great importance. Notwithstanding the county-wide responsibility for waste disposal, problems can arise when county planning authorities formulate waste disposal policies within a structure plan area which do not take into account the relationship between the volume of waste produced and the number of sites available. For instance, the highly populated south east produces far more waste per capita than other areas of the country but is also subject to far greater pressures in relation to the land available in which to dispose of that waste. Therefore, although the matter is of a strategic nature structure plans can do little other than give 'a general indication of the areas in which additional provision is to be made, having regard to the objectives of any waste disposal plans'.

Local plans

Whereas structure plans can give a strategic background to the policies for waste disposal, it is the local plan which should contain 'sites and specific policies for the disposal, storage or treatment of waste' (Circular 22/84). In addition to waste disposal policies contained in general local plans, there is the additional power under the Town and Country Planning Act 1990, s. 36, to prepare subject plans dealing specifically with waste disposal. Experience has shown that very few local planning authorities are willing to do this. This has now been reinforced by a duty to make a waste local plan (see the Planning and Compensation Act 1991, s. 27, sch. 4).

Waste disposal plans
In an attempt to counteract this reluctance, in October 1990, the DoE issued proposals to oblige county authorities to prepare waste disposal development plans. It is proposed that all counties will be required to prepare such a plan with specific reference to amounts of waste, options for disposal and site licensing. It is hoped that they will form the basis of the development plan and that any land-use development plan will be 'consistent in terms of the nature, quantity and distribution of waste with those identified or forecast'.

Development control matters

In addition to the powers local planning authorities have to take account of waste disposal in development planning, they also have control over specific development involving the disposal of waste. The difficulties involved in the control of the development of land for waste disposal purposes require considerations peculiar to the subject. The decomposition of seemingly innocuous matter can and has led to the unforeseeable danger of the leaking of poisonous gases from the site. Moreover, planning controls may have to regulate the everyday workings of the site and the care which is required after a site has been closed.

The need for planning permission
Unsurprisingly, the disposal of waste upon land requires planning permission as either a material change of the use of land or an engineering operation on land (see the 1990 Act, s. 55(1)). Furthermore, s. 55(3)(b) provides that where a site is already used for the deposit of waste it will specifically involve a material change of use requiring planning permission where either the superficial area of the deposit is extended or the height of the deposit is extended and exceeds the level of the land adjoining the site (see *Duckworth* v *Haslingden UDC* [1973] JPL 196).

Exemptions under the General Development Order
Certain activities are deemed to be granted automatic planning permission under the Town and Country Planning (General Development) Order 1988 (SI 1988 No. 1813). Part 6 of Schedule 2 allows for the carrying out on agricultural land of excavation or engineering operations reasonably necessary for the purposes of agriculture (Class A). This is subject to a provision that no waste material shall be brought onto the land from elsewhere except where the material is to be used for the construction of a building or hardstanding and it is to be incorporated into the development forthwith. This would allow for the infill of inert materials to provide a foundation for further development.

Parts 21 to 23 of Schedule 2 allow for the tipping of waste onto mine or ancillary mining land, again with the proviso that the only waste tipped is produced on the site and is not imported from elsewhere.

Application procedure

As the nature of the use of land for a waste disposal tip is particularly sensitive there are strict rules governing the publicity requirements on an application for planning permission. The development of a waste disposal site is classed as a bad neighbour development under the 1990 Act s. 65. The section provides that where an application is made for development which is considered to be within the designated class of bad neighbour development, an advertisement should be published in a local newspaper and a notice stating that an application has been made and that it is bad neighbour development should be posted on the application site for not less than seven days within the month preceding the consideration of the application by the local planning authority (ss. 65(2), (3) and (8)). The rationale behind this wide duty of public notification is that such developments are far more likely to cause public concern and thus require a far greater degree of public participation (see also *R v Rotherham MBC, ex parte Rankin*, below).

Statutory consultees

As the disposal of waste onto land affects other areas of control, Article 18 of the General Development Order provides that certain bodies must be consulted on planning applications. Thus the Health and Safety Executive are consultees in addition to the National Rivers Authority.

Planning conditions

The Town and Country Planning Act 1990, s. 72, allows for the imposition of conditions regulating the development or use of any land. This power in some ways overlaps with the control of waste disposal licences under the present system and there is often some confusion as to which powers should properly control the different elements of a waste disposal site. Planning conditions will attempt to control matters more concerned with the visual appearance of the site rather than the scientific and technical considerations which are controlled under the waste disposal licensing provisions. Schedule 5 provides that planning permission for a development consisting of the winning and working of minerals can be controlled by 'any such aftercare condition as the mineral planning authority thinks fit'.

Waste disposal under the Control of Pollution Act 1974

The Control of Pollution Act introduced a comprehensive system of licensing for the disposal of waste which supplemented the existing controls over land use in the Town and Country Planning Act.

The organisation of waste disposal administration

The control of waste disposal is organised on a county-wide basis (COPA, s. 30). Thus, in non-metropolitan areas the county councils operate as waste disposal authorities, whereas in the majority of metropolitan areas it is the metropolitan district council. In Wales the district council is the waste disposal authority. Greater Manchester, Merseyside and London have their own waste disposal authorities. The disposal of waste is not to be confused with the collection of waste which is the duty of the district councils and London borough councils.

These authorities have both administrative and regulatory functions. They are empowered to grant licences and arrange for the disposal of controlled waste (s. 1) as well as having powers of enforcement for ensuring the licensing system operates effectively.

What is waste?

The Control of Pollution Act governs the licensing of activities concerning the disposal of controlled waste. Controlled waste is defined in s. 30 as household, industrial and commercial waste or any such waste. The term 'waste' is further defined as including:

(a) any substance which constitutes a scrap material or an effluent or other unwanted surplus substance arising from the application of any process;

(b) any substance or article which requires to be disposed of as being broken, worn out, contaminated or otherwise spoiled.

This definition has given rise to interesting questions as to its proper meaning.

At first, it may be thought that identifying what is waste material is a fairly simple process. However, one person's waste can be another person's raw material, or as one commentator put it (JEL [1990] 259):

the odd newspaper blowing down the street may be gathered by boy scouts to be recycled or even used by a vagrant to keep warm. Even at the same moment in time, one person may regard an object as waste, while another has a use for it.

This issue of the reusability of waste materials was adjudicated upon in two recent cases. Firstly, in *R v Rotherham Metropolitan Borough Council, ex parte Rankin* [1990] JEL 251, Safety Kleen UK had applied for planning permission to build a distribution, waste extraction and recycling centre. No notification was given to any of the nearby residents as to the nature of the development. Mr Rankin argued that as the development was dealing with waste disposal it was bad neighbour development and required the appropriate notification procedure under what is now the Town and Country Planning Act 1990, s. 65. The nature of the process involved the provision of equipment and solvent to clean paint–spraying equipment. Any solvent collected was recycled. Mr Rankin said that as used solvents were taken in by the factory they were to be regarded as trade waste. On the other hand, Safety Kleen argued that far from being waste they were raw materials which were an essential part of their operation.

Schiemann J held that the term waste should be given its ordinary meaning and that on these particular facts the treatment and recycling of solvents could amount to the treatment of waste. He did also accept however that in this case it could be said that 'the solvents are perhaps rightly regarded as being both trade waste and raw materials'.

In environment law terms, part of the difficulty with this decision was that it did not specifically decide the definition of waste in the Control of Pollution Act. However, in *Kent County Council* v *Queenborough Rolling Mill Co Ltd* [1990] JEL 257, that point was specifically addressed. The company were alleged to have deposited waste on land without a licence. They occupied a site close to the Swale estuary which was liable to subsidence. To prevent erosion, parts of the site were filled in regularly with inert materials. The material which was alleged to be waste came from a disused site which was being cleared by a demolition company. The material consisted of old china, pottery, chalk, china clay and ballast. All these different types of material were selected and used for different things. The company used the ballast, china, china clay and broken pottery to fill in an area of subsidence by the estuary. The magistrates decided that that material did not amount to waste. They did however state a case for the Divisional Court as to whether or not they were correct.

The defendant company argued that the material was not waste because it was put to a useful purpose and therefore could not be unwanted. On the other hand, the Council argued that it was the nature of the material which itself brought it within the definition contemplated by the Act. Pill J held that although the material was put to a purpose it was not a relevant consideration in deciding whether or not it was waste. The important factor was the nature of the material when it was discarded.

Finally, in a decision of the European Court of Justice, *Vessoso* and *Zanetti* cases 206 and 207/88 (1990) 2 LMELR 133, the matter was adjudicated upon from a European perspective. In this case, a similar situation arose to that in the *Ex parte Rankin* decision. The two named Italians had been charged with collecting, transporting and storing waste without authorisation which was contrary to an Italian presidential decree. It was argued on behalf of the two individuals that the material was not waste at all but recyclable raw material and therefore not subject to the decree. In its judgment, the European Court invoked the framework Directive on Waste 75/442. It stated that the definition of waste was properly concerned with the potential health hazards that the materials could bring. They concluded by finding that although recycling was to be encouraged, the material could still be waste notwithstanding its future use.

Although not explicit in any decision of the courts, it is clear that one of the reasons that the definition of waste includes recycling activities is that many of the environmental problems which arise from the disposal of waste can also arise from the recycling of waste material. Thus, where waste is recycled there may still be problems of contamination, gas leakage, etc. The hazards that are brought about by recycling have to be controlled under environmental legislation as much as planning legislation and thus the definition of waste has been extended to include such activities.

Aside from this general definition of waste contained within COPA, there are also more specific definitions relating to controlled waste contained in the Collection and Disposal of Waste Regulations 1988 (SI 1988, No. 819).

Regulation 3 and sch. 1 define what is to be treated as household waste and this includes waste produced by domestic properties, campsites, residential hostels, prisons and royal palaces. Regulation 6 and sch. 3 define waste which is to be treated as industrial waste as including waste from factories, laboratories, imported waste and clinical waste. Regulation 7 and sch. 4 lay down that commercial waste includes waste from offices and premises used for the purposes of trade or business, sport and local or central government.

As a particular category of controlled waste, s. 17 provides that where waste is so dangerous or difficult to dispose of that special provision has to be made, then that waste is to be subject to tighter controls as 'special waste'. The Control of Pollution (Special Waste) Regulations 1980 (SI 1980, No. 1079 as amended by SI 1988 No. 1794) list certain substances which fall within the category of special waste. They include substances dangerous to life or which are easily ignited, radioactive waste and certain medical products.

Waste disposal licences

Under COPA, s. 3(1), it is an offence to:

(a)   deposit controlled waste on any land or cause or knowingly permit controlled waste to be deposited on any land; or
(b)   use any plant or equipment, or cause or knowingly permit any plant or equipment to be used, for the purpose of disposing of controlled waste; where there is no waste disposal licence in force.

The offences are ones of strict liability and where it is alleged that a specific breach of a condition has occurred then it is not necessary to show that the knowledge extended to the breach of that condition. In *Ashcroft* v *Cambro Waste Products Limited* [1981] 3 All ER 699, the defendant was charged with knowingly permitting the deposit of controlled waste in contravention of a condition of a waste disposal licence. He argued that although he knew of the deposit of the waste, he did not know that that was in breach of the condition. The court held that it was sufficient for the prosecution to prove that the defendant knowingly permitted the deposit of the controlled waste and the burden of proof was then shifted to the defendant to show that he had complied with the conditions of the licence. Causing means that there is to be a direct relationship between the activity of the defendant and the offence complained of. Any break in the chain of causation will be enough to avoid liability (see, in relation to water pollution, *Southern Water Authority* v *Pegrum* [1989] Crim LR 442 and *Alphacell Limited* v *Woodward* [1972] AC 824).

Exemptions

Section 4(2) of COPA exempts household waste from a private dwelling from the need for a licence if it is disposed of within the curtilage of the dwelling by or with the permission of the occupier.

Section 3 provides that exemptions can be made under regulations drawn up by the Secretary of State. The Collection and Disposal of Waste Regulations 1988 (SI 1988 No. 819), (Reg. 9 and sch. 6), provide for situations where although waste is deposited on land that will not be an offence as no authorisation is required. This includes the deposit of construction or demolition waste for the purposes of construction being undertaken on the land and the deposit of waste on the premises on which it is produced, pending its disposal elsewhere. There are many other categories, but to fall within the exemptions, the presence of the waste must not give rise to an environmental hazard. It is an environmental hazard if it has been deposited in such a manner or in such a quantity as to give a material risk of death, injury or impairment of health or to threaten pollution of any water supply.

Applications for a waste disposal licence

All applications for a waste disposal licence have to be made in writing to the waste disposal authority (COPA, s. 5). Where the disposal of waste requires planning permission and that planning permission is in existence, the waste disposal authority have only two grounds for refusal, namely refusal for the purpose of preventing the pollution of water and refusal because of a danger to public health (s. 5(3)). Where no planning permission is in force but it is required, the waste disposal authority have no discretion concerning the grant of a licence—they must refuse it. There is an anomaly in COPA in that an existing use certificate does not appear to be covered under s. 5(2). Many uses which would be subject to control under the licensing system are uses commenced prior to 1964. It has been the practice of waste disposal authorities to attempt to control these uses even though there is no specific provision in the Act. As a matter of planning law, an existing use certificate is not a planning permission and therefore waste disposal licences should not be issued. As a matter of practice, the waste disposal authorities will often issue a quasi-licence which operates as guidance to owners of waste disposal sites with existing use certificates.

There is no statutory specified form of application other than a requirement that it be in writing. To supplement this, Waste Management Paper No. 4/88 gives examples of information to be included in an application as well as a specimen application form. The status of a waste management paper is somewhat similar to that of a Circular in planning guidance. Papers however tend to concentrate more on scientific and technical issues rather than policy.

Statutory consultees

There is a statutory obligation upon a waste disposal authority to consult with two bodies, the waste collection authority and the National Rivers Authority (s. 5(4)(a)). The reason for this is clear, where a collection authority has to work in conjunction with a waste disposal authority their views will often be pertinent as to the suitability of a particular site for the disposal of waste. Secondly, where one of the statutory reasons for refusal is that there is a danger to any watercourse, the National Rivers Authority have an obvious role. Any representations made by either of these bodies have to be taken into account if made within 21 days from the receipt of the application by the body, or if necessary any longer period agreed between the parties.

The power of the NRA as a statutory consultee can be seen in the fact that where the NRA cannot agree with the waste disposal authority as to the suitability of a particular site, they are entitled to refer the matter to the Secretary of State for his final decision (s. 5(4)(b)). In practice, it is often appropriate to consult the NRA informally before approaching the waste disposal authority as, where they are wary about the possibilities of water pollution, there will be little hope of a successful application.

Conditions

Waste disposal authorities are entitled to grant a licence subject to conditions. They may impose any condition they think fit (COPA, s. 6(2)). The section then gives examples of areas to which conditions may apply including:

(a) the duration of the licence;
(b) the supervision by the holder of the licence of activities to which the licence relates;
(c) the types of waste dealt with;
(d) precautions to be taken;
(e) any steps needed to comply with planning permission;
(f) hours of operation;
(g) works in connection with the site before activities commence or whilst they are continuing.

Any aftercare conditions may only be imposed through the planning system. Waste Management Paper No. 4/88 gives examples of model conditions relating to many different types of waste disposal. The role of conditions is purposive to COPA itself; that is to say that they have to reflect the object of the Act rather than attempting to control any other matters outside of the Act. Thus, theoretically at least, there should be no overlap between the conditions imposed under COPA and those under a planning permission.

In *Attorney General's Reference (No. 2 of 1988)* [1990] JEL 80, the Court of Appeal had to consider a condition on a site licence which stated that the site had to be operated '. . . so as to avoid creating a nuisance to the inhabitants of the neighbourhood'. The Court held that such a condition was not lawful for two reasons. Firstly, it identified the purposes of COPA in relation to waste disposal as being to avoid pollution of water, to prohibit activities prejudicial to human health and to control aspects of amenity. Somewhat surprisingly, they decided that such a condition was too wide to relate to those purposes. Secondly, as there was another statute specifically controlling the existence of nuisances within an area (i.e. the Public Health Act 1936 and its statutory nuisance provisions), further attempts to control it should be avoided.

Sections 3(1) and (2) provide that persons commit an offence where they deposit controlled waste on land unless the land is occupied by the holder of a waste disposal licence and unless the deposit is in accordance with the conditions, if any, specified in the licence. A loophole in the drafting of these sections was identified in *Leigh Land Reclamation Limited et al* v *Walsall MBC* [1991] 191 ENDS Report 37. In that case, the operators of a site were discovered not to have complied with conditions relating to the compaction of waste after deposit and the use of inert material to cover daily deposits. The difficulty with trying to prove an offence under s. 3(1) and (2) was pointed out by the defendant company which claimed that, although the deposit of the material was controlled waste and the conditions in the site licence had been breached, the conditions did not directly relate to any deposit on land. Rather, they were more concerned with the site's conditions at the time of deposit. The court held that for there to be an offence under s. 3, there was a need to demonstrate that it was the actual deposit which breached any conditions.

Supervision of licences

Once a licence is in force the waste disposal authority is under a statutory duty to supervise it (s. 9(1)):

(a)   for the purpose of ensuring that the licensed activities do not pollute water or become a danger to public health or seriously detrimental to the amenities of the locality; and
(b)   to ensure that any conditions contained within a licence are complied with.

To enable the authorities to properly carry out this supervisory role, s. 9(2) gives them the power to carry out work in an emergency if it is necessary to do so on land, plant, or equipment to which the licence relates. Furthermore, in carrying out those emergency works, they are entitled to recover any money spent from the holder of the licence, or in the case of cancellation or revocation of that licence, from the last holder. It would be sufficient to avoid liability for a licence holder to show that there was no emergency which required such works to be carried out.

In a situation where the supervisory functions indicate that conditions are not being complied with but there is no emergency, the waste disposal authority may serve a notice requiring compliance with any condition within a certain time and, in the event of non-compliance, this enables them to revoke the licence. This was an often under-used power because there is no ability to suspend a licence in part. Where there is no serious chance of pollution of water or harm to public health or problems with amenity, then the revocation of a licence could be seen as a particularly harsh step to take. This latter procedure can be exercised without any prejudice to prosecution under COPA, s. 3.

Variation and revocation of licences

A waste disposal licence can be varied by the holder of a licence or the waste disposal authority which issued it. Such variations will occur when the circumstances surrounding the activities carried on under the licence have changed from the initial grant of the licence.

The authority can serve a notice on the holder specifying a variation of conditions where it is desirable and unlikely to cause unreasonable expenditure for the licence holder. Where, however, such modification is required so that there is no pollution of water, danger to public health, or serious detriment to amenities, the authority are under a duty to serve such a variation notice (s. 7(1)(b)).

A licence holder is also entitled to ask for the variation of conditions on the licence (s. 7(1)(a)). Any variation of the licence requires consultation once again with the statutory consultees. In an emergency, however, if it is appropriate to do so, the authority can postpone the reference and where they are of the opinion that the variation will not affect statutory consultees then they can disregard them (s. 7(2)). Although in most difficult situations the variation of conditions can take into account new technology etc., there will be occasions when it is not possible to remedy a problem with the variation or modification of a condition. In those situations, s. 7(4) provides that where the continuance of licensed activities would cause pollution of water, danger to public health, or serious detriment to amenities, the authority are under a duty to serve a revocation notice on the licence holder.

The transfer and surrender of licences

Section 8 provides for the situation in which the holder of a licence wishes to transfer it to another person. The only requirement on a transfer of a licence is that original holders of a licence must give notice to the authority that they propose to transfer it, specifying the transferee and its name and address. Circumstances may arise where the authority are unhappy about the new licence holder and may therefore, within eight weeks of receiving the transfer application, give notice that they decline to accept the transferee as the holder of the licence. The licence automatically ceases in such circumstances, 10 weeks after the authority have received the transfer notice.

In a situation where licence holders wish to relinquish their responsibilities under the licence, he can cancel the licence at any time by delivering it to the authority and giving notice that they no longer require the licence. It should be noted that although the responsibilities under the Act may be relinquished, those conditions relating to the aftercare of the site in a planning permission cannot be given up.

Appeals

There is a right to appeal to the Secretary of State in situations where:

(a)   an application for a disposal licence or modification of a disposal licence
is rejected;
(b)   there is a conditional grant of a disposal licence;
(c)   licence conditions are modified;
(d)   a licence is revoked.

During the consideration of an appeal against a variation or a revocation notice,
the effect of a notice is suspended unless the authority include a statement
within the notice that it is their opinion that the notice is necessary for preventing
the pollution of water, or a danger to health, or that for any other reason
the suspension should not apply. However, if the Secretary of State determines
that the authority have acted unreasonably in including such a statement, this
decision can be reversed and can negate the suspension at any time up to
the appeal and at the same time compensation of any consequential loss awarded.
Thus, the reluctance of authorities to take such a potentially high financial
risk ensures that it will only be in the most serious of cases that suspension
will not occur.

Miscellaneous powers

Section 1 of the Act imposes a duty on authorities to ensure that adequate
arrangements are made for the disposal of controlled waste. Consequently, s. 2
provides that they are under a duty to prepare a waste disposal plan which
assesses the adequacy of the arrangements made.

The plan must contain specified information as laid down under s. 2 including
the types and quantities of waste, the methods of disposal and the sites and
equipment which are to be used. As such, there is a strategic nature to the
waste disposal plan which is supposed to indicate a proper provision for disposal
of the waste over a set period. There are also provisions for public participation
and consultation with statutory bodies and affected persons. There is no
requirement for approval by the Secretary of State unless there is disagreement
amongst waste disposal authorities.

The Control of Pollution (Special Waste) Regulations 1980

These Regulations (SI 1980, No. 1079) were introduced partly to implement
EEC Directive 78/319. The regulations define special waste and set up a system
of consignment notes which should trace the progress of waste from where
it is created to its place of final disposal. The Regulations are the subject of
a comprehensive review issued as a draft consultation document in 1990, so
changes can be expected in the next 12 to 18 months and only a brief outline
of the existing Regulations will be given. As stated earlier, the definition of
special waste relates to its danger to life, its low ignition point and other chemical
compounds.

Part II of the regulations sets up a consignment notice system which means
that a consignment note has to be prepared containing details of the waste
and its destination before waste is allowed to be taken away from the place

where it was created. Once drawn up, the consignment note has to be sent to the waste disposal authority not less than three days nor more than a month before the waste is set to be transferred. The waste carrier must then complete a separate note saying that they have collected the waste. This is to be confirmed in a separate certificate by the waste producer which must also specifically contain a statement that the carrier was told of any precautionary measure required. The carrier of the waste then keeps a copy of the consignment note whilst giving all other parts of the note to the operator of the waste disposal site. The operator of the site then completes the final part of the note, keeps one copy and gives a copy to the authority and the carrier.

Such a system is supposed to maintain strict control over all parts of the transportation process. It is however rather complicated and in the case of regular consignments the controls are eased to take into account the ease of enforcement. If any party to the consignment note system is found to have breached the system then they are liable to fines and imprisonment.

The failings of the Control of Pollution Act 1974

Although the Control of Pollution Act 1974 provided the first system of comprehensive waste management in Britain, and indeed was used as the basis for the framework Directive on Waste 75/442, the practical effect of the Act was somewhat disappointing. The second report of the House of Commons Environment Committee on toxic waste contained some of the strongest words ever issued by a Parliamentary Committee when referring to the state of waste management in Britain:

> Never, in any of our enquiries into environmental problems, have we experienced such consistent and universal criticism of existing legislation and of central and local government as we have during the course of this inquiry.

After what would have appeared to be a bright future in 1974, what went wrong?

(a) Organisational difficulties

The Control of Pollution Act attempted to create a system of regional waste disposal authorities with the responsibility of operating sites themselves and at the same time regulating private sites by means of the licensing system. The inherent conflict between the nature of their administrative duties and regulatory functions proved to be the foundation of many difficulties. The perception that the WDAs were acting as both 'poacher and gamekeeper' sought to undermine confidence in the waste disposal industry in the public at large.

(b) A lack of guidance on acceptable standards

The second area of difficulty concerned the disparity between enforcement/control standards in different parts of the country. Evidence submitted to the Committee had shown that different authorities had used different control standards when setting down conditions for site licences. The patchy nature of these controls had given rise to considerable levels of concern; as the Environment Committee put it:

> Against this laissez faire background, it is not surprising to find that there is no consistency of standards between one Waste Disposal Authority and another. In many, the standards are extremely low encouraging the operation of contractors who have no regard for the potential dangers to the environment.

One of the main reasons for this 'laissez-faire' approach was the lack of Central Government guidance. The Department of the Environment is given the task of supplying waste disposal authorities with scientific guidance as to the manner in which this system ought to be controlled. The Department of the Environment were committed to producing some 13 waste management papers in the 1980s. This target was missed and the final papers that were produced were not produced on time. The waste management papers were always intended to introduce uniformity into the system of control; as Duncan Lawrence put it ([1989] 3 Env. Law 4):

> these examples of Central Government complacency and neglect send clear signals out to the local authorities that waste regulation is not taken seriously in this country. This does nothing to engender the professionalism, technical competence and status that is required for efficient waste regulation.

(c) **Lack of strategic plans**
The introduction of the concept of waste disposal plans under s. 2 of the Control of Pollution Act was also a mandatory element of the framework Directive on Waste (75/442). As at 1 October 1989, only 23 waste disposal authorities out of a possible 79 had completed their plans. After being forced into action, the Department of the Environment specifically instructed them to supply the details of the plans, unfortunately this had little effect. Where the plans provide a strategic background to the disposal of waste within an area, no long term planning can take place where there is little policy background.

(d) **The need to prove deposit related offences**
Essentially, the Control of Pollution Act controls the deposit of waste. However, problems often arise where waste is treated, kept, or stored. Having to prove that waste was deposited often led to anonymous fly-tipping with subsequent problems of clean up.

(e) **The ability to surrender a licence**
Where site operators have a free right to surrender disposal licences, they can effectively abandon waste disposal sites without any subsequent responsibilities for supervision. Thus, where an operator was financially or technically incompetent to deal with the problems that had arisen on the land, then by merely giving notice to the waste disposal authority they could shift responsibility

onto the public sector. Alternatively, where a site had ceased to be profitable, an operator could avoid further costs by surrendering their responsibilities.

The Environmental Protection Act 1990—Closing the loophole?

In order to meet some of these problems, the Environmental Protection Act introduced a wide range of new powers.

(a) Separation of the organisational and regulatory functions of the waste disposal authorities

Waste regulation authorities will replace waste disposal authorities in England and Wales and will have sole responsibility for the regulation of sites within their area. The operational arm will be subjected to tendering from the private sector and will be at arms length from the regulation authority.

(b) Creation of a new system of control

Whereas the Control of Pollution Act referred to waste disposal licences, the Environmental Protection Act controls waste management licences. This includes the treating, keeping or disposing of waste as well as the depositing of waste.

(c) The certificate of completion

To avoid the problem of site operators abandoning on-going responsibility for site maintenance after the final deposit of waste has taken place, there is now a facility for the surrendering of a licence only in very specific circumstances. It is hoped that in such circumstances the proper aftercare of a site will be maintained.

(d) Duty of care/code of practice

One of the fundamental problems facing waste disposal authorities in the enforcement of the waste disposal legislation was identifying who had the responsibility for waste at various stages of its life. The Royal Commission on Environmental Pollution in their Eleventh Report in 1985 stated that as an extension of the polluter pays principle it must be the producer of the waste who ensures that it is properly handled and disposed of. Under the Control of Pollution Act, where waste was transferred to a 'cowboy operator', the responsibility for that waste was transferred along with it. The Environmental Protection Act meets such problems by imposing a duty on all those who deal with waste to take reasonable care to manage waste properly. This duty of care is fleshed out by a code of practice which gives some guidelines as to what would amount to reasonable care.

Generally, the Act seeks to extend the Control of Pollution Act and close the loopholes which were exploited during the 1970s and 1980s. In widening the powers of enforcement and the procedure for an application for a licence, there is a much stricter control over all aspects of the waste disposal system.

Implementation of the Environment Protection Act 1990

Unlike other parts of the EPA, Part II, which relates to waste management, did not have any timetable for implementation when the Act was passed in November 1990. Some guidance had been given in draft form but very little information other than that was available. Experience with COPA and more specifically in the case of waste disposal, the Control of Pollution (Amendment) Act 1989, suggested that there could be long delays before the Act came fully into force.

The reason for the absence of any detailed timetable was simple. Part II of the EPA is only a framework within which further regulations can be added to flesh out more detailed procedures. This secondary legislation is fairly complex and the necessary manpower to administrate the drafting of these regulations is unavailable.

More recently, however, a general draft timetable has been published which sees the new duty of care being formally introduced from April 1992 and a new licensing system from April 1993 onwards. A number of other areas in Part II have not yet been timetabled and the waste management papers which are to act as statutory guidance when deciding an application for a waste management licence will not all be available at the time of implementation (see p. 282). Thus, there are still many question marks surrounding the likely full implementation date of all of Part II.

Reorganisation of the waste disposal authorities

Section 30 and Schedule 2 implement the proposals to separate the regulatory and organisational functions of the old waste disposal authorities. In a move echoing the separation of the water authorities into the National Rivers Authority and the water services companies, waste disposal will be separated into the waste regulation authorities (WRA) and the arm's length local authority waste disposal contractors (LAWDC), which will be a private company, whether formed by the old waste disposal authority or a joint venture between a private company and the waste disposal authority, or an unconnected private company. The Department of the Environment has issued draft guidance which suggests that there should be a very definite separation of the functions of the WRAs and the LAWDCs, although they also state that the two separate functions will not justify two different complements of staff. It suggested that the cost behind such a change will not be high.

The form of the WRAs would be on the same geographical basis as the existing waste disposal authorities, i.e. mostly on a county or metropolitan basis, but Greater Manchester, Merseyside, and Greater London will have their own authorities. In Wales the district council acts as the WRA. One anomaly that is continued in the EPA is that Wigan is allowed to control its own waste disposal, even though it is within the Greater Manchester area.

Section 31 allows the Secretary of State to establish regional authorities by the merging of existing WRAs. Under the Control of Pollution Act, a similar power was used to create the South Yorkshire Joint Hazardous Waste Unit.

It is hoped that amalgamating associated authorities will resolve the difficulties caused. The problems of disposing of waste do not necessarily fall within neat geographical boundaries.

As the Second report of the House of Commons Environment Committee stated, 'a present pattern of waste disposal authorities based upon historic administrative area boundaries does not lend itself to the most effective way of organising the safe disposal, in suitable sites, of the waste generated by densely populated industrial areas'. In the report of the Department of the Environment's Working Group on Waste Paper in May 1990, the Department stressed that they felt that they would prefer that approximately 10 groups regulated waste disposal nationally. This again bears an uncanny resemblance to the 10 regions of the National Rivers Authority which regulate water pollution.

The collection authorities under the Environmental Protection Act remain the same as under the Control of Pollution Act, that is to say, the district councils.

Under s. 51 of the EPA the WRAs still have a residual twofold function. They must arrange for the disposal of controlled waste collected within their area and to arrange for the provision of places where deposits of household waste can be made free of charge. They are also responsible for waste recycling and credit schemes (ss. 55 and 52(1)).

The licensing system

In a move away from the previous system of waste *disposal* licences, because of the connotations of control over only one part of a waste operation, the EPA has introduced a new extended system of waste *management* licences. The concept of waste management applies to each individual stage of the waste process rather than the final disposal. Section 35 provides that a waste management licence is needed to authorise the treatment, keeping or disposal of controlled waste on land or by means of mobile plant.

Section 33 of the Act makes it an offence:

(a) to deposit controlled waste or knowingly cause or knowingly permit controlled waste to be deposited in or on land unless there is a waste management licence in force and the deposit is in accordance with it;

(b) to treat, keep or dispose of controlled waste, or knowingly cause or knowingly permit controlled waste to be treated, kept or disposed of in or on land or by means of mobile plant except where there is a waste management licence in force;

(c) to treat, keep or dispose of controlled waste in a manner likely to cause pollution of the environment or harm to human health.

Thus, the Act widens the Control of Pollution Act offences considerably. However, the addition of the word 'knowingly' to the causal link between an act and the offence has to a certain extent weakened the definition.

The introduction of the phrases 'pollution of the environment' and 'harm to human health' (s. 33(1)(c)) replace the narrow concepts of 'pollution of water' and 'danger to public health' under COPA. The two phrases are defined in s. 29 as follows:

'pollution of the environment' means pollution of [land, water or air] due to the release or escape from:
 (a) the land on which controlled waste is treated;
 (b) the land on which controlled waste is kept;
 (c) the land in or on which controlled waste is deposited;
 (d) fixed plant by means of which controlled waste is treated, kept or disposed of;
of substances or articles constituting or resulting from the wastee and capable (by reason of the quantity or concentrations involved) of causing harm to man or any other living organism supported by the environment.

'Harm' includes any harm to the health of living organisms or any other interference with the ecological systems of which they are a part. In the case of humans, harm includes offence to any of their senses or harm to property. The sheer width of this definition is astounding. Most waste disposal operations affect one of the five senses, it might be terrible to look at, it might smell, there might be noise etc. The fact that this has to give rise to an offence does not make it clear whether this is a subjective or objective test. To define harm in a subjective sense would ensure that enforcement would almost be at the whim of any individual who wished to complain. No doubt some form of balancing exercise involving competing rights will ensure that there is adequate protection.

The level of maximum fines has been raised to £20,000, and there is now a more serious offence in relation to 'special' waste (s. 33(9)).

However, the existing loophole under the Control of Pollution Act exploited by *Leigh Land Reclamation Limited et al* v *Walsall MBC* (see p. 272) has now been closed by making it an offence to contravene any condition of a waste management licence without any reference to the deposit of waste (s. 33(6)).

Application procedures

Section 35 governs the general provisions relating to waste management licences and applications for them. Section 35(2) states that only an occupier of the land or the operator of a mobile plant can apply for a licence. There are no definitions within the Act of occupiers or operators but it is assumed that both terms relate to the ability to directly control the activities of the waste operation. The application is to be made to the relevant WRA and the licences will be different in the case of an occupier—'a site licence', and a plant operator—'a mobile plant licence' (s. 35(12)).

Section 36 governs how applications are to be made. The application is to be made to the relevant WRA (s. 36(1)) but in the case of mobile plant to the WRA where the operator has its principal place of business. The Secretary of State is empowered to make regulations governing the application procedure and these will introduce a far greater uniformity of standards.

In keeping with the principles outlined in other areas of the Act, s. 41(1) provides for regulation to be drawn up in respect of fees to be paid in respect of licence applications.

The criteria for the grant of a licence

The EPA widens the criteria to be taken into account when the WRA are considering whether or not to grant a licence. Firstly, there must be a planning permission in force; this now extends to an established use certificate under of the Town and Country Planning Act 1990, s. 192 (s. 36(2)).

If the WRA are satisfied that the application may give rise to pollution of the environment or harm to human health then they may reject the application if it is necessary to do so (s. 36(3)). Where there is no planning permission in force because there are permitted development rights under the General Development Order then a further factor can be taken into account that there will be serious detriment to the amenities of the locality which renders it necessary to reject the application (s. 36(3)(c)).

One of the defects under COPA was that anybody could apply for a licence even though they may not have the scientific or financial capability to cope with any environmental problems occurring. Thus, EPA, s. 36(3), provides that where the WRA is not satisfied that the applicant is a fit and proper person then they are entitled to reject the application; the definition of a fit and proper person is contained in s. 74. Thus, an applicant is to be treated as not being fit and proper if:

(a)   the management of the licence will not be in the hands of a technically competent person; or

(b)   the applicant does not have the finance or the necessary financial obligations to discharge their licence obligation; or

(c)   the applicant or a relevant person has committed a relevant offence.

Guidance as to the factors to be taken into account to judge technical competence will be contained within regulations to be drawn up by the Secretary of State. Clearly, information will have to be supplied to the WRA relating to previous experience in the waste disposal field and the applicant must be able to demonstrate that there is enough financial support to adequately meet any requirements laid down in conditions.

To ensure that individuals with a criminal record relating to environmental offences do not get an opportunity to operate further sites, there is a restriction upon those who have been convicted of a 'relevant offence'.

Section 74(7) provides that a relevant person shall be treated as having been convicted of a relevant offence if:

(a)   any person was convicted of a relevant offence whilst the employee of the applicant;

(b)   a company of which the applicant was the director, manager, secretary, etc. was so convicted;

(c)   where the applicant is a company, an officer of the company has been convicted.

These provisions were criticised as covering far too wide a range of people, which might mean that the innocent would be included as relevant people as well as the guilty. Thus, s. 74(4) provides that even where the relevant person has been convicted of an offence the WRA have a discretion to ignore it. The Rehabilitation of Offenders Act 1974 applies to all relevant offences so that a person rehabilitated under those provisions is entitled to be treated as a person who has not been convicted and will not therefore be required to disclose any convictions on an application.

Where the WRA propose to issue a licence then it must consult with the NRA, the HSE and, in the case of land, which is part of a site of special scientific interest, the relevant Nature Conservancy Council and the local planning authority (s. 36(6)). These bodies may make representations within 21 days or any longer time agreed between the bodies. Where the NRA disagrees with the WRA about the issue of a licence then the matter can be referred to the Secretary of State as under COPA (s. 36(5)).

Further factors to take into account will be Central Government guidance issued under waste management guidance papers (ss. 35(7) and (8)). To avoid the problems of the lack of proper guidance and consequential disparity of standards, the Department of the Environment has issued a timetable for the publication of the waste management papers. These are:

Waste Management Paper	**Date of issue**
Landfill gas	September 1991
Waste management options	January 1992
Licensing	April 1992
Waste disposal plans	July 1992
Special waste	August 1992
Clinical wastes	October 1992
PCBs	January 1993
Metal finishing wastes	March 1993

Landfilling waste

Completion standards	April 1992
Design and preparation	1993
Operation	1993
Monitoring	1994
Restoration	1994
Post-closure pollution control	1994
Recycling	August 1991
Environmental assessment	1993
Solidification	1993

The effect of these papers must be taken into account by the WRAs (s. 35(8)).

The grant of a licence

When dealing with an application for authorisation, a WRA can either:

(a) grant a licence subject to conditions; or
(b) refuse a licence (s. 35(3)).

When granting a licence, the WRA can impose appropriate conditions relating not only to continuing activities under the licence but also to requirements which are to be complied with before the activities start or after the activities cease. Thus, aftercare conditions relating to purely environmental matters can be included (s. 35(3)). Section 35(4) provides that conditions may require the applicant to carry out works that require the consent of another person, thus including works carried out on leasehold premises which require a landlord's consent.

Supervision and enforcement

Section 42 puts WRAs under a duty to supervise waste management licences to ensure that pollution of the environment, harm to human health or detriment to the amenities of the locality does not occur and to ensure that the licence conditions are being complied with. The default powers available include the revocation or partial revocation of a licence (s. 42(6)). The effect of a partial revocation is to ensure that although certain conditions contained within a licence are revoked, other conditions are complied with. Thus, enforcement action coupled with ongoing responsibility can ensure that proper consideration is taken of the overall environmental effect of an operation. Secondly, s. 42(6)(c) gives the WRA power to suspend a licence so far as it authorises the carrying on of the activities specified in the licence or the activity specified by the authority in suspending the licence.

Where the waste management activities make it likely that pollution of water is to be caused then the WRA are under a statutory duty to consult with the NRA as to the discharge of their supervisory duty (s. 42(2)).

Emergency works
Under s. 42(3), a WRA performing their supervisory duty may, in an emergency, carry out work on land or in relation to plant and recover their expenditure from the licence holder or, if such licence has been surrendered, from the former holder.

Variation of conditions
A licence can be varied by means of the modification of conditions (s. 37). This can be done by the WRA where, in their opinion, the modification is desirable and is unlikely to require a reasonable expense on the part of the

licence holder. Moreover, it can be done on request by the licence holder (s. 37(1)). These powers are in addition to the powers under s. 42(5), which can be used where licence conditions are not being complied with.

Revocation and suspension notices

In addition to the powers contained within s. 42, the WRA have the power to revoke and suspend licences where there has not been a breach of any condition imposed on the licence.

Section 38(1) provides that where there is a licence in force and it appears to the authority:

(a)   that the holder of a licence has ceased to be a fit and proper person by reason of being convicted of a relevant offence; or

(b)   that the licence activities would cause pollution of the environment, harm to human health or serious detriment to the amenities of the locality; and

(c)   that the pollution, harm or detriment cannot be avoided by modification under s. 37

the WRA can revoke the licence partially or entirely.

This particular section covers unforeseen circumstances which would give rise to particular environmental problems. Thus, where a licence holder or relevant person is convicted of an offence relating to waste disposal, the WRA are entitled to revoke any part of the licence, or all of it, as may be appropriate (s. 38(3)).

Where more serious environmental consequences are anticipated there is a new power contained under s. 38(6) which provides for the suspension of a waste management licence either partially or wholly. This power can be exercised in one of three ways:

(a)   Where the licence holder has ceased to be a fit and proper person by reason of the management of the licence being in the hands of a technically incompetent person.

(b)   Where serious pollution of the environment or serious harm to human health has resulted from or is about to be caused by the licensed activities.

(c)   Where continuing to carry out those activities will cause or continue to cause serious pollution to the environment or serious harm to human health.

The extreme nature of the power means that it will be exercised only in the most extreme of circumstances and this is reflected in that there are rights of compensation if the Secretary of State decides that the WRA have acted unreasonably (s. 43(7)).

Section 38(9) allows the authority when suspending a licence to impose measures on the licence holder which are not specifically related to the conditions and responsibilities contained within the original licence. Thus, where situations have arisen which fall outside the control of a licence, the holder may be required to rectify these. Section 38(10) and (11) makes it a criminal offence to fail to comply with the requirements of a suspension notice. There are stricter penalties where the breach relates to special waste.

Revocation and suspension notices take effect by means of a notice served on the holder of a licence which states the time at which the revocation is to take effect or, in the case of suspension, the period at which the suspension is to cease (s. 38(12)).

Transfer and surrender of licences

Where a licence is transferred under EPA, s. 40, there is a more formal power than that contained in COPA. Where a licence is to be transferred, both the existing holder and the proposed transferee have to make a joint application to the WRA for a transfer, pay an appropriate fee and provide any information laid down by regulations (s. 40(2) and (3)). However, the only criterion which the WRA are entitled to consider is whether or not the proposed transferee is a fit and proper person; if that criterion is met, the authority are under a mandatory duty to transfer the licence (s. 40(4)).

Whereas under COPA there was no power controlling the relinquishment of a licence under s. 39, a licence can only be surrendered under EPA if the authority accepts the surrender (s. 39(1)). It is open to the holder of a site licence to apply to surrender the licence; it must pay a fee and provide accompanying information (s. 39(3)). The authority is then required to inspect the land and determine whether or not it is likely that the condition of the land resulting from the site activities will cause pollution to the environment or harm to human health (s. 39(5)). Only where the authority are satisfied that the land is unlikely to cause pollution or harm can they accept the surrender and only then after referring the matter to the NRA. If there is a disagreement between the two enforcement bodies as to the proposal to surrender the licence then the matter may be referred to the Secretary of State (s. 39(7)). The WRA have a period of three months in which to decide an application after which it is deemed to be refused (s. 39(10)). Where the authority are satisfied that there will be no pollution or harm they are under a duty to issue to the applicant a certificate of completion stating that they are of such an opinion (s. 39(9)). Where the operator possesses a certificate of completion, the WRA are in the position of having continuing responsibility for the site.

Appeals

There are wide-ranging rights of appeal contained in s. 43. An appeal can be made where:

(a) an application for a licence or a modification of the conditions of a licence is rejected;
(b) a licence is granted subject to conditions;
(c) the conditions of a licence are modified;
(d) a licence is suspended;
(e) a licence is revoked under ss. 38 or 42;
(f) an application to surrender a licence is rejected; or

(g)   an application for the transfer of a licence is rejected.

There are powers of call in by the Secretary of State, who may appoint a person to deal with any appeal which can be in the form of a private hearing (s. 43(2)). Any decision of the WRA relating to the continuing authorised activities on a site is ineffective where an appeal is pending (s. 43(4)), unless it was a suspension notice (s. 43(5)), or the notice contains a statement that it is the authority's opinion that the continuing activities should be suspended for the purpose of preventing pollution or harm to human health (s. 42(6)).

The duty of care

Section 34 of the EPA sets out the duty of care to be taken with respect to waste. The new duty relates to the keeping, transfer and control of waste. Its introduction was primarily prompted by the RCEPs Eleventh Report, *Managing Waste: The Duty of Care*, in which it was said:

> the first task is for society to identify where the responsibility lies for ensuring that wastes are properly handled and disposed of. In our judgment, this must rest with the individual or organisation who produces the wastes. The producer incurs a duty of care which is owed to society, and we would like to see this duty reflected in public attitudes and enshrined in legislation and codes of practice.

They went on to stress the need to assign responsibility for the waste from person to person relying upon the competence of those handling the waste at any particular time to do so safely and without harm to the environment.

The aim or the duty is to provide a 'cradle to grave' approach to the management and disposal of waste. COPA never fully dealt with waste throughout its life and thus where problems arose it was not easy to allocate responsibility to the person responsible in the disposal chain.

The duty is imposed upon any person who imports, produces, carries, keeps, treats or disposes of controlled waste or, as a broker, has control of such waste. Therefore, responsibility should attach to the person responsible at any time during the waste disposal chain.

The standard of the duty is that any person to whom the duty applies should take reasonable steps to:

(a)   prevent any person contravening the law with regard to unauthorised deposits, treatment or disposal of waste;
(b)   prevent the escape of waste;
(c)   secure that the waste is only transferred to an authorised person;
(d)   ensure that a sufficient written description of the waste accompanies it on transfer to another person.

There is also a residual duty. The Secretary of State (s. 34(5)), has the power to make regulations with respect to the making, retention and furnishing of documents or copies in relation to the first four duties. This will enable log-books to be established.

The only exception to the duty applies to occupiers of domestic property as respect to household waste produced on the property (s. 34(2)). The liability imposed by the Act is criminal and breach of the duty will be punishable by a fine of up to £2000 in the magistrates' court and unlimited in the Crown Court. What is reasonable in particular circumstances will differ depending upon the role of the waste holder.

The provisions of s. 34 are to be backed up by a statutory code of practice (s. 34(10)). This code of practice will lay down steps for waste holders to take, in showing that their actions have been reasonable. A code of practice has been issued in draft form and brief comment will be made upon it although the final version may well change. A technical breach of the code of practice will not in itself be an offence; however, it will give rise to a presumption that the duty has been breached. However, where the code is complied with, the WRA may still show, in the circumstances, that an offence has been committed.

(a) The prevention of breach of s. 33

The purpose of the code of practice is to give guidance on the sorts of situations whereby it would be clear to the reasonable person that waste was not being dealt with effectively. The code goes on to suggest a number of examples where a waste holder consigning waste to another person should take account of the evidence suggesting that illegal disposal might take place. The onus is placed upon the waste holder to take reasonable proactive steps to ensure that no breach occurs:

> A producer may notice a carrier's lorry is returning empty for further loads in a shorter time than they could possibly have taken to reach and return from the nearest lawful disposal site; or a producer may notice his carrier apparently engaged in the unlawful dumping of someone else's waste. Producers or carriers may know or suspect breaches of licence conditions in the subsequent treatment or disposal of waste they consigned to licensed sites. . . what is reasonable will depend on the knowledge and expertise of the parties.

Although the standard is objective in the sense of the reasonable person, it is also subjective, in that there is a degree of imputed knowledge on the waste disposal industry.

(b) Prevention of escape

This duty is directly related to the correct packaging of waste. The responsibility for preventing escape rests with the producer of the waste or any holder who takes out the waste and then repackages it. Specially designed containers which take into account the potential hazards of a particular type of waste should be used, e.g., fire resistant packaging for inflammable wastes.

(c) Transfer to authorised persons

A holder of controlled waste must take reasonable measures to secure that waste is only transferred to a list of people considered to be authorised (see also s. 34(3)). These include:

(i)   the waste collection authority;
(ii) a holder of a waste management licence;
(iii) anyone exempt under regulations from the requirement to hold a waste management licence;
(iv) any person registered as a carrier of waste under the Control of Pollution (Amendment) Act 1989 (see p. 292).

The code suggests that minimal checks are made upon title documentation that the holder/carrier of waste is purporting to rely on.

(d) Describing waste

To ensure that complete and appropriate control is maintained throughout a transportation of waste, there has to be an adequate written description of the waste transferred at each stage of transfer. The code states that the nature of the description will depend upon the nature of the waste, the hazard it presents, the intended disposition of the waste and how far this has already been established. Where the risk imposed by waste is low then it would be sufficient to have a 'simple description'.

In July 1991, the Government supplemented the previous draft with a new Circular and consultation paper. However, it is clear from the consultation paper that the role of the duty of care has shifted from a proactive prevention approach to a reactive mechanism to be used as a supplement to the other prosecution powers under s. 33. The Circular states that there should be no extra enforcement activities solely relating to the duty of care and any enforcement work should be part and parcel of their existing responsibilities to supervise and enforce the waste management regime and illegal disposal.

Miscellaneous powers

Miscellaneous powers include power for a WRA to prepare waste recycling plans (s. 49). These involve:

(a)   an investigation as to the appropriateness of dealing with waste by recycling;
(b)   a decision as to the arrangements needed;
(c)   the preparation of a plan;
(d)   periodic revisions and modifications of that plan.

The plan must include information in relation to the kinds of quantities of controlled waste and the manner in which it is to be dealt with, along with an estimate of the costs or savings which can be attributed to dealing with it in the ways suggested in the plan. There are requirements as to publicity within the area (s. 49(5)) and the plan must be kept available for inspection by members of the public at reasonable times and they must be able to take copies for a reasonable charge.

There are further provisions as regards the preparation of waste disposal plans (s. 50). These reflect the concern of the Department of the Environment over the neglect of such plans under the Control of Pollution Act. The major difference contained within EPA (s. 50(11)) provides that the Secretary of State can give a time-limit by which a WRA are to perform their duty in preparing the plan.

Powers to require removal of unlawful waste

Section 59 gives WRAs power to require the removal of unlawfully deposited waste. Thus, where an offence has been committed under s. 33 the authority can serve a notice requiring the occupier to remove waste from land within a specified period of not less than 21 days from the service of the notice or to take within that period steps to eliminate or reduce the consequences of the deposit.

There is a right of appeal to a magistrates' court within 21 days (s. 59(2)) and an appeal will be successful where it can be shown that the appellant neither deposited nor knowingly caused or permitted the deposit of the waste or there is a material defect in the notice (s. 59(3)). The effect of an appeal is to suspend the requirement until the court's decision (s. 59(4)).

Where waste on land requires removal because of the need to prevent pollution of land, water or air or harm to human health or where there is no occupier or the occupier did not make or knowingly permit the deposit of the waste, the authority have a discretion whether to remove the waste themselves and to recover their costs from the occupier or from the person depositing the waste, unless that person can show that the costs were incurred unnecessarily (s. 59(8)).

Duties of WRAs in respect of closed landfills

The WRA have powers of control over sites which have not been subject to a site licence. Thus, any contaminated land within their area can be inspected to detect whether or not there is anything affecting the land so that it causes pollution or harm to human health (s. 61(1)). This duty to carry out inspections from time to time on closed landfill sites arises in respect of any land on which controlled waste has been deposited under a licence or at any time or where the authority has reason to believe that there are concentrations or accumulations of landfill gases or noxious liquids (s. 61(3)). Where such landfill sites are, in the opinion of the authority, likely to cause pollution or harm to human health, they are under a duty to carry out works or take other steps on the land or adjacent land to avoid such harm or pollution (s. 61(7)). In such circumstances, the costs or any part of such costs can be recovered from the owner of the land unless the costs were incurred unreasonably. There may, of course, be instances when the owner of the land is not responsible for the build-up of pollution. Thus, where costs are sought from the owner, account has to be taken of any hardship suffered by the owner in paying costs (s. 61(10)).

Contaminated land registers

Section 143 of EPA provides that it is the duty of district and London borough councils in England and Wales to compile and maintain public registers of past and present 'contaminative uses' of land. Such uses are to be more fully defined within regulations yet to be drawn up. This reflects activity which has taken place within the EC and also in the United States and Canada. It is estimated that there are approximately 50 to 100,000 potentially contaminated sites within the UK and it is hoped that the registers containing details of such sites will be set up by the end of 1994.

One of the primary functions of the register will be to warn potential purchasers of land of possible contamination on a site. In normal situations, the rule of *caveat emptor* applies to purchasers of land and thus, where particularly polluting activities have been carried out on a site and concealed, there is a danger that polluters can pass on the responsibility of contamination to an innocent purchaser. Where there is a register of such contamination it has been suggested that no unknowing purchases will be made. Indeed, the Department of the Environment hope that a search of the registers will become a standard procedure before purchase.

Unfortunately, there is a negative side to the contaminated land registers. Where an entry is made in the register on a previously acceptable site there may well be a blight upon the use of the land and certainly upon any valuation put on that land. The types of contaminating uses which would be included in a register have been outlined in draft in a consultation paper issued by the DoE and these include:

Chemical works	Timber treatment works
Engineering works	Brick works
Docks	Mineral workings
Garages	Paint manufacturers
Ministry of Defence land	Paper and printing works
Scrap yards	Metal processing industries
Power stations	

The Registers are to be compiled from local knowledge supplemented by surveys, aerial photographs and other maps and plans. The entry on the Register will refer simply to the contaminative uses both past and present, the name of the present occupier and the details of any site assessment carried out. Most importantly, although there will be details of any remediation carried out, such sites will remain on the Register.

It has been suggested that there will be a major blight upon the value of any land placed upon the Register. Investigating the full nature of a contamination problem may cost tens of thousands of pounds. There is a question mark over who will be willing to pay for these investigations as Central Government have made it clear that they will not be funding the clean-up.

The introduction of the contaminated land register was a direct consequence of a report of the House of Commons Environment Committee on toxic waste and contaminated land. The Department of the Environment defined contaminated land as '. . . . land which represents a natural or potential hazard to health or to the environment as a result of current or previous uses'. One of the major concerns was that a lot of effort had been directed towards the use of derelict land and:

> little or no thought has been given to the big, central questions; who ought to pay for the clean up of contaminated sites (and how can they be made to do it?) How can contamination be prevented? Should contaminating chemicals be destroyed, or is it enough just to cover them up? How clean is clean and how safe is 'safe enough?'.

Many of these problems have been looked at and attempts have been made to deal with the issue in both the new waste disposal regime under Part II and also the integrated pollution control system under Part I of the Act.

Overlap with integrated pollution control

As the disposal, treatment, keeping or storage of waste is a particularly hazardous activity, with potentially harmful consequence to the environment, it has now been brought within part A of the Environmental Protection (Prescribed Processes and Substances) Regulations 1991 (SI 1991 No. 472). Thus, it is possible to control such activities under an authorisation granted by HMIP. They will control:

(a)   the destruction by burning in an incinerator of any waste chemicals or waste plastic arising from the manufacture of a chemical or the manufacture of plastic;

(b)   the destruction by burning in an incinerator, other than incidentally in the course of burning other waste, of waste associated with halogens, heavy metals, nitrogen, phosphorus and sulphur;

(c)   the destruction by burning of any other waste, including animal remains in large plants; and

(d)   the cleaning of metal containers used for storage or transport purposes or of chemicals for reuse. Furthermore, certain incineration processes are contained within part B of the regulations and will therefore fall under local authority control.

However, to avoid the overlap of controls between the WRAs and HMIP/ local authorities, s. 33(3) gives power to the Secretary of State to exempt certain activities from the prohibition on unauthorised or harmful deposit, treatment or disposal of waste etc. It is thought that such exemptions will be made in relation to those processes controlled by HMIP but where waste incineration falls within part B of the regulations there will be the requirement for both an authorisation from the local authority and a waste management licence issued by the WRA. Notwithstanding this desire to keep controls separate, HMIP also has a more formal role in the control of waste disposal matters. They are expected to supervise the performance of WRAs and to advise on the methods of control used.

As to final disposal in or on land, no condition can be attached to any authorisation to regulate such activities which are more properly regulated under either COPA or Part II of the EPA (s. 28). However, to ensure that there is proper notification of the WRA, the local authority or HMIP are under a duty to notify them where they are authorising an activity whenever the authorised process involves the final disposal of controlled waste by depositing it in or on land (s. 28(1)).

How this notification procedure will work in practice is unclear. There is some danger that this particular administrative loophole could lead to communication difficulties between the regulatory bodies. It could potentially mean that there is a period of time when a Part I process is disposing of waste in or on land without any regulatory control.

Future changes

The pace of change of the law relating to the disposal of waste in its widest sense will certainly not slow down with the introduction of Part II of the EPA.

Control of Pollution (Amendment) Act 1989
The Control of Pollution (Amendment) Act 1989 provides powers to deal with enforcement difficulties relating to fly-tipping on open sites. The Act was introduced as a private member's bill although it did have Government support in the light of the Second Report of the Environment Committee on toxic waste. It aims to deal with the problem of fly-tipping by ensuring that all those carrying waste are registered. Therefore, it will be a criminal offence for any person who is not a registered carrier of controlled waste, in the course of any business, to transport any such waste (s. 1). This is subject to exemptions made under s. 1(2) and further regulations to be made by the Secretary of State (s. 1(3)). There are also various defences in s. 1(4) which include emergencies and circumstances in which the defendant neither knew or had reasonable grounds for suspecting that the waste was controlled waste and took reasonable steps to ascertain the nature of the waste or in which he acted on instructions from his employer (s. 1(4)). The Act is fleshed out by further regulations relating to the registration of carriers and the information which may be required in relation to applications, conditions and charging (s. 2). There are further provisions governing who may hold such a licence which are similar to those concerned with the fit and proper person definition under EPA, s. 74 (s. 3(1)). Apart from this situation and that where there has been a contravention of regulations, there are no other reasons to refuse an application.

There is to be a system of appeals (s. 4) and enforcement will be by means of stopping and searching vehicles where it 'reasonably appears' that controlled waste is being carried by non-registered carriers (s. 5).

It is hoped that the Act will enable waste authorities to intercept the unauthorised deposit of controlled waste before it is dumped.

The Act received its commencement order on 22 July 1991 under the Control of Pollution (Amendment) Act 1989, Commencement Order 1991 (SI 1991 No. 1618). The implementation process is in two stages. The first stage deals with the registration of waste carriers under s. 2, to be introduced from 14 October 1991. From 1 April 1992, s. 1 will be implemented.

The special waste regulations

A consultation paper was issued in January 1990 concerning a redrafting of the special waste provisions. This is taking place in tandem with the EC amendments to the definition of waste under the framework Directive 75/442.

The draft regulations propose a change to the definition of special waste by reference to four different groups. Firstly, waste may be special by reason of possessing characteristic properties which make them dangerous or difficult to dispose of; secondly, there may be substances which if present within waste would cause them to be dangerous or difficult to dispose of; thirdly, there are characteristic properties which will give rise to substances or materials being special waste such as those which are toxic, exotoxic, flammable or infectious; finally, there will be a list of household waste which will fall under one of the other three groups.

There will be a number of amendments to the existing consignment notice procedure to take into account problem areas of the legislation. These will include a special form of consignment note which will only be obtained from disposal authorities, new definitions of the term holder, carrier and consignee and, finally a requirement that there must be a contractual agreement entered into before special waste can be removed from premises. There are further prohibitions on mixing special waste and for the setting up of a register of consignment notes.

To ensure that there is proper guidance on this new system, the Department of the Environment have indicated that there will be a revision of Waste Management Paper No. 23, which deals with test methods for special waste. These regulations will ensure that there is far tighter control over special waste than has previously been the case.

The Draft Directive on Civil Liability for Damage Caused by Waste

The EC has also been active in proposing new changes to the law on waste disposal. This draft Directive seeks to impose strict liability for damage caused by waste. The rationale behind the Directive is to ensure that liability for damage will be the responsibility of the producer of the waste from the moment that it is produced until it has been transferred to a licensed installation.

Article 2(1) of the draft Directive defines 'the producer' of waste as:

any natural or legal person whose occupational activity is to produce waste and/or anyone who carried out preprocessing, mixing or other operations resulting in a change in the nature or composition of this waste, until the moment when the damage or injury to the environment is caused.

In certain circumstances the producer of waste will be someone other than the person who has generated it. Thus Article 2(2) includes importers of waste and those having effective control over it. Such persons will be responsible only where the producer of waste cannot be identified within a reasonable period.

The draft Directive extends to cover not only personal injury and damage to property but also introduces the new concept of purely environmental harm. Liability will include the costs of restoring the different sectors of the environment to their state before the injury occurred. The liability will be strict (i.e. no fault) and without limit in financial terms. The remedies which accrue not only include a right to compensation for steps taken to prevent the pollution but also for the restoration and payment of other damages.

The right to restore the environment to its prior condition is restricted to public authorities or the person suffering the damage. Otherwise, under Article 4(4), amenity and action groups have a right to bring an action for the costs that they have incurred in preventing or remedying environmental harm.

The first restriction on the Directive is that it is not supposed to be retrospective. Article 13 of the draft Directive specifically provides that the Directive is only to apply to damage arising from an incident giving rise to damage or injury to the environment taking place after the Directive comes into effect. This is understood to mean that there is no retrospective liability. However, the nature of waste disposal in the UK ensures that such a definition does not adequately clarify the situation. The issue would seem to be: when does the incident actually occur? Where, for example, cylinders containing hazardous material are dumped and then after some months of decay, begin to leak into a nearby watercourse and continue to so leak for a longer period, it is arguable whether the incident causing the damage took place when the cylinders were dumped or when the leakage first occurred or whether the 'incident' continues to take place for so long as the leakage continues. Where drums of waste were deposited before the date of implementation of the Directive and seepage had been continuing for some time since, the damage to the environment may still be subject to the Directive. Thus, in situations where there is latent damage, the Directive does not seem to provide a full answer.

Recently, there have been amendments made by the European Commission to the Draft Directive. These amendments include the redefinition of environmental damage to a wider definition, that of 'impairment of the environment'. Secondly, there has been a move away from holding the waste producer solely responsible and the new draft seems to suggest that in certain situations the transporter of waste would be jointly liable with the producer. Finally, there is now an obligation imposed upon waste producers to ensure they are properly insured or they have sufficient financial security to pay any compensation under the Directive.

THIRTEEN
Water pollution

This chapter is about the protection of the water environment. It will concentrate on the control of pollution of inland and coastal waters and will not seek to cover the very wide range of environmental and other issues that arise from the activities of the water industry. Some of these issues, such as the provision of a clean water supply, will be covered briefly here, since, although they do not directly concern the protection of inland and coastal waters, they have a significant impact on water pollution policy and controls. Others, such as the effects of land drainage on the landscape and on nature conservation, will be relevant to Chapter 15. Marine pollution, where different controls apply, will not be covered.

There is a degree of coherence in water pollution control which is arguably lacking in other areas. For the most part control is exercised through a sophisticated and relatively public regulatory system operated by the National Rivers Authority (NRA) under the Water Act 1989. The provisions of the Water Act replaced the Control of Pollution Act 1974 (COPA) on 1 September 1989 (the 'transfer date' in the legislation, when the new organisational structure of the water industry came into force). The system involves the setting of water quality objectives and a requirement that consent is obtained from the NRA for discharges of trade and sewage effluent to controlled waters. Discharges from certain hazardous processes are controlled by Her Majesty's Inspectorate of Pollution under the integrated pollution control provisions of the Environmental Protection Act 1990. Discharges to sewers, which have as much in common with waste disposal as with water pollution and which have their own, more basic, regulatory system operated by sewerage undertakers, are dealt with in Chapter 14.

The consent system is backed up by a general offence of causing water pollution which applies where pollution is caused by matter other than trade and sewage effluent. It is also supported by further regulatory and administrative controls, notably in relation to the prevention of harm, and by the common law.

The legislation on the water industry was consolidated into five separate Acts which all received the Royal Assent in July 1991. These come into force on 1 December 1991. Since (as befits a consolidation) there will be no change in the substance of the law, the references to the existing law are retained in this and the next chapter, and destinations of the most important sections are as stated in a postscript to this chapter.

Water pollution

Pollutants of water come in many forms, such as:

(a)   deoxygenating materials, for example, sewage and other organic wastes, such as silage, farm wastes, and wastes from a number of heavily polluting industrial processes (e.g. food processing and the production of smokeless fuel, textiles, paper and dairy products);

(b)   nutrient enrichment by such things as fertilisers, which may give rise to eutrophication, causing an accelerated growth of plants and algae and leading to a decline in water quality;

(c)   solids, which may impede flows, or block out light for growth;

(d)   toxic materials; some materials, such as heavy metals, pesticides or nitrate, are toxic to humans, animals, plants, or all three, often depending on the level of the dose received;

(e)   materials which cause an impact on amenity, such as car tyres or shopping trolleys, or old boots in canals;

(f)   disease-carrying agents, such as bacteria;

(g)   heat, which may affect biological conditions and also deoxygenates water.

The effect of any potential pollutant will vary according to the size, temperature, rate of flow and oxygen content of the receiving waters, as well as the local geology and the presence of other pollutants and any resulting synergistic effects. The use made of a stream is also of enormous importance in deciding whether it can be said to be polluted, and this factor has a large impact on the attitude of the regulatory bodies towards the setting of standards and their enforcement. It is not sufficient to look at pollution of surface waters, since 35% of domestic water supply is taken from ground waters. As a result the control of water pollution encompasses the control of liquid discharges to land.

The sources of pollution are also varied:

(a)   There are over 30,000 separate industrial discharges where there is consent for discharge to waters. Many of these will involve toxic materials or organic pollutants.

(b)   There are over 4,300 sewage works with discharge consents. The organic content of these discharges makes them highly polluting, and they have had a particularly important role in the history of water pollution.

(c)   Agricultural pollution is significant; discharges of farm wastes are of increasing importance, and the increase of pollution incidents has averaged 12% per year in the 1980s, reaching 4,141 in 1988 (*Water Pollution From Farm Waste 1988*, ADAS/MAFF, 1989). A new phenomenon of recent years has been discharges of wastes from fish farms. Run-off from pesticides and fertilisers also create major problems.

(d)   Discharges of waste waters from mines are often highly contaminated (and *abandoned* mines are entirely exempt from the regulatory system).

(e)   Accidents are frequent, particularly from the storage and transport of hazardous chemicals and such things as fertilisers.

(f)   Leachate from waste sites, including disused ones, is also significant.

The Department of the Environment River Quality Survey already takes place every five years to give an accurate national picture of water pollution. The 1985 Survey (covering the period 1980–1985) showed a slight deterioration in overall river quality, although this may to some extent have been due to changes in the recording system. However, closer analysis reveals that there was a significant deterioration in some areas, matched by an improvement in others. Given that the period in question coincided with a deep industrial recession and the increased utilisation of alternative disposal routes for wastes, this position reflects a serious problem. The main causes of deterioration were discharges from sewage works, and agricultural pollution. The latter is reducing the quality of many once clean rural rivers. Other significant polluters were identified as discharges from mines, run-off from waste tips and fish farms. This illustrates that one issue for the next decade is how to control non-point discharges and that more inventive legal mechanisms than those used in the past are needed.

The water industry

The water industry has traditionally been thought of as including a wide range of rather different matters: water collection, treatment and supply; the provision of sewers, sewage works and sewage disposal; water pollution control; the regulation of bodies providing water services; fisheries; navigation; flood defence and land drainage; recreational activities; and conservation responsibilities. From this list it is clear that in reality this is a set of industries, connected in the sense that they all relate to the water cycle, but separate in their objectives. Not all of these matters are relevant to the themes of this book; pollution control is only one function of the water industry, but its place in relation to these other activities needs to be understood.

The industry has historically been dominated by water supply and sewage disposal. Up to the Second World War these tasks were largely carried out by municipal authorities. However, activities such as fishing and pollution control increasingly came to be organised on a river basin basis through a number of specialist, river-related institutions, such as catchment boards (for land drainage), fisheries boards and internal drainage boards, although major responsibility for pollution control still rested with the local authorities through their public health functions.

These trends led to an attempt to create a more logical system. The River Boards Act 1948 established 32 river boards, organised on a catchment area basis, which took over a number of regulatory functions. In 1963 the Water Resources Act converted these boards into 27 river authorities, which had a range of regulatory functions, including pollution control and responsibility for the new system of licensing abstractions of water. Water supply and sewage disposal remained in general a local authority function, although the number of water supply undertakings was steadily reduced over the years.

The Water Act 1973 established a fully integrated system of river and water management. Ten regional water authorities became responsible for all water related functions within river basin areas. These included the management of water provision, water treatment and water supply, sewerage, sewage works and sewage disposal, land drainage and flood defence, pollution control, inland fisheries, recreational uses of water and ecological and amenity matters. The idea was to set up a completely planned and integrated service as opposed to the fragmented system then in existence (prior to 1973, there were 27 river authorities, 157 water supply undertakings and no less than 1,393 sewage authorities). The only real exception was the retention of 29 private water companies responsible for water supply in defined areas.

However, this system came to be seen as ineffective. For a start, the industry was clearly massively underfunded, with the result that capital and other works were postponed and the quality of service declined. In consequence, the problem of water quality was never really addressed and this contributed to a general decline in standards. A particular cause of these declining standards was the inadequacy of many sewage works operated by the regional water authorities themselves, which came to be seen as acting the part of both poacher and gamekeeper in relation to water pollution. This conflict of interest led to specific changes in the Water Act 1989.

The Water Act 1989

The Water Act 1989 carried out a fundamental restructuring of the water industry. The main impetus was undoubtedly the Government's policy of privatisation. One stated aim of this was to increase accountability, though exactly whether this means the industry should be accountable to the public, the Government, or to shareholders is unclear. A further aim was to remove the previous cash limits on public spending that had restricted the regional water authorities, thus opening the way for improvements in the quality of water services, but at a cost to the consumer of those services, who will pay for them.

Originally it was intended to privatise the whole industry en bloc, but the inadequacy of the proposed regulatory mechanisms, particularly those for pollution control in an age of increased environmental awareness, led to the privatisation of the operational end of the industry only (i.e. water supply, sewerage services and certain recreational services) in the form of 10 water services companies. These double as water undertakers and sewerage undertakers in areas corresponding with the old regional water authority ones. The 29 water companies remain as statutory water companies, having responsibility for water supply only.

The position of Director General of Water Services was created to exercise regulatory functions in relation to water supply and sewerage provision. The NRA was created as a wide-ranging and independent regulatory agency with responsibility for tackling water pollution amongst other things. Unlike the old regional water authorities, it has no operational responsibilities in relation to sewage works to conflict with its environmental protection role. For a more detailed explanation of the NRA, see p. 32.

Water pollution controls

The modern system of control really begins with the Rivers (Prevention of Pollution) Act 1951, a rather rudimentary control system in which consent from the river board was required for industrial or sewage discharges into most inland waters. Prior to that, there had been the Rivers Pollution Prevention Act 1876, which imposed an absolute prohibition on pollution but proved almost totally unworkable. The Clean Rivers (Estuaries and Tidal Waters) Act 1960 extended the controls to tidal and estuarial waters and the Rivers (Prevention of Pollution) Act 1961 ensured that a large number of discharges that had hitherto been exempted were controlled, such as those commenced prior to 1951. The Water Resources Act 1963 extended the system to discharges to certain underground waters. However, the system remained essentially secret and with little public accountability. Control over sewage effluents was also compromised because of the local authorities' control of the river authorities.

The next major step forward was in the Control of Pollution Act 1974, which again extended the geographical coverage of the controls so that most discharges to inland, underground, tidal or coastal waters out to the three-mile limit were covered. More importantly, COPA introduced some advanced provisions on public participation in decisions, established public registers of information and allowed for private prosecutions, which had previously been excluded. In addition a more sophisticated set of preventative and remedial measures was introduced.

However, the Control of Pollution Act did not come into force immediately. Like much environmental legislation its implementation relied on commencement orders, and the main measures were not brought into force until the mid-1980s: a delay mainly due to the Government's worries over the economic cost of the new controls, particularly in relation to underperforming sewage works operated by the regional water authorities. Even when the Act was brought into force, the transitional provisions meant that the full impact was not immediately felt, and indeed certain of the provisions never were implemented.

The Water Act 1989 created the NRA, and continued the process of refining and improving the law. The system of consents set out in the Control of Pollution Act remains roughly the same, though with a few amendments. Important changes include the introduction of statutory water quality standards for the first time, the introduction of a system of charging for trade and sewage discharges, and the improvement of the available preventative and remedial powers.

The Environmental Protection Act 1990 does not alter the main structure of water pollution law, but, under the Act, Her Majesty's Inspectorate of Pollution takes the lead role in relation to processes subject to integrated pollution control, thus robbing the NRA of total control over discharges to inland and coastal waters.

Throughout this period the emphasis has been on flexible standards, with most consents being set on an individualised basis by reference to the effect of a discharge on the receiving waters. Particular emphasis was placed on biochemical oxygen demand (BOD) and the level of suspended solids, rather than on such things as metals and toxic substances, especially in relation to sewage discharges. In a sense, the method of setting consents could almost be described as a 'rule of thumb' method. This approach is changing in response to EC Directives and the establishment of the NRA.

Scotland

It should be noted that in Scotland a different system applies. Regional councils are responsible for the provision of the water supply and for sewerage and sewage disposal. Apart from the three island councils, which are all-purpose authorities, water pollution is the responsibility of the seven river purification boards. These are independent catchment area bodies with their own budgets financed out of precepts on the regional councils, and with one third of their members appointed by each of the following, namely, regional councils, district councils and the Secretary of State.

The Water Act 1989 did not make any institutional changes, but in sch. 23 it did amend the Control of Pollution Act 1974, which still remains in force in Scotland. Unfortunately, this has meant that there are slightly different wordings for some sections on each side of the border. Whilst water pollution law is thus very similar in Scotland, it cannot always be guaranteed that it is exactly the same.

A further difference was enacted in the Environmental Protection Act 1990. The river purification boards are given a greater role in relation to integrated pollution control than the NRA and will have joint responsibility for operating the system alongside Her Majesty's Industrial Pollution Inspectorate.

Pollution policy

Until 1989, it was difficult to identify a coherent national water pollution policy. The Department of the Environment had overall responsibility for all water matters, but most policy decisions were left to the regional water authorities, with the DoE appearing more preoccupied with financial matters than with water quality. The one national body in this area, the National Water Council, was abolished in 1983 as superfluous. Of course, there were often unspoken aims, such as that of getting treatable wastes into the sewerage system if possible, and cleaning up waters for economic reasons, since the public water supply was increasingly taken from them. In addition, EC standards effectively laid down a set of priorities, leading to such things as a policy to minimise the discharge of dangerous substances and if possible to cut them out entirely— effectively a 'precautionary' policy.

The establishment of the NRA has meant that the opportunity can be taken to establish a truly national policy on water pollution—or at least one applicable to England and Wales. At a general level, this is being done through the NRA's First Corporate Plan, published in September 1990. This sets out a number of aims on water pollution, such as the assessment of the present quality of waters, the establishment of classification systems so that comparisons can be made, the review of existing policy in relation to the granting of consents and compliance with them, increased attention to prevention of harm in such areas as farm pollution, and a more rigorous enforcement policy involving greater use of prosecution. Most of these things are already happening. The plan also has a range of policies on other aspects of the water cycle, including aquifer protection, conservation issues, recreational opportunities and water resources. This process is a good example of environmental policy being set by a body other than Central Government.

More specifically, the NRA is currently involved in trying to establish uniformity and consistency on such things as sampling, setting of consents and public participation, where in the past there have tended to be different attitudes in different regions. In the Kinnersley Report (*Discharge Consent and Compliance Policy: A Blueprint for the Future*, National Rivers Authority, July 1990), the NRA suggests some mechanisms for unifying the totally different procedures and levels of consents that it inherited from the 10 regional water authorities. It is establishing a national strategy for reviewing all existing consents on a catchment area basis, and this will include bringing sewage works consents into line with industrial consents. However, for the time being it remains the case that consents are mainly set on an individualised basis, with the main determinant being the perceived effect on the receiving waters.

In addition to the activities of the NRA, the Royal Commission on Environmental Pollution is currently looking at fresh water quality and its report is expected in 1991.

The EC and water pollution

The EC has had an enormous impact on water pollution law and policy over the last few years. The First Action Programme on the Environment in 1973 picked out water pollution as a priority matter, and there has been a steady stream of Directives since. In addition, more recent Directives on such diverse things as Environmental Impact Assessment (85/337) and Access to Environmental Information (90/313) and the Regulation on the European Environmental Agency (1210/90) have had an indirect impact on water.

Although much of the justification for interference with national laws on water pollution has been related to the aim of establishing a common market in which one country's producers are not effectively subsidised by having to obey less stringent environmental laws than those in other countries, more recent Directives, such as that on Urban Waste Water Treatment (91/271), have tended to emphasise straightforward environmental protection more openly. Nevertheless, it remains the case that EC law only covers water pollution in a selective way: not all pollutants in all waters are yet covered.

The EC water Directives tend to follow two basic models (see Somsen 'EC Water Directives' [1990] 1 *Water Law* 93):

(a)   those which adopt emission standards, which are mainly used for reducing dangerous substances; and
(b)   those which impose quality objectives on waters which are mainly set according to the use that is to be made of those waters.

For a full discussion of all the EC Directives relating to water and their implementation, see Haigh, *EEC Environmental Law and Britain*, 2nd Revised Edition, 1989.

Dangerous substances

One of the first water Directives, and arguably the most important, is 76/464 on Dangerous Substances in Water. This is a framework Directive passed with the aim of reducing or eliminating specified dangerous substances from water. It covers essentially the same waters as those controlled by the NRA.

The Directive includes two Lists—a 'black list' and a 'grey list', respectively Lists I and II. The 'black list' includes exceptionally toxic or persistent substances, such as organohalogens, organophosphorous compounds, mercury, lead, known carcinogens and many pesticides, and it is sought to eliminate pollution from these sources. The 'grey list' includes many other heavy metals, cyanide, ammonia and other substances where pollution should be reduced. In 1982 the Commission published a list of 129 'black list' substances for future action—still far more than the equivalent British 'Red List'.

For 'black list' substances, any discharge must be subject to a consent by a competent national authority, and emission standards on the discharge must be set which do not exceed limit values set by the EC. Alternatively, the emission standards may be set by reference to quality objectives for the receiving waters laid down by the EC, which must be kept to at all times. Only Britain has adopted the second approach (see below). These EC standards and objectives are to be set in 'daughter Directives', although at present only a few of these have been agreed (e.g. Mercury 82/176, Cadmium 83/513 and Lindane 84/491). Until a 'daughter Directive' is agreed, 'black list' substances are treated as if they were on the 'grey list'.

For 'grey list' substances, all discharges require a consent which sets emission standards with the aim of achieving environmental quality objectives, most of which are at present set at a national level. Member States must introduce a reduction programme for these substances in setting these quality objectives.

It was Directive 76/464 which first demonstrated the differences between Britain and the rest of the EC over standard setting. Britain's system of a decentralised setting of non-uniform consents by reference to the quality of the receiving waters was seen to be directly contradictory to the EC desire for uniform, centrally set emission standards for dangerous substances. After much argument, this led to the agreement of the alternative approaches for 'black list' substances in the Directive explained above. The same conflict has also led to delays in the process of agreeing 'daughter Directives', since unanimity is at present required on the setting of the limit values and environmental quality objectives (although a proposal to allow qualified majority voting on these matters is currently being debated).

Directive 76/464 has had an enormous impact on British pollution control. Having claimed that it set its consents by reference to quality objectives for the receiving waters, the British Government was forced to introduce such a system on a formal basis, and water quality objectives were introduced for the first time in the late 1970s, at first by administrative action. This was insufficient for compliance with EC law and statutory water quality objectives have now been introduced in the Water Act 1989, ss. 104 and 105.

The Directive also led to specific changes in relation to controls over dangerous substances. For example, whilst many existing discharges were given deemed consent when the Control of Pollution Act 1974 was finally brought into force, those involving dangerous substances were subject to specified emission standards. The new rules providing for control by Her Majesty's Inspectorate of Pollution of prescribed substances discharged to sewers are also a result of this Directive. In general, 'black list' and 'grey list' substances are in future to be subject to integrated pollution control.

A similar story attaches to Directive 80/68 on Groundwater, except in this case List I substances are to be prevented from entering ground waters, whilst List II substances should be limited, in both cases by a consent system.

One problem with the emission standards approach is that it does not work well for pollution from non-point (i.e. diffuse) sources, nor where there are multiple polluters in one catchment area. Directive 86/280 (which mainly concerns the setting of limit values and environmental quality objectives for DDT, carbon tetrachloride, and pentachlorophenol) attempts to tackle this issue by requiring all *sources* of 'black list' substances to be monitored.

Quality approaches

For the quality approach there are a number of stages:

(a)   water with particular uses must first be identified (this is usually left to the discretion of the Member States);

(b)   the EC must establish a number of parameters; these are normally expressed either as Imperative (I) Values, which must be kept to, or Guide (G) Values, which Member States must try to achieve;

(c)   environmental quality objectives must be set for the waters, having regard to the parameters;

(d)   a competent national authority must be established for monitoring purposes and uniform sampling techniques are set by EC Directives (e.g. 79/869 on Sampling Surface Water for Drinking);

(e)   procedures are established for updating the I and G Values in the light of new knowledge.

Directives which have adopted this approach include those on Surface Water for Drinking 75/440, Shellfish Waters 79/923, Water Standards for Freshwater Fish 78/659, Bathing Water 76/160 and Drinking Water 80/778. However, the Commission is currently proposing a draft Directive that would cover the quality of *all* waters irrespective of their use or function.

The Directive on Surface Water for Drinking lays down three classes of waters (A1, A2 and A3), and 46 relevant parameters that waters must comply with to fall within any class (see **Water supply** below).

The two Directives on Freshwater Fish and Shellfish lay down standards for waters designated by Member States. The power to designate these waters was delegated to the regional water authorities—another example of a decentralised implementation of policy. But, there is no duty to designate and the main effect of these Directives has been to increase sampling and monitoring of relevant waters.

The Directive on Bathing Water lays down 19 parameters (mainly bacteriological) with which all 'traditional' bathing waters must comply, within specified percentile compliance rates. It covers fresh and marine waters. The Directive is very vague as to precisely which waters are covered, but unlike the previous two Directives there is no need for any designation for the Directive to apply. The British response was unenthusiastic; identification of the relevant waters was left to the regional water authorities and only 27 were initially identified—less than, for example, land-locked Luxembourg. No doubt the reason was the fear of the cost of cleaning up discharges of sewage effluent to the sea. In consequence of a reasoned opinion on non-implementation from the EC Commission, and intense EC and public pressure, the number of designated beaches is now over 400. Nevertheless, Britain is being taken to the European Court of Justice over non-implementation of the Directive. This action relates to a failure to reach the required standards at Blackpool, Formby and Southport beaches.

It is clear that this particular Directive has led to significant changes in priority in relation to expenditure on sewage outfalls and the whole policy of sewage discharges to the sea. This process of change is now being speeded up by the recently agreed Directive on Urban Waste Water Treatment 91/271. This lays down a series of dates by which urban areas will have to have sewage treatment systems. For Britain, which has followed a long-standing 'dilute and disperse' policy of discharging virtually untreated sewage into the sea, and thus has a large number of marine sewage outfalls, it will require at least secondary treatment of sewage discharged from most urban areas, and more stringent standards in sensitive areas. At present it appears that only 2% of UK sewage outfalls into the sea receive secondary treatment, so the cost of implementing this Directive will be very high. The Directive also requires all Member States to cease dumping sewage sludge in the sea by 1998, as agreed at the Conference for the Protection of the North Sea in March 1990. Britain is the only country currently carrying out this practice.

The Directive on Drinking Water is probably the best known of the water quality Directives. It lays down 62 parameters relating to the quality of all water provided for human consumption, except for natural mineral waters (see

80/777). It led directly to the setting in Britain of the first statutory standards of wholesomeness for drinking water, in the Water Supply (Water Quality) Regulations 1989 (SI 1989 No. 1147).

Apart from the delay in complying with the Directive until well after the formal date set for compliance, argument has centred over the provisions for derogating from the Directive, because of problems in some areas in complying with the standards on lead, nitrate and certain pesticides. For example, the Government sought to grant derogations for nitrate levels by reference to Article 9 of the Directive, which refers to geological conditions. This was argued by the Commission to be an inaccurate interpretation of Article 9, since nitrate levels result from self-induced effects on the soil. Formal infringement proceedings have now been commenced before the European Court of Justice in relation to the Directive.

The Directive on Nitrate also adopts a quality approach. (This Directive was agreed by the EC Council in June 1991, although the official text has yet to be approved.) It requires Member States to designate 'vulnerable zones', which are defined in the Directive as being where inland or ground waters intended for drinking are likely to contain more than 50mg/l nitrate if protective action is not taken; or where any inland or coastal waters are liable to suffer from eutrophication if protective action is not taken. Within these designated 'vulnerable zones', very detailed regulatory requirements are laid down in the Directive. This Directive introduces a far more interventionist system than that which is currently being operated through the provisions on nitrate sensitive areas in the Water Act 1989 (see p. 327).

Finally, there are two other Directives worth a mention in the light of their different approaches to control. Directive 73/404 on Detergents sets a product standard by prohibiting the marketing of detergents with average biodegradability of less than 90%. Directive 78/176 on Titanium Dioxide sets standards in relation to a specific industry.

The EC has thus had a great impact on British water pollution practice. Whilst there have been many arguments about technical matters, such as the levels laid down for nitrate in drinking water and the need for a Bathing Water Directive at all, most of the standards required have been introduced in one way or another, although normally belatedly. A formal system of water quality classifications and objectives, statutory regulations on drinking water quality, the introduction of specific standards for dangerous substances, and a dramatic shift in relation to the discharge of sewage effluent to the sea can all be attributed to EC initiatives. The general approach to pollution control has also been altered significantly.

Perhaps the greatest impact, however, has been the great publicity that has been engendered by having specific standards set at EC level against which Governmental action can be measured. This has certainly contributed to the intensity of the debate over nitrate. EC requirements also had an impact on the proposals for the privatisation of the water industry. It became clear that the EC would not accept a private pollution regulator as a 'competent authority' for the purposes of Directives, and this was one reason for the creation of the NRA (and also a separate Drinking Water Inspectorate).

Water supply

Strictly speaking the provision of a clean water supply is a consumer protection rather than an environmental protection measure. However, a brief summary of the law on the quality of the water supply is necessary because its requirements often dictate what must be done in the way of pollution control. For example, a major reason for protecting inland waters against pollution is to protect against pollution of water sources, or to reduce the cost of treatment for use. To this end it is an offence to pollute any waterworks, including a spring or well likely to be used for human consumption (Water Act 1945, s. 21), and by-laws may also create offences of polluting water supply sources (Water Act 1945, s. 18).

In addition, EC Directive 75/440 on Surface Water for Drinking has imposed significant controls on the quality of inland waters. This Directive seeks to ensure that surface waters that are abstracted for drinking are fit for that purpose and divides such waters into three categories—A1, A2 and A3. Classification in these categories depends upon the waters meeting the limits set out in the Directive. Any water of below A3 quality should not be abstracted for drinking except in exceptional circumstances. These requirements are implemented in British law by the Surface Waters (Classification) Regulations 1989 (SI 1989 No. 1148) (which set out categories DW1, DW2 and DW3 corresponding to those in the Directive), and by the Water Supply (Water Quality) Regulations 1989 (SI 1989 No. 1147).

Water is supplied by the privatised water undertakers under the regulatory oversight of the Director General of Water Services and the Secretary of State. Under s. 52 of the Water Act 1989, domestic water must be 'wholesome' and this is officially defined for the first time in the Water Supply (Water Quality) Regulations 1989. These lay down a large number of specific criteria with which water must comply. In each case the limits have been set so as to conform to EC Directive 80/778 on Drinking Water. Publicly available information on water quality must be provided under the Regulations. A Drinking Water Inspectorate has been established within the Department of the Environment with responsibility for monitoring the provisions relating to water quality.

There are other controls on the quality of the water supply. It is an offence under the Water Act 1989, s. 54 to supply water unfit for human consumption, although prosecutions may only be brought by the Secretary of State or the Director of Public Prosecutions. There is also strict civil liability for supplying unsafe water under the Consumer Protection Act 1987 and the possibility of an action at common law for breach of statutory duty or negligence (see *Read* v *Croydon Corporation* [1938] 4 All ER 631, where a ratepayer successfully sued in negligence for water supplied to his household which caused his daughter to contract typhoid).

Consents for the discharge of trade or sewage effluents

A consent is required from the NRA for:

(a)   any discharge of trade or sewage effluent into 'controlled waters';

(b) any discharge of trade or sewage effluent through a pipe from land into the sea outside the limits of 'controlled waters';
(c) any discharge where a prohibition is in force.

It is an offence under s. 107(1) to 'cause or knowingly permit' such a discharge, although there is a defence if it is carried out in accordance with a consent. This means it is also an offence to breach any conditions attached to a consent, a point made explicit by s. 107(6). There is no need to show that the discharge has polluted the receiving waters because the offence consists of discharging otherwise than in accordance with the consent.

'Trade effluent' is defined in s. 124 and includes any effluent from trade premises (these include agricultural, fish farming and research establishments), other than domestic sewage or surface water. 'Sewage effluent', also defined in s. 124, includes any effluent, other than surface water, from a sewer or sewerage works. Under the Water Act 1989, the discharge must be of effluent, so it seems that if trade materials, such as fuel oil or silage liquor, escape they are covered by the general pollution offence (see below). But there is some doubt here since effluent is defined in s. 189 to mean 'any liquid' and is not specifically limited to wastes.

A further problem relates to the interpretation of the word 'discharge'. This word is not defined in the Act. It is capable of carrying either an active meaning (i.e. that the release of materials has to be part of a deliberate trade or sewage process) or a passive meaning (as in the discharge of blood from a wound). It is suggested that it carries an active meaning, because otherwise potential dischargers would be in the impossible position of having to apply for a consent for something that was not meant to happen. The effect of this reasoning is that accidental and non-routine emissions of trade or sewage effluent do not require a consent and are covered by the general water pollution offence (see below).

Controlled waters

The meaning of 'controlled waters' is given in s. 103. There has been a change in the meaning of this phrase since its usage in COPA and it now includes virtually all inland and coastal waters. Controlled waters are made up of four sub-categories:

(a) relevant territorial waters (i.e. the sea within a line three miles out from the baselines from which the territorial sea is measured, despite the extension of the territorial limit to 12 miles in the Territorial Sea Act 1987);
(b) coastal waters (i.e. the sea within those baselines up to the line of the highest tide, and tidal waters up to the fresh water limit as defined by the Secretary of State on maps produced for that purpose);
(c) inland waters (i.e. rivers, streams, underground streams, canals, lakes and reservoirs, including those that are temporarily dry); and
(d) ground waters (i.e. any waters contained in underground strata or in wells or boreholes).

The only waters that are excluded are land-locked waters that do not drain into other controlled waters. However, the Secretary of State has power to include or exclude specific waters by order. This has been done in the Controlled Waters (Lakes and Ponds) Order 1989 (SI 1989 No. 1149), which includes any reservoirs, apart from those intended for public water supply, which would otherwise be excluded. Water supply mains and pipes, and sewers and drains (where separate controls on discharges apply), are also excluded from the definition of controlled waters.

The prohibition is a new device introduced by the Water Act 1989. It is designed to cover those cases where the type of discharge is not necessarily harmful and thus the blanket requirement of a consent is not justified. By prohibiting discharges on a selective basis, control can be exercised over just those situations where it is required.

There are three situations where a prohibition may apply:

(a) Where the NRA by notice prohibits a discharge of trade or sewage effluent from a building or fixed plant to any land or land-locked waters outside the definition of controlled waters (this could include some agricultural activities, but it does not appear to cover slurry spreading).

(b) Where it prohibits a discharge of matter other than trade or sewage effluent from a drain or sewer. Trade and sewage effluent are automatically covered by the need for a consent, so the intention here is to restrict such things as discharges of dangerous substances from a storm drain.

(c) In addition, any such discharges involving substances prescribed by regulations *automatically* invoke the prohibition. In relation to the first two categories, the prohibition can only come into force three months after notice to the discharger, unless the NRA is satisfied that there is an emergency.

General pollution offence

There is a general offence under s. 107(1)(a) of causing or knowingly permitting any poisonous, noxious or polluting matter or any solid waste to enter controlled waters. As is common within the flexible definitions of British pollution control, the words 'poisonous, noxious or polluting' are not defined, but the wording is very wide and appears to include an entry which could cause harm to plants or animals. It also appears to include an entry of material containing disease-carrying bacteria.

This general offence complements the more specific offence of discharging trade or sewage effluent without consent. Obviously it covers any entry of polluting matter which is not trade or sewage effluent. But, unlike COPA, where the general and the specific offences were made exclusive of each other by s. 31(2)(e), under the Water Act this exclusivity has been removed, so an illegal discharge of trade or sewage effluent also amounts to an offence under the general offence if it causes pollution. Indeed, because of the evidential problems of providing a legal sample to prove a breach of a discharge consent, it is normal for the general offence to be charged even for discharges of trade or sewage effluent.

The general offence also covers accidental and non-routine escapes of trade or sewage effluent because, whilst the specific offence requires a 'discharge', the general offence only requires an entry. In addition, non-point discharges, such as agricultural run-off, are potentially covered by the general offence.

There is a further offence in s. 107(1)(e) of substantially aggravating pollution by impeding the proper flow of inland, non-tidal waters.

For all s. 107 offences the potential penalties are the same. On summary conviction there is a maximum fine of £20,000 (this was raised by the Environmental Protection Act 1990, s. 145(1) from the previous maximum of £2,000), and/or three months in prison. On conviction on indictment, there can be an unlimited fine and/or a two year jail sentence. The normal six month period for a summary prosecution to be brought is also extended to 12 months in the Water Act 1989, s. 121, as it is for all offences in the Water Act Part III, Chapter I. For the actual practice of enforcement, see p. 324.

Defences

A number of common defences to these water pollution offences are set out in s. 108. A discharge or entry made in accordance with the following is a defence:

(a)   a consent from the NRA, or the equivalent consent granted or deemed to have been granted under COPA or earlier legislation;

(b)   an authorisation in relation to integrated pollution control granted by HMIP under Part I of the Environmental Protection Act;

(c)   a waste management licence or a waste disposal licence from the waste regulation authority (except where the offence is of discharging trade or sewage effluent or where a prohibition is in force);

(d)   a licence permitting dumping at sea granted by the Ministry of Agriculture, Fisheries and Food under the Food and Environment Protection Act 1985;

(e)   an Act of Parliament;

(f)   any statutory order (such as a drought order).

It is also a defence if the entry or discharge was made in an emergency in order to avoid danger to life or health: in such a case the discharger must inform the NRA as soon as reasonably practicable and take reasonable steps to minimise any pollution. It must be assumed that only a danger to human life or health would suffice.

In addition, s. 108 excludes from the operation of s. 107 sewage effluent from vessels (which is covered under by-laws), solid refuse from mines where the NRA has given consent for its deposit, and water from abandoned mines. There is also a block exemption order relating to certain discharges which had never required a consent until COPA came into force. This granted transitional exemption for these discharges, but it is being progressively withdrawn and few discharges are now covered.

There are some complex provisions in s. 108(7) and s. 108(8) relating to responsibility for discharges from sewage works. In essence, sewerage undertakers are responsible for discharges from sewers and works, unless the pollution is caused by an illegal (i.e. unconsented) discharge into the sewer which could not reasonably have been prevented. In such a case, the original discharger to the sewer is committing an offence under s. 107 as well as under the Public Health (Drainage of Trade Premises) Act 1937 (see Chapter 14).

Under COPA, there was a defence to the general offence if it was committed by a farmer who was acting in accordance with good agricultural practice. This was defined in a Code of Guidance issued by the Minister of Agriculture, Fisheries and Food. The defence has been repealed by the Water Act 1989. In its place is a non-binding Code of Good Agricultural Practice for the Protection of Water issued jointly in 1991 by MAFF and the Secretary of State, after consultation with the NRA. This code has no legal effect. Contravention does not amount to a criminal offence, and compliance does not afford a legal defence, but obviously conformity with the Code will affect any decision whether to prosecute and the level of any fine imposed.

There is no Crown Immunity under the Water Act 1989 (s. 192), thus reversing the position under COPA.

Meaning of 'cause or knowingly permit'

The offences under s. 107 require that the defendant 'cause or knowingly permit' the relevant discharge or entry. This phrase has been interpreted in many cases and it is clear that it lays down an offence of strict liability. Indeed, *Alphacell* v *Woodward* [1972] AC 824, a case on this wording in the Rivers (Prevention of Pollution) Act 1951, is one of the leading cases in criminal law on the meaning of strict liability.

In *Alphacell* v *Woodward*, settling tanks at a paper factory overflowed into the River Irwell. The biochemical oxygen demand (BOD) of the discharge was well above the level permitted in the consent. Although the magistrates made a specific finding that there was no negligence (a strange finding since pumps which should have stopped the overflow were blocked), the House of Lords held that there was no need to prove negligence or fault. Alphacell were guilty of the general offence by carrying on the activity which caused the pollution. As long as their activity was itself intentional all that needed to be shown was a causal link between it and the discharge. The directness of the entry was also irrelevant; in this case the entry was via a channel into the river.

This test has been reiterated most recently in *Southern Water Authority* v *Pegrum* [1989] Local Government Review 672. In this case effluent from the defendants' pig farm ran into tanks and from there into specially built lagoons. Owing to a fissure in one of the lagoons, when it reached a certain level it leaked, polluting a nearby stream. The Divisional Court held that, as long as the farmers carried on an active operation such as this, and there was no effective intervening cause of the pollution, such as a trespasser or an Act of God, the general offence of causing pollution under COPA s. 31 (which involved identical wording) had been committed. The defence that the lagoon was filled by heavy rain was rejected on the grounds that it required something quite out of the ordinary to break the causal link.

Similarly, in *Wrothwell Ltd v Yorkshire Water Authority* [1984] Crim LR 43, it was held that a director of a company who had poured herbicide into what he thought was a drain leading to the public sewer, but which in fact led to a nearby stream, was guilty of causing pollution to the stream, despite the unintentional nature of his action.

Two cases illustrate some limitations. In *Impress (Worcester) Ltd v Rees* [1971] 2 All ER 357, fuel oil from a tank was released into the River Severn. The defendant successfully pleaded that this was an act of a trespasser, although it seems that the burden of proof was on the defendant to prove the defence. In *Price v Cromack* [1975] 1 WLR 988, a farmer had a contract permitting an animal products firm to discharge waste into lagoons on his land. One lagoon wall failed and the resulting escape severely polluted the River Perry. The farmer was charged with causing pollution, but was acquitted on the ground that he had only permitted the accumulation rather than causing the pollution. This is a good illustration of the fact that there are two separate offences here, causing pollution and knowingly permitting it, and the prosecutor has to be careful to allege the correct one. It appears that the farmer was possibly charged with the wrong offence, since he was arguably guilty of knowingly permitting the pollution.

The effects of these offences being of strict liability are many. Any excess over the requirements of a numerical consent will amount to an offence, no matter how small it is. There is a very high success rate on prosecution. But the main effect is that the prosecuting bodies have tended to dilute the potency of the offence by exercising discretion over whom to prosecute (see p. 324).

The consent system

The system for acquiring a consent is set out in the Water Act 1989, sch. 12. It involves a higher degree of public involvement than many other licensing-type systems.

Consents which have already been granted under COPA or earlier legislation are simply translated into valid consents for the purposes of the Water Act 1989. However, they may be varied or revoked in the future under the terms of sch. 12 (see below).

A consent is required for each discharge, so if a factory has three discharge pipes it needs a consent for each one. The applicant applies to the NRA, which has a discretion as to the details required. Normally the applicant will have to state the place, nature, quantity, rate of flow, composition and temperature of the proposed discharge. It is an offence under the Water Act 1989, s. 175, to give incorrect information.

The NRA must publicise the application in a local newspaper and in the London Gazette and notify any relevant local authorities and water undertakers, at the applicant's expense. However, this publicity may be dispensed with if the NRA considers that the discharge will have 'no appreciable effect' on the receiving waters. Great use was made of this dispensation by the regional water authorities in the past, so that an estimated 90% of all applications were exempted from publicity in this way. Guidance on this vague and subjective discretion is given in DoE Circular 17/84, which suggests a complex set of tests to be considered, the main one being that a change is not to be considered appreciable if there is less than a 10% increase on all relevant parameters, unless some significant environmental amenity is affected. This is a good example of the use of administrative methods to define a legal requirement; it is objectionable that the operation of such an important publicity procedure rests on a rather restrictive interpretation given in a Departmental Circular.

Under sch. 12, para. 1(7), an applicant may apply to the Secretary of State for a certificate of exemption from these publicity requirements. Such a certificate will be granted if the Secretary of State is satisfied that publicity would be contrary to the public interest or would prejudice information about a trade secret to an unreasonable degree. A certificate will also exempt the discharge and discharger from the provisions of the public register under s. 117. It seems that this exemption is rarely used.

The NRA must take into account written representations made within six weeks of the notice appearing in the London Gazette. It has the power to grant consent, either unconditionally or subject to conditions, or to refuse consent. If it proposes to grant a consent it must inform anyone who made representations and wait a further 21 days. This is to enable an objector to request the Secretary of State to call the matter in.

A fee for making an application for a new or revised consent was introduced from 1 October 1990. The intention is that the NRA should recover the overall costs incurred in processing applications. A standard charge of £350 is payable for each new or revised consent. There is a reduced charge of £50 for certain minor discharges of sewage effluent or cooling waters and for those surface water discharges which require consent (Scheme of Charges in Respect of Applications and Consents for Discharges to Controlled Waters, 1991).

Conditions
The NRA may attach 'such conditions as it may think fit' and sch. 12, para. 2(3) includes a non-exhaustive list. This includes such things as the quality, quantity, nature, composition and temperature of the discharge, the siting and design of the outlet, the provision of meters for measuring these matters, the taking and recording of samples by the discharger, and the provision of information to the NRA. Frequently the most significant conditions will relate to biochemical oxygen demand, levels of toxic or dangerous materials, and suspended solids, although the NRA has recently suggested, amongst other recommendations relating to consents, the introduction of a more sophisticated test based on the total organic carbon in the discharge (*Discharge Consent and Compliance Policy: A Blueprint for the Future*, National Rivers Authority, 1990). For industrial discharges it is normal to attach absolute numerical limits for the various parameters covered in the consent, with the result that any excess amounts to a breach of the consent. For sewage discharges a test based on 95% compliance is more normal (see p. 321).

The Water Act 1989 has altered the law so that conditions requiring a specified treatment process are legal. It remains to be seen whether such conditions will be imposed, since in the past it has been Government policy to require compliance with environmental standards whilst giving a discharger a choice of methods to achieve the standard. It is permissible for conditions to be staggered so that they get progressively stricter. This was accepted in *Trent River Authority v F. H. Drabble & Sons Ltd* [1970] 1 WLR 98 and is now specifically covered in sch. 12, para. 3.

A consent attaches to the discharge and is not personal to the applicant, so the benefit can be passed on to a new owner (sch. 12, para. 2(4)).

There is a procedure for granting a retrospective consent in para. 5. This involves the payment of the relevant fee and the same publicity requirements as for any other application. However, the paragraph is not fully retrospective since it affords no immunity for offences committed before the consent was granted. It enables the NRA to formalise the legal position in relation to a discharge and also to attach conditions to an existing discharge.

A significant problem under COPA was the position of new pollutants. This phrase covers substances which the discharger introduces into the discharge after the consent has been obtained, or new substances unknown at the time the consent was set, or substances which were only later traceable or later considered to be polluting. Such substances would not be mentioned in the consent, and it appeared that discharging them may not have been in breach of the consent, since there was a breach only if the conditions were not met.

It seems that this possible loophole has been removed by the Water Act 1989, which requires that the discharge must be 'under and in accordance with' the consent in order for the defence in s. 108 to apply. However, to make matters clear, the NRA has also recommended that all consents should include a general condition excluding the discharge of any substance not specified in the consent.

Revocation and variation

Under sch. 12, para. 6 it is the duty of the NRA to review consents from time to time. A variation or a revocation can be made simply by notifying the discharger. Alternatively the Secretary of State may direct that a variation take place. No compensation is payable except in one case considered below. There is no provision for public participation in relation to a variation or revocation. This power to make variations or revocations is a wide one which reflects the need to cater for new circumstances, such as a new polluter in the catchment area, or a newly-perceived pollution threat, or a change in EC or international obligations. It also reasserts the position that no one has a right to pollute.

However, there are limits on when a variation or revocation can be made. A period will be stipulated in the original consent (this is normally two years, and cannot be less than two years) and a variation or revocation cannot take place within that period (measured from the setting of the original consent or the last variation), except with the permission of the discharger. Exceptionally, the Secretary of State may direct a modification within the two-year period in order to give effect to an EC or international obligation, or to protect public health or flora and fauna dependent on an aquatic environment, but there is no right to vary early solely because the discharger has been in breach of the consent, or in order to cater for a new pollutant: both are situations where such a right would be desirable. The NRA will have to pay compensation to the discharger if a direction is made on the public health or protection of flora and fauna ground within the two-year period.

Transitional provisions

In any regulatory system, when a new Act comes into force the transitional provisions are of importance. For the Water Act, because most discharges were already covered by the provisions of COPA, the transition was fairly straightforward. Existing consents were simply translated into Water Act consents. Only new or varied discharge consents require the publicity procedures.

This hides a continuation of a transitional provision from COPA. Some discharges which did not require a consent before that Act were deemed to have been granted consent for the current level of discharge under COPA, s. 40(4), as long as an application was made. These applications are slowly being decided by the NRA but the process is not yet complete. Such discharges include many pre-1974 discharges to estuaries, which are effectively permitted to continue with their previous discharge uncontrolled.

Annual charges for discharge consents

The NRA is empowered to make annual charges for discharge consents under the Water Act 1989, sch. 12, para. 9, although any such scheme requires the approval of the Secretary of State and the consent of the Treasury. Accordingly, the Scheme of Charges in Respect of Applications and Consents for Discharges to Controlled Waters 1991 has been made. It came into force on 1 July 1991 and incorporates the existing fee for applications.

The basic philosophy underpinning the Scheme is that of cost-recovery charging, i.e. that the NRA should recover from dischargers the actual cost of its activities connected with discharges. This includes the sampling of discharges, inspection of discharges, discharge-related impact monitoring, work on the review of consents, laboratory services and direct administration connected to these matters. Expenditure on general water quality monitoring, general administration and pollution incidents is not recovered by these charges, but will come from the general budget of the NRA. It is estimated that about £41m will be recovered through charges annually out of the NRA's current annual expenditure of £71m on water quality activities, thus increasing the Authority's independence from Government.

Further principles are that the charges are uniform throughout the country and are not to vary locally; that they relate to what is consented to rather than to the actual discharge; and that they are set according to a formula which has three separate elements—the volume of the discharge, its content, and the nature of the receiving waters. For each of these three elements broad bands have been devised, each being accorded a weighted value (i.e. a number of units). For volume, there are eight broad bands, with larger volume discharges having a higher value than lower ones. There are exceptions for emergency discharges, intermittent discharges and rainwater drains. For content, there are seven bands, reflecting the relative complexity and cost of monitoring the discharge. For receiving waters, there are four bands, with estuarine waters having a higher weighting than inland watercourses, which in turn are weighted more highly than discharges to groundwaters.

Each discharge thus has three separate values, which are multiplied together to give a final figure in terms of a number of units. This final figure is then multiplied by a national financial factor, so that all dischargers know in advance what their charge is going to be. This financial factor will be varied annually, but since the figure for the first nine months is £202.50, it can be expected that most dischargers will face a significant annual bill for their discharges.

At present there is no proposal for additional charges for 'Red List' or other hazardous substances on the grounds that the presence of these in a discharge will tend to take it into the more highly weighted categories as far as content is concerned. In a way, therefore, the polluter pays principle is being partially operated in relation to these charges. However, the White Paper (*This Common Inheritance*, 1990, Cm. 1200, para. 12.25 and Annex A) suggests that the Government is looking at charging methods related to the pollution load, or environmental effect, of a discharge, and is commissioning studies to look at such a system. This would be far more in keeping with the true meaning of the polluter pays principle.

The role of the Secretary of State

The Secretary of State has a general, and very wide, power under the Water Act, s. 146 to issue directions of a general or specific nature to the NRA in relation to pollution control, amongst other matters. The supplementary power of the Secretary of State to require information from the NRA in ss. 118 and 149 should also be noted. The reason for the width of the s. 146 power is the fact that large policy-making powers have effectively been delegated to the NRA, making some mechanism for central control desirable. The use of directions to achieve this should be compared with the use of Circular guidance in other areas of environmental law, since they fulfil similar purposes.

This power is only exercisable, except in an emergency, after consultation with the NRA, but it could be used if the NRA failed to act on a certain matter. It is envisaged that it will be used to give effect to EC or international obligations if there is no other way of achieving this. Directions made under s. 146 must be listed in the NRA's Annual Report: otherwise there is no requirement for them to be published.

At any stage the Secretary of State may call in an application for decision (sch. 12, para. 4). This is an unfettered discretion and ousts the jurisdiction of the NRA to consider the consent. It is rarely exercised.

Appeals

The applicant or discharger has a right to appeal to the Secretary of State against a refusal of consent, the attachment of unreasonable conditions, any adverse variation or revocation of a consent, or the setting of the period in which a consent cannot be varied. An application is deemed to have been refused if no decision is given within four months.

An appeal is a general rehearing of the matter in issue and the Secretary of State has the same powers as the NRA originally had. Unlike the system of planning appeals, which accords enormous opportunities for argument on policy, it seems that this appeal right will be rarely used, since there is no perceived difference in policy between the Secretary of State and the NRA.

The procedures for called in applications and for appeals are set out in the Control of Pollution (Consents for Discharges etc.) (Secretary of State's Functions) Regulations 1989 (SI 1989 No. 1151). These regulations retain the procedures for other applications with modified wording, and also provide for the rights of objectors. One significant change is that the discretion not to publicise where there is no appreciable effect on the receiving waters does not apply.

A final power of the Secretary of State is that the NRA must apply to the Secretary of State if it wishes to make any discharges. Similar procedures apply as for ordinary consent applications (Control of Pollution (Discharges by the NRA) Regulations 1989 (SI 1989 No. 1157)). Given the limited operational activities of the NRA, few such applications will be necessary.

How are consents set?

The NRA, or the Secretary of State on appeal, has a wide discretion in setting the consent and it will be set by reference to a variety of factors. Although sch. 12 is silent as to the factors which must be taken into account, applying ordinary public law principles, the NRA must have regard to all material considerations. In addition, certain requirements appear from other sections of the Act.

As stated before, it is important to grasp the individualised and flexible nature of these consents, although uniformity and consistency is now being sought by the NRA. Relevant matters include:

(a)   The water quality objectives and standards set for the receiving waters under s. 105 (see below). This emphasises that one of the crucial elements in fixing a consent is the effect on the receiving waters. This in turn depends on the use that is intended for those receiving waters.

(b)   Any other effects on the receiving waters, such as on a fishery, or downstream user. In particular, regard will be had to whether the waters are used for abstraction for water supply or irrigation.

(c)   Any relevant EC standards for the emission concerned or for the quality of the receiving waters.

(d) Any 'cocktail' effect of the discharge. The NRA will consider not only the immediate effect of the discharge but also any impact the discharge will have in combination with the current contents of the waters and any potential future discharges.

(e) The desirability of minimising discharges of hazardous substances as far as possible.

(f) The NRA's environmental duties laid out in s. 8 (see p. 33).

(g) The specific duty in relation to sites of special scientific interest set out in s. 9 (see p. 351).

(h) Any objections and representations made and the results of any consultation carried out.

(i) Certain informal standard tests for particular types of discharge. For example, fairly 'normal' standards for sewage works were suggested by the Eighth Report of the Royal Commission on Sewage Disposal in 1912 and these were applied for many years. The NRA is now seeking to establish some uniformity of standards across the country for all types of discharge.

(j) Any other material considerations.

Water quality standards

The Water Act 1989, ss. 104–105 introduced statutory water quality classifications and objectives for the first time. There are effectively two different processes involved, although these do get intertwined. The first is the setting of classificatory systems for waters under s. 104. It is permissible to have different classifications for different purposes and areas, and this process has been started by the Surface Waters (Classification) Regulations 1989 (SI 1989 No. 1148), which classify inland waters (i.e. fresh waters) into three categories according to their suitability as drinking waters. The classification is based on the mandatory values in EC Directive 75/440 on Surface Water for Drinking. To qualify as within any category, the specified limits must not be exceeded.

In accordance with EC Directive 76/464 on Dangerous Substances in Water, a further set of classifications has been established relating to dangerous substances. These are set out in the Surface Waters (Dangerous Substances) (Classification) Regulations 1989 (SI 1989 No. 2286). These regulations specify annual mean concentrations of a limited range of substances (mainly, but not all, 'Red List' substances), listed in DS1 (for inland waters) and DS2 (for coastal waters), which should not be exceeded. In order to comply with EC law, these classifications have also been issued as initial water quality objectives under s. 105, this action having been taken by the Secretary of State under the powers in s. 146. In so doing, the Secretary of State dispensed with the publicity requirements set out in s. 105(4).

The second process is that water quality objectives for individual stretches of controlled waters may be set by the Secretary of State (s. 105). The water quality objectives, which will formally replace the non-statutory objectives currently in operation, will become of crucial importance in the setting of discharge consents and other decisions about water pollution.

The procedure for setting a water quality objective involves at least three months publicity of the proposed objectives 'in such manner as the Secretary of State considers appropriate for bringing it to the attention of persons likely to be affected by it' (i.e. these provisions are less specific than many other publicity provisions in relation to pollution control). The NRA must also be notified. All representations and objections must be considered, and the Secretary of State may modify the proposals in the light of these representations. A public local inquiry may be held under s. 120.

The Secretary of State may review and, in the light of the review, vary water quality objectives by going through the same procedures, but this may only take place five years after the water quality objective was last set or varied, or alternatively, if the NRA requests a review, which it may only do after consulting relevant water undertakers.

The requirements for classifications were deliberately left vague in the Act, leaving a wide discretion to the Secretary of State. In addition, no time scale for the introduction of water quality objectives was put into the legislation, though it is expected that they will be in force from 1992.

Under s. 106 the NRA and Secretary of State are placed under a duty to exercise their powers under the Act so as to achieve the water quality objectives at all times, so far as it is practicable to do so. This does not mean that they are in breach in failing to do so, merely that powers in relation to the setting and variation of consents, remedial and enforcement powers, and powers in relation to preventative controls should be exercised to achieve these water quality objectives if practicable. Under the Environmental Protection Act 1990, s. 7(2)(c), a similar duty is placed on HMIP to try to achieve water quality objectives when considering authorisations for integrated pollution control.

Whilst it remains true that, in relation to water pollution, consents have tended to be set on an individualised basis, these statutory water quality standards merely put on a formal footing what has been happening for a number of years. The British approach to water pollution has tended over the years to concentrate on the environmental effects of a pollutant, as opposed to laying down uniform emission levels without regard to the effect on the environment.

The development of water quality objectives owes a great deal to the existence of the EC. In holding out for a system based on localised consent standards, rather than one based on uniform emission standards or limit values, in relation to EC Directives on water, the British Government was forced to show how this worked, as there were at the time no formally set river quality objectives. Thus, in 1978 the National Water Council developed a system of river quality objectives, which was adopted by the regional water authorities (see *River Water Quality: The Next Stage*, National Water Council, 1978).

The National Water Council's classification had five basic classes of river waters (there was a similar but separate classification for estuaries):

1A   High quality waters suitable for all abstraction purposes with only modest treatment. Capable of supporting game or other high class fisheries. High amenity value.

1B   Good quality waters usable for substantially the same purposes as 1A though not as high quality.

2   Fair quality waters viable as coarse fisheries and capable of use for drinking water provided advanced treatment is given. Moderate amenity value.

3   Poor waters polluted to the extent that fish are absent or only sporadically present. Suitable only for low grade industrial abstractions.

4   Bad quality waters which are grossly polluted and likely to cause a nuisance.

This administrative method of implementing EC Directives was clearly insufficient to satisfy EC law (see *Commission* v *Belgium* [1982] CMLR 627, which requires implementation of EC Directives to be done by legislative means), so it became inevitable that a statutory system be adopted.

Public registers

For the first time, the Control of Pollution Act 1974 provided for public registers of a range of environmental information relating to water pollution, although these provisions were not implemented until 1985. Prior to that the system tended to be operated with a fair degree of secrecy about consents and samples taken. The relevant provisions are repeated in the Water Act 1989 with some amendments.

Under s. 117, a public register must be kept by the NRA of all applications for consent, consents actually granted, any conditions attached to a consent, notices of water quality objectives served under s. 105 and certificates issued under sch. 12, para. 1(7) exempting applicants from the publicity requirements of the Act. Prescribed details of authorisations granted for the purposes of integrated pollution control must also be recorded on the water registers. In addition, the results of any samples of the receiving waters or of effluent, and any information produced by analysis of them, must be registered. This requirement is worded more widely than under COPA, and samples taken by *any* person must be registered; this seems to include samples taken by a discharger as a condition of consent.

Section 117 requires that the register is open for inspection by any member of the public free of charge at all reasonable times and that reasonable facilities for taking copies are afforded on payment of a reasonable fee. The Control of Pollution (Registers) Regulations 1989 (SI 1989 No. 1160) specify the detailed shape of the registers, including a requirement that details of any sample must be entered on the register within two months of the date of the sample.

The public register provides an invaluable database for groups and individuals wishing to monitor water quality. It can be used to mount a private prosecution (as in *Wales* v *Thames Water Authority* [1987] 1/3 Environmental Law 3, where the Water Authority was successfully prosecuted for pollution from a sewage works in reliance on the information which it had itself recorded on the register), or to provide evidence for a civil claim, or to provide general information on the state of the water environment. The admissibility of the registers as evidence seems quite clear now that they are kept by the NRA (see p. 323).

It is possible to obtain a certificate of exemption from the Secretary of State exempting an applicant from the requirements of the register in relation to an application, a consent, any conditions attached or any sample of effluent from the discharge (sch. 12, para. 1(7)). This involves satisfying the Secretary of State that registration would either prejudice a trade secret to an unreasonable degree or would be contrary to the public interest. Circular 13/85 suggests that such a situation will be rare, and the existence of the certificate itself must be registered, but the exemption does illustrate a particularly property-based view of the control of pollution.

In addition, s. 174 prohibits the NRA or any officer from disclosing information obtained under the Act. Any person who does disclose such information without the permission of the person or company which provided it is guilty of an offence and liable, on summary conviction, to a fine not exceeding the statutory maximum (currently £2,000), and on conviction on indictment, to imprisonment for up to two years or an unlimited fine, or both. Of course, this restriction does not apply to matters required to be entered on the register. Nor does it apply to such things as the disclosure of information for criminal proceedings, or in pursuance of an EC obligation, and a range of other matters listed in s. 174. It also does not apply where a company has ceased trading.

Integrated pollution control

For those processes prescribed for Part I of the Environmental Protection Act 1990 (i.e. those processes subject to integrated pollution control), the NRA loses its powers in relation to consents for discharges to controlled waters. Instead, HMIP has responsibility for operating and enforcing the system of authorisations for processes set up under the 1990 Act. Acting in accordance with an integrated pollution control authorisation will be a defence to the water pollution offences under s. 107 of the Water Act 1989.

However, the NRA does not lose all its control over water pollution. In deciding whether to grant an authorisation, HMIP must consult with the NRA and, in setting the authorisation, HMIP must take into account such things as any relevant water quality objectives set under the Water Act 1989. Most importantly, under s. 28 of the Environmental Protection Act, the NRA may effectively dictate certain matters to HMIP where a release into controlled waters is concerned:

(a)   Under s. 28(3)(a), the NRA may certify its opinion that a release will result in, or contribute to, a failure to achieve a statutory water quality objective. If it does so, HMIP cannot grant an authorisation at all.

(b)   Under s. 28(3)(b), the NRA may dictate whatever conditions it thinks are appropriate. If it does so, HMIP must include these conditions, though it may make them more onerous and it may add others.

(c)   Under s. 28(4), the NRA may require HMIP to vary any conditions of an authorisation if it considers such a variation appropriate. If it does so, HMIP must vary the conditions as required, using its powers under s. 10 of

EPA. This can be done at any time by serving a notice on the holder of an authorisation.

Since the NRA has responsibility for controlled waters, and HMIP has responsibility for all prescribed processes, there was always going to be a conflict where the two controls overlapped. The NRA's position was that it should be the decision-making body in relation to controlled waters, with HMIP having powers to make directions to it. However, this was not accepted in the legislation, and HMIP was given the lead role. In particular, the NRA has no effective policing powers in relation to prescribed processes (with the exception of the right to bring a prosecution for breach of the 1990 Act), even though it is ultimately responsible for water quality. The EPA provides some extensive administrative provisions on the enforcement of the system, such as prohibition notices, yet the NRA will be unable to use these and will have to rely for enforcement on HMIP.

The significant powers given to the NRA under EPA, s. 28, provide one resolution of this conflict. But it must be said that they do take away some of the internal logic of the integrated pollution control system by allowing the NRA effectively to interfere with the terms of an authorisation, thus potentially upsetting any balance HMIP was trying to reach.

In Scotland, the potential conflict between Her Majesty's Industrial Pollution Inspectorate and the river purification boards was resolved in a different way, with both bodies having a role as enforcing agency for integrated pollution control. The exact division of responsibilities and any rights of veto, or duties of consultation, will be prescribed in regulations made by the Secretary of State under EPA, s. 5.

Sewage discharges

Sewage discharges have always caused problems, firstly because of their potent polluting power and secondly because of the conflict of interest between regulator and regulated. These points were seen at their clearest in the 1970s and 1980s when capital expenditure cuts led to a number of badly underperforming sewage works at a time when the regulator and regulated was the same body, the regional water authority. However, the same conflict also existed prior to that; the local authorities which ran the sewage works also provided members for the rivers authorities, for example, and thus exercised an influence on their decisions.

Under the Water Act 1989, the conflict of interest is removed, and sewerage undertakers are treated similarly to other dischargers in requiring a consent from the NRA, although there are still some differences in treatment. One slight difference relates to the offences under s. 107. Because sewerage undertakers treat wastes discharged into the sewers by other people, they have a special defence under s. 108(7). This operates if the contravention of their discharge consent was due to an unconsented discharge made into the sewer by another person which they could not reasonably have prevented.

A more significant difference is that sewage works have traditionally had their consents set on different terms from other dischargers. The standard practice for other dischargers has been to set absolute numerical limits, with the result that any breach of the limit amounts to a criminal offence. For sewage discharges, the conditions of consents have normally been set by reference to 'look-up tables' intended to ensure a 95% compliance rate over a rolling 12 month period. This leeway was allowed for in recognition of the variable quality of sewage effluents and the comparative lack of control that sewage works operators could exercise over them.

However, the result is that it is difficult to prove the offence under s. 107, since a single sample which exceeds the consent will not amount to a breach, and a number of legal samples over a 12 month period are needed. This problem was exacerbated in the short term by the Water Act 1989, sch. 26, para. 25(7), one of the transitional provisions, which required that only samples taken by the NRA after 1 September 1989 (the transfer date) could be used as evidence of discharges from sewage works. The effect was to impose a one year moratorium on prosecutions of sewerage undertakers for breach of consent conditions involving a percentile compliance rate.

This exemption did not apply to breaches of the higher absolute consent limits that were also set for many works, and three prosecutions were brought by the NRA for such breaches in its first year of operation. In addition, now that the exemption has expired, the NRA has commenced proceedings in a number of other cases and is considering many more.

For the future, the NRA has suggested that it will remove the special treatment of sewage works by requiring absolute limits for them. However, it is also suggested that some percentile compliance tests be retained in addition to those absolute limits, in order to provide greater control over discharges (*Discharge Consent and Compliance Policy: A Blueprint for the Future*, National Rivers Authority, 1990).

An understanding of the present position requires some explanation of the position prior to the Water Act 1989. Between 1951 and 1985 (when the relevant provisions of the Control of Pollution Act 1974 came into force), consents had been set and monitored in virtual secrecy, though they tended to follow the biochemical oxygen demand (BOD) and suspended solids standards recommended by the Eighth Report of the Royal Commission on Sewage Disposal in 1912. Under the 1974 Act, because of the conflict of interest within regional water authorities, a special procedure was established whereby consents were formally set by the Secretary of State (through HMIP after 1987). Similar procedures for applying for consent to those set up for industrial discharges were provided for in regulations. However, most sewage works consents were already in existence, which meant that under COPA, s. 40 there was no need for a new application and hence the publicity requirements were rarely used.

In the 1970s and 1980s many consents were relaxed. For example, the National Water Council had commenced a review of consents in the late 1970s which led to the relaxation of some sewage works consents. This review was never completed and the results never published. Consents were also relaxed in the 1980s in anticipation of the implementation of COPA and the consequent availability of a right to bring private prosecutions, and again in the run-up to water privatisation in order to protect the sewerage undertakers. Notwithstanding these events, there was evidence that up to a quarter of sewage works were still regularly exceeding their consents in 1989 and some private prosecutions were successfully brought (e.g. *Wales* v *Thames Water Authority* [1987] 1/3 Environmental Law 3).

Radioactive discharges

Under the Control of Pollution (Radioactive Waste) Regulations, 1989 (SI 1989 No. 1158), the radioactivity of a discharge is to be ignored for the purposes of the Water Act 1989. In other words, the non-radioactive elements of a discharge or entry are dealt with under the Water Act and the radioactive elements under the Radioactive Substances Act 1960 by HMIP or the Minister of Agriculture, Fisheries and Food.

Sampling and enforcement powers

NRA officers have wide rights of entry to property under the Water Act 1989, s. 147, to ascertain if any powers or duties require implementation, or to inspect for breaches of controls. Reserve powers of entry under a warrant from a magistrate are granted in ss. 178–179 for cases of difficulty.

The power in s. 147 includes a right to take samples of water or effluent or to install monitoring equipment. However, under s. 148, a sample of effluent from a discharge taken on behalf of the NRA is not admissible in legal proceedings unless it is a 'legal sample' (i.e. it is taken in accordance with s. 148(1)(a), which requires that the occupier of the land concerned be informed as soon as reasonably practicable that the sample is a legal sample, and it is divided into three parts, of which one is given to the occupier, one sent for analysis and one retained for future comparison). This does not mean that the discharger has to be present when the sample is taken; nor does it mean that no prosecution can be brought without a sample. The requirement for a legal sample also applies only to samples of effluent, not to samples of the receiving waters, and only to those taken 'on behalf of the Authority', so a privately taken sample would be valid, although its scientific accuracy may be challenged. It is also worth noting that a private sample taken by trespassing on the discharger's land, although potentially admissible, may be excluded as improperly obtained evidence at the discretion of the court, although in the light of the cases on such evidence this is unlikely (see the Police and Criminal Evidence Act 1984, s. 78).

All of this raises a problem of proof. Legal samples cost approximately five times more than routine samples, so are not normally taken. Most samples entered on the public register will not therefore be admissible in evidence. Their status—whether legal or not—should be recorded on the register.

There is also a potential problem relating to the admissibility of the register itself, since it is fairly clearly hearsay evidence. It appears that samples taken by the NRA are admissible under the Criminal Justice Act 1988, s. 24. This section also seems to avoid any problem relating to self-incrimination where the discharger's own data are used, as that data will count as a confession (see the Police and Criminal Evidence Act 1984, ss. 76 and 82).

Enforcement policy

A central issue relating to water pollution, and indeed of this whole book, is whether the rules are actually enforced by the regulators (see Chapter 6 for a general survey of attitudes towards enforcement by regulatory bodies). The NRA is currently attempting to establish a national prosecution policy and the signs are clear that although there has been no change in the law in the Water Act 1989, the traditional recipe of a conciliatory approach to enforcement with low prosecution rates is being rapidly reformulated.

In its first year of operation, the NRA successfully prosecuted in 370 cases of water pollution. This compares with total reported prosecutions of between 91 and 254 for each year from 1980 to 1987 (Birch, *Poison in the System*, Greenpeace, 1988). Of course, because of the strict liability nature of the offences, most prosecutions are successful. Another emerging trend is an increased willingness to bring a prosecution in the Crown Court, where fines may be higher. This has resulted in several fines of over £10,000 in 1990 and 1991, most notably the £1m fine imposed on Shell (*National Rivers Authority* v *Shell (UK)* [1990] 1 Water Law 40). There has, as yet, been no reported case of a sentence of imprisonment being imposed.

The level of fines imposed by magistrates has also risen. Before the Environmental Protection Act 1990 raised the maximum fine on summary conviction, under s. 107 of the Water Act 1989, to £20,000, the maximum was £2,000. However, this was rarely imposed before 1989 and the average fine was estimated to be around £250. This has clearly increased in 1990, most possibly as a result of great publicity as to the costs of environmental pollution, so that a fine of over £1,000 would now be expected.

However, it remains the case that most prosecutions are for accidental or other unusual incidents, rather than for consistent breaches of consent. This characteristic was noted by Greenpeace in its Report, *Poison in the System* (1988), and results in the largest category of prosecutions being related to agricultural escapes.

For prosecutions of sewage works the picture is still unclear. Not only is there the difficulty of proving failure by reference to the 95% compliance rate, but, prior to the creation of the NRA in 1989, prosecution was effectively limited to private prosecutions, so experience in this area is as yet limited. Private prosecution remains a possibility under the Water Act 1989. Whilst sparingly used, its availability remains a threat to dischargers, particularly in the light of the information on the public registers.

Preventative and remedial powers

One of the special features of the regulatory system on water pollution is the extent of powers in relation to the prevention of harm. The exercise of these powers is undoubtedly aided by the presence of water quality objectives against which action may be justified.

Under s. 115, the NRA has widely drafted powers to prevent pollution incidents where there is a threat of water pollution, to clean up after them and to carry out remedial or restorative works. For example, s. 115 covers such things as diverting a potential pollutant spilt in an accident in order to prevent it from entering a watercourse, cleaning up the effects of a spillage, and restocking a river with fish. The rights of entry conferred by s. 147 may be used to further the use of s. 115.

The NRA can recover the costs incurred in these works or operations from anyone who has caused or knowingly permitted the pollutant to be present in controlled waters, or who has caused or knowingly permitted the pollutant to be a threat to controlled waters. It is arguable that this wide formulation will cover requiring existing owners to clean up contaminated sites. There are two exceptions: no expenses can be recovered in relation to waters from an abandoned mine (these are also exempted from the criminal provisions in the Act) and these powers cannot be exercised so as to impede or prevent the making of a discharge in pursuance of a consent. In this second case the NRA is limited to a consideration of whether the consent should be varied, though it should be noted that there is no power to override the two-year period of immunity against variation merely on the grounds that a discharger has committed a breach or an act of pollution.

Section 115 is mainly used for accidental acts of pollution, although it can be used where there has been a breach of the conditions of a consent. It is particularly useful because the potential cost may act as a greater deterrent than the threat of prosecution. The costs of a clean-up operation are likely in many cases to be higher than the potential fine. For example, in *National Rivers Authority* v *Shell (UK)* [1990] 1 Water Law 40, in which Shell were fined £1m for a major leak of oil into the River Mersey, Shell was reported as having paid over £1.4m in clean-up costs.

Precautions against pollution

Under s. 110, the Secretary of State is empowered to make regulations concerning precautions to be taken in relation to any poisonous, noxious or polluting matter to prevent it from entering controlled waters. Such regulations may prevent anyone having custody or control of poisonous, noxious or polluting matter, unless the steps required in the regulations or specified by the NRA are carried out. These regulations may create additional criminal offences and administrative remedies in relation to breaches, although these may not have penalties higher than for the pollution offences under s. 107.

There was a similar provision in COPA, but no regulations were ever made under it. The Control of Pollution (Silage, Slurry and Agricultural Fuel Oil) Regulations 1991 (SI 1991 No. 324) have been made under s. 110. They introduce precautionary controls over the design and operation of some potentially very polluting activities by imposing specific controls over silage making operations, slurry stores and agricultural fuel oil stores. All new or substantially altered facilities are covered by the new standards (many of which are performance standards rather than strict design requirements), though it is possible for the NRA to bring existing activities under control if it is satisfied there is a significant risk of pollution to controlled waters. These Regulations have the potential to complement the planning system in preventing pollution problems arising. However, control is exercisable over operational details in a more specific way than is possible through the planning system, oversight and monitoring will be carried out by a more specialist body, and the controls relate to agricultural matters not normally covered by planning powers.

Water protection zones

Under s. 111, the Secretary of State may designate water protection zones by order. Such an order may effectively establish a system of local law within the zone with regard to water pollution. In s. 111(2) it is envisaged that an order under this section may either prohibit or restrict specified activities within the designated zone with a view to preventing or controlling the entry of poisonous, noxious or polluting matter into controlled waters, or provide for a system whereby the NRA determine prohibited or restricted activities. It is not possible to require the carrying out of positive works. An order may also include provisions relating to procedures for obtaining consent for such restricted activities from the NRA, with criminal sanctions being available for breaches.

The procedure for the making of an order are set out in sch. 7. This requires that the NRA must apply for an order by submitting a draft to the Secretary of State. Fairly precise publicity requirements are laid down, including a duty to notify any local authority and water undertaker within the designated area. The Secretary of State may modify the order and has a power (not a duty) to hold a public inquiry before making it. In England, the Secretary of State must consult with the Minister of Agriculture, Fisheries and Food.

Similar provisions were included in COPA but were never used, and no water protection zones have yet been designated under the Water Act either. They would be excellent tools for protecting certain sensitive areas and for combating non-point discharges, such as pesticide or fertiliser run-off, and would enable steps to be taken to protect against groundwater pollution. However, the use of these powers has always been strongly opposed by agricultural interests. Significantly, there is no specific provision in the Act for an order to include compensation payments, but it may include such supplemental and consequential provision as the Secretary of State 'considers appropriate'.

One limitation, in s. 111(5), is that a water protection zone should not concern itself with nitrate. This is because protection against nitrate is provided for in s. 112: a section which was hurriedly written into the Act during its passage in response to public worries about nitrate in groundwaters used for water supply and the pending action against the British Government in the European Court of Justice for non-compliance with EC Directive 80/778 on Drinking Water. From a legal point of view it is difficult to see why the nitrate problem could not have been tackled through the designation of water protection zones, and it is hard to avoid the conclusion that specific nitrate sensitive area provisions are something of a political gesture.

Nitrate sensitive areas

The powers in relation to nitrate are set out in s. 112, which provides that an area may be designated a nitrate sensitive area by order with a view to preventing or controlling the entry of nitrate into controlled waters as a result of agriculture. In this case the designation is made by the Secretary of State and the Minister of Agriculture, Fisheries and Food acting jointly if the area is in England, and by the Secretary of State for Wales alone if it is in Wales. An order can only be made if requested by the NRA, which must identify controlled waters likely to be affected and the agricultural land likely to result in the entry of nitrate into waters. It must also appear to the NRA that its other powers are inadequate to control nitrate pollution before applying for an order. The consent of the Treasury is required before an order is made.

There are two types of order that may be made, respectively imposing voluntary and mandatory controls. Voluntary controls are available where *any* nitrate sensitive area has been designated: the Minister of Agriculture, Fisheries and Food may enter into a management agreement with any owner of an interest in agricultural land, with compensation payable. Such an agreement will bind those deriving title from the original party.

A mandatory order is similar to an order designating a water protection zone. However, there are significant differences. In nitrate sensitive areas the order may require positive obligations, such as the construction of containment walls around agricultural stores, as well as prohibitions and restrictions on activities. If consent is required, it is obtained from the Minister responsible for the designation, not the NRA. In addition, the order may provide for compensation to be paid to anyone affected by the obligations. No guidelines on the criteria for awarding compensation are set out in the Act.

The procedure for making a mandatory order is set out in sch. 11. This requires that the NRA must apply for an order by submitting a draft to the relevant Minister. Once again, precise publicity requirements are laid down, including a duty to notify any local authority and water undertaker within the designated area, and to notify any owner or occupier appearing to the relevant Minister to be likely to be affected by the compensation provisions. The relevant Minister may modify an order and has a power (not a duty) to hold a public inquiry before making an order.

The Government has made public its intention to use only the voluntary methods initially, in keeping with its stated preference for such methods. It had designated 10 trial areas in the Nitrate Sensitive Areas (Designation) Order 1990 (SI 1990 No. 1013), which explains the types of agreement that may be reached within the designated areas and also sets out compensation arrangements.

The newly-agreed EC Directive on Nitrates goes quite a bit further than current Government policy. It lays down some very specific requirements on restrictions and would necessitate the use of mandatory orders. It may also require some redrafting of the Water Act, since it includes measures relating to discharges from sewage works as well as to agriculture, which is all that is covered by s. 112.

Planning controls

Local planning authorities have the ability to make important decisions relating to water pollution through the town and country planning system. However. it is clearly recommended in Central Government guidance, such as Circular 1/85 on planning conditions, that planning powers should be used mainly for locational and siting decisions and that matters about the regulation of pollution should be left to the specialist regulators to control through the specialist consent systems.

However, it is clear that potential water pollution arising from a proposed development would be a material consideration in any planning decision, and the NRA is made a statutory consultee under the General Development Order in relation to all applications for planning permission. Equally, permission may be refused because of inadequate sewerage in the area. Of course, the NRA will also have an important role to play in the making of development plans. The generous exemptions for agricultural activities and buildings may be of significance in the context of increasing evidence of water pollution by agriculture.

Other water pollution offences

There are a number of other offences which may be committed in relation to water pollution. A few of the main ones are considered here: to these should be added offences involving the dumping of waste or the disposal of litter and many by-laws of a local or specific nature.

Under the Water Act 1989, s. 109(1), it is an offence to remove any part of the bed of inland waters so as to cause it to be carried away in suspension. Section 109(2) provides for an offence of causing or permitting vegetation to be cut or uprooted so as to fall into inland waters, and then failing to take reasonable steps to remove it. In both cases the NRA may grant its consent subject to any conditions it considers appropriate. The offences are summary only, with a maximum fine of £1,000.

Under the Water Act 1989, s. 114, the NRA has powers to make by-laws in relation to the washing or cleaning of anything in controlled waters, or in relation to sanitary appliances on vessels. The maximum fine for an offence under these by-laws is currently £1,000. By-laws affecting vessels made under the Rivers (Prevention of Pollution) Act 1951 remain in force.

Under the Salmon and Freshwater Fisheries Act 1975, s. 4(1), it is an offence to cause or knowingly permit any liquid or solid matter to flow or be put into waters containing fish so as to cause those waters to be poisonous or injurious to fish, their food or their spawning grounds. This offence is more limited than the Water Act 1989, s. 107; it requires proof of the presence of fish and injury to them. A prosecution cannot be brought except by the NRA or anyone who has obtained a certificate from the Minister of Agriculture, Fisheries and Food (or, in Wales, the Secretary of State) that they have a material interest in the waters affected. The maximum fine on summary conviction is also less than for s. 107 (£2,000 rather than £20,000) although the penalties for conviction on indictment are the same. In the Public Health Act 1875, s. 68, there is a specific offence relating to the pollution of water by the gas manufacture industry, which is effectively superseded by s. 107. Section 113(4) of the Water Act 1989 provides that a consent under the 1989 Act is a defence to the offences under the Salmon and Freshwater Fisheries Act 1975, s. 4, or the Public Health Act 1875, s. 68.

Under EPA, s. 140, the Secretary of State is given powers to make regulations to prohibit the importation, use, supply or storage of any substance or article for the purpose of preventing it causing pollution of the environment, or harm to the health of humans, animals or plants. This very wide power includes the power to order the disposal or treatment of restricted articles. It replaces the similar power under COPA, s. 100. That section was used to make regulations banning the supply of lead weights for use by anglers (see Control of Pollution (Anglers' Lead Weights) Regulations 1986 (SI 1986 No. 1992)), prohibiting the supply and use of PCBs (see Control of Pollution (Supply and Use of Injurious Substances) Regulations 1986 (SI 1986 No. 902)), and prohibiting the supply of tri-organotin compound paints (see Control of Pollution (Anti-Fouling Paints and Treatments) Regulations 1987 (SI 1987 No. 783)).

Statutory nuisances

In addition to the normal statutory nuisance provisions listed in Part III of the EPA (see p. 151), two further statutory nuisances are provided for in the Public Health Act 1936, s. 259. Section 259(1)(a) provides that any pool, pond, ditch, gutter or watercourse which is in a state that is prejudicial to health or a nuisance is a statutory nuisance. This will cover small ponds and ditches which are not within the consent system as well as controlled waters. Section 259(1)(b) covers any watercourse which is silted up or choked so as to obstruct the proper flow of water and thus causing a nuisance or which is prejudicial to health. This is limited to watercourses which are not normally navigated. The normal procedures for statutory nuisance apply to these situations, thus creating an alternative course of action for a local authority or individual wishing to clean up a grossly polluted watercourse.

Water pollution and the common law

The common law still plays a significant role in the control of water pollution. Indeed, for various technical reasons it is probably of greater use for water pollution than for other forms of pollution and may be used to produce, directly or indirectly, environmental improvements.

One right which has already been mentioned is the right of private prosecution for breaches of the criminal law. This has been available for many water pollution offences since 1985 as a result of the removal by COPA of the restrictions on it. More significant, however, are the various civil law claims that may be brought. For example, the Anglers' Cooperative Association is estimated to have been involved in over 1,000 cases involving water pollution since the Second World War. The two main remedies available are damages to compensate an owner of the river bed, the river banks, or a fishery for any losses caused, and an injunction to restrain future breaches of the law.

There are a number of reasons why water pollution cases have proved easier to bring in nuisance than air pollution cases:

(a)   Causation is easier to show because of the defined channels in which water normally flows.

(b)   Many rural landowners have the money to bring an action: indeed, pollution to fisheries will often justify an action in commercial terms, as the recent claim by pop star Roger Daltrey for the loss of an estimated 500,000 fish from his fish farm, caused by the bursting of an upstream fertiliser storage tank, illustrates (*Beju Bop Ltd* v *Home Farm (Iwerne Minster) Ltd* [1990] 1 Water Law 90). Damages of £500,000 were claimed, although the case was settled out of court for £150,000.

(c)   There are a number of campaigning and amenity bodies concerned with water problems, far more than are concerned with air or noise pollution.

(d)   The acquisition of evidence is more straightforward, particularly since the advent of the public registers, which may provide evidence relating to the quality of the receiving waters before and after an incident and also relating to discharges. Nevertheless, there will still be problems with an individual acquiring scientifically valid evidence (see Macrory, *Water Law*, Ch. 5:2).

Riparian rights

The usefulness of the civil law in this area stems mainly from the nature of riparian rights. Owners of land adjoining a watercourse (including estuaries), termed riparian owners, normally own the river bed, but not the water itself. However, as a natural incident of the soil itself, they have the right to receive the water in its natural state, subject only to reasonable usage by an upstream owner for ordinary purposes (*Chasemore* v *Richards* [1859] 7 HLC 349). Owners of other property rights such as fisheries have the same right.

The most authoritative statement of this principle was given by Lord Macnaghten in *Young & Co* v *Bankier Distillery Co* [1893] AC 698. He stated:

A riparian proprietor is entitled to have the water of the stream, on the bank of which his property lies, flow down as it has been accustomed to flow down to his property, subject to the ordinary use of the flowing water by upper proprietors, and to such further use, if any, on their part in connection with their property as may be reasonable in the circumstances. Every riparian owner is thus entitled to the water of his stream, in its natural flow, without sensible diminution or increase, and without sensible alteration in its character or quality.

This means that any interference with the natural quantity or quality of the water is an actionable nuisance. The strictness of this test was shown in *Young & Co v Bankier Distillery Co.* An upstream mineowner discharged water into a stream from a mine. This altered the chemistry of the water from soft to hard and thus altered the quality of the downstream distillery's whisky. The water had not been made impure, but the distillery obtained an injunction because the nature of the water had been changed. The case illustrates the relative nature of the definition of water pollution and indeed emphasises that the common law does not lay down any absolute standards in relation to water quality. It is worth noting, however, that this test only applies where the upstream usage is not ordinary; a good example of the balancing process the law of nuisance tries to carry out.

Some of the technical difficulties relating to the law of nuisance, such as the causation question and the locality doctrine, have also been neatly answered in the water pollution cases. Because there is no need to show damage, it follows that an action can be brought against any upstream polluter, even if only one of many and responsible for only a part of the whole pollution. All that needs to be shown is that the polluter is contributing to the pollution (*Crossley v Lightowler* [1866] 11 Ch App Cas 478).

Liability will also arise in nuisance for polluting percolating ground waters, as long as causation can be shown (*Ballard v Tomlinson* [1885] 29 ChD 115).

Damages will be recoverable for any loss to the downstream owner. This will include such things as any clean-up costs, the cost of restocking the water with fish, and any loss of profits.

Injunctions are also available for water pollution, though they will normally be suspended to allow the defendants time to correct matters. For example, in *Pride of Derby Angling Assoc. v British Celanese Ltd* [1952] Ch 149, injunctions and damages were obtained against British Celanese Ltd (for industrial effluent), Derby Corporation (for untreated sewage), and the British Electricity Authority (for thermal pollution from a power station).

It is important to note that acting within the terms of a discharge consent does not act as a defence to a nuisance action, since the private law system of nuisance operates separately from the public regulatory mechanisms.

Other common law claims may also be available. In *Jones v Llanrwst UDC* [1911] 1 Ch 393, the owner of a river bed claimed successfully in trespass for deposits of solid wastes. In *Scott-Whitehead v National Coal Board* [1987] 53 P&CR 263, Southern Water Authority was held liable in negligence for the loss of a farmer's potato crop. The loss was caused by saline water abstracted in accordance with an abstraction licence granted by the Authority: the salinity in turn was caused by an upstream colliery discharge permitted by the Authority, which was not being diluted properly in the circumstances of the 1976 drought. The judge held the Authority liable for not warning the farmer of the potential damage to his crop if he used excessively saline water, although the exact reasoning behind this decision must now be reassessed in the light of the restriction on the liability of public authorities for negligence in the exercise of their duties in *Murphy v Brentwood DC* [1990] 2 All ER 908.

Finally, it is often stated that a prescriptive right to acquire an easement to pollute can be acquired. Whilst this remains true as a matter of principle, such an occurrence will be rare owing to the fact that it is not possible to acquire a prescriptive right where the act relied upon to gain the right is illegal. In most water pollution cases the polluting activity will be illegal.

Postscript

In July 1991 Royal Assent was given to five Acts which consolidate the law on the water industry. These are the Water Industry Act 1991, Water Resources Act 1991, Water Companies Act 1991, Land Drainage Act 1991 and Water Consolidation (Consequential and Amendments) Act 1991. These Acts do not change the substance of the law, except to give effect to some very minor amendments recommended by the Law Commission in its Report No. 198 (Consolidation of Legislation Relating to Water, Cm. 1483, 1991). They come into force on 1 December 1991, when the Water Act 1989 will be repealed.

Most of the material relevant to this book is in the Water Resources Act 1991. The provisions on the structure of the National Rivers Authority are in Part I and Schedule 1. Those on water resources are in Part II. Control of Pollution is in Part III. Specific destinations of the current sections are as follows:

Section in Water Act 1989	Section in Water Resources Act 1991
103	104
104	82
105	83
106	84
107	85, 86, 87
108	87, 88, 89
109	90
110	92
111	93, 96, sch. 11
112	94, 95, 96, sch. 12
113	99
115	161
116	97
117	190
124	221
146	102
147	169, 172
148	209
174	204
sch. 12	sch. 10
sch. 12, para. 8	91

The general environmental duties laid down in the Water Act 1989, ss. 8–10 are in both the Water Industry Act 1991 (ss. 3–5) and the Water Resources Act 1991 (ss. 16–18).

Sewerage services are in the Water Industry Act 1991, Part IV. The provisions of the Public Health (Drainage of Trade Premises) Act 1937 are re-enacted in ss. 118–141.

FOURTEEN
Disposal of waste to sewers

In this book disposals of waste to the sewerage system are dealt with in a self-contained chapter because they are a separate form of waste disposal with their own particular and unique regulatory regime. The treatment of wastes at sewage works is an integral part of general policies on waste disposal and protection of the natural environment. The alternative to such disposal (waste minimisation apart) is often some form of direct discharge to the environment, so sewage treatment offers an important weapon in the search for the best practicable environmental option (BPEO).

There are other links with environmental protection that justify detailed consideration of sewage disposal. Sewage treatment is only an intermediate step in the ultimate disposal of waste and the operators of sewers and sewage works must dispose of their own wastes. This will often (though not always) be after a treatment process and will involve a combination of liquid discharges into watercourses or the sea, the dumping of sludge on land or at sea, and incineration. Indeed, sewage works have been responsible for the low quality of many of our inland and coastal waters (see *River Quality Survey*, DoE, 1985). The Government announced a commitment to phase out the dumping of sewage sludge at sea by 1998 at the Third International Conference for the Protection of the North Sea in March 1990.

Sewerage and sewage treatment have always been closely related with the water industry and most books have tended to treat discharges to sewers as a part of the law on water pollution. This can be explained on the grounds that discharges to sewers are liquid and that most sewage works themselves discharge into watercourses, but it also relates to the historical institutional connections. Sewerage, public water supply and the prevention of water pollution have often been carried out by the same bodies, most notably between 1974 and 1989 when the 10 regional water authorities in England and Wales carried out all functions in relation to water and sewage on an integrated basis. This included regulating discharges both to the sewers and to surface waters.

Since 1 September 1989 there has been a reversion to a system of split responsibilities under the Water Act 1989. Private water and sewerage undertakers provide the public water supply and own and operate the sewerage network and the sewage works, as well as regulating discharges to sewers, whilst the National Rivers Authority regulates abstractions from and discharges to the natural environment and has responsibility for combating surface water pollution.

Trade effluent discharges

The sewerage undertaker plays its most important environmental protection role in the regulation of trade effluent discharges, although since 1989 certain dangerous discharges have been regulated by Her Majesty's Inspectorate of Pollution (see below). Measured in terms of pollutant load, a far greater quantity of industrial effluent is discharged into the sewers than directly into surface waters or by any other disposal route.

The regulatory regime relating to discharges to sewers is an old and somewhat rudimentary one, though there have been periodic developments designed to bring it more up-to-date. It involves a rather basic system of individualised consents set by the operators of the sewers, involving little input from other bodies or from the public at any of the various stages of policy-making, standard-setting, consent-setting or enforcement. The legislation is still contained mainly in the Public Health (Drainage of Trade Premises) Act 1937, though this Act has been amended in significant ways by the Public Health Act 1961, ss. 55-70, the Control of Pollution Act 1974, ss. 43-45, the Water Act 1989, Part II, Chapters III and IV and Schs. 8 and 9, and the Environmental Protection Act 1990. From 1 December 1991, the law will be consolidated in the Water Industry Act 1991, though the substance of the law will not change.

It is a criminal offence to discharge any trade effluent from trade premises into sewers unless a trade effluent consent is obtained from the sewerage undertaker (Public Health (Drainage of Trade Premises) Act 1937, s. 2(5)). 'Trade effluent' and 'trade premises' are defined widely in s. 14 to include all liquid discharges from industry, shops, research establishments, launderettes and agriculture, except for domestic sewage. It is also an offence to breach the terms of a consent. This is a unique system of control in that it is the only example in this country of a private body exercising regulatory functions with regard to environmental protection.

Applying for a trade effluent consent

The discharger applies for a trade effluent consent by serving a trade effluent notice on the sewerage undertaker at least two months prior to the commencement of the discharge. This notice is effectively an application and must state the nature and composition of the proposed effluent, the maximum daily volume and the maximum rate of discharge in order to enable the sewerage undertaker to establish its likely effect.

The sewerage undertaker then has a discretion whether to grant or refuse consent, though if the sewerage system can cope with the discharge, it is normal for consent to be granted subject to conditions. The scope of these conditions is laid down in the Public Health Act 1961, s. 59. They may include such matters as the place of discharge, the nature, temperature and composition of the discharge (including requirements as to the elimination or maximum concentration of any specified constituent), the rate and timing of discharges, and ancillary matters such as the fixing of meters to register the volume of the discharge, the monitoring of the nature and volume of the discharge and the keeping of records. Most importantly, conditions on the payment of effluent charges will also be included.

It is not permissible to attach conditions which require the fitting of specified treatment plant; the normal practice is to specify the effluent standards that must be met and to leave it to the discharger to determine how to meet those standards, albeit often with advice from the sewerage undertaker. One reason for this is the widespread belief that most effluent is better and more efficiently treated at the sewage works than at each factory, but it also reflects the policy of preserving some element of choice for producers.

How are consents set?

Since discharges to sewers are distinct from other discharges in being to an artificial environment, the matters that are taken into account in setting a consent differ from other consents and licences. In particular, environmental protection is only one factor.

The objectives of trade effluent control are set out clearly in a booklet produced by the Water Authorities Association in September 1986 entitled *Trade Effluent Discharged to the Sewer*. They are that the system of control seeks:

(a) to protect the sewerage system and the personnel who work in it;

(b) to protect the sewage works and their efficient operation (for example, most sewage works operate by a biological process and care has to be taken not to neutralise that process).

(c) to protect the environment generally from the residues of the sewage treatment process or from direct discharges from parts of the system such as storm drains; and

(d) to ensure that dischargers pay a reasonable charge for the cost of the treatment.

In addition, the booklet stresses that it is important for correct information on discharges to be kept, so that dischargers can know how to improve their trade effluent control and sewerage undertakers can plan for future sewerage provision and operate the treatment process efficiently.

With these factors in mind, the consent will in general be set by reference to the receiving capabilities of the sewer and sewage works. If the works are already overburdened, the consent may be refused or subject to tight limits, whereas if there is spare capacity at the works, the limits will be much more generous. Certain pollutants, such as heavy metals or persistent chemicals, may be unsuitable for sewage treatment and may be banned from the discharge. The discharger may then have to pre-treat the effluent to remove these constituents, or find an alternative method of disposal. Other relevant matters are taken into account, such as the sewerage undertaker's own potential liability for discharges from the works under the Water Act 1989 and the requirements of EC law, especially in the light of the adoption of the Urban Waste Water Treatment Directive 91/271 (see Chapter 13).

The sewerage undertaker has a power to vary a consent unilaterally by giving two months' notice to the discharger (Public Health Act 1961, s. 60). This enables it to take steps to meet the terms of the consent for the sewage works set by the NRA. Variation is currently happening with great frequency, as sewerage undertakers try to renegotiate consents inherited from the regional water authorities and establish a uniform system for their areas.

Variation of a consent is, however, possible only after two years have elapsed from the grant of the consent or the last variation. Exceptionally, a variation may be made within this period if it is necessary to provide proper protection for people likely to be affected by the discharge. In this situation, compensation will be payable to the discharger unless the variation was necessary as a result of a change of circumstances unforeseeable at the time of the grant of the consent, or its last variation (COPA, s. 45).

The discharger has a right of appeal to the Director General of Water Services against a refusal or variation of consent or the imposition of conditions, except that there is no appeal against trade effluent charges (1937 Act, s. 3). An appeal against a deemed refusal may also be brought if no decision is given on the trade effluent notice within two months. (It used to be the case that such a failure to determine an application led to an automatic consent, but that rule was removed by the Water Act 1989.) As with planning appeals, an appeal is effectively a rehearing and the Director General may make any decision that the sewerage undertaker could have made. There is a further right of appeal to the High Court on a matter of law.

An alternative to seeking a consent is for the discharger and the sewerage undertaker to reach an agreement for the reception or disposal of trade effluent under the 1937 Act, s. 7. Such an agreement may provide for the discharger to pay for works necessary to treat the wastes, such as an extension to a sewage works. It must have a provision enabling the sewerage undertaker to vary or terminate it (COPA, s. 43).

Trade effluent charges

Trade effluent charges are levied for discharges to sewers and a charges scheme may be made under the Water Act 1989, s. 76. All the sewerage undertakers currently use a similar formula based on the so-called 'Mogden Formula', in which charges are calculated according to the volume and strength of the effluent, as measured by the chemical oxygen demand (COD) and the solids content. Dischargers are therefore advised to consider whether their processes can be changed so as to minimise wastes, and thus costs. No extra charges are currently levied by the sewerage undertakers in relation to metals or other hazardous items; undesirable levels of these are controlled by the consent limits rather than by charging mechanisms. However, levels of charges are likely to rise substantially as a consequence of the fact that sewerage undertakers will themselves be liable for charges for their own discharges from sewage works. The charging system thus operates in tandem with the consent system to reduce discharges. To a limited extent it encourages the reduction of pollution, although it does not make dischargers fully responsible for the environmental costs of their discharges. It remains to be seen whether a system of incentive charging will be introduced in this area: that would require legislation.

Public participation

Public rights in relation to the trade effluent system are very limited. There is no right for a member of the public to be informed of an application for a trade effluent consent and no right to participate in the decision whether to grant one, or in any appeal. Under the Water Act 1989, sch. 8, para. 3(5), which inserts a new s. 7A in the 1937 Act, all consents, variations, agreements and directions by the sewerage undertaker or the Director General, and all decisions by the Secretary of State (effectively HMIP in this context) must be placed on a public register.

However, this is a limited right, since there is no public right to information on any samples taken. Indeed, it is a criminal offence under the Public Health Act 1961, s. 68, for an employee of the sewerage undertaker to disclose information furnished under the 1937 Act or the 1961 Act. There is also no right of private prosecution for breach of a consent, except by a 'person aggrieved' or with the consent of the Attorney-General. Many of these restrictions may have to change in the near future in the light of EC Directive 90/313 on Freedom of Access to Information on the Environment, though it is unclear whether the sewerage undertakers answer to the description of a public body under the Directive, or whether sewers satisfy the definition of the environment.

'Red List' substances

In order to ensure compliance with EC Directives, such as 76/464 on Dangerous Substances in Water, an additional control was introduced from 1 September 1989 in the Water Act 1989, sch. 9, for specified dangerous substances. The Secretary of State was empowered to prescribe certain substances or processes for which HMIP was effectively made the consenting body. Currently 24 such substances (the 'Red List' substances) are listed in sch. 1 to the Trade Effluents (Prescribed Processes and Substances) Regulations 1989 (SI 1989 No.1156), as amended by SI 1990 No. 1629, and five processes involving asbestos or chloroform are listed in sch. 2.

All discharges where any of these substances or processes are present in more than background concentration must be referred to HMIP, which may then issue a direction (against which there is no appeal) to the sewerage undertaker on whether to grant a consent and on any conditions it might impose. Before deciding an application, HMIP must provide the sewerage undertaker and the applicant with an opportunity to make representations.

Existing discharges covered by the regulations are also reviewable by HMIP. As with ordinary trade effluent discharges, a review may not normally be made within two years of the previous review. However, review is possible within two years if there has been a contravention of a consent or agreement, to give effect to an international or EC obligation, or to protect public health or aquatic flora and fauna. Compensation is payable in some of these circumstances, unless the review resulted from a change of circumstances unforeseeable at the time of the setting of the consent or the previous review.

This system is itself undergoing change as a result of the introduction of integrated pollution control by the Environmental Protection Act 1990. Control over discharges to sewers in the course of processes prescribed for the purposes of integrated pollution control will be exercised by HMIP under powers in EPA Part I (see sch. 15, para. 28). These new powers will come into force on the date when an authorisation is either granted or refused. However, a consent from the sewerage undertaker will still be required in addition to the authorisation from HMIP.

Enforcement

The penalty for the offence of discharging without consent, or in breach of a condition, is, on summary conviction, a fine not exceeding the statutory maximum (at present £2,000), and on conviction on indictment, an unlimited fine (1937 Act, s. 2(5A)).

Enforcement of the legislation is by the sewerage undertaker. In the past this has led to a conciliatory approach to enforcement, since officials have seen themselves as problem-solvers rather than as police officers. Indeed, one of the main surveys of enforcement attitudes (Richardson, Ogus and Burrows, *Policing Pollution*, 1983) was a survey of trade effluent control officers. This approach is reinforced by the requirement for a 'legal sample' to be taken in order for it to be admissible as evidence in court (1937 Act, s. 10). (For the meaning of 'legal samples', see p. 323.)

Discharges from sewage works

Under the Water Act 1989, sewerage undertakers have consents set for their own discharges and may be prosecuted by the NRA or any individual if they breach them. They are responsible for all discharges from their sewers or works, subject only to a defence that the breach was caused by an illegal discharge to the sewer that they could not reasonably have been expected to prevent (Water Act 1989, s. 108(7)). This means that sewerage undertakers are ultimately responsible if they are unable to treat adequately discharges they have permitted. They thus have an incentive to restrict discharges to those which are treatable.

Domestic sewage discharges

Some discharges are prohibited entirely by the Public Health Act 1936, s. 27 (although a trade effluent consent is a defence). These are discharges of anything liable to damage the sewer, or to stop its flow, or to prejudice the sewage works treatment; any chemicals or liquids over 110 °F which will be dangerous or a nuisance; and any petroleum spirit, including motor oils. For example, drainage of used car oils is an offence under this section. The maximum penalties are, on summary conviction, a fine of up to £2,000, and, on conviction on indictment, an unlimited fine and/or up to two years imprisonment.

Otherwise, there is no restriction on discharges of domestic sewage. There is a right of connection to the public sewer conferred on owners and occupiers by the Public Health Act 1936, s. 34 with very limited powers of refusal. These do not include the potential overloading of the system: as Upjohn J stated in *Smeaton* v *Ilford Corporation* [1954] 1 Ch 450, 'they [i.e. now the sewerage undertakers] are bound to permit occupiers of premises to make connections to the sewer and to discharge their sewage therein'. Powers to requisition sewers for domestic purposes are set out in the Water Act 1989, s. 71.

However, it is permissible for the local planning authority to refuse planning permission on the grounds that the local sewage works are overburdened or inadequate, since that is a material consideration. Alternatively, it could seek to gain some planning gain in relation to the provision of sewers by the use of conditions, or an agreement under the Town and Country Planning Act 1990, s. 106 (see p. 196 for the limitations on this course of action).

FIFTEEN
The conservation of nature

This chapter looks at the laws which set out specifically to protect plants, animals and habitat. This has become a popular subject in recent years, partly as a result of the dramatic growth of interest in all things connected with nature and conservation, but also as a consequence of the appalling rate of decline in and loss of the natural environment. The Wildlife and Countryside Act 1981, the major piece of legislation in this area, reflects this popularity: it still holds the record for the number of amendments tabled to a Parliamentary Bill and its controversial passage brought nature conservation firmly into the arena of political debate, where it has stayed.

At the outset, a distinction must be made between nature conservation and matters of amenity and landscape. Even though these topics are often closely related, it is possible to distinguish between those laws which are justified as a matter of straight wildlife protection and those which relate more to human uses of the environment. It must also be borne in mind that the preservation of a balanced ecosystem and the survival of many species depends as much on the responses to the other environmental threats covered in this book, such as pollution and development, as on the specific methods of protection mentioned in this chapter, which would probably be useless if applied in isolation.

History

A brief history of nature conservation will help to explain the current structure of the law. Up to less than 200 years ago, the need to protect wildlife was normally perceived solely in human terms, such as the desirability of preserving game and quarry species and protected areas in which to hunt them. There is little doubt that an incidental benefit of this human-centred approach was the protection of other animals and plants and the preservation of whole areas (for example the New Forest) in a fairly natural state, but there were few laws designed specifically to protect wildlife.

From Victorian times, the tendency was to enact legislation outlawing unwelcome activities in response to particular problems as they were identified. The rationale for this intervention was as much based on concern about cruelty as on any positive desire to conserve nature for its own sake. Some good examples are the Sea Birds Protection Acts of 1869, 1872 and 1880, passed to combat the slaughter of birds at places such as Flamborough Head, and various pieces of legislation intended to restrict the international trade in feathers for clothing and hats. However, there was no grand design underlying these restrictions. The weight of conservation fell on voluntary organisations—indeed Britain had the world's first developed conservation movement—and no official bodies were established to monitor or enforce the legislation that did exist. This unplanned approach persisted; the Protection of Birds Act 1954, which established protection for birds that was far stronger than that for other animals and plants, was a Private Member's Bill brought forward on behalf of the Royal Society for the Protection of Birds.

These voluntary organisations gradually developed a strategy which became, and remains, the typical approach to nature conservation. This is the designation of selected areas or sites that are specially protected. The first modern uses of this technique related to the protection of common lands for recreational purposes, but it was soon used for the development of nature reserves, even though at this time they were seen as a somewhat peripheral interest of the nature conservation movement. For example, the National Trust acquired parts of Wicken Fen in 1899, the Norfolk Naturalists Trust was founded to buy Cley Marshes in 1926 and the Royal Society for the Protection of Birds bought its first nature reserve (on Romney Marsh) in 1929. However, in the absence of any legislative protection for such sites, their safety lay in the exercise of ordinary property rights. After all, the property owner's freedom to exclude others and to use the land for any purposes is one mechanism for controlling land use in limited areas. The limitations of this approach are well illustrated by the RSPB's first reserve, which had to be abandoned when developments on neighbouring land destroyed its natural interest.

The post-war period

In the immediate post-war period, the site designation approach was adopted as a matter of national policy. The beginning of the modern age of nature conservation can be traced to that time in the publication of two influential reports, *Conservation of Nature in England and Wales* from the Wildlife Conservation Special Committee (the Huxley Committee, Cmd. 7122) and *Nature Reserves in Scotland* from the Scottish Wild Life Conservation Committee (the Ritchie Committee, Cmd. 7184), many of whose recommendations were accepted and acted upon.

A specialist national nature conservation body—the Nature Conservancy— was established and one of its main roles was to create a series of protected sites across the nation, rather than the somewhat random series produced by private acquisition. The two main habitat protection measures, the national nature reserve (NNR) and the site of special scientific interest (SSSI) both date from this period. The scientific basis of nature conservation was emphasised and it was linked firmly to education and research on the natural environment. Nature conservation was also split from amenity, recreation and landscape matters, which had their own separate institutions and laws, and it is worth reflecting that the powers for nature conservation at that time were both stronger and met with far less opposition than those for recreation in the countryside.

Current policy

Many of the features of this post-war structure remain, but the climate in which they operate has changed radically, with the result that many of the similarities the current system has with that structure are illusory. There have been devastating changes in both the urban and rural environments and these have altered the role of site designation dramatically from an educational to a safeguarding one. One result has been the expansion of the NNR and SSSI system way beyond that envisaged, or indeed considered necessary, by the Huxley and Ritchie Committees, in order to ensure that at least a basic pool of key sites is protected.

Another result is that general environmental awareness has now shifted the focus of policy away from the designation and protection of certain key sites towards the protection of the wider countryside. It is now accepted that there is little future in having isolated and ever-decreasing areas of protected wildlife in an otherwise barren countryside, and so nature conservation is increasingly seen as a factor to weigh in the balance when considering all rural policies. This adds to the political dimension which nature conservation has rapidly acquired.

In addition, the enjoyment of nature has emerged as a major leisure pursuit, blurring the distinction in the public mind and in policy between nature conservation as a scientifically justified discipline and as a recreation. There has been an undreamt-of increase in voluntary activity in relation to the countryside, resulting in large numbers of reserves and sites protected by voluntary bodies and non-statutory designations. There has also been an increase in international activity on the environment, mainly through conventions such as the Washington Convention on International Trade in Endangered Species (usually known as CITES) (which is implemented in Britain through the Wildlife and Countryside Act 1981), and the pressure on the Government to carry out internationally agreed policies is immense. Nowhere is it greater than in relation to the EC, which has an important Directive on Wild Birds and a proposed Directive on Habitat Protection. The Wild Birds Directive (79/409) required changes in British law and led to the Wildlife and Countryside Act 1981, effectively the first major Government sponsored measure on nature conservation and one that has revealed some severe differences in philosophy between the political parties.

From this brief historical survey it can be seen that the protections offered by the law can be divided into four rough categories:

(a) protecting individual animals and plants;
(b) habitat protection through the designation of key sites;
(c) the use of grants and incentives; and
(d) incidental protection.

(a) Protecting individual animals and plants

This is still done on a somewhat ad hoc basis, though a degree of coherence is provided by the Wildlife and Countryside Act 1981. Nature conservation is not the only aim being pursued; there is still a large element of protection against cruelty, and important exceptional provisions relate to game and quarry species.

(b) Habitat protection through the designation of key sites

This has been a favoured technique, and a bewildering array of legislative designations has built up, the special rules and protections differing for each one. There is quite a degree of overlap here and many designations are cumulative. In *Nature Conservation in Great Britain* (1984), the Nature Conservancy Council sets out its policy that 10% of the country be covered by one designation or another, so that a bedrock of essential sites may be protected.

(c) The use of grants and incentives in the wider countryside

The realisation that the protection of isolated sites is insufficient, both in scientific terms and in terms of the expectations of people who are interested in nature, has led to the search for general policies conducive to nature conservation, especially as part of agriculture and forestry policy.

(d) Incidental protection

It remains clear that nature conservation interests are often served by taking advantage of legal powers which were not designed with nature conservation in mind. The best example is the purchase of private nature reserves by voluntary bodies, but another good example is the nature conservation value of the large tracts of land used for Ministry of Defence training grounds.

Nature Conservancy Council (NCC)

The NCC came into existence in 1949 as the Nature Conservancy, established by Royal Charter on the recommendations of the Huxley and Ritchie Reports. After several further incarnations, it was established in the Nature Conservancy Council Act 1973 as an autonomous body independent of Government Departments, although Council members were appointed by the Secretaries of State. It received annual grant in aid from the Treasury and had to submit annual reports and accounts. The separation of the NCC from its active research ecology side (now the Institute of Terrestrial Ecology) and the increasingly political nature of site protection turned the NCC into what could almost be described as a pressure group within Government. In one sense, therefore, it was largely unaccountable for many of its decisions; in another it could be said to be accountable to the interests of wildlife and ecology.

Prior to the Environmental Protection Act 1990, the NCC was a single national body, with headquarters in Peterborough, and with responsibility for nature conservation matters throughout Great Britain. Under the EPA, from 1 April 1991, the NCC (and hence responsibility for nature conservation) was split into three national bodies; an NCC England (called English Nature), a Countryside Council for Wales, combining the functions of the NCC and the Countryside Commission in the principality (i.e. combining nature conservation with amenity and recreational matters), and an NCC Scotland. In the case of Scotland, a Scottish Natural Heritage Agency is being established by the merger of the NCC Scotland and the Countryside Commission for Scotland (see the Natural Heritage (Scotland) Act 1991). The intention is that these three bodies inherit the NCC's existing responsibilities within the relevant geographical areas. Any reference to the NCC in this book is a reference to the relevant body in its own national area.

The three national NCCs retain a similar independence to the old NCC. The members are appointed by the Secretary of State and they receive an annual grant in aid from the Treasury. A limited form of accountability is ensured by an annual report and presentation of accounts to Parliament. They are not Crown Bodies (see EPA 1990, sch. 6).

A Joint Nature Conservation Committee of the three new bodies has been established (EPA 1990, s. 128(4)). This body has no executive functions, but will carry out important roles in relation to the international responsibilities of the old NCC (e.g. under the Ramsar Convention and other conventions) and those affecting the whole of Great Britain. It will also seek to monitor the retention of uniform standards between the three national bodies (for example, the preservation of common criteria for the designation of SSSIs). During the debates on the Environmental Protection Bill, the adequacy of the powers and staffing of this new umbrella committee was greatly discussed and the scope of its powers evolved in response to criticism, illustrating the ill-considered nature of the reforms.

The Joint Nature Conservation Committee relies on the national NCCs for its funding, staffing and other resources, but it does have an independent chair and three other independent people appointed by the Secretary of State, in addition to two representatives from each national NCC and the chair of the Countryside Commission. Significantly, the first chair of the Joint Nature Conservation Committee, Sir Frederick Holliday, resigned in July 1991 over what he saw as unreasonable Government interference. The particular issue which caused his action was Government support for a controversial clause in the Natural Heritage (Scotland) Act 1991 requiring a separate committee to review the designations of existing SSSIs in Scotland.

The national NCCs are the Government's statutory advisers on nature conservation issues. They have specific responsibilities for advising on species and habitat protection, the dissemination of knowledge about nature conservation, the support and conduct of research into nature conservation, and the safeguard of protected sites. In particular they are responsible for the selection and management of NNRs and for the designation and oversight of SSSIs. They are statutory consultees in relation to a large number of public decisions.

One effect of the dismantling of the NCC is bound to be the loss of uniformity in the implementation of the law. This is inevitable given the wide discretions under the legislation, and also in the light of previous attitudes to nature conservation in Scotland and Wales. As the outgoing Chairman of the NCC, Sir William Wilkinson, put it when presenting the NCC's 16th Annual Report, 'As a result of the Government's attitude, nature conservation has been set back three, or possibly up to five, years '.

The protection of individual animals and plants

The common law is generally unsympathetic to wild creatures, according them no rights of their own. However, property rights may usefully be exercised in order to protect them. Wild animals are subject to the qualified ownership of the landowner whose land they are on, whilst wild plants are part of the land itself. As a result, anyone who kills or injures a wild animal or picks a wild plant commits the torts of trespass and interference with property. Whilst the normal remedy would be damages for the value of the item taken (and thus is of little practical use), it would be possible to seek an injunction to restrain continued breaches. An owner of a nature reserve could in theory use these property rights to protect against threats to the wildlife on it. In addition, a person who uproots plants may commit the crimes of theft and criminal damage, though there is an exception in the Theft Act 1968, s. 4(3) for picking flowers, fruit, foliage and fungi.

As a consequence of the limitations of the common law, the main protection for wild creatures is statutory. The Wildlife and Countryside Act 1981, Part I, consolidated and updated the law in this area: it covers most birds, but only a few animals and plants. Two more specific conservation Acts are the Conservation of Seals Act 1970 and the Badgers Act 1973. There are numerous pieces of legislation relating to hunted species, such as deer, game birds, wildfowl, rabbits and of course fish, though in all these Acts protection of individual animals is incidental. Reference to specialist books is recommended.

The chosen method of control is to establish blanket criminal offences of interfering with specified wildlife, together with a long list of exceptions and defences for acceptable activities, many of which require permission or a licence from an official body. The strongest provisions relate to wild birds (a legacy of the historical influence of the voluntary bodies here, but also a result of the EC Directive on Wild Birds 79/409, which requires certain legislative protections) in the sense that they are reverse listed—i.e. the Act applies unless they are exempted in the Schedules covering pest and quarry species. Animals and plants are covered only if specifically listed in other Schedules. As with all Schedules under the Act, the Secretary of State has powers to vary them by order to include or exclude species (s. 26). Schedules 5 and 8 are being formally reviewed in 1991, as part of the formal quinquennial review provided for in s. 24(1).

Wild birds

It is an offence to kill, injure or take any wild bird and this is backed up by offences of taking, damaging or destroying a nest whilst it is in use or being built and taking or destroying eggs (s. 1(1)). It is also an offence to be in possession of a wild bird or egg, live or dead (s. 1(2)). There are further offences relating to illegal methods of killing or taking wild birds (s. 5) and the sale or advertising for sale of wild birds (s. 6). For these purposes a bird is presumed to be wild unless proved otherwise.

Birds are divided into two categories. Rarer birds are listed in sch. 1 and are specially protected. This means that the maximum penalty for committing

any of these offences is increased from the normal £200 to £1,000 (s. 1(4)).
In addition, intentionally disturbing a Schedule 1 bird on or near its nest,
or disturbing its dependent young, is an offence (s. 1(5)).

Areas may be designated as bird sanctuaries by the Secretary of State, but
only with the consent or acquiescence of the owners and occupiers. By-laws
may be made for bird sanctuaries which create extra offences, including
unauthorised access to the site (s. 3).

There are a number of exceptions and defences to these various offences.
Game birds (i.e. pheasant, partridge, grouse and ptarmigan) are excluded from
the protection provided by the Act, apart from that relating to illegal methods
of killing or taking them (s. 27). Wildfowl listed in sch. 2, Part I may be killed
or taken outside the close season (s. 2(1)). (The close season can be varied
by the Secretary of State and there is also a power to provide for special protection
periods in the event of bad weather in the open season.) Pest species listed
in sch. 2, Part II may be killed or taken and their nests or eggs destroyed,
but only by the owner or occupier of the land or any other authorised person
(s. 2(2)).

Under s. 4, there are defences relating to the killing of injured birds and
where the action is an 'incidental result of a lawful operation and could not
reasonably have been avoided', or where it is necessary for crop protection,
disease prevention or the protection of public health and safety. None of these
defences requires permission, though the last three are only available to owners
and occupiers and other authorised persons.

Section 16 also includes a long list of further exceptions which apply if
a licence has been obtained from the appropriate official authority. It includes
such things as the carrying out of research, educational activities, ringing of
birds, falconry and keeping bird or egg collections.

Animals
Only the animals listed in sch. 5 are protected by the legislation. This includes
all bats, reptiles and amphibians, but only the rarest mammals, fish, butterflies
and other forms of life.

For those animals which are protected, there is a range of offences similar
to those for wild birds. It is an offence to kill, injure or take any scheduled
wild animal (s. 9(1)), or to have in one's possession any such animal, live or
dead, or any part of one (s. 9(2)). Additional offences relate to intentionally
damaging or obstructing places of shelter or protection (s. 9(4)), the sale or
advertisement for sale of wild animals (s. 9(5)), illegal methods of killing or
taking any wild animal (s. 11(1)), and illegal methods of killing or taking animals
listed in sch. 6 (s. 11(2)). For all these offences the maximum penalty is £1,000.
In ss. 10 and 16 there are similar provisions relating to defences and licences
to those available for wild birds.

Plants
Section 13 makes it an offence for anyone other than the owner, occupier
or other authorised person intentionally to uproot any wild plant. In addition,
it is an offence intentionally to pick, uproot or destroy any of the rare wild

plants listed in Schedule 8. The sale or advertisement for sale of Schedule 8 plants is also an offence.

Introducing foreign animals or plants to Great Britain

A final section of the 1981 Act worth mentioning is s. 14, which makes it an offence to introduce into the wild any animal not normally resident in Great Britain or any wild animal or plant listed in Schedule 9. This section aims to protect against the ecological havoc wrought by alien introductions such as grey squirrel, coypu and giant hogweed.

Habitat protection

Although there is a rapidly growing number of protective designations for areas of habitat, the main ones remain the interrelated categories of NNR and SSSI. Both were originally introduced in the National Parks and Access to the Countryside Act 1949 on the recommendation of the Huxley and Ritchie Committees. The NNR powers remain essentially those enacted in 1949, but the SSSI provisions have been significantly altered and strengthened by the Wildlife and Countryside Act 1981, Part II. This reflects the changing role of SSSIs in the light of the enormous environmental changes since 1949.

Two preliminary points need to be made about the 1981 Act, the passage of which would justify a book by itself. First the whole structure of Part II rests on the policy of voluntariness favoured by the Conservative Government. This is the view that compulsory controls should only be used as a last resort, because they will only serve to antagonise landowners, who are seen as having the main responsibility for site protection. Pursuant to this policy, the favoured mechanism of control is the management agreement: the NCC is to seek to enter into agreements with landowners to protect the site, with compensation being paid for losses incurred by owners. In order to achieve this, many of the legal requirements focus on a duty to notify the NCC of threats to sites.

Secondly, Part II was significantly altered during its passage through Parliament. Originally the Government intended to confer statutory protection only on the limited number of sites to be accorded Nature Conservation Order status, leaving the majority of SSSIs protected by the narrow existing limitations on development in the planning system. Many saw this as wholly inadequate, particularly when the NCC released statistics showing that between 10 and 15% of SSSIs had suffered significant damage or loss in 1980 alone, the majority of the damage being caused by agriculture rather than urban-type developments. Statutory powers relating to *all* SSSIs were hurriedly introduced. One effect is that the provisions on SSSIs (and the confusingly similar Nature Conservation Orders) are not well drafted and many detailed matters remain particularly unclear, although there have subsequently been drafting amendments in the Wildlife and Countryside (Amendment) Act 1985, the Wildlife and Countryside (Service of Notices) Act 1985 and the Environmental Protection Act 1990.

The difference between NNRs and SSSIs can best be explained by saying that NNRs are actively controlled and managed by the NCC, whereas in SSSIs the occupier of the land retains control subject to a number of restrictions on use decided by the NCC. In one sense, therefore, the NNRs are the top tier of sites which merit extra controls and the expenditure of money on positive management. However, since they are all designated as SSSIs and benefit from the restrictions on them, it is clearer if the protections available to SSSIs are explained first.

Sites of special scientific interest (SSSIs)

It is important to understand the function of SSSIs. In an explanatory paper, *The Selection of Sites of Special Scientific Interest*, the NCC explains that they are a representative sample of British habitats, with each site seen as 'an integral part of a national series' established with the aim of 'maintaining the present diversity of wild animals and plants in Great Britain'. The NCC emphasises that selection is on scientific grounds rather than to enhance amenity or provide recreation. For biological sites, the best examples of various habitat types (including natural, semi-natural and man-made landscapes) are chosen, determined on the basis of 'naturalness, diversity, typicalness and size', along with sites catering for rare habitats and species. A geographical spread is ensured by selecting typical sites within sub-regional areas. (See, in general, *Guidelines for Selection of Biological SSSIs*, NCC, 1989.) Geological SSSIs are treated differently, the intention being to 'conserve those localities essential to the continued conduct of research and education in the earth sciences', again in the context of a national representative series (see *Geological Conservation Review*, NCC).

Currently there are 5,435 SSSIs, ranging in size from over 10,000 hectares down to 1 hectare. They cover 1.6 million hectares, or about 7% of the land area of Great Britain, though the proportion is far higher in some areas.

The NCC is given a wide discretion both to formulate reasonable criteria for designation and to carry out the task of individual selection. The 1981 Act, s. 28(1), states:

Where the Nature Conservancy Council are of the opinion that any area of land is of special interest by reason of any of its flora, fauna, or geological or physiographical features, it shall be the duty of the Council to notify that fact—

(a)   to the local planning authority in whose area the land is situated;
(b)   to every owner and occupier of any of that land; and
(c)   to the Secretary of State.

One effect of this definition is that the list is not unchanging. New SSSIs will be designated as new information about sites is acquired, and as the importance of safeguarding certain habitats increases. It must also be understood that, in an age when sites are being damaged and destroyed, one site may become of greater importance simply because of the loss of another site. The NCC will denotify a site which loses its scientific interest.

Section 28 talks of a *duty* to designate. This is a very rare example of a piece of environmental legislation where a duty rather than a power to act is given. The strength of the duty is especially unusual given the largely unaccountable nature of the designating bodies. It has potentially important consequences, suggesting that an action could be brought to compel the NCC to designate if evidence was produced to show that it did consider a site to be of special importance. This would make it illegal to refuse to designate on political or tactical grounds, though acquiring the necessary evidence would be difficult.

Conversely, the duty suggests that it would be very difficult for a successful challenge to be mounted against an unwelcome designation. Although s. 28(2) does give owners and occupiers three months to make representations to the NCC about a proposed designation (which has interim effect from the date of the original notification, as a result of an amendment made by the Wildlife and Countryside (Amendment) Act 1985), it is difficult to see that this right confers much of value.

It is up to the NCC to define the boundaries of the SSSI and it appears from *Sweet* v *Secretary of State and Nature Conservancy Council* [1989] 1 JEL 245 (actually a case about s. 29, as to which, see below) that it is permissible for land of lesser intrinsic scientific interest to be designated if it is part of the same environmental unit as land which is of interest. However the position of surrounding buffer lands is less clear and it must be doubted whether they could be designated. One geographical limitation is that SSSIs cannot be designated for waters below the low water mark (thus excluding many estuaries), although inland waters are included within the definition of land in the Act.

In carrying out the notification to owners and occupiers, the NCC must specify the features of the land which are of special interest and must also specify any operations which are likely to damage those features. These are called 'potentially damaging operations' and it is clear from the decision in *Sweet* that a very wide interpretation will be given to this phrase. It can include virtually anything that has an impact on the site and 'operations' is not limited to its meaning under the Town and Country Planning Act 1990. In *Sweet*, it was held to include:

cultivation, including ploughing, rotavating, harrowing and reseeding; grazing; mowing or other methods of cutting vegetation; application of manure, fertilisers and lime; burning; the release into the site of any wild, feral or domestic animal, reptile, amphibian, bird, fish or invertebrate, or any plant or seed; the storage of materials; the use of materials; the use of vehicles or craft likely to damage or disturb features of interest.

Such things as drainage, building operations and the application of pesticides are clearly covered. One thing which is not covered, however, is doing nothing, and on many sites this is potentially bad for the nature conservation interest.

This process of notification is a lengthy one, since every owner and occupier, which includes approximately 30,000 people, must be notified in relation to the whole of each site. The NCC has still not finished the process, started in 1981, of notifying all the sites which existed at that time. This is important because, until it does so, the protection of the 1981 Act does not apply to those sites.

Once they have been notified, owners and occupiers are placed under a reciprocal duty. They must notify the NCC in writing before carrying out any potentially damaging operation. However, four months after this notification, or earlier if the written consent of the NCC is obtained, the operation can go ahead unimpeded—unless of course it requires and fails to get planning permission, which must still be sought for operations and material changes of use as defined in the Town and Country Planning Act 1990. It is an offence 'without reasonable excuse' to carry out a potentially damaging operation either without notifying the NCC, or within the four month period, but the maximum penalty is only a £1,000 fine. The restrictive effect of designation as an SSSI is therefore to impose a four month ban on potentially damaging operations.

Liability for the commission of the offence is strict, but it can only be committed by owners and occupiers of the SSSI. They should know about the designation, either because they have been notified, or because it is a local land charge (s. 28(11)). There are two specific defences available; that the operation was carried out in an emergency, and that planning permission had been granted by the local planning authority. This does not include a permission granted by the General Development Order (s. 28(8)).

These provisions illustrate the 'voluntary' mechanism which is favoured by the Conservative Government. The whole purpose of the reciprocal notification requirement and the four month ban is to give the NCC an opportunity to arrange a management agreement with the owner or occupier.

Specific duties in relation to SSSIs are imposed in a number of pieces of legislation, most notably in the Water Act 1989, s. 9. The NCC must notify 'relevant bodies' (i.e. the NRA, water and sewerage undertakers and internal drainage boards) of SSSIs that may be affected by their activities. If a relevant body is notified, it must consult the NCC over any operation or activity it intends to carry out which it thinks is likely to damage or destroy the SSSI. In addition, the NRA is obliged to consult the NCC before authorising anything it thinks is likely to damage the SSSI. This includes granting abstraction licences, discharge consents and land drainage consents. A published Code of Practice suggests that *all* operations should be notified to the NCC, rather than just those the 'relevant body' *thinks* will damage the SSSI, otherwise detrimental ones may inadvertently be missed (Code of Practice on Conservation, Access and Recreation, July 1989).

These duties are wider than the normal ones imposed on owners and occupiers. They apply to all operations, not just to potentially damaging operations notified by the NCC, and they cover activities in the vicinity of an SSSI which may affect it, such as drainage works, or an upstream discharge. However, these duties are ultimately entirely unenforceable, since there is no remedy if the relevant body fails to consult with the NCC. This reflects the fact that the real purpose of these duties is to bring the matter to the attention of the NCC so that it may give advice (it does not normally offer a management agreement to public bodies, considering that their general environmental duties should suffice to make them responsible).

Nature conservation orders

Section 29 provides stronger powers for areas subject to a nature conservation order. Even so, they have been sparingly used. Only 40 have been made, mainly to protect sites imminently threatened with destruction.

The powers in relation to nature conservation orders are superficially similar to those on SSSIs, but there are significant differences. The order will list potentially damaging operations which must be notified to the NCC before being carried out, and a three month ban is imposed. The NCC can extend this ban to 12 months by offering a management agreement, or by offering to purchase the interest of the person seeking to carry out the operation. At the end of the 12 months, the operation can go ahead. Once again, the purpose of this ban is to enable the NCC to conclude a management agreement, or terms for the purchase of the site.

It is an offence to carry out a potentially damaging operation without notifying the NCC, or within the period of the ban. The offence carries a maximum fine of £2,000 on summary conviction, or an unlimited fine for a conviction on indictment, and it can be committed by anyone, not just owners and occupiers. Thus, contractors, trespassers or visiting members of the public could be prosecuted under this section, a position justified by the publicity given to a nature conservation order (see below).

Certain ancillary arrangements differ from s. 28. The NCC is authorised to enter land to see if an order ought to be made, or to see if an offence against one has been committed (s. 51), powers which are not available for SSSIs. Anyone can prosecute for a s. 29 offence (under s. 28 it is only the NCC and anyone who has the permission of the Director of Public Prosecutions). A convicting court has powers to make a restoration order (s. 31), ordering that the offender carry out specified works for the purpose of restoring the land to its former condition, although in many cases this power will be next to useless because the damage will be irreversible. Compensation is also payable to the owner or occupier for any reduction in the value of an agricultural holding as a result of an order, and for any loss directly attributable to the ban on operations (s. 30).

These wider powers are complemented by a much more complex system for making nature conservation orders. After consulting the NCC, the Secretary of State is empowered to designate areas by order. They must be of special interest and national importance, or required to ensure the survival in Great Britain of a plant or animal, or to comply with an international obligation. Although it is arguable that all SSSIs are of national importance, it is apparent that the Secretary of State has in practice refused to designate some SSSIs under s. 29 on the grounds that the land was not of national importance, even when the NCC has requested it. It is clear from *Sweet* v *Secretary of State and Nature Conservancy Council* [1989] JEL 245 that it is permissible to designate the whole of an environmental unit even though only part of it is of national importance.

Schedule 11 provides for the making of an order. It comes into effect immediately it is made. It must then be notified to owners, occupiers and the local planning authority and must be publicised generally for any objections to be made. Twenty-eight days are allowed for representations to the Secretary of State, who must appoint an inspector or hold a public inquiry if any objections are not withdrawn. The Secretary of State has a discretion to confirm the order, or to amend or revoke it.

Despite their complexity, nature conservation orders provide the NCC with few extra powers not available for all SSSIs. They are basically used to provide more time for the NCC to negotiate a management agreement where the owner or occupier is being awkward. They also serve notice of intent to use whatever powers are available to protect the site. This may include compulsory purchase (see below). Indeed, in *Sweet* the land was eventually purchased compulsorily in 1989 as part of a new national nature reserve.

National nature reserves (NNRs)

NNRs owe their existence to the National Parks and Access to the Countryside Act 1949, s. 15, which defines them as areas managed for study or research into flora, fauna or geological or physiographical interest, or for preserving such features which are of special interest. Before declaring an area an NNR, the NCC must consider that it is expedient in the national interest to manage the area as a NNR.

Designation as an NNR is a simple process; the NCC merely declares that an area is one. In order to do this it has to have control of the site so that it can manage it. Control may be achieved either by buying the land, leasing it, or entering into a nature reserve agreement with the owner under the National Parks and Access to the Countryside Act, s. 16. Such an agreement is enforceable against successors in title. In addition, the Wildlife and Countryside Act 1981, s. 35 permits the NCC to declare an NNR on land which is of national importance and which is being managed by an approved body (meaning a voluntary conservation organisation).

The NCC also has powers to seek a compulsory purchase order if it is unable to conclude a satisfactory management agreement with the owner (1949 Act, s. 17), or if an unremedied breach of an agreement occurs. An order will require the approval of the Secretary of State. These compulsory powers are intended as reserve powers only and are very rarely used. However, they remain the only compulsory powers available to the NCC: if a maverick landowner were to refuse to enter into a management agreement on an SSSI and refused to sell the property, a compulsory purchase order would be the only remaining weapon.

There are no additional statutory restrictions on the use of a NNR other than those imposed on all SSSIs, since the nature reserve agreement will cover anything extra. However, the NCC is empowered to make by-laws for the protection of the reserve (1949 Act, s. 20). They require confirmation by the

Secretary of State and the procedures for making them are set out in the 1949
Act, s. 106. These by-laws may include wide restrictions on such things as
entry to the reserve, taking, killing or interference with animals, plants or the
soil, dropping of litter and lighting fires. Shooting of birds can also be restricted
in areas surrounding the reserve. By-laws may not restrict the rights of the
owner or occupier, public rights of way (though this does not include rights
of navigation—*Evans* v *Godber* [1974] 3 A11 ER 341), or statutory undertakers
and some other public bodies carrying out their statutory functions.

There are 241 NNRs, but it cannot be assumed that they are necessarily
the very best sites. Designation of a site as an NNR imposes heavy costs on
the NCC, which has accordingly to be selective, and it has tended to follow
a policy of opportunism. Given a chronic shortage of money, it will buy or
take control of sites that are threatened or available, rather than those which
are in safe hands, such as those owned by a voluntary conservation body.
Notwithstanding this, the NCC does have a list of proposed nature reserves,
and has published *A Nature Conservation Review* (Ratcliffe, 1977 and updated),
a description of around 900 key sites representing the range of British flora
and fauna, which provides a list of possible future NNRs.

Local nature reserves

Under the National Parks and Access to the Countryside Act 1949, s. 21, local
authorities are given the same powers to designate and manage local nature
reserves as the NCC has in relation to NNRs. A local nature reserve must
have local, as opposed to national, importance and the local authority must
consult with the NCC before designation.

Marine nature reserves (MNRs)

MNRs are the counterparts to NNRs in tidal and coastal waters and may
be designated for any area of land or water from the high tide mark to a
line three miles from the baselines established for measuring the territorial
sea (see the Territorial Sea Act 1987). They are provided for in the Wildlife
and Countryside Act 1981, s. 36, and may be designated on the same grounds
of conservation and study as NNRs. They are actively managed by the NCC.

There are a number of differences from NNRs. Some stem from the absence
of property rights over most of the potential area of MNRs, others are a
consequence of the limited vision of MNRs in the 1981 Act. Designation of
an MNR is by the Secretary of State on the application of the NCC. There
is a lengthy procedure, similar to that for nature conservation orders, in which
the proposed designation and any by-laws are publicised, followed by a period
for representations from interested parties, with the possibility of a public inquiry
and of a judicial review both being catered for (see Wildlife and Countryside
Act 1981, sch. 12). Only two MNRs have ever been designated (around the
islands of Lundy and Skomer), although this may reflect the fact that the
NCC's priorities lay elsewhere in the 1980s.

In common with NNRs, the main additional control conferred by MNR status is the power of the NCC to make by-laws. These may be made as part of the original designation, or may be issued separately, but in either case require confirmation by the Secretary of State. The 1981 Act, s. 37, sets out the range of possible by-laws, which is much more limited than the range for NNRs. Restrictions may be introduced on the killing, taking and disturbance of plants and animals and on the deposit of litter. The by-laws may also prohibit or restrict access by people or vessels to the MNR, but this is limited by the provision in s. 37(3) that by-laws may not restrict any lawful right of passage by vessels, except for pleasure boats. This is an important limitation, since most boats will be able to take advantage of the right of passage in tidal waters, and there are no proprietary limitations on access in such waters. In addition, it must be noted that MNRs cannot take any real advantage from the protection relating to SSSIs, since SSSIs cannot be designated below the low water mark.

Limestone pavements

Limestone pavements are rare landscape features limited to a small number of areas in North-West Europe. In the light of the devastating damage that has been done to them, particularly in gathering stone for garden rockeries, specific powers to protect them were introduced in the Wildlife and Countryside Act 1981, s. 34.

There are two distinct controls. Under s. 34(1), the NCC or the Countryside Commission must notify limestone pavements of special interest to the local planning authority. Amongst other things this will then be taken into account in any planning application. Under s. 34(2), the Secretary of State, a county planning authority or a National Park Authority may by order prohibit the removal from, or disturbance of, any limestone on a site notified under s. 34(1), if they consider it is likely to be adversely affected by such acts. The making of a limestone pavement order is subject to the same procedures as a nature conservation order (1981 Act, sch. 11). It is an offence without reasonable excuse to remove or disturb any limestone on or in an area subject to an order, although it is a defence to have planning permission to do so. The penalty is a maximum fine of £2,000 on summary conviction and an unlimited fine on conviction on indictment. It was originally intended to protect most areas of substantial pavement, but the cumbersome nature of designation has meant that only six orders have ever been made, mainly (as with nature conservation orders) to deal with threats of imminent damage.

This dual form of protection differs from all other conservation designations. But it must be noted that this is the form that the Government originally proposed in 1981 should apply to SSSIs, with only a few specially protected areas having extra restrictions and the ordinary SSSIs being protected only by notification to the local planning authority.

EC Wild Birds Directive 79/409

Under the Wild Birds Directive, Member States are required to take measures to maintain a sufficient diversity of habitats for *all* European bird species. They are also required to take special measures to conserve the habitats of certain listed rare or vulnerable species and of all regularly occurring migratory species. These special measures should include the designation of special protection areas for such birds (Article 4).

Apart from the requirement to designate special protection areas, the Directive does not state how these objectives are to be reached, giving a degree of flexibility to Member States. In this country, the intention is that protection is provided mainly through the town planning and SSSI systems. All special protection areas will be notified as SSSIs before being designated. It should be noted that designation as a special protection area (or as a Ramsar site—see below) does not impose any additional domestic legal requirements on owners and occupiers to those applicable to all SSSIs.

However, this method of protection may have to be changed as a result of the decision of the European Court of Justice in the *Leybucht Dykes* case (*Commission* v *Germany, The Times*, 20 March 1991). This important case establishes that reduction in the area of a special protection area is only justified on very limited grounds, and not on grounds such as economic or recreational pressures, thus effectively creating a strong presumption against development in such an area. At the very least this requires a strengthening of the current guidance to local planning authorities on the importance to be attached to special protection areas in planning decisions, and it may well require a complete re-evaluation of the role of these areas in this country.

There is also a crucial gap in the legislation on SSSIs. Local authority areas, and hence the areas of SSSIs, do not normally stretch beyond the low water mark, thus meaning that there is no effective SSSI protection for parts of many special protection areas (and also Ramsar Convention sites), because they include areas below low water mark (e.g. the Wash). It appears that Britain is potentially in breach of its EC and international obligations in relation to such sites. It is also clear that estuarine sites in particular are under great pressure; an NCC report has shown that 56 out of 136 estuarine SSSIs suffered damage between 1986 and 1989 (see *Nature Conservation and Estuaries in Great Britain*, NCC, 1991), many through permanent developments.

The NCC has produced some extensive criteria for qualification as a special protection area (see *Protecting Internationally Important Bird Sites*, NCC, 1990). It has identified a total of 218 candidate sites and is considering the merits of a further 43, but so far the Government has designated only 40.

Draft Habitats Directive

The EC also has a draft Directive on the Protection of Natural and Semi-Natural Habitats and of Wild Fauna and Flora (see OJ 1988 C247/3 and COM(90) 59 final). This ambitious Directive aims to conserve habitats, with particular attention to threatened species. Member States will be required to establish special protection areas, with the objective of creating by the year 2000 a network within Europe similar to the British SSSI system. Given the number of sites identified under the Wild Birds Directive and the Ramsar Convention, the number of potential sites in this country could easily run into hundreds.

This draft Directive has run into opposition in the EC, possibly because of its failure to identify the cost of the proposals, but it may help to implement the rather vague undertakings in two other international conventions to which Britain is a party. These are the Berne Convention on the Conservation of European Wildlife and Natural Habitats and the Bonn Convention on the Conservation of Migratory Species of Wild Animals.

The Ramsar Convention

The Ramsar Convention on Wetlands of International Importance Especially as Waterfowl Habitat (1971) was the first international convention dealing solely with habitat. It came into force in 1975 and currently there are 52 Contracting Parties, of which the UK is one.

The Convention establishes a number of protections, though it can be criticised for being too general and unenforceable. First it imposes on the Contracting Parties a general duty to promote the conservation of wetlands and waterfowl, especially by establishing nature reserves. Secondly it adopts a site designation approach and provides for the compilation of a list of wetlands of international importance. Contracting Parties are under a duty to formulate their planning so as to promote the conservation of wetlands included in the list. Each Contracting Party must designate at least one site within its territory and deletion or reduction in size of a site is allowed only on the grounds of 'urgent national interests'. Guidelines on the definition of international importance have been drawn up, although ultimately it is up to each Contracting Party to decide whether and where it will designate. In addition to these powers, there are provisions under the Convention for the monitoring of wetlands, the establishment of a database, the funding of projects, educational work and publications. It also provides for a Ramsar Bureau, which is based in Switzerland.

'Wetland' is interpreted very widely to include 'areas of marsh, fen, peatland or water, whether natural or artificial, permanent or temporary, with water that is static or flowing, fresh, brackish or salt, including areas of marine water the depth of which does not exceed six metres'. Designation may also include adjacent areas of land, such as coasts, riverbanks and islands.

As with the Wild Birds Directive, the implementation of the Ramsar Convention is through the planning and SSSI systems. All sites will be designated as SSSIs before becoming Ramsar sites. The NCC has identified 154 candidate sites (many of them the same as the special protection areas under the Birds Directive), but as yet the Government has only designated 45. Nevertheless, this recognises the UK's unique importance for coastal and wetland species.

Management agreements

The NCC has a power to enter into management agreements with owners and occupiers of SSSIs (Countryside Act 1968, s. 15). This has been extended by the Environmental Protection Act 1990, sch. 9 to enable agreements to be made with owners or occupiers of land adjoining an SSSI, which will be of use, for example, in wetland areas to control drainage. There is a similar power to make nature reserve agreements for NNRs (National Parks and Access to the Countryside Act 1949, s. 16), although these normally provide for the NCC to manage the land itself.

Management agreements underpin the voluntary approach to nature conservation favoured by the current Government. They are effectively contracts in which owners or occupiers of land agree to manage it in the interests of nature conservation in return for payment from the NCC. They normally provide for positive management of the site as well as for restrictions, but it appears that only restrictive arrangements in the agreement will be binding on successors in title (s. 15(4)).

Prior to the Wildlife and Countryside Act 1981, little use was made of management agreements—only 70 were in force in 1980/81. But since the 1981 Act, numbers have grown, so that in the financial year 1988/89 the NCC paid out over £6.4m on management agreements on SSSIs (see NCC 15th Annual Report).

Standard rates of compensation have been established in financial guidelines made by Ministers under the 1981 Act, s. 50 (these are set out in the Appendix to Circular 4/83). These are generous to landowners, because they are based on the principle of compensation for profits forgone, which will include such things as lost agricultural grants or lost revenues had the land been converted to a more profitable use. The owner or occupier also has a choice between a lump sum payment or an index-linked annual payment.

There is little doubt that the cost of management agreements has proved more expensive than the Government originally anticipated. Only £600,000 was originally provided for them in 1981 although this figure has risen considerably since. It is also clear that lack of money has caused the NCC to be inhibited in negotiations. For example, in 1982 in Romney Marsh the NCC pulled out of negotiations when no extra Government money was provided for a potentially expensive agreement (see *Cash or Crisis*, Rose and Secrett, 1982). However, when the current figures for damage to SSSIs are considered (see below), it appears that the strategy of relying on management agreements has had some success in reducing damage caused by agricultural activities (although wider issues connected with the profitability of agriculture are probably of great significance too).

Planning permission

In addition to any controls specific to SSSIs and NNRs, planning permission will be required for operations and material changes of use which fall within the definition of development in the Town and Country Planning Act 1990,

s. 55 (see p. 174). Where the application site is an SSSI, the General
Development Order, Article 18 requires the local planning authority to consult
with the NCC before making a decision. The objective is the familiar one
of informing the NCC in advance of a potential threat to the site, so it may
give advice or offer a management agreement. Prior to the 1981 Act, this was
the *only* legal protection for SSSIs. These formal requirements are supplemented
by administrative practice in Circular 27/87, which encourages consultation
over developments outside an SSSI which are likely to damage it and over
sites of nature conservation interest, even if not designated. A new Planning
Policy Guidance Note on nature conservation is awaited, and the signs are
that this will include some stronger guidance on the protection of sites, especially
those of international importance in the light of the Leybucht Dykes case (see
p. 356).

These requirements are very limited in practice. Many activities likely to
damage SSSIs, such as those relating to agriculture, forestry and works carried
out by statutory undertakers, are not covered by the need for planning
permission, either because they are not development or because they are granted
exemption. In any case, the local planning authority is not bound by the NCC's
advice—it is just one material consideration to be taken into account. The
economic and other arguments in favour of the development may well outweigh
the need to protect the SSSI. For example, in 1990 Havering DC granted
outline planning permission for a large theme park on Rainham Marshes, the
largest SSSI in Greater London. The Secretary of State refused to call the
application in, even though this would be the largest ever loss of SSSI land
to a development with planning permission should it go ahead. In another
example, Poole BC granted itself planning permission for housing on Canford
Heath, an SSSI within the town's boundaries. After an unsuccessful High
Court challenge (see *R* v *Poole BC, ex parte Beebee* [1991] 192 ENDS Report
40), the Secretary of State took the almost unprecedented step of revoking
the planning permission under the Town and Country Planning Act 1990,
s. 100.

If planning permission is granted for development, it acts as a defence to
a prosecution for damaging an SSSI (1981 Act, s. 28(8)). This exempts existing
mineral and peat extraction permissions in SSSIs from the 1981 Act. These
are in sites which tend not to have been identified as of importance when
the permission was originally granted. The NCC's options are limited: revocation
of the planning permission entails a liability to pay compensation, a management
agreement would have to compensate for lost profits, and purchase would
normally be at the market price.

Loss and damage to SSSIs

It is now clear that, despite the strengthening of the law relating to SSSIs
in the 1981 Act, damage and loss to sites is still continuing, though at lower
levels than before the Act (see p. 348). In its 16th Annual Report, the NCC
identifies 430 incidents of damage in 1989/1990. The continuing losses illustrate
that the traditional British approach to environmental issues identified in Chapter

5, of balancing the various factors and reaching a compromise, simply does not work when it comes to safeguarding key nature conservation sites.

However, it is significant that the causes of the damage, especially the more serious and permanent damage, are changing. A large proportion is now caused by activities which are not covered properly by the 1981 Act, rather than by agricultural activities which must be notified to the NCC. These causes show that there are a number of defects in the Act which require addressing. Two of these are the problems relating to the grant of planning permission and the omission of marine areas referred to earlier. But, in addition, those who are neither owners nor occupiers cannot commit an offence under s. 28, thus exempting from control some damaging recreational activities; there are no powers to combat neglect of a site if the occupier refuses a management agreement; and it is unclear whether commoners and those with sporting rights are covered by the definition of owner or occupier (overgrazing by commoners is a significant cause of damage). Such a lack of clarity is unfortunately symptomatic of the law on nature conservation.

Bibliography

This bibliography is intended as slightly more than just a list of books mentioned in the text. Because of our sparing use of references (which we think often only serve to distract the reader), we have sought to identify, with brief comments, some of the more important pieces of writing on each area.

As the book tries to illustrate, there is a need to be familiar with policy aspects of environmental protection as well as with the law; indeed the two are often indistinguishable. Obviously one way to achieve this is to read official publications, but often the best way to get an insight into what is really happening in any area is to read literature produced by environmental organisations. We recommend Rose, *The Dirty Man of Europe: The Great British Pollution Scandal* (Simon & Schuster, 1990).

For a clear picture of the whole range of current policies and issues, *This Common Inheritance: Britain's Environmental Strategy* (Cm. 1200, 1990), the recent White Paper on the environment, is most informative. A set of booklets entitled *Environment in Trust*, produced by the Department of the Environment in 1989, provide at-a-glance summaries of some of the main points. A good antidote is Secrett and Porritt, *The Environment: The Government's Record* (Friends of the Earth, 1989).

Any Report by the Royal Commission on Environmental Pollution or the House of Commons Select Committee on the Environment is worth reading. Both bodies have a firm grasp of the policy issues and are not frightened to challenge the adequacy of the existing situation.

There is not much written which attempts to cover the whole of environmental law. It is a sign of the rapid changes in environmental law that Hughes' *Environmental Law* (Butterworths, 1986) has now become out-of-date. It does, however, include a wealth of detail on the law, and has some good material on issues such as minerals and energy and the environment. The *NSCA Pollution Handbook 1991* (National Society for Clean Air and Environmental Protection, 1991) provides an overview of the new legislation with a particular emphasis on air pollution.

A set of essays entitled 'Law, Policy and the Environment', a special issue of the *Journal of Law and Society*, edited by Churchill, Gibson and Warren, 1991, includes background material on many of the major areas of law. In particular the article by Churchill, 'International Environmental Law and the UK', is an excellent survey of the role of international law using some topical examples, which neatly fills the gap in this subject left in the text of this book.

Journals

Of course, one of the most important things in environmental law is keeping up-to-date. There are a number of journals which attempt to do this, though one thing that any environmental law researcher quickly discovers is just how difficult it is to establish what has happened recently and what is going to happen next. This is perhaps a good illustration of the secrecy traditionally surrounding policy-making in this country (though the difficulties pale into insignificance when compared with those involved in finding material on EC proposals). There are many Consultation Papers currently being produced by Government on proposed changes in the law. These often summarise the current position and the reasons for change. The problem is finding out about their existence.

Since environmental law includes news and policy from a wide range of sources, the best way to keep up is to read *ENDS Report* (Environmental Data Services Ltd), a topical monthly digest of a wide range of news on environmental matters, with good coverage of legal and policy developments.

Land Management and Environmental Law Report (Wiley), is now in its third year of publication. It appears bi-monthly and attempts to cover all areas of environmental law through articles and current survey. *Water Law* (Chancery Law Publishing Ltd) is also bi-monthly, and as its name suggests, covers those things connected to the water industry, also through articles and current survey.

The Journal of Environmental Law (Oxford University Press), is published twice a year and includes more lengthy and reflective articles. It can be said to fill the need for a more academic journal, though a great disadvantage is the slowness with which it is published. There is also *Environmental Law*, the journal of the UK Environmental Law Association (UKELA), published four times a year and including short articles and items of news.

All these journals—and the *Journal of Planning and Environment Law* (Sweet & Maxwell)—include summaries and reports of cases, usually with illuminating comments. These are often the only places to find environmental law cases.

Chapter 2

Chapter 2 covers some general principles of public law. For more detailed coverage of these issues see Wade, *Administrative Law*, 6th ed., (Oxford University Press, 1988). For the non-lawyer, Harte, *Landscape, Land Use and the Law* (E & FN Spon, 1985), provides a sound introduction to public and private law concepts, though only in the context of land use.

Chapter 4

The starting point for any reading about EC environmental law and policy is Haigh, *EEC Environmental Policy and Britain*, 2nd rev. ed. (Longman, 1989). This excellent book has some brief introductory chapters about the scope and structure of the EC environmental policy, but the major part of the book consists of an analysis of each Directive which could be said to be within the sphere of environmental policy. As a book to complement the reading of the text of any Directive this one is invaluable. It also has an excellent chapter on approaches to pollution control. The first edition (1984), also had an interesting account of the dispute between Britain and the rest of the EC over the adoption of limit values for environmental quality objectives, particularly in relation to Directive 76/464 on Dangerous Substances in Water.

For a more legalistic look at the legal basis of EC policy, a new book is Krämer, *EEC Treaty and Environmental Protection* (Sweet & Maxwell, 1990), written by the Head of Application of Community Law in Directorate-General XI in the EC Commission. Also see Krämer, 'The Implementation of Community Environmental Directives Within Member States: Some Implications of the Direct Effect Doctrine' [1991] JEL 39, which puts forward some interesting views on the width of the doctrine of direct effects.

There are a number of books on the general constitutional law of the EC. The easiest to read is Steiner, *Textbook on EEC Law*, 2nd ed. (Blackstone Press, 1990). This should be used to supplement any shortcomings in the explanations in this book on the general law of the EC.

Keeping up with changes in EC law is almost impossible. Very few people have the time to look through the pages of the *Official Journal or Europe*, though this is really the only way to do it. It is often a better bet to scan the reports of current events in the general environmental journals. There cannot really be any greater indictment of the secrecy that surrounds the decision-making processes in the EC! The only thing that makes this less disturbing is the fact that most pieces of environmental legislation take such a long time to get agreed that their import is known long before they are adopted.

Other recommended publications: Haigh and Baldock, *Environmental Policy and 1992* (European Cultural Foundation, 1989); Lomas, 'Re-use and Recycling; Developments in Europe', [1989–90] 1 Land Management and Environmental Law Report 160; Somsen, EC Water Directives [1990] 1 Water Law 93.

Chapter 5

Chapter 5 attempts to tackle a number of more theoretical issues that have been consistently ignored in environmental writings, although Rehbinder and Stewart, *Environmental Protection Policy* (De Gruyter, 1985), provides an excellent reference point. On standards, see Haigh, *EEC Environmental Policy and Britain*, 2nd ed., Chapter 3. There is also some interesting material in Wood, *Planning Pollution Prevention* (Heinemann Newnes, 1989) and Department of the Environment Pollution Paper No. 11, *Environmental Standards—The UK Practice* (1975). For a sound explanation of general legal principles, see Waite, 'Criminal and Administrative Sanctions in English Environmental Law', [1989-90] 1 Land Management and Environmental Law Report 38 and 74.

On the British approach to pollution control, see Vogel, *National Styles of Regulation* (Cornell University Press, 1986), a comparison of British and American approaches. It is also useful to read Ridley, *Policies Against Pollution: The Conservative Record and Principles* (Centre for Policy Studies, 1989), which includes an explanation of Government policy in the late 1980s, though (interestingly) one that does not always correspond with what is happening in the 1990s.

Pearce, Markandya and Barbier, *Blueprint for a Green Economy* (Earthscan Publications, 1989) is probably the best place to start reading about environmental economics, though also see Bowers, *Economics of the Environment: The Conservationists' Response to the Pearce Report* (British Association of Nature Conservationists, 1990).

Chapter 6

Anyone looking from some wider reading material on the enforcement of environmental law will find a number of extremely useful works. Most of these studies have tended to concentrate on the socio-legal aspects of empirical studies. Two seminal articles by Carson investigated the use of enforcement mechanisms in the Factory Inspectorate and described how the Factory Inspectorate first incorporated the idea of 'moral blame' in making any decision to prosecute for the breach of strict liability offences. (See 'White Collar Crime and The Enforcement of Factory Legislation' (1970) 10 British Journal of Criminology 383 and 'Some Sociological Aspects of Strict Liability' and 'The Enforcement of Factory Legislation' (1970) 33 MLR 39.)

Following on from these and other works, a number of in-depth studies were carried out by the SSRC Centre for Socio-legal Studies, Wolfson College, Oxford. Two further works were produced as a result, Richardson, Ogus and Burrows, *Policing Pollution—A Study of Regulation and Enforcement*, (Clarendon Press, 1982) and Hawkins *Environmental and Enforcement Regulation and the Social Definition of Pollution* (Clarendon Press, 1984). Both these studies examine the work of the water industry, the former looking specifically at the discharge of trade effluents into public sewers whereas the latter deals with the discharge of the trade effluents directly into watercourses. The final work in the series, Hutter, *The Reasonable Arm of the Law* (Clarendon Press, 1988) examines the enforcement processes of Environmental Health Officers. All three works support the view that the enforcement of strict liability offences relies heavily upon the individual officers view of the offender and the offence.

More recently, the activities of enforcement agencies in Scotland have been examined. Rowan-Robinson, Watchman and Barker, 'River Pollution: A Case for a Pragmatic Approach to Enforcement' [1988] JPL 674 and *Crime and Regulation: A Study of the Enforcement of Regulatory Codes* (T and T Clark, 1990) examine the factors influencing enforcement activities in a wide range of fields, not exclusively environmental.

Chapter 7

The Royal Commission on Environmental Pollution has long campaigned for free access to environmental information. See generally: *Three Issues in Industrial Pollution* (The Second Report, Cmnd. 4894, 1972); *Pollution in some British Estuaries and Coastal Waters* (The Third Report, Cmnd. 5054, 1972); *Air Pollution Control: An Integrated Approach* (The Fifth Report, Cmnd. 6371, 1976); *Agriculture and Pollution* (The Seventh Report, Cmnd. 7644, 1979). More specifically, however, *Tackling Pollution—Experience and Prospects* (The Tenth Report, Cmnd. 9149, 1984) gives a good introductory account of the arguments for and against disclosure. For a more informal essay (editor, Wilson) *The Secrets File* (Heinemann Educational Books, 1984) provides good anecdotal evidence of the use and abuse of secrecy. More particularly, Frankel, *How Secrecy protects the Polluter*, Chapter 3, suggests that there are real benefits to be gained from a greater degree of openness. These works are largely made up of contributions from members of the Campaign for Freedom of Information in Britain whose periodical *Secrets* gives up-to-date briefings on access to official information of all types. Indeed, the success of the organisation is demonstrated by the two Acts of Parliament introduced by their lobbying—the Local Government (Access to Information) Act 1985 and the Environment and Safety Information Act 1988.

The Government replied to the criticisms contained in the Royal Commission's Tenth Report in Pollution Paper No. 23, which gives an overview of present Government policy on access to environmental information. Other recommended reading: Birtles, 'The European Directive on Freedom of Access to Information on the Environment' [1991] JPL 607; Birkenshaw, *Government and Information* (Butterworths, 1990), Burton, 'Access to Environmental Information—The UK Experience of Water Registers', (1989) 1 Journal of Environmental Law 192.

Chapter 8

This chapter looks at the law of tort from a single perspective and therefore does not attempt to cover all aspects of that particular field. More specialised works include Rogers, *Winfield and Jolowicz on Tort* (13th ed., Sweet & Maxwell, 1989), Dias, *Clerk and Lindsell on Tort* (16th ed., Sweet & Maxwell, 1989 and 1991 supplement).

For a more general read about the protection of private rights see Pugh-Smith, *Neighbours and the Law* (Sweet & Maxwell, 1988).

There are a number of articles dealing with the narrower area of the overlapping nature of the common law and the protection of the environment: McLaren, 'Nuisance—Law and the Industrial Revolution—Some Lessons from Social History', 3 Oxford Journal of Legal Studies, (1983) 3 OJLS 155; Ogus, Richardson, 'Economics and the Environment: A Study of Private Nuisance' [1977] CLJ 284. Both these deal with the socio-legal aspects of common law control.

Other recommended reading for those interested in the practical aspects of the common law include Croft, 'The Environmental Protection Act 1990—Part III, Statutory Nuisance—Consolidation or Change?' 3 LMELR 2, and Waite, 'Private Civil Litigation and the Environment', 1 LMELR 113.

Chapter 9

There are many excellent books on the law relating to town and country planning which cover it in far greater detail than could be attempted in the confines of one chapter. They tend to vary between those which see the subject as a set of rules and those which put it in its policy context. Quite simply, the best book is Grant, *Urban Planning Law* (Sweet & Maxwell, 1982, supplement 1990), though it is now awkward to use because of the need to cross-reference between the original text and the supplement. This large book combines clear explanations of the law with analysis of its difficulties, as well as providing coverage of the practical context and policy factors that are so important in planning law.

Those who wish to get an immediate impression of what planning law is all about would be best advised to supplement *Grant* by familiarising themselves with the Planning Policy Guidance Notes and Circulars and to ensure that they look at a few copies of development plans. In addition, some useful pieces on the direction of planning law are: Grant and McAuslan, 'The Scope of Planning: Back to the Future?', *Development & Planning* (editors Cross and Whitehead, Policy Journals, 1989); Garner, 'The Decline of Planning Control' [1985] JPL 756; McAuslan, 'Planning Law's Contribution to the Problems of an Urban Society' [1974] 37 MLR 134 and McAuslan, *Ideologies of Planning Law*, (Pergamon Press) especially Chapters 1 and 6.

Other good textbooks on planning law are: Moore, *A Practical Approach to Planning Law*, 2nd ed. (Blackstone Press, 1990 and supplement 1991). This is the clearest of the standard textbooks, but is rather too much orientated towards the exposition of principles through cases and hence fails fully to convey the central role that policy plays in the subject; Heap, *An Outline of Planning Law*, 9th ed. (Sweet & Maxwell, 1987—a tenth edition is expected). This is a solid but a rather uncritical explanation of the law, though it is very full in its coverage; Telling, *Planning Law and Procedure*, 8th ed. (Butterworths, 1990), is more readable, but less complete than Heap. Purdue, Young and Rowan-Robinson, *Planning Law and Procedure* (Butterworths, 1990) is a very full practical guide to the area.

All of these books use the space available to explain the law on matters not covered in this book, such as advertisements, compensation, listed buildings and conservation areas, although a good introductory book on this last area is Ross, *Planning and the Heritage* (E & FN Spon, 1991).

An excellent and stimulating book which analyses the public law issues underlying the development control system is Alder, *Development Control*, 2nd ed., (Sweet & Maxwell, 1989).

Two good books on the relationship between planning and pollution control are: Miller and Wood, *Planning and Pollution* (Oxford University Press, 1983) and; Wood, *Planning Pollution Prevention* (Heinemann Newnes, 1989). Both include some interesting case studies of the application of the law in practice, and the second book also carries material on the USA by way of comparison.

The *Journal of Planning and Environment Law* (JPL), includes most important cases in the area. It has the advantage of having comments on the cases by Professor Purdue. It is, however, somewhat misnamed since its contents almost exclusively relate to the planning side of the title.

The law on enforcement is undergoing some quite significant changes. There are quite a few books which look at enforcement from a practical view, but the best supplement to what is written here is the Carnwath Report, 'Enforcing Planning Law' (HMSO, 1989), on which most of the changes in the Planning and Compensation Act 1991 are based.

Keeping up-to-date is crucial in the planning area. *The Encyclopaedia of Planning Law* (Sweet & Maxwell), includes all the relevant statutory and non-statutory material and is updated each month. It also has the distinct advantage of Professor Grant's annotations and analysis. The June 1991 supplement includes a masterly analysis of the potential ramifications of the new s. 54A.

Chapter 10

For a critical evaluation of the historical development of environmental law the Royal Commission on Environment Pollution Reports provide a good background to the introduction of integrated pollution control. The Fifth Report, *Air Pollution Control: An Integrated Approach* (HMSO, Cmnd. 6371, 1976), the Tenth Report, *Tackling Pollution—Experience and Prospects* (HMSO, Cmnd. 9149, 1984) and the Twelfth Report, *Best Practicable Environmental Option* (HMSO, Cmnd. 310, 1988) all trace the development of the principles of integrated pollution control. Other works of interest include UKELA's 'Best Practicable Environmental Option—A New Jerusalem?' (1987). Also see 'Best Practicable Environmental Option and its Antecedents' [1986] JPL 643.

For a more practical guide to the legal intricacies of the IPC system under the EPA see Waite, 'Integrated Pollution Control and Local Authority Air Pollution Control—The New Regime' 3 LMELR 11. Also HMIP's 'Integrated Pollution Control—A Practical Guide' (HMSO, 1991) is helpful in giving a view of the enforcement bodies thinking.

For a view of how integrated pollution control systems have developed elsewhere in the world see 'Integrated Pollution Control in Europe and North America' (edited by Haigh and Irwin, Institute for Environmental Policy, 1990).

Chapter 11

Good introductory background works on air pollution include Ashby and Anderson, *The Politics of Clean Air* (Clarendon Press, 1981) and Elson, *Atmospheric Pollution* (Basil Blackwell, 1987). Royal Commission on Environmental Pollution's Reports in 1976 and 1984 also provide a good overview of the legislation historically.

Other areas which may be of interest include the overlap between planning and environmental regulations (see Wood, *Planning Pollution Prevention* (Heinemann Newnes, 1989) and Forster, 'Plugging the Gaps—The Revision of the Ozone Layer' Protocol 2 (1990) LMELR 74. Finally, for an overview of the workings of the local authority air pollution control system see Waite, 'Integrated Pollution Control and Local Authority Air Pollution Control—The New Regime' 3 LMELR 11.

Chapter 12

There have been many articles and books dealing with the area of waste disposal, however, as of yet, there are few on the wider area of waste management. The starting point for any research should be the Royal Commission on Environmental Pollution's Eleventh Report—*Managing Waste: The Duty of Care* (HMSO, Cmnd. 9675, 1985). This Report not only deals with waste management law and practice but also some of the wider issues surrounding the disposal of waste in Britain. Other helpful official publications include, House of Lords Select Committee on Science and Technology, Fourth Report, Session 1988-90, *Hazardous Waste Disposal* (HMSO, 1989), House of Lords Environment Committee Second Reports Session 1988/9, *Toxic Waste* (February 1989), House of Commons Environment Committee First Report Session 1988-90, *Contaminated Land* (January 1990).

For an excellent article dealing with the problems of defining waste see Purdue, 'Defining Waste', (1990) 2 Journal of Environmental Law 250, which provides an analysis of the *ex parte Rankin* and *Queensborough Rolling Mill Company*. For a short discussion of the problems in the enforcement of the Control of Pollution Act 1974, see Hawke, 'Waste Management Law and Enforcement' (Leicester Polytechnic Law Monographs, 1989). This contains a good overview of the old system and provides a quick guide to its defects. Other recommended articles include Burnett-Hall, 'Waste and Contaminated Land' 135 Sol J 254, and Cuckson, 'Waste Regulation and Recycling' 3 LMELR 6.

Chapters 13 and 14

There are good existing books on water pollution law. The best detailed coverage is Howarth, *Water Pollution Law* (Shaw and Sons, 1988, supplement 1990). Howarth, *The Law of Aquaculture* (Fishing News Books, 1991), though on a restricted subject matter, is also a most impressive book.

On the policy side the Annual Reports of the National Rivers Authority are worth looking at, and should be compared with Birch, 'Poison in the System' (Greenpeace, 1988). Future NRA policy is explained in 'Discharge Consent and Compliance Policy: A Blueprint for the Future' (National Rivers Authority, 1990). Up-to-date information is provided by *Water Law* (Chancery Publishing) and, in news form, the NRA's monthly publication *The Water Guardians*.

The history of the water industry from its early days to privatisation in 1989 is well covered in Kinnersley, *Troubled Water* (Hilary Shipman, 1988). Recommended writings on the current law are: Howarth, 'Water Pollution:

Improving the Legal Controls' [1989] Journal of Environmental Law 25; Waite, 'Water Pollution Law After the Water Act 1989' [1989] 1 LMELR 146; Macrory, 'The Privatisation and Regulation of the Water Industry' [1990] 53 MLR 78.

Chapter 15

There is, as yet, no book which analyses the *law* on nature conservation in great detail. Though Denyer-Green, *Wildlife and Countryside Act 1981: the Practitioner's Companion* (RICS, 1983), remains a useful guide to the 1981 Act, it does not grapple with the more recent areas of difficulty. For some recent thoughts on nature conservation in the light of the 1990 Act, see Ball, 'The Environmental Protection Act 1990 and Nature Conservation' [1991] 3 LMELR 81.

However, there is a wealth of information on the state of our natural heritage and on nature conservation policy. As far as the former is concerned, the Annual Reports of the NCC (now English Nature) are of enormous interest. The NCC also publishes a wide range of literature on specific issues, and a general strategy is set out in 'Nature Conservation in Great Britain' (NCC, 1984). The starting point for any reading on the shape of modern nature conservation must be the Huxley Report, *Conservation of Nature in England and Wales* (Cmnd. 7122, 1947), which sets out all the arguments as to why nature conservation is important. There are many good books on the history of nature conservation (and also landscape protection). A stimulating introduction to the science of nature conservation is Moore, *Bird of Time: The Science and Politics of Nature Conservation* (Cambridge University Press, 1987), written by a former Chief Scientist at the NCC who had a special involvement in the drawing up of the current SSSI criteria. Adams, *Nature's Place: Conservation Sites and Countryside Change* (Allen and Unwin, 1986), provides another readable summary of conservation history.

Shoard, *The Theft of the Countryside* (Temple Smith, 1980), is a book which caused enormous controversy when it first appeared in the run-up to the Wildlife and Countryside Act 1981, and it provides a polemical view of what was (and arguably still is) happening in the countryside. The story is taken on further by Pye-Smith and Rose, *Crisis and Conservation Conflict in the British Countryside* (Penguin, 1984), and Lowe, Cox, MacEwen, O'Riordan and Winter, *Countryside Conflicts: The Politics of Farming, Forestry and Conservation* (Temple Smith Gower, 1986), which includes a number of case studies in the light of the Act. International instruments on wildlife protection are well explained in Lyster, *International Wildlife Law* (Grotius Publications Ltd, 1985).

Index